VISUAL QUICKSTART GUIDE

FINAL CUT EXPRESS HD

FOR MAC OS X

Lisa Brenneis

 Peachpit Press

Visual QuickStart Guide
Final Cut Express HD for Mac OS X
Lisa Brenneis

Peachpit Press
1249 Eighth Street
Berkeley, CA 94710
510/524-2178
800/283-9444
510/524-2221 (fax)

Find us on the World Wide Web at: www.peachpit.com
To report errors, please send a note to errata@peachpit.com
Peachpit Press is a division of Pearson Education

Copyright © 2005 by Lisa Brenneis

Editor: Judy Ziajka, Karyn Johnson
Production Editor: Connie Jeung-Mills
Illustrations: Jeff Tolbert
Compositor: Owen Wolfson
Indexer: Emily Glossbrenner
Cover Design: The Visual Group

ISBN 0-321-35026-X

9 8 7 6 5 4 3 2

Printed and bound in the United States of America

Dedication

For my folks, Jon and Aida Brenneis—from you I learned that if you treat your friends like family and your family like friends, you'll build a large friendly family.

You are the best.

Acknowledgments

Thanks to the Peachpit Press people: editor Karyn Johnson, editor-in-chief Nancy Davis and executive editor Marjorie Baer; editor extraordinaire Judy Ziajka; production editor Connie "A-Team" Jeung-Mills; compositor Owen Wolfson; and Tonya Engst, Jeff Carlson, Jill Marts-Lodwig, Lisa Theobald, and Kelly Ryer, the editors of the previous editions, who built a fine foundation for this edition.

Thanks to my dad, Jon Brenneis, for generously allowing the use of images that appear in this book.

Thanks to the whole Final Cut Pro team at Apple Computer, particularly Mary Massey, Brian Meaney, Erin Skitt, John Malm, and Paul Saccone—genuinely kind, helpful people who work very hard.

Thanks to my collaborator and friend Brett Spivey who, on top of everything else, concocted the compositing and special effects chapters with me.

Thanks always to Lauren Coyne (sharp eyes, sharp mind, sharp pencil) for all the great help.

Thanks to all the men and women of the Final Cut Pro discussion forums: 2-pop.com, LAFCPUG.org, and Creative Cow. You lead the FCP community by example, and I am indebted to you. Keep posting.

Thanks to the deejays at Internet radio beacon KEXP.org (Seattle), where they play the best damn music by real bands. Top fuel for weary fact-jockeys.

Thanks to a group of very important people who defy classification: Michael Wohl, Andrew Baum, Cawan Starks, Ross Jones, Philip Hodgetts, Josh and Michelle Mellicker, Larry Jordan, Elina Shatkin, Tom Wolsky, Bill Davis, Kevin Monahan, Michael Horton, Ken Stone, Ned Soltz, Lowell Kay, Michael Rubin, Steve Martin, Ramy Katrib, Ben Gardiner, Nick Meyers, Fred Huff and Kit Gray.

We lost another major mentor this year— Charles McConathy, founder of Promax Systems. Charles helped create these amazing personal digital video systems we enjoy today. Charles's passion for assembling something useful out of a jumble of parts that didn't communicate very well extended into his tireless and generous efforts towards building a human community of digital video users.

Finally—eternal gratitude to the late Ralph Fairweather.

TABLE OF CONTENTS

Chapter 3:   **Presets and Preferences**   **39**

INTRODUCTION

When the two Steves started Apple back in 1976, they dreamed of making a computer that people could use as a tool to change the world. In 1999, Apple released Final Cut Pro—a program worthy of the founders' vision. A worldwide community has formed around this tool, and people are making movies who weren't able to before. Final Cut Pro changed the way stories are told, because it changed who's telling them.

In 2003, Apple debuted Final Cut Express, a lower-cost, entry-level, nonlinear editing and effects program built using the same code base as Final Cut Pro 3; followed by Final Cut Express 2, which is based on Final Cut Pro 4—are you starting to see a pattern here?

This book covers Apple's third program version, Final Cut Express HD 3.0, known as Final Cut Express HD (or just "FCE HD" to its friends and fans). FCE HD offers a light sprinkling of refinements throughout the program and another significant bump in real-time performance. FCE HD's big news is indicated in the application's name change: Limited high-definition video (HDV) capture, edit and output via FireWire—without an additional hardware card.

FCE HD also ships with two significant helper applications—LiveType, an animated titling program, and Soundtrack, a kind of musical Erector Set you can use to generate custom tracks from loops. LiveType and Soundtrack had previously been available only to Final Cut Pro users.

This book, *Final Cut Express HD for Mac OS X: Visual QuickStart Guide*, is adapted from my *Final Cut Pro HD for Mac OS X: Visual QuickPro Guide*. This edition describes the operation of Final Cut Express HD. I've carefully revised the Final Cut Pro HD material to accurately reflect the way Final Cut Express HD works, so if you are using an earlier version of Final Cut Express, you might want to seek out a copy of an earlier edition.

Who should use this book

Final Cut Express HD for Mac OS X: Visual QuickStart Guide is designed to be used by intermediate to advanced Mac users with a little basic knowledge of video editing terms and procedures; explaining basic video production and editing is beyond the scope of this book. Final Cut Express (FCE) is designed to be easy to use, and it's simpler than Final Cut Pro, but it's still a professional-level video editing and compositing program. If you are not new to the Macintosh, but you're completely new to video editing, consider some basic training in the fundamentals of video editing before you plunge into this program. If you haven't done so already, try Apple's free iMovie program—it's a great way to get a taste of basic video editing in a stripped-down program that's a lot easier for beginners to use.

What's in this book

The first part of the book starts with a quick feature overview of the entire program, followed by hardware setup, program installation, and preferences specification, and it ends with a chapter devoted to FCE's project structure and clip handling.

The next section introduces the Capture, Browser, and Viewer windows—the tools you use for capturing, importing, and organizing media in preparation for an edit.

The third part of the book details the variety of ways you can use FCE's editing tools to assemble and refine an edited sequence. This section covers basic editing procedures and the operation of the Timeline, Canvas, and Trim Edit windows.

The fourth section is devoted to using the program's special effects and compositing tools. You'll find an overview chapter plus chapters devoted to creating motion effects, using filters, and creating titles and other generator effects.

The final section includes two chapters on finishing your FCE project: one discusses rendering techniques and strategies; the other lays out your options for outputting a final product.

How to use this book

This guide is designed to be a Final Cut Express user's companion, a reference guide with an emphasis on step-by- step descriptions of specific tasks. You'll encounter the following features:

◆ **"Anatomy" sections** introduce the major program windows with large, annotated illustrations identifying interface features and operation. If you're not a step-by-step kind of person, you can pick up quite a bit of information just by browsing these illustrations.

◆ **"FCE Protocol" sidebars** lay out the protocols (the programming rules) that govern the way Final Cut Express works. These sections are highly recommended reading for anyone interested in a serious relationship with this program.

◆ **Sidebars** throughout the book highlight production techniques, project management ideas, and suggestions for streamlining your workflow.

◆ **Tips** are short bits that call your attention to a neat trick or a cool feature, or warn you of a potential pitfall in the task at hand.

Learning Final Cut Express

Here are some tips to help you get up and running in Final Cut Express ASAP.

Basic theory

Two sidebars, one in Chapter 1 and another in Chapter 4, are referred to throughout this book. You don't absolutely have to read these to operate the program, but understanding some of the basic concepts underlying the design of the program will make Final Cut Express much easier to learn.

"What Is Nonlinear Nondestructive Editing?" in Chapter 1 explains how nondestructive editing works and how it affects the operation of Final Cut Express.

"FCE Protocol: Clips and Sequences" in Chapter 4 explains the protocols governing clip and sequence versions, which are key to understanding how Final Cut Express works.

FCE is context sensitive

The Final Cut Express interface is context sensitive, which means that the options available in the program's menus and dialog boxes can vary depending on any of the following factors:

♦ The external video hardware attached to your system

♦ The setup configuration you specify when you install the program

♦ The program window that is currently active

♦ The program selection that you just made

The logic behind the context-sensitive design is sound: to simplify your life by removing irrelevant options from your view. However, because the interface is context sensitive, the menus and dialog boxes in your installation of Final Cut Express may occasionally differ from those in the illustrations shown in this guide.

Keyboard commands

Final Cut Express was designed to support a wide variety of working styles ranging from heavy pointing, clicking, and dragging to entirely keyboard-based editing. More keyboard commands are available than those listed in the individual tasks in this book. You'll find a comprehensive list of keyboard commands in Appendix B.

Shortcut menus

Final Cut Express makes extensive use of shortcut menus. As you are exploring the program, Control-clicking items and interface elements is a quick way to see your options in many areas of the FCE interface, and it can speed up the learning process.

Refer to the manual

Final Cut Express 1 did not come with a printed manual; Apple has partially remedied that situation by including a 100-page (more or less) printed program overview. The most comprehensive FCE reference document is still the onscreen help document, *Final Cut Express Help*. This 992-page PDF is installed with FCE and is accessed from FCE's Help menu. FCE HD features are covered in *New Features in Final Cut Express HD*, a 16-page PDF.

Apple's manual is a valuable reference tool, but be warned: you'll occasionally run across stray references to Final Cut Pro features that don't exist in Final Cut Express, or FCE features that don't operate as described. I'll occasionally refer you to specific sections of the official manual that cover a topic in more detail than this book can accommodate. (Still, Apple did miss a few items covered here, and unlike the electronic-only manual, you can scribble notes in this Visual QuickStart Guide.)

Check out the Knowledge Base

Apple posts a steady stream of valuable Final Cut Express articles and updates in its online Knowledge Base. The company also posts information about FCE "known issues" (that's corporate-speak for bugs) as Knowledge Base articles. See Appendix A, "Online Resources," for information on locating the Knowledge Base.

The Web is your friend

Using the World Wide Web is an essential part of using Final Cut Express. Apple, as well as the manufacturers of the video hardware you'll be using with Final Cut Express, relies on the Web to inform users of the latest developments and program updates and to provide technical support. You'll find a starter list of online resources in Appendix A and specific URLs sprinkled throughout this book. There are some great sources of information, technical help, and camaraderie out there. If you get stuck or encounter difficulties getting underway, go online and start asking questions. After you've learned the program, go online and answer questions. Helping other people is a great way to learn.

Where to find more information

Check out Appendix A, "Online Resources," for a list of helpful web sites.

Go forth and experiment

If you're new to video production—or even if you're experienced but new to Final Cut Express—it would be wise to test your brand-new DV post-production system on a short, noncritical project before you plunge into that feature-length masterpiece that haunts your dreams. By knocking out a series of short projects, you build up your skills quickly as you learn from your mistakes. Have fun, keep moving, and don't be afraid to experiment.

WELCOME TO FINAL CUT EXPRESS

Welcome to Apple's Final Cut Express—a combination digital video editing, compositing, and special effects program. Final Cut Express is based on Final Cut Pro, Apple's wildly popular professional digital video editing program.

Final Cut Express is tightly integrated with Apple's G4 and G5 processors, FireWire high-speed data transfer technology, and QuickTime multimedia format. FCE is designed to capture only DV-format video via FireWire, but allows you to export to most QuickTime formats. Final Cut Express provides professional editing functionality in a variety of styles, from strictly drag-and-drop edits to entirely keyboard-based editing.

Soon you'll be spending plenty of time working with clips, audio levels, and other editing minutiae, so let's start with the big picture. This chapter provides an overview of Final Cut Express features and tracks a basic FCE project from start to finish. You'll be introduced to the main interface windows used for editing and for creating effects, plus learn how to customize the arrangement of these windows.

Your First Final Cut Express Project: Start to Finish

Here's a roadmap you can use to chart a course through your first FCE project. This flowchart describes the production pathway of a typical DV project from hardware setup through output of the finished program. At each step, you'll find pointers to sections in this book that describe that part of the process in more detail.

YOUR FIRST FINAL CUT EXPRESS PROJECT

1. **Set up hardware, install FCE, and choose an initial Easy Setup:** Use a FireWire cable to connect your DV camcorder to your computer. If you hook up your hardware before you install FCE, the program will select the correct initial settings automatically. (If you've already installed FCE, don't worry—those settings are easy to define at any time.)

   See Chapter 2, "Installing and Setting Up."

2. **Capture DV:** Use the controls in the Capture window to capture raw video and audio from your DV camcorder and save it to a hard disk.

   See Chapter 5, "Capturing Video."

3. **Import other media elements:** Add music or sound effects, or graphics elements such as digital stills or graphics created in Photoshop.

   See Chapter 6, "Importing Digital Media."

ROUGH CUT

4. Rough assembly: Review your raw video in the Viewer and select the portions you want to use by marking In and Out points. Assemble the selected portions into a *rough cut* in an empty sequence in the Timeline. If your project includes narration, be sure to edit a *draft* narration into your rough cut. If you plan to base the rhythm of your cut on a piece of music, you should edit the music into the rough cut as well.

See Chapter 9, "Basic Editing."

5. Fine cut: Revisit your rough cut and make fine adjustments to edit points directly in the Timeline or in the Trim Edit window or by opening sequence clips and making adjustments in the Viewer.

See Chapter 11, "Fine Cut: Trimming Edits."

FINISHING

6. Finishing: When your fine cut is complete, use FCE's text generators to add titles, apply the Color Corrector filter to tweak the video's color balance, and fill out the audio tracks with effects and music.

See Chapter 14, "Compositing and Effects Overview."

OUTPUT

7. Output: Output your finished program to DV tape or to a DVD-mastering program like Apple's iDVD, or export it in a compressed QuickTime format for distribution in another digital format like streaming web video or CD-ROM.

See Chapter 19, "Creating Final Output."

YOUR FIRST FINAL CUT EXPRESS PROJECT

What Is Nonlinear, Nondestructive Editing?

Final Cut Express is a nonlinear, nondestructive editing program.

In a tape-based *linear* editing system, constructing an edit means selecting shots from one tape and then recording them in order on another tape. Once you've recorded the shots, you're limited to the shots as recorded and in the order recorded. If you want to go back and extend the length of a shot in the middle of your edited program, you'll also have to re-record every shot that came after it, because you can't slip the back end of your program down the tape to make room. A computer-based *nonlinear* editing system uses the computer's random-access capabilities to allow editors to swap, drop, trim, or extend shots at any point in an edited sequence, without having to reconstruct any other portion of the program.

Some nonlinear computer editing programs, like iMovie, offer random access but modify the original media files on your hard disk when you change a clip (in iMovie's case, when you empty the Trash). This is called *destructive* editing.

Nondestructive editing is a basic concept that distinguishes Final Cut Express from other digital, nonlinear editing systems like iMovie. When you edit on a digital, nonlinear editing system like Final Cut Express, constructing a digital edit means constructing a playlist, much like a playlist you would construct in iTunes.

In iTunes, your archive of song files is stored in the iTunes Library; an iTunes playlist is just a set of instructions that tells the iTunes jukebox how to sequence playback of songs you select. A single song file can appear in multiple playlists, and deleting a song from a playlist doesn't delete the actual song file from the Library. In Final Cut Express, sequences operate like iTunes playlists.

An FCE sequence is a collection of instructions to the program to play a certain bit of Media File A, then cut to a bit of Media File B, then play a later bit of Media File A, and so on. The full length of each file is available to the editor from within the edited sequence. That's because in Final Cut Express, the *clip*—the basic media element used to construct edited sequences— is only a set of instructions referring to an underlying media file. When you play back an edited sequence, it only looks as though it's been spliced together; in fact, Final Cut Express has assembled it on the fly. Since you're viewing a simulation of an edited sequence and the full length of each captured file is available at the edit point, extending a shot is simply a matter of rewriting the editing program's playlist to play a little more of Media File A before switching to Media File B. In Final Cut Express, you do this by modifying the clip's length in your edited sequence.

Nondestructive editing is key to editing in a program like Final Cut Express, which allows you to use media source files multiple times across multiple projects or to access the same source file but process it in a number of different ways. Having many instances of a clip (which, in Final Cut Express, is just a set of instructions) all referring to the same media file saves disk space and offers flexibility throughout your editing process.

When you reach the limit of Final Cut Express's ability to assemble your edited sequence on the fly, it's time to render. The rendering process computes all the modifications, superimpositions, and transitions applied to the clip into a single new media file that resides on your hard disk and plays back as part of your edited sequence.

For more information on protocols governing clips, see Chapter 4, "Projects, Sequences, and Clips."

Touring Your Desktop Post-Production Facility

Four program windows form the heart of the Final Cut Express interface: the *Browser*, the *Viewer*, the *Canvas*, and the *Timeline* (**Figure 1.1**).

Because the program combines so many editing and effects-creation capabilities in a single application, each of these windows performs multiple functions. Final Cut Express's elegant use of tabbed windows to stack multiple functions in a single window makes maximum use of your screen real estate.

A small, floating Tool palette contains tools you can use to make selections, navigate, and perform edits in the Timeline and the Canvas.

YOUR DESKTOP POST-PRODUCTION FACILITY

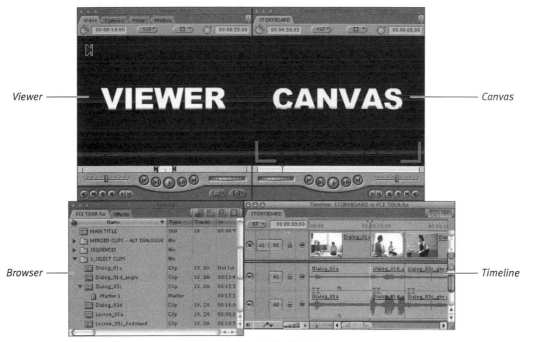

Viewer — VIEWER   CANVAS — Canvas

Browser —

Timeline —

Figure 1.1 The four main program windows in Final Cut Express.

Useful features

Following are a few useful features that apply throughout the program:

◆ **Tabbed windows:** Every major window in Final Cut Express uses tabs. In the Viewer and User Preferences windows, tabs give you access to multiple functions within the window (**Figure 1.2**). In the Canvas, Timeline, and Browser, tabs provide access to multiple sequences or projects (**Figure 1.3**). You can drag a tab out of the Browser, Viewer, Canvas, or Timeline and display the tab as a separate window. You can also return a tab to its original window by dragging the tab back to the tab header of the parent window. You can find out more by reviewing "Creating Custom Screen Layouts" in Chapter 3.

◆ **Tooltips:** You can use tooltips to identify most of the controls in the Viewer and Canvas windows and on the Tool palette (**Figure 1.4**). Tooltips also display the keyboard shortcut for a tool or button. Rest the pointer over the button and wait a moment, and a label will appear. Activate tooltips on the General tab of the User Preferences window.

Figure 1.2 Tabs give you access to multiple functions in the Viewer window.

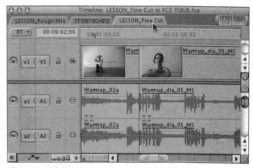

Figure 1.3 Tabs give you access to multiple sequences in the Timeline.

Figure 1.4 Rest the pointer over a button in the Tool palette, and a tooltip—a label with the tool's name—will appear. Tooltips also display keyboard shortcuts for tools and buttons.

YOUR DESKTOP POST-PRODUCTION FACILITY

Menus, shortcuts, and controls

Final Cut Express offers several methods for performing video editing tasks. Some people work fastest using keyboard shortcuts; others prefer to use the menu bar or shortcut menus as much as possible. Apart from the menu bar and window buttons, you can use several other means to access Final Cut Express's functions; experiment to find out which control methods work best for you:

◆ **Shortcut menus:** Shortcut menus can speed your work and help you learn Final Cut Express. Control-click an item in one of the four main interface windows and select from a list of common functions specific to that item (**Figure 1.5**). Control-click often as you learn your way around the program just to see your options in a particular area of the FCE interface.

◆ **Keyboard shortcuts:** You'll find a complete list of keyboard shortcuts in Appendix B. You may find that these shortcut keys help you work more efficiently.

◆ **Timecode entry shortcuts:** Final Cut Express provides a number of timesaving shortcuts for timecode entry. See "FCE Protocol: Entering Timecode Numbers" in Chapter 8.

Customizable interface

FCE's flexible interface can be custom-tailored to suit your needs. You can create and save custom screen layout configurations to facilitate different editing and effects-creation tasks. Personalize and save anything from a single custom shortcut button to an entire screen layout for a multi-monitor setup.

See "Customizing Final Cut Express" in Chapter 3.

Onscreen help

Onscreen help for FCE is a 980-page PDF file, *Final Cut Express Help*. The PDF has a couple of advantages over the printed manual. The PDF index entries are hyperlinked; you can jump to a listing by clicking its page number. The PDF is also illustrated in full color.

To access onscreen help:

◆ Choose Help > Final Cut Express Help.

✔ Tip

■ The Documentation folder on the Final Cut Express HD application disk contains additional reference materials that will help you master the program: a quick reference guide to keyboard shortcuts and interface parts, a FAQ, and a PDF version of the printed FCE manual.

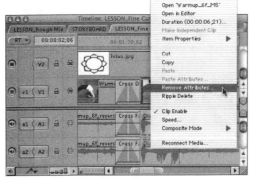

Figure 1.5 Control-clicking a sequence clip in the Timeline calls up a shortcut menu with a list of functions related to that clip.

Editing and Effects Windows

The following brief descriptions of the features and functions of each of the four main windows are simplified summaries of the full list of features. Final Cut Express's designers went all out to support a wide variety of editing styles, and they have produced a very flexible editing system.

The Browser

The Browser (**Figure 1.6**) is the window where you organize and access all the media elements used as source material for your projects. It also contains your projects' sequences: the data files that contain edited playlists.

The Browser's Effects tab is your source for effects, filters, and generators, including the text generator (**Figure 1.7**).

The Browser is not like a folder on your computer's Desktop—it's not a collection of actual files. Instead, a Browser item is a *pointer* to a file on your hard disk. It's important to keep in mind that file storage is independent of Browser organization. That means you can place the same clip in multiple Browser projects, and each instance of the clip will refer to the same media file on your hard drive. For detailed information about the Browser, see Chapter 7, "Organizing Clips in the Browser."

EDITING AND EFFECTS WINDOWS

You can display more than 40 sortable columns of information

Different projects appear on separate tabs

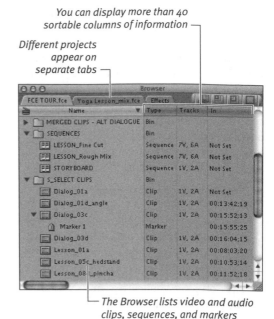

The Browser lists video and audio clips, sequences, and markers

Figure 1.6 Use the Browser window to organize the media elements in your projects.

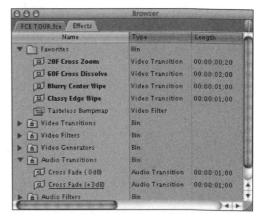

Figure 1.7 The Browser's Effects tab displays Final Cut Express's effects, filters, and generators, as well as your own customized effects.

The Viewer

The Viewer is bursting with functions. When you're editing, the Viewer acts as your source monitor; you can review individual video and audio clips and mark edit points. You can also load clips from the current sequence into the Viewer to refine your edits, apply effects, create titles—and, as they say, much, much more.

The FCE interface offers a stack of tabs in the Viewer that organize and display audio and video plus provide controls for any effects you want to apply to a clip. Here are quick summaries of the functions available on each tab.

The Viewer's Video tab

◆ **Video tab (Figure 1.8):** View video frames and mark and refine edit points. This is the default playback window for a video clip.

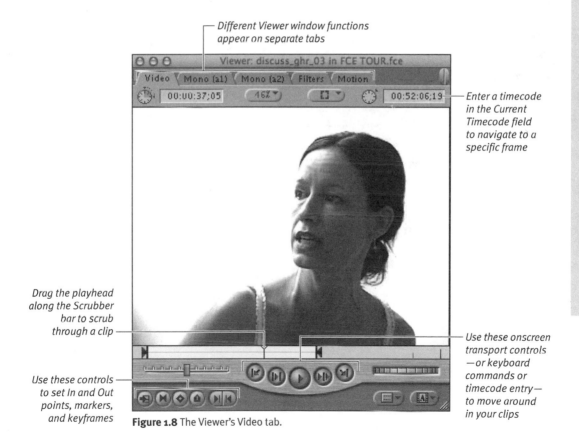

Different Viewer window functions appear on separate tabs

Enter a timecode in the Current Timecode field to navigate to a specific frame

Drag the playhead along the Scrubber bar to scrub through a clip

Use these onscreen transport controls —or keyboard commands or timecode entry— to move around in your clips

Use these controls to set In and Out points, markers, and keyframes

Figure 1.8 The Viewer's Video tab.

The Viewer's Audio tab

◆ **Audio tab** (**Figure 1.9**): Audition and
mark edit points in audio-only clips.
Set level and pan or spread settings. The
Audio tab displays the audio portion of
an audio+video clip. Clips with two channels display two audio tabs.

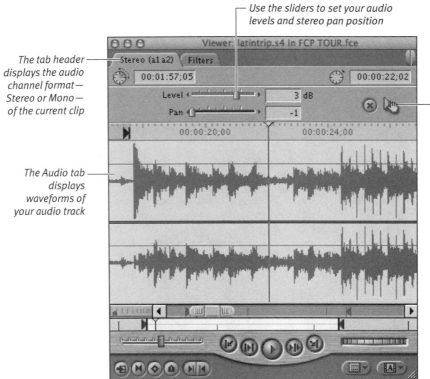

*Use the sliders to set your audio
levels and stereo pan position*

*The tab header
displays the audio
channel format—
Stereo or Mono—
of the current clip*

*Drag this hand
icon. It's your
handle for
performing
drag-and-drop
audio edits*

*The Audio tab
displays
waveforms of
your audio track*

Figure 1.9 The Viewer's Audio tab contains a few controls that don't
appear on the Video tab.

The Viewer's Effects tabs

◆ **Controls tab** (**Figure 1.10**): Adjust the settings for a generator effect, such as the text generator.

◆ **Filters tab:** Adjust the settings for any filter effects you have applied to a clip.

◆ **Motion tab:** Apply and modify motion effects.

◆ **Color Corrector tab:** Use onscreen controls to adjust the settings for the Color Corrector filter. This tab appears only on clips with the Color Corrector filter applied.

For more information on the Viewer, see Chapter 8, "Working with Clips in the Viewer."

To learn about creating effects, see Chapter 14, "Compositing and Effects Overview."

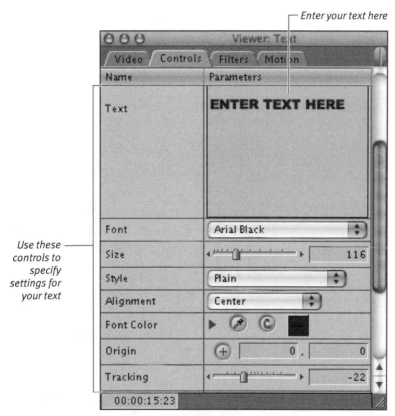

Enter your text here

Use these controls to specify settings for your text

Figure 1.10 A text generator on the Viewer's Controls tab. The Controls tab contains the tools you need to adjust the settings for a generator effect. The Filters tab and the Motion tab each perform this function too, but for different classes of effects.

EDITING AND EFFECTS WINDOWS

The Canvas

The Canvas is a monitor where you view playback of your edited sequence. The Canvas and the Timeline work together; the Canvas always displays the frame at the current position of the Timeline's playhead.

The Canvas (**Figure 1.11**) looks similar to the Viewer and has many of the same controls. You can use the controls in the Canvas to play sequences, mark sequence In and Out points, add sequence markers, and set keyframes.

Multiple open sequences appear on separate tabs

Drag the Canvas playhead along the Scrubber bar to scrub through a sequence

The Canvas and Viewer transport controls operate in the same way; you can also edit with keyboard commands or timecode entry

Figure 1.11 The Canvas window.

In addition to using the Viewer-like marking controls, you can perform various types of drag-and-drop edits in the Canvas edit overlay (**Figure 1.12**), which appears automatically when you drag a clip into the Canvas. You can also use the Canvas's Image+ Wireframe mode to plot motion effects.

For more information on the Canvas, see Chapter 10, "Editing in the Timeline and the Canvas."

Learn about applying motion effects in Chapter 15, "Motion."

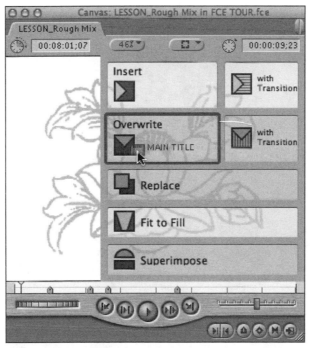

Figure 1.12 The Canvas window, with the Canvas edit overlay displayed. Drag a clip from the Viewer or Browser and drop it on the type of edit you want to perform.

EDITING AND EFFECTS WINDOWS

The Timeline

The Timeline displays your edited sequence as clips arrayed on multiple video and audio tracks along a time axis (**Figure 1.13**). The Canvas and Timeline are locked together; you view Timeline playback in the Canvas. If you have multiple sequences open, both the Timeline and the Canvas will display a tab for each sequence. You can edit by dragging clips directly from the Browser or the Viewer and dropping them in the Timeline; see Chapter 10, "Editing in the Timeline and the Canvas."

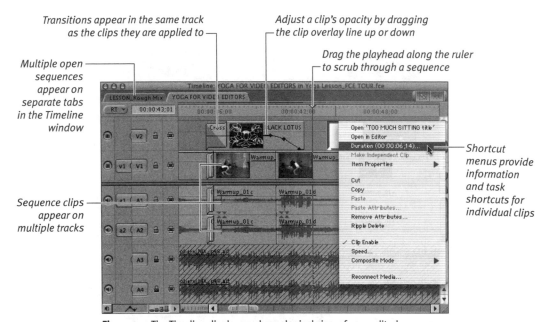

Transitions appear in the same track as the clips they are applied to —

Adjust a clip's opacity by dragging the clip overlay line up or down

Drag the playhead along the ruler to scrub through a sequence

Multiple open sequences appear on separate tabs in the Timeline window

Shortcut menus provide information and task shortcuts for individual clips

Sequence clips appear on multiple tracks

Figure 1.13 The Timeline displays a chronological view of your edited sequence.

Editing and Effects Windows

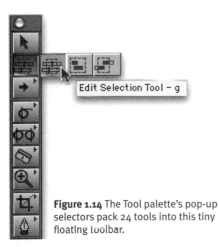

Figure 1.14 The Tool palette's pop-up selectors pack 24 tools into this tiny floating toolbar.

The Tool palette

The Tool palette (**Figure 1.14**) contains tools for selecting and manipulating items in the Timeline, Canvas, and Viewer. For a listing of each tool, see Chapter 9, "Basic Editing."

The Voice Over tool

Use the Voice Over tool (**Figure 1.15**) to record audio inside Final Cut Express. Specify a section of your sequence in the Timeline; then record voice-over as you play. See "Recording Audio with the Voice Over Tool" in Chapter 12.

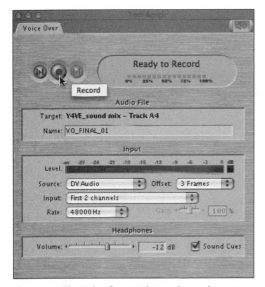

Figure 1.15 The Voice Over tool records synchronous audio directly into FCE.

EDITING AND EFFECTS WINDOWS

15

Input and Output Windows

Although you perform most editing tasks in Final Cut Express's main editing and effects windows, you'll need to use a couple of other windows to shape your program's input and output.

Capture

Use the Capture window (**Figure 1.16**) to capture video and audio media in Final Cut Express. Capture supports a range of capturing options, from live video capture on the fly to project recapture with full device control. Capture functions are explained in detail in Chapter 5, "Capturing Video."

Print to Video

Use Print to Video to output a Final Cut Express sequence or clip to videotape. The Print to Video function lets you configure pre- and post-program elements such as color bars and a 1-kHz tone, leader, slate, and countdown. Print to Video's loop feature allows you to print your sequence multiple times automatically.

For more information on the Print to Video window, see Chapter 19, "Creating Final Output."

Figure 1.16 The Capture window supports three capturing techniques, including automated project recapture.

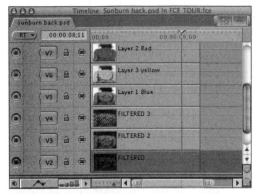

Figure 1.17 When you import a layered Photoshop file into Final Cut Express, you can maintain control over the Individual layers.

Import and export options

Final Cut Express's media handling is based on Apple's QuickTime, and that means you have a lot of import and export format options. If QuickTime can handle it, so can Final Cut Express.

◆ You can import QuickTime-compatible media files into a Final Cut Express project.

◆ You can import an iMovie project and convert it into an FCE project.

◆ You can import audio directly from a CD.

◆ You can import still images in a full range of formats.

◆ You can import a layered Adobe Photoshop file (**Figure 1.17**). Final Cut Express preserves the layers, importing the file as a sequence. Each layer in Photoshop corresponds to a video track in the sequence.

◆ You can export clips, sequences, or portions of either as QuickTime movies or in a variety of image and sound formats, including export to iDVD.

INPUT AND OUTPUT WINDOWS

The Final Cut Express HD Suite

Final Cut Express HD ships with a suite of two special-purpose applications. Each application is independent, but has been designed to work closely with the program.

 Soundtrack: Use Soundtrack's library of high-quality loops and *one-shots* (non-looping musical figures and sound effects) to assemble royalty-free music tracks. You can adjust pitch and tempo of any element in real time. Truly twenty-first century.

 LiveType: Select a prefabricated animated type sequence from LiveType's library to create complex animated titles, or edit the stock animated fonts in the library to create your own customized library. You can even borrow the motion paths from a LiveType animated font to animate graphic or video elements in your FCE sequence.

This book's coverage of LiveType and Soundtrack is limited to importing and exporting material between these applications and FCE. Individual PDF manuals are available from the Help menu of each application.

Do You Need Final Cut Pro?

Final Cut Express is a very capable video editing program, but if you need any of the following features, you should learn more about Final Cut Pro, Apple's professional-grade digital editing program.

If you're knee-deep in a Final Cut Express project before you realize that the feature you need is available only in Final Cut Pro, fear not. Open a Final Cut Express project in Final Cut Pro and you'll find your FCE project intact—you can pick up where you left off and enjoy FCP features.

- **If you need to capture and edit video in a format other than DV or HDV:** Final Cut Pro allows you to capture and edit HD, SD, DV, and analog video and film-based projects.

- **If you need to log your video footage before capture:** Final Cut Pro supports logging your shots as you review your footage and then capturing all or selected clips in a batch process.

- **If you work with large amounts of source video and need to save storage space:** Final Cut Pro allows you to capture and edit in OfflineRT, a compressed format that requires much less storage space. FCE offers a number of options for trimming media files over the course of your project.

- **If you want to import and export project data for use in other editing systems:** In Final Cut Pro, you can export an Edit Decision List (EDL), used for re-creating your edit on another editing system. You can export your audio tracks in Open Media Framework (OMF) format for finishing in an audio program like Digidesign's Pro Tools. FCE also supports After Effects plug-ins.

THE FINAL CUT EXPRESS HD SUITE

INSTALLING AND SETTING UP

This chapter walks you through the process of assembling the necessary hardware, hooking everything up, and installing Final Cut Express. Topics include Final Cut Express system requirements as well as hardware selection and configuration for both a basic setup and a more full-featured system.

The chapter ends with suggestions for optimizing performance, including recommendations for running Final Cut Express on a minimal "base-case" system and tips for troubleshooting Final Cut Express.

The perfect time to get the latest news on Final Cut Express and your hardware options is *before* you commit to a particular system. Apple's official Final Cut Express web site has a Resources page, and there's also a bustling community of resources for Final Cut Pro. FCP web sites, FCP user group meetings, and reputable vendors are my favorite sources. See Appendix A for a list of some useful sites.

System Requirements

Final Cut Express has the same basic system requirements as its big brother Final Cut Pro, but because fast CPUs and built-in FireWire ports have spread throughout the Macintosh product line, FCE wannabes can keep pace on just about any recent Mac. If you're unsure whether your Power Mac makes the grade, go to the AppleSpec page at Apple's web site and look up its complete specifications at `http://www.info.apple.com/support/applespec.html`.

Apple is continuously testing and qualifying third-party software and third-party external devices for compatibility with Final Cut Express. To review the latest list of Apple-approved video hardware and software, go to the Final Cut Express web site at `http://www.apple.com/finalcutexpress/qualification.html`.

✔ Tip

■ If you want to make use of FCE's real-time effects, you'll need more RAM and a speedier CPU. See the sidebar "Real-Time System Requirements."

Real-Time System Requirements

FCE's real-time technology (dubbed "RT Extreme" by Apple marketing wizards) performs its effects-previewing magic without additional hardware, so you'll need a fast G4 to see the show. You'll need a 500-MHz or faster single-processor Power Mac G4 system (or any model dual-processor G4 system) with at least 512 MB of RAM to see any real-time previewing at all. FCE has been programmed to check the processor speed of your Mac and to scale the quantity and quality of real-time effects available. Macs with faster processors (or dual processors) can process and preview multilayer scaling, motion effects, and selected transitions.

For more information on real-time system capabilities, see Chapter 18, "Real Time and Rendering." Why are real-time effects discussed in the rendering chapter? Because you can preview all sorts of FCE effects while you edit your show, but you still have to render many of them before you can output a full-resolution final program.

Software requirements:

◆ Mac OS X 10.3.7 or later

◆ QuickTime 6.5.2 or later

Minimum hardware requirements:

◆ Power Mac G4 with a 500-MHz processor and an AGP graphics card

◆ 384 MB of RAM (though more is always welcome)

◆ DVD drive (required for installation)

◆ 40-GB A/V (audio/video-rated) drive

◆ True color (24-bit) display

FCE application disk space requirements:

◆ 1 GB for the FCE application installation

◆ 5 GB for Soundtrack media

◆ 9 GB for LiveType media

DV hardware requirements:

◆ FireWire-equipped camcorder or DV deck for video capture

◆ FireWire cable plus any additional cables you may need for connecting your camcorder or deck to an external TV monitor and speakers

What's the Difference Between DV and Digital Video?

When you refer to *digital video*, you could be talking about any video format that stores image and audio information in digital form—it's digital video whether you store it on a DV tape or on a DVD disc.

DV is a specific digital video format whose identifying characteristic is that the conversion from analog to digital information takes place in the DV camera. So *DV* is a camera-based digital video format.

There are a few different flavors of DV, the differences between them come down to tape format and tape speed:

◆ DV usually refers to MiniDV, used by most consumer digital camcorders.

◆ DVCAM prints the same DV bitstream to a larger, more robust tape stock.

◆ DVC Pro uses a professional-grade tape as well, and it supports a high-quality mode—DVC Pro 50—which digitizes at twice the data rate as DV.

◆ HDV uses the same miniDV tape stock to record compressed digital video with frames sizes up to 1080:1440 pixels at data rates similar to standard DV rates.

SYSTEM REQUIREMENTS

Hardware Selection and Connection

You'll need a few additional items to transform your Macintosh into a video production studio. This section describes two possible setups. The basic system is the bare minimum required; the recommended setup is, well, highly recommended for anyone with more than a passing interest in making movies.

Basic hardware configuration

A basic hardware configuration (**Figure 2.1**) includes a DV camcorder or deck, a computer, and a high-resolution computer monitor. The beauty of the basic system is its simplicity: a DV camcorder connected to your Macintosh with a FireWire cable—that's all there is to it.

Here's a rundown of the function of each piece of the system.

DV camcorder or deck: The DV camera or deck feeds digital video and audio into the computer via FireWire and records DV output from Final Cut Express. During video capture, you must monitor audio through your camera or deck's audio outputs; computer speakers are muted.

Computer: Final Cut Express, installed on the Mac, captures and then stores digital video from the DV camera or deck on an A/V hard drive. Qualified Macs are equipped with FireWire; no additional video digitizing card is needed. You use your computer's speakers to monitor your audio. You edit your DV footage with Final Cut Express and then send it back out to tape through FireWire to your DV camcorder or deck.

High-resolution computer monitor: You view the results of your work on the computer's monitor.

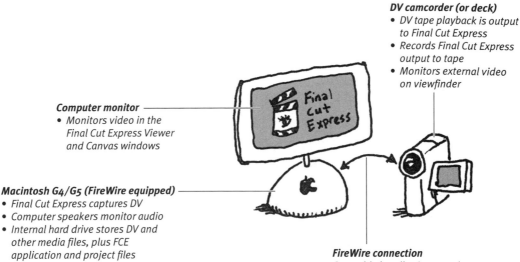

DV camcorder (or deck)
- DV tape playback is output to Final Cut Express
- Records Final Cut Express output to tape
- Monitors external video on viewfinder

Computer monitor
- Monitors video in the Final Cut Express Viewer and Canvas windows

Macintosh G4/G5 (FireWire equipped)
- Final Cut Express captures DV
- Computer speakers monitor audio
- Internal hard drive stores DV and other media files, plus FCE application and project files

FireWire connection
One cable handles input and output of:
- Digital video
- Digital audio
- Device control
- Timecode

Figure 2.1 A basic FCE hardware setup.

Recommended setup

A recommended setup (**Figure 2.2**) adds a dedicated hard drive to store your media and enhances your monitoring capabilities with the addition of an NTSC or PAL video monitor and external speakers.

Dedicated hard drive: Adding a dedicated drive for your media improves the performance as well as the storage capacity of your system. For more information, see "Storage Strategy for Final Cut Express" later in this chapter.

NTSC monitor: Most DV camcorders feature a built-in LCD display that you can use as an external video monitor, but if you're producing video to be viewed on television, you should preview your video output on an NTSC monitor as you edit. A real studio monitor is best, but even a consumer TV will give a much more accurate idea of how

your program looks and sounds. Connect the NTSC or PAL monitor to your video deck or camcorder using the component, S-video, or composite output jacks.

External speakers: Monitoring audio output from your video camcorder or deck with external speakers provides higher-quality audio output.

✔ Tip

■ If you plan to use an external NTSC or PAL monitor as you edit, connect your external speakers to monitor the audio output of your camcorder or deck, so that the audio from the external speakers will be synchronized with the video displayed on the video monitor. You need to do this because audio from your computer's built-in audio outputs will be slightly out of sync with the NTSC or PAL monitor.

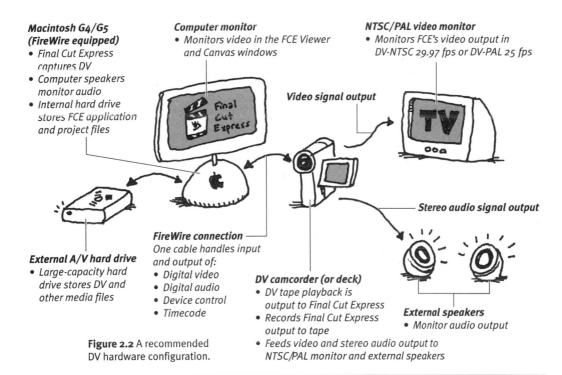

Figure 2.2 A recommended DV hardware configuration.

HDV: HD for the Masses

FCE's big sister Final Cut Pro has been able to handle even uncompressed HD formats for years, but the cost of HD cameras, additional hardware and storage requirements has limited the number of users able to take advantage of this power.

Now JVC and Sony have started to offer HDV cameras with retail prices under $5000. These inexpensive cameras make entry-level HD video available to those thousands of us with more limited means.

With Final Cut Express HD and iMovie HD, Apple joins Sony and JVC in a serious campaign to bring HD to the Mac and the masses by offering entry-level video editing software that can handle HD without additional hardware.

Final Cut Express HD (and even the latest edition of iMovie) can now capture HDV via FireWire, edit using Apple's new Apple Intermediate Codec format, and then output via FireWire—all without an additional hardware card.

To celebrate their latest achievement, Apple rechristened Final Cut Express 3 "Final Cut Express HD."

HD capture without a hardware card? What's the catch?

Here's the scoop:

HD is the first video standard that's digital all the way from acquisition through final playback. Now video developers are freed from the constraints of analog video broadcast standards—and new HD formats are popping up faster than Las Vegas suburbs.

High definition video is a growing family of formats with a wide variety of frame sizes and frame rates ranging from ultra-compressed HDV 720p (1280 x 720-pixel frame size and a data rate of 19 Mb/s) to uncompressed 10-bit 1080i60 (1920 x 1080-pixel frame size and a data rate of 932 Mb/s).

HDV uses MPEG-2, a compression algorithm that reduces the size of the HDV datastream by reducing the number of frames that contain complete picture information. One of these complete frames (called I-frames) is followed by a sequence of reduced-image-data frames (called B-frames and P-frames). HDV operates at data rates ranging from 19Mb/s to 25 Mb/s—that's a data rate that FireWire can handle. As you capture, FCE converts the HDV footage to Apple Intermediate Codec (AIC) format. AIC generates complete image and audio information for each frame—that's a frame rate that FCE can handle. For more information, see Apple's *New Features in Final Cut Express HD* PDF.

Storage Strategy for Final Cut Express

Digital video files are big—really, really big. In the Olde Days (five years ago), big hard drives were an expensive proposition; these days, $300 will get you a reliable 120-GB FireWire drive that will store 8 hours of DV. If you're going to edit anything substantial at all, consider additional hard drive storage for your system.

Here are some overall considerations when selecting a storage option:

Any storage system you select must be fast enough to keep up with required data transfer rates (some experts recommend a minimum transfer rate of 7 or 8 MB per second). Many storage formats do meet the speed requirement, but as you weigh your speed/capacity/price trade-offs, don't shortchange yourself in the speed department.

Hard disk storage is available in a variety of formats, and the number of formats is always growing. Rather than present a variety of specific hard disk options, here's a set of strategic questions to help steer you to the storage option that's best for you.

How much space do I need?

DV requires 3.6 MB of storage space per second of program material.

That's 216 MB of space per minute of DV.

Or 1 GB of space per 5 minutes of DV.

When calculating your storage needs, remember that a good rule of thumb is to add the final program lengths of the total number of projects you want to keep online and then multiply by four to accommodate any render files, undos, scratch copies, and test exports you may generate while editing. Be more generous if you want to capture much more footage than you ultimately use.

Do I need a dedicated drive just for media storage?

A dedicated drive for storing your media will improve the performance of your system because it contains no operating system software, other applications, or other files that can fragment the disk. Fragmentation can interfere with the continuous data flow of video and audio to and from the disk.

Here's another reason to keep your media files and program files on separate drives: your media drive, because it works harder, is more likely to crash than your program drive. In the event of a media drive crash, you may lose your media files, but you won't lose your edit data, which should make it easier to recover from the crash. A dedicated drive or drives for media storage is almost always a great investment.

Should I go with internal or external storage?

What kind of workflow do you anticipate? Whether to invest in internal drives (which could be less expensive) or external drives (which allow you to switch between projects quickly by swapping out drives on your workstation, or to move a project and its media from one workstation to another quickly) depends on your individual needs.

HARDWARE SELECTION AND CONNECTION

Connecting a DV camcorder

Connecting a DV camcorder or deck to your computer couldn't be simpler. All you need is a single FireWire cable, which transmits device control data, timecode, video, and audio between the DV device and your Mac.

To connect a DV device to your computer with FireWire:

1. Start with a 6-pin to 4-pin FireWire cable (**Figure 2.3**). Plug the 6-pin connector into the 6-pin Apple FireWire port (**Figure 2.4**) and the 4-pin connector into your video device's DV port. (FireWire ports on external devices are sometimes labeled IEEE 1394, DV IN/OUT, or iLink.) Both connectors snap into place when properly engaged.

2. Turn on the DV camcorder or deck.

3. Switch the DV device to VCR mode (sometimes labeled VTR).

continues on next page

Figure 2.3 A 6-pin to 4-pin FireWire cable. The 6-pin (big) end goes into your Mac's FireWire port; plug the 4-pin (small) end into your DV camcorder.

Figure 2.4 The FireWire logo identifies the FireWire ports on the back of your computer.

FireWire Cables: Handle with Care

Before you hook up your FireWire connectors, take a careful look at the connector ends (the 4-pin connector is the smaller end). The connectors are easy to hook up, but the 4-pin connectors and ports can be especially fragile. Before connecting a 4-pin connector to its corresponding port, be sure to align it properly by matching an indent on the connector to the indent in the port. Do not force the two together.

The 6-pin connector (the larger end) plugs into one of the FireWire ports on the back of your Mac. Don't try to force the 4-pin connector into the computer's 6-pin FireWire port.

New in FCE HD: Monitor Full-Screen Video on a Computer Display

FCE HD introduces a new option for external video display—Digital Cinema Desktop. You can use the Digital Cinema display option with a single display to enjoy gorgeous full-screen monitoring, or you can attach a second computer display to your Mac and use it as a dedicated video monitor.

Digital Cinema's full-screen playback is wonderful for editing on a PowerBook because you don't need to tie up your FireWire port with the deck or camcorder that's feeding your external video monitor.

The playback quality is decent enough for rough edit monitoring, and you can skip the FireWire traffic jam that ensues when you're trying to get FireWire drives and your external video device all hooked up and playing nicely together on the PowerBook's single FW bus.

To enable full-screen monitoring, choose View > Video Out > Digital Cinema Desktop Preview, and then switch in and out of full-screen preview using the external video keyboard shortcut, Cmd-F12. (You can use the customizable keyboard feature to reassign your full-screen preview toggle to something more convenient; try Shift-1.)

If you're working in HDV format, you can monitor your HDV output on a computer display rather than an expensive HD broadcast monitor. This is good news for entry-level HD producers and others looking for a low-cost way to monitor HD video. For more information, see Apple's *New Features in Final Cut Express HD* PDF.

✔ Tips

- If your DV device is Apple FireWire compatible, connect it to the computer and turn it on before installing Final Cut Express to allow the installation program to automatically receive setup information from your DV camcorder or deck.

- Whenever you want to use a DV deck or camcorder with Final Cut Express, connect and turn on the device before opening the application so FCE can detect the device.

- If you want to use a camcorder as your playback/record deck, you must switch it to VCR mode. In VCR mode, the camcorder uses the video and audio connectors or FireWire for input and output. Because a camcorder in Camera mode has switched its inputs to receive information from the CCD sensor and microphone, Final Cut Express cannot record to the camcorder while it is in Camera mode.

- For more information on controlling your deck or camcorder during video capture, see Chapter 5, "Capturing Video."

- For more information on controlling your deck or camcorder as you output to tape, see Chapter 19, "Creating Final Output."

FCE Protocol: Disk Names

When naming hard drives, partitions, and folders that you intend to use with Final Cut Express, you should observe a special naming requirement: give each hard disk a name that does not contain the entire name of another disk or partition. For example, naming disks "Inferno" and "Inferno 1" could cause FCE to have trouble finding your files later.

HARDWARE SELECTION AND CONNECTION

Connecting an external NTSC or PAL video monitor

Final Cut Express is designed to use the audio and video outputs of your DV deck or camcorder to feed an external NTSC or PAL monitor. Because the monitor receives output from Final Cut Express through your device's outputs, you must have your device on and the FireWire connection to your computer established, or you won't be able to view output on your monitor while you work in Final Cut Express.

To connect an external NTSC or PAL monitor:

1. Position your video monitor at a comfortable viewing distance from your location in front of the computer.

2. *Do one of the following:*

   ◆ Connect the audio and video outputs of your video deck or camcorder to the audio and video inputs of your NTSC or PAL monitor.

   ◆ If you are using additional external speakers, or if your video monitor has no speakers, connect only the video output from your video device to the video input of your monitor. Use your video device's audio outputs to feed your external speakers.

3. After you install Final Cut Express, you can check or modify your viewing settings by choosing View > Video Out (**Figure 2.5**).

✔ Tip

■ For more details on FCE's video output settings, see the next section, "FCE Protocol: Controlling External Video Output."

Figure 2.5 Choose View > Video Out to check or modify your external video output settings.

FCE Protocol: Controlling External Video Output

The external video display options in Final Cut Express require a little explanation. Using an external video monitor while editing is really the best way to work, so the program assumes you'll be working in this way and was designed to output video and audio via FireWire whenever a video device is connected to the system.

Here's the catch: you can preview real-time effects on your computer only when that video output is disabled.

These View > Video Out menu options control video output mode:

◆ View > Video Out > Canvas Playback disables the FireWire video output, thus enabling real-time effects preview in FCE's Canvas window.

◆ View > Video Out > Digital Cinema Desktop Preview switches that Canvas playback in and out of full-screen preview mode. Digital Cinema mode also allows real-time effects preview.

◆ View > Video Out > Apple FireWire (NTSC or PAL) opens the video output feeding your DV camcorder, but disables real-time effects preview on the computer monitor.

Two additional View menu options help you manage external video device switching:

◆ View > Video Out > Refresh Video Devices re-scans all your input/output busses and detects your external video devices—convenient when you've forgotten to power up your camera before launching FCE.

◆ View > Video Out > Toggle Last switches you between the last two video output modes selected. The keyboard shortcut is Command-F12; that's important to remember when you want to return to the FCE interface from Digital Cinema full-screen preview mode.

If you watch FCE's output through an external NTSC or PAL monitor, you may see a difference in the Canvas window's playback quality. FCE gives CPU priority to the FireWire output to ensure that there are no dropped frames in that output signal, so the Canvas may play back at 15 frames per second (fps).

One day soon, you'll be able see your effects previewed in real time on your video monitor, but for now you'll have to choose.

HARDWARE SELECTION AND CONNECTION

Installing Final Cut Express

It's a good idea to set up and connect your additional hardware before you install Final Cut Express, because the type of DV deck or camcorder you use with Final Cut Express determines how the software is configured during installation. If you have not yet installed and configured the additional hardware you will be using with your computer, read "Hardware Selection and Connection" earlier in this chapter. If your system is already configured with capture hardware and a camcorder or deck, proceed with the installation instructions in this section.

If you don't have your hardware yet, it's okay to install Final Cut Express.

It's also important to install your software in the recommended order.

Installation Options for the FCE Suite of Applications

Final Cut Express ships with a pair of helper applications—LiveType and Soundtrack. Both LiveType and Soundtrack require big media libraries, which push the minimum disk space required to 15 GB for a default FCE installation. Soundtrack's library of music loops can be installed on another drive, but that 9 GB of LiveType media will be installed on your boot drive—unless you take steps. Here are a couple of options:

◆ Install the LiveType data into a folder on another drive (call the folder LiveType Data), and then create an alias for that folder. Put the alias on your boot drive here: Library/Application Support/LiveType/(your alias, which must be called *exactly* LiveType Data). The alias will direct LiveType to the location of its stock media folder.

◆ Install individual LiveType fonts from the application DVD on an as-needed basis. LiveType supports this option; you can preview the fonts and textures without installing the multi-gigabyte LiveType data.

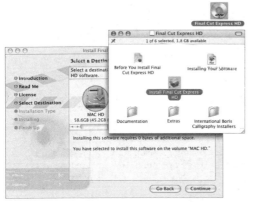

Figure 2.6 The Final Cut Express application DVD and installer. Don't forget to check out the *Installing Your Software* PDF document.

Figure 2.7 If you install FCE in the Applications folder, any user of the computer can use the software.

Figure 2.8 You can install FCE in a private application folder within your Home directory.

Where to install FCE?

Here's a recommended installation configuration for a Final Cut Express system with two hard drives available.

You should leave your fastest drive completely free for media files only. Media files include captured audio and video, as well as rendered media files and any computer-generated graphics or motion graphics.

Keep your Final Cut Express project files on the same drive as the application.

You should also back up your project files to removable media with such frequency that your behavior seems obsessive to a casual observer. Go ahead—let 'em laugh.

To install Final Cut Express:

1. Be sure any external video hardware is connected and turned on before you start the installation procedure, so that Final Cut Express can automatically detect your video capture equipment.

2. Insert the Final Cut Express disc into your DVD drive (**Figure 2.6**); then follow the onscreen installation instructions.

3. After reading the obligatory licensing agreement and read-me file, choose an installation location from the Install Final Cut Express dialog box. Normally, you should choose the Applications folder on the startup disk; installing FCE in this folder gives all users of your computer access to the program (**Figure 2.7**).

   However, if you want exclusive use of Final Cut Express, install the program in a private application folder you create inside your Home directory (**Figure 2.8**).

INSTALLING FINAL CUT EXPRESS

✔ Tips

■ For each user, Final Cut Express creates a separate Final Cut Express User Data folder and generates a separate Custom Settings folder and Final Cut Express Prefs file (**Figure 2.9**).

■ One big benefit of personal FCE Preference files is that your individual Scratch Disk preferences stay put, even when you're sharing your FCE system with the masses. As long as you remember to log in to your own identity before you start work, your preferences will load from your User Data folder when you launch FCE.

■ Final Cut Express relies on QuickTime for its functionality, which is installed automatically under Mac OS X 10.2 and later. However, it's a good idea to check Apple's web site for the latest information on QuickTime updates and Final Cut Express version compatibility before you install FCE.

■ You don't need to upgrade to QuickTime Pro to use Final Cut Express.

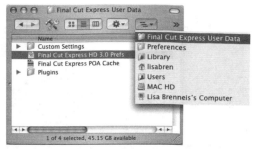

Figure 2.9 For each user, FCE creates a Final Cut Express User Data folder. You can find it in each user's Preferences folder (in the user's Library folder).

Upgrading to Final Cut Express HD

Here are a couple of tips for users upgrading to Final Cut Express HD from an earlier version:

◆ You can open and update project files from FCE 1 and 2.

◆ Final Cut Express 2 switched to a new kind of clip-handling structure: a master-affiliate clip relationship. You can rename and relink any member of a master-affiliate clip group, and all clips in that group will be modified. Final Cut Express 1 projects updated in FCE HD will retain FCE 1's clip-handling structure, which dictates that separate instances of clips shall be independent of one another.

For more information on FCE's clip-handling grammar, see Chapter 4, "Projects, Sequences, and Clips." For details on project upgrade procedures, see Chapter 9 of Apple's *Final Cut Express Help* PDF.

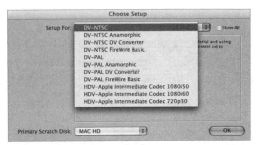

Figure 2.10 In the Choose Setup dialog box, pick the Easy Setup that matches your system's video format and hardware.

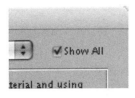

Figure 2.11 Check Show All to display the complete list of Easy Setups available.

Figure 2.12 After you choose an Easy Setup, a brief description of the setup and a summary of its settings appear below its name.

Registering and choosing an initial setup

Be sure any external video hardware is connected and turned on before you launch Final Cut Express for the first time, so that FCE can detect your DV camcorder and streamline the initial setup process. With the standard hardware setup, your initial setup selections should correctly configure all your Final Cut Express audio and video settings automatically.

To register and choose your initial setup:

1. Open the Final Cut Express application and enter your registration information and serial number.

2. In the Choose Setup dialog box, choose an Easy Setup from the Setup For pop-up menu (**Figure 2.10**). Choose the setup that matches your system's video format and hardware. FCE constructs a short list of Easy Setups based on your hardware format; check Show All to display a complete list of setups available (**Figure 2.11**).

   For more information, see "How to choose an Easy Setup" in Chapter 3.

   A brief description and summary of your selected Easy Setup appears below the pop-up menu (**Figure 2.12**).

   continues on next page

3. From the Primary Scratch Disk pop-up menu, choose the disk you want to use to store your captured video, audio, render, and cache files (**Figure 2.13**).

   It is recommended that you save captured media files on a different disk than the disk where Final Cut Express is installed. For more information, see "Setting Scratch Disk Preferences" in Chapter 3.

4. Click OK.

   If you didn't connect a DV camcorder or deck during launch, Final Cut Express displays the External Video dialog box notifying you that it can't find an external device. Click Continue to dismiss it. If the dialog box appears and you did connect a device, see "Troubleshooting" later in this chapter.

   Final Cut Express is now configured to use a standard set of preferences and preset controls based on information you supplied. You may want to review the default preference settings before you dive into a project. For details on modifying preferences, read "Specifying User Preferences and System Settings" in Chapter 3.

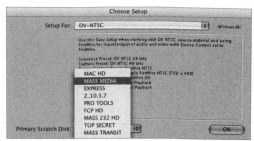

Figure 2.13 From the Primary Scratch Disk pop-up menu, choose the disk you want to use to store your captured media.

Figure 2.14 If you see scroll bars on the edge of the Canvas's image area, you're zoomed in too far for optimum playback performance, and your external video playback will be disabled. Choose Fit to Window from the Canvas View pop-up menu to bring the entire frame back into view.

Optimizing Performance

Trying to eke out the best possible performance from Final Cut Express? Here's a rundown of settings and maintenance tips that can help FCE perform more efficiently.

Settings

◆ Turn off file sharing.

◆ Avoid running processor-intensive operations in other open applications while you're working in Final Cut Express (especially when capturing video).

Display

◆ Make sure the entire image area is visible in windows playing video. If you see scroll bars on the edge of the Viewer or the Canvas (**Figure 2.14**), you're zoomed in too far for optimum performance.

◆ Don't place program windows so that they split across dual monitors.

OPTIMIZING PERFORMANCE

Disk maintenance

◆ Store project files on your startup disk, and store media and rendered files on a separate hard disk.

◆ Maintain 10 percent free space on each disk drive. If you fill your disk to the last megabyte, your performance will take a dive—and that's the *best*-case scenario.

◆ Defragment disk drives regularly, especially those you use for capturing. You can use a defragmentation utility; or make a complete backup of your data, erase the disk, and restore your data.

◆ When a project is finished and archived, delete all files from the disk you used to create the project and then defragment the drive. This helps prepare the disk for the next project.

◆ Final Cut Express performs poorly if you try to work with remote media files over a network connection. Copy files from the network to a local disk before importing them.

◆ It's a good idea to run Disk First Aid, a component of Apple's Disk Utility application, once or twice a month to check your drive's data directory.

OPTIMIZING PERFORMANCE

The Bottom Line: Running FCE on a "Base-Case" Mac

To get the best performance possible from Final Cut Express running on a slower G4, you'll have to give up a little flexibility in your display options, but you may find that the improved responsiveness and playback quality are worth it.

1. Eliminate display scaling. Scaling the video to match the size of the playback window in the Viewer or the Canvas is handled by the computer's video card, but it takes a lot of processing power to pull off. To reduce the card's demands on your CPU, set your display option to match DV's native display format: 50 percent, non-square pixels. Go to the Zoom pop-up menu in the Canvas, set the View size to 50 percent, and then uncheck the View as Square Pixels box.

2. In the Monitors preference pane, set your monitor resolution to 1024 by 768 or lower and your color depth to Millions.

3. On the General tab of the User Preferences window, reduce the number of undos as well as the number of recent items. These changes will free up more RAM.

4. Keep your projects lean by deleting old versions of sequences that you no longer need to reference. Smaller projects reduce the amount of RAM necessary to track an open project file.

5. Reinitialize your drives. Quite often, old drive software and/or drivers will impair performance.

Troubleshooting

You probably won't encounter any of these problems. But if you run into snags after installing Final Cut Express and configuring your hardware, the following tips may help.

Many of the tips presented here involve checking and adjusting preferences. But before you start changing individual preferences, try this: choose Final Cut Express > Easy Setup and make sure you're still using the correct Easy Setup for your video format and hardware.

Also, make sure you're running the latest version of Final Cut Express by checking Apple's web site.

You'll find a complete guide to setting preferences and presets in Chapter 3, "Presets and Preferences."

You can't establish a device control connection with your camcorder or deck.

◆ Make sure the FireWire cable connecting your computer and DV camcorder is connected properly.

◆ Verify that the camcorder is set to VCR mode.

◆ If your device has a Local/Remote switch, be sure it's set to Remote.

◆ Turn the device off and back on and then restart Final Cut Express.

You can't control certain functions of your camcorder or deck.

◆ Make sure the FireWire cable connecting your computer and DV camcorder is connected properly.

◆ If you are using a device with FireWire, try switching the device control protocol from Apple FireWire to FireWire Basic.

◆ If your device has a Local/Remote switch, make sure it's switched to Remote.

You see a "Missing scratch disk" warning.

◆ Make sure your scratch disks are powered up and mounted properly. You should see your disks on the Finder Desktop.

◆ Make sure your designated Capture Scratch folder is in its proper location.

◆ If you are sharing Final Cut Express with other users on a multiuser system, make sure you are logged in as the current user—FCE creates a separate set of preference settings for each user.

TROUBLESHOOTING

You don't hear audio on your computer's speakers when playing video from your camcorder or deck.

◆ Make sure your audio cables are connected properly.

◆ When you enable your external video output to monitor video externally (by choosing Apple FireWire from the View menu), your audio and video are routed to your external monitor or video device, and your computer's speakers do not receive any audio. Make sure your external monitor and speakers are on and that the volume is turned up. To disable external video output, choose View > Video Out and select Canvas Playback or Digital Cinema Desktop Preview.

Video is not visible on an external NTSC or PAL monitor.

◆ Make sure your cables are connected properly and that your monitor is on.

◆ Verify that the camcorder is set to VCR mode.

◆ Confirm that external video output is enabled by choosing View > Video Out > Refresh Video Devices to re-scan all your input/output busses. Then choose View > Video Out and make sure the Apple FireWire option is checked.

◆ Make sure the Capture window is closed.

You notice dropped frames on your NTSC or PAL monitor during DV playback from the Timeline.

Like the common cold, dropped frames are frequently a symptom of an overworked system. Refer to Appendix A, "Solutions to Common Problems and Customer Support," in Apple's *Final Cut Express Help* PDF for a comprehensive list of possible causes of dropped frames. Here are a few easy things to try first:

◆ In the Canvas, choose Fit to Window from the View pop-up menu to ensure that the image area displays the entire frame.

◆ Reduce the Canvas or Viewer view size to 50 percent.

◆ Disable Show as Square Pixels in the Zoom pop-up menu.

◆ Set Audio Quality Playback to Low Quality and reduce the number of Real-Time Audio Mixing tracks specified on the General tab in the User Preferences window.

◆ Turn off AppleTalk and file sharing.

◆ Make sure your media drives are fast enough to feed media files to FCE and that the drives have not become so fragmented that their performance is impaired.

PRESETS AND PREFERENCES

3

Final Cut Express's designers have carefully organized the tools you use to configure settings and preferences. The goal of this organization is to make it much easier for editors using the most common hardware and video formats to configure FCE—and much more difficult for users to unintentionally modify individual settings within a preset configuration.

This chapter explains Easy Setups—FCE's streamlined configuration feature—and then walks you through your preference options in the User Preferences and System Settings windows.

FCE's preset principle is balanced by a highly customizable interface. At the end of this chapter you'll learn about options for reconfiguring Final Cut Express's interface to complement your personal working preferences.

About Easy Setups, Presets, Settings, and Preferences

FCE preference settings are accessed from three menu choices: Easy Setup, User Preferences, and System Settings (**Figure 3.1**).

◆ **Easy Setup:** Capture, device control, and sequence settings are all organized into preset configurations, and these Audio/Video presets are grouped into master presets called *Easy Setups.* For more information, see the next section, "Using Easy Setups."

◆ **User Preferences and System Settings:** Unlike your Easy Setup preset, which is largely dictated by your hardware and video formats, a preference is a setting that specifies how *you* want to work with your media in Final Cut Express. FCE preferences are divided between two windows: User Preferences and System Settings. The settings in these windows affect all your Final Cut Express projects.

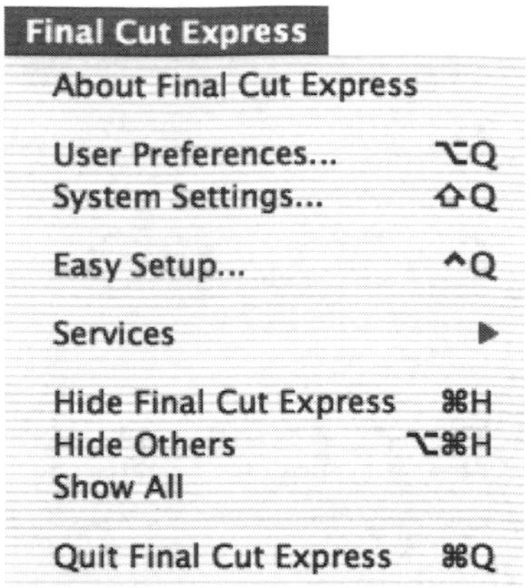

Final Cut Express

About Final Cut Express	
User Preferences...	⌥Q
System Settings...	⇧Q
Easy Setup...	^Q
Services	▶
Hide Final Cut Express	⌘H
Hide Others	⌥⌘H
Show All	
Quit Final Cut Express	⌘Q

Figure 3.1 Access preference settings from three Final Cut Express menu choices: Easy Setup, User Preferences, and System Settings.

How to "Trash Your Prefs"

FCE has made setting up preferences simple, but you still may find that you need to delete your FCE preferences files (or "trash your prefs") to force FCE to restore all your program settings to their default values. You will need to delete three files:

1. First, go to **User/Library/Preferences/** and remove the file called com.apple.FinalCutExpress.plist.

2. Then go to **User/Library/Preferences/ Final Cut Express User Data/** and remove the other two preferences files, called Final Cut Express HD 3.0 Preferences and Final Cut Express POA Cache.

After deleting the files, relaunch Final Cut Express with all your external hardware on and connected. You'll see the Choose Setup dialog box. Here's your chance to reset your preferences from scratch.

EASY SETUPS/PRESETS/SETTINGS/PREFERENCES

Using Easy Setups

An Easy Setup is a single preset configuration of multiple Final Cut Express settings: a Device Control preset, a Capture preset, a Sequence preset, and video and audio playback settings. The beauty of a preset is that you can configure all your settings correctly with a single selection.

You selected an Easy Setup as part of the initial setup process. Your selected Easy Setup becomes your default setup, so all projects and sequences use these settings until you change them.

Once you have an Easy Setup that works for your Final Cut Express system, you shouldn't need to change it unless you change your video hardware or video format. If you do use your FCE system with a variety of different cameras or with footage shot in a different DV format, Easy Setups make it simple to switch configurations quickly and accurately.

In this section, you'll learn how to choose the correct Easy Setup and how to switch to a different Easy Setup.

Modifying the Settings of an Existing Item

If you switch to a different Easy Setup or change your settings on the Timeline Options tab of the User Preferences window, your change will be reflected in new projects, sequences, and items created after you change the settings. Here's how and where you modify the settings of a project, sequence, or clip you've already created:

- **Item Properties:** Control-click the item's icon in the Browser or Timeline; then select Item Properties from the shortcut menu.

- **Sequence Settings:** Control-click the sequence's icon in the Browser; then select Settings from the shortcut menu.

- **Project Properties:** Open the project and then choose Edit > Project Properties.

How to choose an Easy Setup

The Easy Setups window displays the currently selected presets for each setting—Sequence, Capture, and Device Control, plus Audio and Video Playback—that makes up your current Easy Setup, plus a brief description of when you should use the currently selected setup.

FCE's default DV-NTSC (or DV-PAL) setup will be fine for most FCE users, but if you check Show All and then click the Easy Setups pop-up menu, you'll see a long list of other setups to choose from (**Figure 3.2**).

When should you switch to another Easy Setup? The basis for selecting a preset is always *matching*:

◆ You want your Capture preset to match the recorded format of the DV tape you're capturing. If the tape was recorded with 16-bit, 48-kHz audio, then the default DV-NTSC setup is fine. If you're capturing DV with 12-bit, 32-kHz audio, you'll need to switch to an Easy Setup

with the same settings. If you're capturing DV that was shot in anamorphic (wide-screen) format, switch to a setup set that includes anamorphic settings.

◆ Your Sequence preset must match the format of your Capture preset. All Easy setups in FCE take care of this for you.

◆ Your Device Control setting must match the requirements of the video hardware you're controlling. Final Cut Express is pretty good at automatically selecting the correct device control setting, but if you're having trouble controlling your video device from inside FCE, check the Final Cut Express Qualified Devices page at www.apple.com/finalcutexpress/qualification.html. Your equipment may require a different device protocol or an additional helper script.

◆ Your Video Playback settings must match the video format (DV or PAL) of the device you're outputting video to.

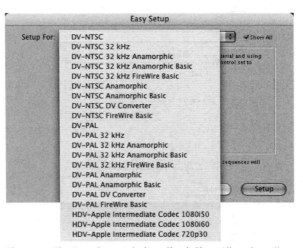

Figure 3.2 The Easy Setup window. Check Show All, and you'll find a long list of Easy Setups to choose from. Choose the one that matches the format of the video you want to capture.

DV-NTSC, FCE's default setup, is designed to complement the recommended settings on most DV decks and camcorders. (The default settings are the same for the two video standards that FCE supports: NTSC and PAL.)

Here are the settings for DV-NTSC:

Sequence preset: DV NTSC 48 kHz

Capture preset: DV NTSC 48 kHz Capture

Device control preset: FireWire NTSC

External video for playback and print to video: Apple FireWire NTSC (720 x 480)

When an Easy Setup offers an alternative to any of these default presets, the alternative is listed in the Easy Setup's name. **Figure 3.3** dissects one example.

✔ **Tip**

■ Unfortunately, many consumer DV camcorders come from the factory set to record audio at the lower-quality 12-bit, 32-kHz setting. FCE assumes you'll be savvy enough to switch your camera settings to 16-bit, 48 kHz—the recommended higher-quality audio setting. Check any source tapes you're capturing and be aware that if your camera is set at 32 kHz, choosing the default Easy Setup will result in a settings mismatch.

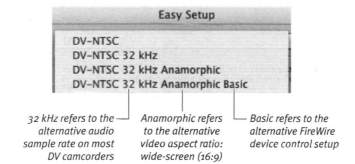

32 kHz refers to the alternative audio sample rate on most DV camcorders

Anamorphic refers to the alternative video aspect ratio: wide-screen (16:9)

Basic refers to the alternative FireWire device control setup

Figure 3.3 An Easy Setup's name indicates which alternatives to the default preset are included. If a default preset is used, it's omitted from the name.

To switch to a different Easy Setup:

1. Choose Final Cut Express > Easy Setup.

2. *Do one of the following:*
   - ◆ Check Show All to see the complete list of available Easy Setups.
   - ◆ Leave Show All unchecked to see a restricted list of Easy Setups.

3. From the Setup For pop-up menu, select an Easy Setup (**Figure 3.4**).

   A summary of your selected Easy Setup appears below the pop-up menu (**Figure 3.5**).

4. Click Setup.

   The new Easy Setup affects only new projects and sequences and doesn't change settings for existing projects and sequences.

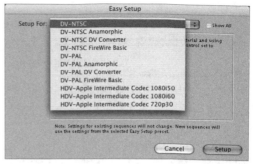

Figure 3.4 From the Setup For pop-up menu, select an Easy Setup.

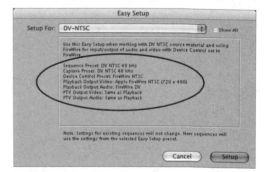

Figure 3.5 A summary of the Easy Setup you chose appears below the pop-up menu.

Apple FireWire vs. Basic FireWire

Apple FireWire is a high-speed serial bus that allows simultaneous transfer of digital video, digital audio, timecode information, and device control, all through a single cable. Nearly all Macintosh models of the past few years include built-in FireWire ports. FireWire's usefulness is not limited to digital video—a wide variety of hard drives, printers, scanners, audio mixers, and other peripheral devices take advantage of FireWire's high speeds and advanced features.

FireWire (IEEE 1394) serial bus technology is currently supported by many professional and consumer-level camcorders and decks. However, not all manufacturers have implemented the full FireWire specification in their products, so some devices don't fully support Final Cut Express's device control. That is why Final Cut Express provides two versions of the FireWire protocol in its Device Control presets: Apple FireWire and Apple FireWire Basic.

If your deck or camcorder uses FireWire, try selecting the Apple FireWire protocol first. With Apple FireWire selected, your device should support the most basic functions like returning timecode and accepting basic transport commands. If you discover that your device does not accurately go to specified timecodes or fails to execute special commands, switch to the FireWire Basic protocol.

Specifying User Preferences and System Settings

The settings in the User Preferences and System Settings windows affect all of your Final Cut Express projects. The User Preferences window contains four tabs: General, Editing, Timeline Options, and Render Control. The System Settings window offers another four tabs' worth of preference settings: Scratch Disks, Memory & Cache, Playback Control, and External Editors. System Settings window preference options are covered in the second half of this section.

To set General preferences:

1. Choose Final Cut Express HD > User Preferences.

   The General tab will appear as the front tab in the User Preferences window (**Figure 3.6**).

2. You can specify settings for the following:

   ◆ **Levels of Undo:** Specify the number of actions that can be undone. Specifying a large number of undos can make significant demands on your available RAM, however.

   ◆ **List Recent Clips:** Set the number of recently accessed clips available on the Viewer's Recent Clips pop-up menu.

   continues on next page

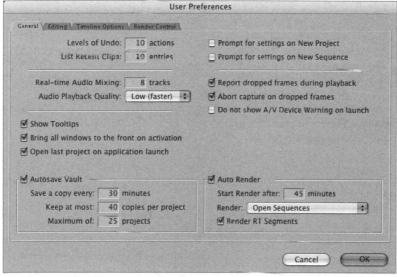

Figure 3.6 Specify a number of general program preferences on the General tab of the User Preferences window.

◆ **Real-Time Audio Mixing:** Specify the number of audio tracks that Final Cut Express mixes in real time. The default setting is eight tracks. The maximum number of tracks you will be able to mix depends on multiple factors. Reduce the number of tracks if you experience audio playback problems, such as video stuttering or audio pops or dropouts.

◆ **Audio Playback Quality:** Choose the quality of sample-rate conversion when you import audio files with sample rates that differ from your sequence's rate. At the lowest playback quality, Final Cut Express can reserve more processing power for real-time mixing operations. If you choose the highest playback quality, your sample-rate-converted audio will sound better, but you won't be able to stack up as many simultaneous audio tracks before FCE needs to mixdown (render) your audio. Higher quality settings will take more processing time, so the default is Low. In general, choose Low when editing. FCE automatically defaults to the highest audio quality during all rendering, audio mixdown, and printing to video, so you won't need to switch the setting here when you're ready to output your program.

◆ **Show ToolTips:** Check this box to toggle the display of tooltip labels on buttons and tools.

◆ **Bring All Windows to the Front on Activation:** Check this box to specify that whenever FCE is in the background, clicking any single FCE window to activate the application will bring all open FCE windows to the front of the Desktop.

◆ **Open Last Project on Application Launch:** Check this box if you want FCE to automatically reopen your last saved project when you launch the application. Uncheck the box if you want FCE to create a new empty project on application launch.

◆ **Autosave Vault:** Check this box if you want FCE to save backup copies of all your open projects automatically at regular intervals. Enter a number to specify a time interval in minutes. For more information, see "Using the Autosave Vault" in Chapter 4.

  ◆ **Save a Copy Every *n* Minutes:** Enter a number of minutes to specify a time interval between backup operations.

  ◆ **Keep at Most *n* Copies per Project:** Enter a value to specify how many autosaved backup copies of each project file you want Final Cut Express to store.

  ◆ **Maximum of *n* Projects:** Enter a value to specify the maximum number of projects you want to back up in the Autosave Vault. If the number of open projects exceeds the number specified here, Final Cut Express will override the maximum you set and autosave all open projects.

◆ **Prompt for Settings on New Project:** Check this box if you want the option to modify project properties each time you create a new project.

◆ **Prompt for Settings on New Sequence:** Check this box if you want to see a list of sequence presets each time you create a new sequence.

USER PREFERENCES AND SYSTEM SETTINGS

- **Report Dropped Frames During Playback:** Check this box if you want Final Cut Express to display a warning dialog box whenever frames are dropped during playback.

- **Abort Capture on Dropped Frames:** Check this box to automatically stop the capture process if dropped frames are detected during a capture.

- **Do Not Show A/V Device Warning on Launch:** Check this box if you want Final Cut Express to ignore any missing external video devices when you launch the application and disable the display of the External A/V warning dialog box.

- **Auto Render:** Check the box to enable the triggering of automatic rendering when FCE is idle for a specified period.

  - **Start Render After *n* Minutes:** Enter a number of minutes to specify how long FCE should be idle before automatic rendering is triggered.

  - **Which Sequences:** Select Open Sequences to render all sequences currently open in the Timeline, select Current Only to render just the active sequence on the front tab of the Timeline, or select Open Except Current to render all open sequences except the active sequence on the front tab of the Timeline.

  - **Render RT Segments:** Check the box to include those sections of your sequence that use real-time effects in the auto-render operation.

✔ **Tip**

- Displaying video on the computer monitor while printing to video or editing to tape taxes the computer's processing power and can cause performance problems. If you notice dropped frames in your output when performing these operations, check out the tips for optimizing performance in Chapter 2, "Installing and Setting Up," before giving up and disabling Desktop video playback. You may want to increase the size of your thumbnail caches if you are working with a large number of clips and want to display thumbnails, or if you are using the Browser's Icon view. If you often scrub through thumbnails in Icon view, you can optimize the performance of this feature by increasing the size of the thumbnail RAM cache on the Memory & Cache tab of the System Settings window.

USER PREFERENCES AND SYSTEM SETTINGS

Setting Editing Preferences

Preference settings on this tab are all directly related to editing and trimming operations. Many of these preferences can be modified without opening the User Preferences window; for example, the Trim preferences can be toggled without leaving the Trim Edit window by using keyboard shortcut equivalents.

To set Editing preferences:

1. Choose Final Cut Express HD > User Preferences.

2. Click the Editing tab. On the tab (**Figure 3.7**), you can specify settings for the following:

   ◆ **Still/Freeze Duration:** Enter a duration (in seconds) to specify a default duration between In and Out points for imported still images, generators, and Adobe Photoshop files. Feel free to change this setting to increase your efficiency—for example, when you're producing a series of freeze-frames of a uniform length. The same Still/Freeze duration also applies to any freeze-frames you create from clips opened in the Canvas or Viewer.

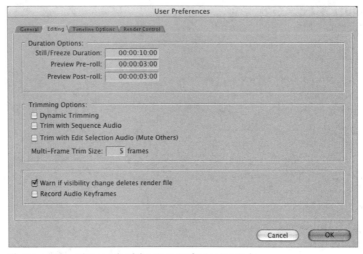

Figure 3.7 The Editing tab of the User Preferences window.

◆ **Preview Pre-roll:** Enter a number of seconds to specify how much media to play before the edit point when you click the Play Around Current button or the Play Around Edit-Loop button.

◆ **Preview Post-roll:** Enter a number of seconds to specify how much media to play after the edit point when you click the Play Around Current button or the Play Around Edit-Loop button.

◆ **Dynamic Trimming:** Check the box to enable Dynamic Trim mode in the Trim Edit window. You can also enable this mode in the Trim Edit window.

◆ **Trim with Sequence Audio:** Check the box to monitor all audio tracks at the playhead position while trimming an edit in the Trim Edit window. Uncheck this option to limit audio monitoring in the Trim Edit window to the selected clip's audio.

◆ **Trim with Edit Selection Audio (Mute Others):** Check the box to monitor only the audio tracks included in the edit selected for trimming in the Trim Edit window.

✔ Tip

■ The two Trim Edit preferences settings listed above apply only when you are using the JKL keys to play back or trim—they have no effect if you're using the spacebar or Transport control buttons. See Chapter 11, "Fine Cut: Trimming Edits" for more information.

◆ **Multi-Frame Trim Size:** Set the multi-frame trim size by specifying the number of frames (up to 99) in this field. The specified number appears in the multi-frame trim buttons in the Trim Edit window.

◆ **Warn if visibility change deletes render file:** Check this box if you want Final Cut Express to display a warning dialog box whenever making tracks invisible would cause render files to be deleted.

◆ **Record Audio Keyframes:** Check the box to enable the real-time recording of audio keyframes in the Viewer's Audio tab as you use the sliders to make level or pan adjustments on the fly. See Chapter 12, "Audio Tools and Techniques" for more information.

Customizing the Timeline Display

The Timeline display options you specify on the Timeline Options tab in the User Preferences window will become the default display settings for subsequent new projects and sequences. If you want to modify the Timeline display options for an existing sequence, you will need to make the change in the Sequence Settings window for that sequence. See "Changing the Settings of an Existing Sequence" in Chapter 4.

To customize your default Timeline display settings:

1. Choose Final Cut Express > User Preferences.

2. Click the Timeline Options tab. On the Timeline Options tab (**Figure 3.8**), you can modify the default settings for any of the following:

   ◆ **Track Size:** Choose a setting to specify a default track size.

◆ **Thumbnail Display:** Select one of three thumbnail display options:

   ◆ **Name:** Choose Name to display just the name of the clip.

   ◆ **Name Plus Thumbnail:** Choose this option to display the first frame of every clip as a thumbnail image, along with the name of the clip.

   ◆ **Filmstrip:** Choose Filmstrip to display as many thumbnail images as possible for the current zoom level of the Timeline.

◆ **Track Display:** Check the boxes next to the Timeline features you want to display by default in new sequences.

   ◆ **Show Keyframe Overlays:** Display opacity keyframe overlays on video clips and audio level keyframe overlays on audio clips in the Timeline.

   ◆ **Show Audio Waveforms:** Display audio waveforms on audio clips in the Timeline.

◆ **Default Number of Tracks:** Specify the number of video and audio tracks to be included in a new sequence.

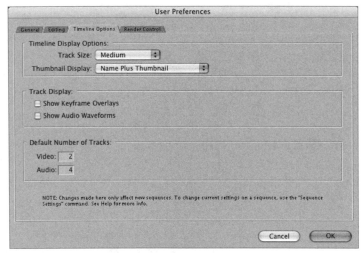

Figure 3.8 Customize your default Timeline display options on the User Preference window's Timeline Options tab.

Specifying Render Control Settings

Render Control tab settings affect the image quality of rendered material in your sequence. You can selectively disable non-critical aspects of render processing that improve image quality but slow your work. Low-resolution/limited-frame-rate rendering is much faster than a high-resolution render process; your Render Control tab settings allow you to control the balance between the quality of the render file and the speed of the rendering process. These Render Control tab settings apply during all FCE operations, including real-time playback, rendering, video output, and QuickTime output, so be sure to specify full-quality rendering before your final output.

The settings you define in this window become the default render quality settings for subsequent new projects and sequences. If you want to modify Render Control settings for an existing sequence, you will need to make the change in the Sequence Settings window for that sequence. See "Changing the Settings of an Existing Sequence" in Chapter 4.

To customize your default Render Control settings:

1. Choose Final Cut Express > User Preferences.

2. Click the Render Control tab. On the tab (**Figure 3.9**), modify the default settings for any of the following; then click OK:

   Render & Playback options:

   ◆ **Filters:** Check this box to include filters when rendering. Filters will be applied only to clips you have specified. Excluding filters from a render quality setting is another way to speed up rendering.

   ◆ **Frame Blending for Speed:** Check this box to enable any motion-smoothing effects you have previously applied to speed-modified clips.

   ◆ **Motion Blur:** Check this box to include motion blur when rendering. Motion blur will be applied only to clips you have specified. Excluding motion blur from a render quality setting will speed up rendering.

   Render options:

   ◆ **Frame Rate:** Set the frame rate for the render quality to 25%, 33% 50%, or 100% of the sequence editing timebase.

   ◆ **Resolution:** Select an option from this pop-up menu to set the resolution (frame size) for the render quality to 25%, 33% 50%, or 100% of the resolution set for the sequence.

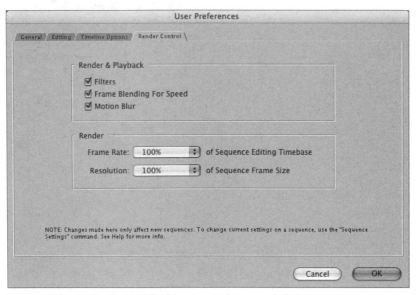

Figure 3.9 The Render Control tab of the User Preferences window.

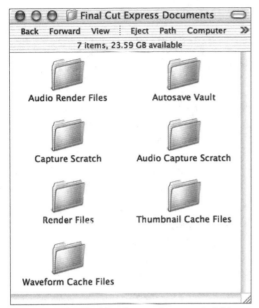

Figure 3.10 The Final Cut Express Documents folder contains a subfolder for each type of media file that your project will generate.

Setting Scratch Disk Preferences

A *scratch disk* is a folder on a hard disk where Final Cut Express stores your captured media source files and render files. The default scratch disk location is the same hard disk where your Final Cut Express application is installed. You can specify multiple scratch disk locations, either to improve performance by capturing audio and video on separate drives (not recommended for DV) or to provide the necessary storage capacity for your project media.

You should assign your scratch disks to your fastest disk drives. For best performance, avoid using the system hard disk as a scratch disk.

When a disk or folder is added to the scratch disk list, Final Cut Express automatically creates a folder on that disk called Final Cut Express Documents. That folder contains subfolders (one for each type of media file your project will generate) named Capture Scratch, Audio Capture Scratch, Render Files, Audio Render Files, Thumbnail Cache Files, and Waveform Cache Files (**Figure 3.10**). If you are capturing DV, your captured media files will be stored in a folder bearing your project's name inside the Capture Scratch folder.

✔ Tip

- Final Cut Express requires that each hard disk have a distinct name that does not contain the entire name of another media drive. For example, the program will not reliably distinguish between two drives named Media and Media 1, but Media 1 and Media 2 are acceptable names. Bear this in mind when you are assigning names to hard drives you are using with Final Cut Express.

FCE Protocol: Scratch Disks

Unless you specify otherwise, Final Cut Express uses the disk with the most available space as its storage area for rendered files. If you specify multiple scratch disks, Final Cut Express will use the next disk in the list with the most available space when the current disk runs out of space. You can specify separate disks for captured video and audio files to obtain better capture quality at higher data rates and improved playback performance. If you're capturing DV, however, you should always specify the same scratch disk for captured video and audio.

SETTING SCRATCH DISK PREFERENCES

To specify Scratch Disk preferences:

1. Choose Final Cut Express > System Settings.

   The Scratch Disks tab appears as the front tab of the System Settings window (**Figure 3.11**).

2. You can specify settings for the following:

   ◆ **Video Capture, Audio Capture, Video Render, and Audio Render:** Check these boxes to specify the types of files to be stored on each disk. Specify more than one disk for increased storage space. When the current disk runs out of space, Final Cut Express automatically switches to the next specified disk for storing capture files or to the disk with the most space available for storing render files.

◆ **Clear:** Click to remove a disk from the list of available disks.

◆ **Set:** Click to choose a disk or a folder on a hard disk. You can specify up to 12 disks.

◆ **Waveform Cache:** Click the Set button to specify a folder or disk to store waveform cache files (graphical representations of audio signals). The default location is the Final Cut Express Documents folder on your scratch disk.

◆ **Thumbnail Cache:** Click the Set button to specify a folder or disk to store thumbnail cache files. The default location is the Final Cut Express Documents folder on your scratch disk. You specify the size of this cache on the Memory & Cache tab.

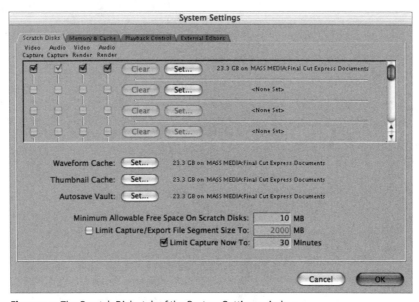

Figure 3.11 The Scratch Disks tab of the System Settings window.

◆ **Autosave Vault:** Click the Set button to specify a folder or disk to store FCE's automatic backup copies of your project files. The default location is the Final Cut Express Documents folder on your scratch disk. For more information on the Autosave Vault, see Chapter 4, "Projects, Sequences, and Clips."

◆ **Minimum Allowable Free Space on Scratch Disks:** Enter a limit value. When disk space falls below this minimum, a disk will no longer be used as a scratch disk, and files will be stored on the next disk in the list.

◆ **Limit Capture/Export File Segment Size To:** Enter a limit value. The default value is 2 GB. Final Cut Express allows the capture and export of single files larger than 2 GB, but if you plan to move your files to another system that has a file size limitation, or if you share media files over a network, you should enable this option. Files that are larger than your specified limit will be spanned (written as separate, but linked, files).

◆ **Limit Capture Now To:** Enter a limit value. The default limit is 30 minutes.

✔ Tip

■ FCE automatically calculates a safer, saner default value for Minimum Allowable Free Space (MAFS) on Scratch Disks. Previous versions of FCE used 10 MB as the default minimum—too low for comfort.

Each time FCE generates a new preference file, it checks the capacity of the first scratch disk selected in the Scratch Disks tab, and automatically sets a default value for MAFS that is based on a percentage of the disk's capacity. FCE allows 5% if the scratch disk is a boot drive, and 1% for a non-boot hard drive. You can always set a higher MAFS. If you're interested in preserving the performance and reliability of your captured source media, you should set a higher minimum. Many users set aside 10 percent of each drive's capacity as "headroom"—and sleep better for it.

SETTING SCRATCH DISK PREFERENCES

Specifying Memory & Cache Settings

Settings on the Memory & Cache tab determine how much of your computer's available RAM can be used by Final Cut Express, and how that assigned RAM will be apportioned.

Final Cut Express makes extensive use of your computer's RAM to support real-time playback and preview. You don't have to set hard memory allocations for applications running in OS X, but it is advisable to set an upper limit on the amount of RAM that FCE can use. If you like to keep multiple applications open while you edit, setting aside some RAM will minimize OS X's use of virtual memory to accommodate the processor load, which helps maintain FCE's performance.

1. Choose Final Cut Express > System Settings.

2. Click the Memory & Cache tab. On the tab (**Figure 3.12**), modify the default settings for any of the following; then click OK:

   ◆ **Memory Usage:** Assign an upper limit to FCE's RAM usage and allocate a percentage of that total for use by the still cache.

◆ **Application:** Use the slider or enter a maximum percentage of total available RAM to make available to Final Cut Express. The total number of megabytes assigned to FCE appears to the right of the percentage slider.

◆ **Still Cache:** Use the slider or enter a percentage value to allocate a portion of the RAM allotted to FCE for use by the still cache. The recommended minimum is 25 MB, but you should increase this value if your projects include large amounts of graphics. The total number of megabytes appears to the right of the percentage slider.

◆ **Thumbnail Cache:** If you use Large Icon as your Browser view, or if you're working on a large project containing many clips and want to display thumbnails in the Browser or Timeline, you should increase the amount of RAM available for displaying thumbnails to improve FCE's performance and the image quality of your thumbnails.

   ◆ **Disk:** Specify the amount of disk space to allocate for storing thumbnails.

   ◆ **RAM:** Specify the amount of memory to allocate for storing thumbnails.

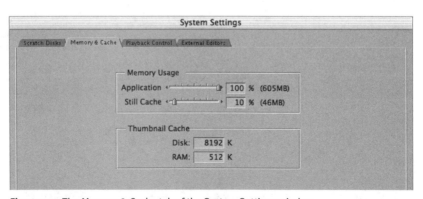

Figure 3.12 The Memory & Cache tab of the System Settings window.

Specifying Playback Control Settings

FCE lets you change the settings that determine the image quality of real-time playback. The options help you strike a balance between the number of effects you can see in real time versus the visual quality of the playback. An overview of these settings follows; for more information, see Chapter 18, "Real Time and Rendering."

✔ Tip

■ As you shift from basic assembly to multilayer effects and finishing work, your playback quality needs may change frequently. You can modify these Playback Control settings directly in the Timeline's RT pop-up menu and save yourself a trip to the System Settings window.

To specify Playback Control settings:

1. Choose Final Cut Express > System Settings.

2. Click the Playback Control tab. On the Playback Control tab (**Figure 3.13**), modify the default settings for any of the following and then click OK:

   ◆ **RT:** Choose a default image-quality level for the playback of real-time effects.

      ◆ **Safe:** Final Cut Express limits real-time effects processing to a level that can be sustained without dropping frames during playback.

      ◆ **Unlimited:** Final Cut Express allows real-time effects processing to exceed the level that your computer can handle without dropping frames during playback. Unlimited playback is useful when quick previewing is more important than image quality or playback integrity.

continues on next page

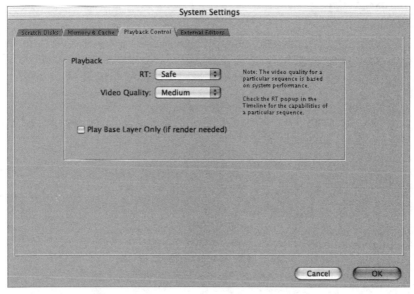

Figure 3.13 The Playback Control tab of the System Settings window.

◆ **Video Quality:** This option is available for DV and other codecs that support playback at multiple quality levels. Choose one of three image-quality levels:

◆ **High:** Full-frame, full-resolution playback, which preserves video interlacing.

◆ **Medium:** High-quality, quarter-frame-resolution playback of noninterlaced video.

◆ **Low:** Low-quality, quarter-frame-resolution playback of noninterlaced video.

◆ **Play Base Layer Only (If Render Needed):** Check this box to play only the base tracks (V1 and all audio tracks up to the real-time audio mixing track limit you set in General preferences) and cuts. Cuts will be substituted for unrendered or non-real-time transitions. Motion will not be applied to clips or sequences when played back in the Viewer. Play Base Layer Only is optimized to allow playback with minimal rendering. Unrendered sections will display the red render status indicator.

Setting External Editors Preferences

When you're coaxing a stack of graphic elements you've created in a layered Photoshop file into a seamless match with your video elements, you can find yourself making many, many trips back and forth between FCE and Photoshop. The External Editors preferences are designed to speed the process of modifying a media file you've created in another application and then imported in to FCE.

In this preferences window, you can specify which application will become the default editing application for each of three different media types: still image, video, and audio.

To specify External Editors preferences:

1. Choose Final Cut Express > System Settings.

2. Click the External Editors tab.

3. Using the Clear and Set buttons, specify an external editing application for the file types listed (**Figure 3.14**):

   ◆ **Clear:** Click the Clear button next to a file type to reset the External Editor for that file type to the default application used by your Mac's Finder.

   ◆ **Set:** Click the Set button, navigate to the folder location of the editing application you want to specify, and then click Open.

The pathname and the application name appear next to the file type on the External Editors tab.

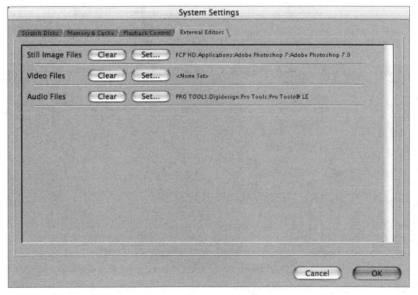

Figure 3.14 The pathname and the application name appear next to the file type on the External Editors tab.

Customizing Final Cut Express

Final Cut Express offers an array of customizable options:

◆ You can create and save custom full-screen layouts.

◆ You can turn any command used in Final Cut Express into a custom button, building custom button bars that can be saved and reloaded or transported to another FCE system.

◆ You can create and save custom filters, transitions, and even motion effects as Favorites.

In this section, you'll learn how to create custom screen layouts and button bars. Learn about working with Favorites in Chapter 14, "Compositing and Effects Overview."

Figure 3.15 Use a screen layout with a wide Timeline to get the big picture of your sequence layout.

Creating Custom Screen Layouts

The power of the Final Cut Express interface lies in its flexibility. You perform a wide range of tasks in FCE: database management, editing, effects design, titling, and many others. Here are a couple of sample screen layouts that can help you make the most of your screen real estate. Final Cut Express saves every detail of your workspace status each time you quit the program, so the next time you relaunch Final Cut Express, each program window will contain the same project, sequence, clip, and frame—just as you left it.

Figure 3.15 is an example of a screen layout with a wide view of the Timeline.

Figure 3.16 is an example of a video-editing layout with large picture-viewing monitors.

Figure 3.16 This screen layout features large monitor views for video editing.

To select a preset screen layout:

◆ Choose Window > Arrange (**Figure 3.17**); then select a screen layout from the four presets and two custom layouts available.

To customize a screen layout:

1. Arrange the four main windows in the layout and sizes you want.

2. Hold down the Option key and choose one of the two custom layouts from the Arrange submenu of the Window menu (**Figure 3.18**).

   The next time you open Final Cut Express, you can choose the layout you created from the Arrange submenu of the Window menu.

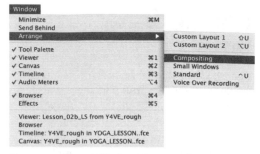

Figure 3.17 Choose Window > Arrange; then select from four preset and two custom screen layouts.

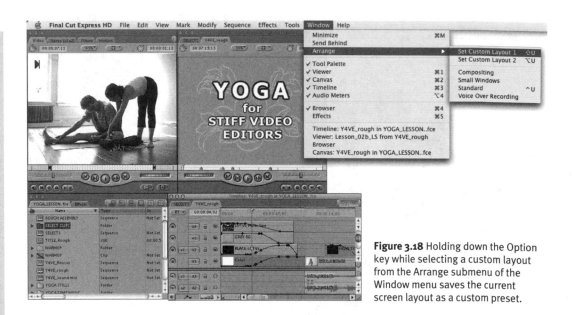

Figure 3.18 Holding down the Option key while selecting a custom layout from the Arrange submenu of the Window menu saves the current screen layout as a custom preset.

Figure 3.19 You can arrange shortcut buttons in the button bar found at the top of major program windows. You can group and color-code buttons and save and load custom button bar sets.

Figure 3.20 Control-click; then choose Show Button List from the button bar's shortcut menu.

Creating Custom Shortcut Buttons

Use FCE's button bar (**Figure 3.19**) to personalize your workspace by adding custom shortcut buttons to the button bars located at the top of the Viewer, Canvas, Browser, Timeline, and Voice Over tool windows. There's a button available for virtually every FCE command.

FCE lets you save multiple button bar toolsets, so you can easily switch to a button bar that complements your current editing task. You can:

◆ Rearrange the button order.

◆ Add spacers to organize your buttons into groups.

◆ Change the color of a button.

◆ Copy or move a button from one window to another.

◆ Save custom button bars.

For all the details on managing custom buttons, see Chapter 5 of Apple's *Final Cut Express Help* PDF.

To create a custom shortcut button:

1. Control-click the button bar area at the top of the window; then choose Show Button List from the shortcut menu (**Figure 3.20**).

   The Button List window appears, displaying a complete list of commands.

   continues on next page

2. To find the command you want to make into a shortcut button, *do one of the following:*

  ◆ Click the expansion triangle next to the name of the command's group to reveal the command in the list.

  ◆ Enter the command's name or a keyword in the Search field. Commands matching the search term are displayed automatically (**Figure 3.21**).

  ◆ Click the Search field to view the command list alphabetically.

3. Drag the command from the list to the button bar location where you want the button to appear (**Figure 3.22**).

  The button appears in the location you've selected (**Figure 3.23**).

4. Close the Button List window.

To delete a button:

Do one of the following:

  ◆ Control-click the shortcut button and then choose Remove > Button from the shortcut menu.

  ◆ Drag the button off the bar and release the mouse button.

  The button disappears in a puff of animated smoke (**Figure 3.24**).

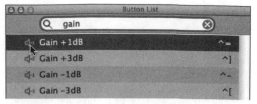

Figure 3.21 Searching the button list for commands containing the word *gain* returns four Gain commands.

Figure 3.22 Drag the command from the list to the button bar.

Figure 3.23 The button appears in the new location. You can use the color-coding options in the button bar shortcut menu to tint the buttons.

Figure 3.24 Drag the shortcut button off the button bar and watch it disappear in a puff of smoke—kinda like Road Runner. Speaking of cartoon animals ...

Projects, Sequences, and Clips

A Final Cut Express project is more than a collection of media files. The real power of Final Cut Express lies in the way the media is controlled by the intelligence of the program's data structuring. To take advantage of that power, you must take control of the data.

This chapter introduces Final Cut Express's system of organizing your video projects. You'll get an overview of Final Cut Express's organizing frameworks: projects, sequences, and clips. You'll also learn how to manipulate that organizational framework so that your projects, sequences, and clips stay sound and organized.

Longer, more complex projects sometimes require a little extra care and feeding, so you'll find project management strategies and techniques for building a project that contains multiple sequences. You'll also find tips on how to delete media files—and how to resurrect deleted files.

Final Cut Express is a nondestructive, nonlinear editing system, and that design has an impact on the way it handles file management. You'll be much more effective as a media manager if you understand how Final Cut Express tracks media files and project data before you use the project management techniques described in this chapter.

"FCE Protocol: Clips and Sequences," found later in this chapter, explains the rules you really need to know to understand how this program constructs edits.

Anatomy of an FCE Project

A Final Cut Express project breaks down into the following key components.

- **Project file:** The top level of the FCE organizing framework, a *project* file stores references (file location information) to all the media files you use to complete a particular program, along with the sequencing information (your *cut*) and all settings for special effects you apply to any clip in the project. The project file contains no media—it's strictly the "brains" of your project—but this one file is your project's most valuable asset. All your editing genius is stored in this modest data file.

- **Sequence:** The middle level of the Final Cut Express organizing framework, a *sequence* is an edited assembly of audio and video clips. A sequence is always part of a project, and you can have multiple sequences in a project, but you can't save a sequence separately from a project. However, you can copy a sequence from one project and paste it into another project.

- **Clip:** The ground level of the FCE organizing framework, the *clip* represents an individual unit of media in Final Cut Express. A clip can stand for a movie, a still image, a nested sequence, a generator, or an audio file. Clip types appear in the Browser's Type column, and each type of clip displays an identifying icon.

Figure 4.1 diagrams the FCE organizing framework.

Figure 4.2 shows how the FCE project structure plays out in the Browser and Timeline windows.

Project item types

On a project's Browser tab, you'll find quite a few different clip types, but you'll also find containers for holding clips: sequences and folders. The Browser's Effects tab contains other types of nonclip project items, audio and video filters and transitions, and generators. See "Browser Window Icons" in Chapter 7 for descriptions of each type of item you'll encounter in a project.

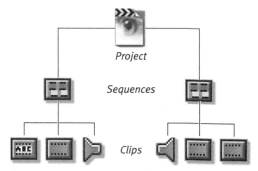

Figure 4.1 The project file is at the top level of FCE's organizing framework. You organize multiple clips and sequences inside a project file.

Each open project appears — as a tab in the Browser

The Type column identifies — project items by type

Sequences appear as items on the project's Browser tab —

Use folders to organize — groups of project items

Each clip represents an — individual unit of media

Clips with added markers — can be expanded to reveal a list of the markers

An offline clip appears with — a red slash through its icon

A project item's icon — identifies its type

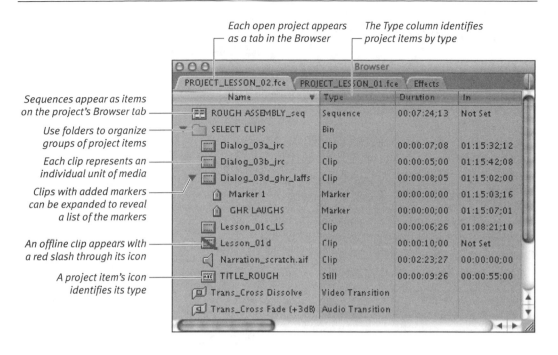

The selected sequence and project — name appear in the Timeline title bar

Each open sequence appears as a tab in the Timeline

Timeline clips — appear on tracks

Linked clips appear — with underlined names

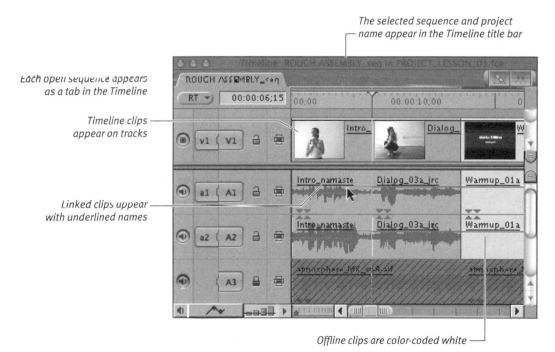

Offline clips are color-coded white —

Figure 4.2 The Browser (top) and Timeline (bottom) interfaces provide a variety of information about your project.

About Projects

Project files store disk location information for all the media files used in a program, along with the sequencing information for your edited program plus the settings for special effects applied to any clip in the project. The data stored in a project file is used to re-create the timing, sequencing, and transitions and effects you specify for a particular cut, *without altering or changing the storage location of your original source files*. (Note: If you haven't read the sidebar "What Is Nonlinear, Nondestructive Editing?" in Chapter 1, please do so now. It's key to understanding how Final Cut Express works.)

To get started in Final Cut Express, you create a new project and then start adding clips and sequences to the Browser window as you shape your project. Sequences can be exported independently as movies or clips, but they can't be saved separately from a project.

To create a new project:

◆ Choose File > New Project (**Figure 4.3**); or press Command-Shift-N.

A new project tab appears in the Browser window (**Figure 4.4**).

To open a project:

1. Choose File > Open; or press Command-O.

2. Locate and select the project file you want to open (**Figure 4.5**).

3. Click Choose.

Figure 4.3 Choose New Project from the File menu.

Figure 4.4 The Browser window with a new, untitled project. Sequence 1 appears automatically when you create a new project.

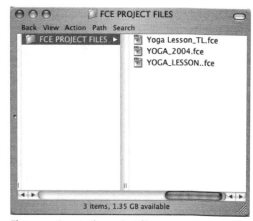

Figure 4.5 Locate the project file you want to open.

Figure 4.6 Choose Save Project As from the File menu.

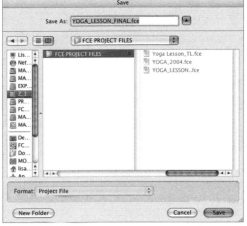

Figure 4.7 After you've typed the new name for your project, click Save.

Figure 4.8 Choose Save All from the File menu.

To save a project:

◆ Choose File > Save Project; or press Command-S.

To save a project with a different name:

1. Choose File > Save Project As (**Figure 4.6**); or press Command-Shift-S.

2. In the dialog box, type a name for the project in the Save As field.

3. Choose a destination folder.

4. Click Save (**Figure 4.7**).

To save all open projects:

1. Choose File > Save All (**Figure 4.8**); or press Command-Option-S.

2. If you created one or more new projects that haven't yet been saved, type a name for the first one in the dialog box.

3. Choose a destination folder.

4. Click Save.

   Repeat steps 2 through 4 for each new project that you want to save. Previously saved open projects are saved automatically.

Using Save As to Protect Your Work

Opening, modifying, and then saving the same project file day after day increases the chance that your precious project file will become corrupt and unusable.

Use the Save As command to back up your project file every day or so. Save As makes a fresh copy of the current version of your project file.

Give the original project file a version number, revert the name of your fresh duplicate to the base name of your project, and then continue working in the new duplicate version.

FCE automatically creates a new, separate capture folder every time you change the name of your project. For this reason, to avoid the complications that arise from changing the name of your project file (multiple capture folders), you'll need to add an identifying version number to your older project file and then be sure that your active project file always has the same original name (**Figure 4.9**).

FCE's vault system, which automatically saves and then archives multiple versions of your project, provides you with a fail-safe backup, but some editors still prefer to retain control over the process. Good habits are hard to break.

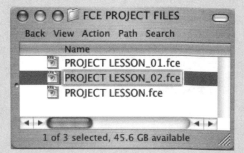

Figure 4.9 Rename your older project file with an identifying version number and use the original project filename for your fresh copy.

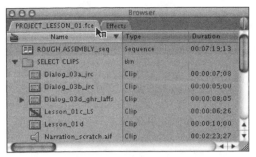

Figure 4.10 Control-click a project's tab to bring up the shortcut menu; note the special pointer.

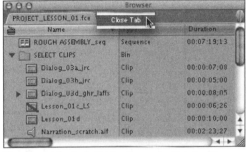

Figure 4.11 Control-clicking the project's tab will result in only one choice; choose Close Tab to close the project.

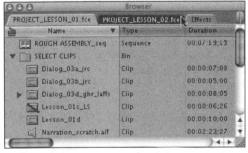

Figure 4.12 Click a project's tab to bring it to the front of the Browser.

To close a project:

Do one of the following:

◆ In the Browser, Control-click the project's tab (**Figure 4.10**); then choose Close Tab from the shortcut menu (**Figure 4.11**).

◆ In the Browser, click the project's tab to bring it to the front (**Figure 4.12**). Then choose File > Close Project.

◆ In the Browser, press Command-W. For all projects you've modified, Final Cut Express will ask which projects you want to close.

✔ Tip

■ To close all open projects, close the Browser window.

Viewing and setting project properties

Each project has a set of properties that are saved with it. The project's properties apply to all sequences in a project and are independent of the project's Sequence presets.

To view or change the properties of a project:

1. In the Browser, click the Project tab.

2. Choose Edit > Project Properties (**Figure 4.13**).

3. In the Project Properties window (**Figure 4.14**), *do any of the following:*

   ◆ Display project durations as timecode or as frames. Choosing Frames displays the total number of frames for clips and sequences in the Browser's Duration column, as well as in the Timeline, Canvas, and Viewer.

   ◆ Set the time mode of all project clips to Source Time (which matches the timecode rate of the clip's source media file) or Clip Time (which starts with the timecode value of the first frame in the clip, then calculates and displays timecode based on the current frame rate assigned to the clip). Source Time and Clip Time are identical in most cases; a speed-modified clip is an example of a clip whose Source Time and Clip Time do not match.

   ◆ Edit the heading labels for the Comment columns that appear in the Browser window.

4. After you make your changes, click OK.

Figure 4.13 Choose Project Properties from the Edit menu.

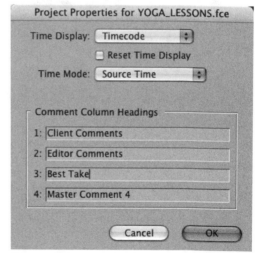

Figure 4.14 You can rename Comment column headings and choose the timecode or frame display format from the Project Properties window.

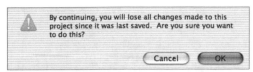

Figure 4.15 After you choose File > Revert Project, you'll see a dialog box warning you that your unsaved changes will be lost.

Figure 4.16 Choose Restore Project from the File menu.

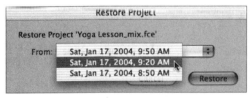

Figure 4.17 Select the archived project you want to restore; then click Restore.

To revert a project:

1. Choose File > Revert Project.

2. In the warning dialog box, click OK (**Figure 4.15**).

   Final Cut Express reverts the current project file to its condition at the last time you saved the file.

To restore a project:

1. Choose File > Restore Project (**Figure 4.16**).

2. In the Restore Project dialog box's pop-up menu, select the archived project file you want to restore (**Figure 4.17**).

3. Click Restore.

   Final Cut Express opens the selected archived project from the Autosave Vault.

✔ Tip

■ If you want to replace the current version of your project with this dated archived version, you should save the archive copy with the same project name as your current version. This will maintain continuity in capture folders and Autosave archives.

Using the Autosave Vault

Final Cut Express's Autosave Vault automatically saves all open projects as you work, at a time interval that you select. The vault stores multiple, dated backup copies of your project. This archive can come in handy. For example, maybe you're at the point in a project where you are trying new approaches to refine your cut, and you want to discard your last experiment. Or maybe you and your collaborator just don't agree, and she's completely recut your program while you were away for the weekend.

Each autosaved version is a backup copy that includes all changes you've made (up to the last autosave time) in the project file that you're currently working on. (That project file is modified only when you invoke the Save or Save All command.) If you haven't made any changes in an open project file since the last backup copy was autosaved, FCE won't archive another backup in the Autosave Vault until you do.

Setting Autosave Vault location and preferences

You can set Autosave preferences on the General tab of the User Preferences window. See "Specifying User Preferences and System Settings" in Chapter 3 for details on your settings options.

The backup copies of your project files are archived in a folder located inside your Final Cut Express Documents folder (**Figure 4.18**). If you want to store your archive of backups elsewhere, specify another location on the Scratch Disks tab of the System Settings window (**Figure 4.19**).

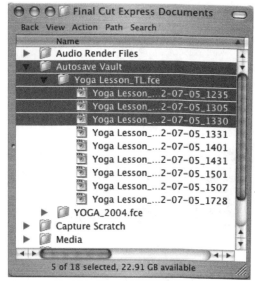

Figure 4.18 In the Autosave Vault, dated backup copies of your project files are archived in a folder.

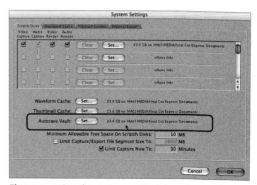

Figure 4.19 Set the Autosave Vault location on the Scratch Disks tab of the System Settings window.

When the number of backup copies in the Autosave Vault reaches the limit you set in User Preferences, FCE deletes the oldest Autosave file (or project folder) to make room for the newest Autosave file, unless the oldest project archived in the vault is currently open. FCE overrides the maximum projects limit you set if the number of open projects exceeds your specified limit when a scheduled autosave occurs.

Using Autosave to recover from a crash

If your computer powers off or crashes while you're working, the last saved version of your project file will open when you relaunch Final Cut Express. The choice is yours—continue to work in your original file, or use the Restore Project command to open your most recent autosaved backup copy. Here's the drill.

To use Autosave to recover from a crash:

1. After you restart, go to the folder where you archived your current original project file (that's the file you just crashed out of) and rename that file so it won't be overwritten and you can return to it, if need be.

2. Launch FCE; then use the Restore Project command to go to the Autosave Vault and open the most recent Autosave backup version of your project file in FCE.

3. After you've checked the integrity of the autosaved file in FCE, save the autosaved project file with your original project name.

You Need Backup

◆ The Autosave Vault should not be used as a substitute for your own systematic archiving of your project files. The Autosave Vault folder is not locked, and the oldest backups are purged regularly.

◆ Be consistent about where you store your project files. Make sure that all files relating to a project are stored in the same place.

◆ Back up project files on your FCE system and again on a removable disk or in another safe location to avoid losing files in case of a power outage or another technical problem. Project files contain the results of all your time and hard work. Without the editing information in the project files, your media files have no sequencing information. Protect it. Okay   end of lecture.

Undoing Changes

You can undo every type of action you perform in your projects, sequences, and clips, as well as redo actions that you have undone. FCE can store up to 32 actions across multiple projects—you set the number of undos on the General tab of the User Preferences window.

To undo the last action:

◆ Choose Edit > Undo (**Figure 4.20**); or press Command-Z.

To redo the last undone action:

◆ Choose Edit > Redo; or press Command-Shift-Z.

To specify the number of actions that can be undone:

1. Choose Final Cut Express > User Preferences.

2. On the General tab of the User Preferences window, set the levels of undo actions to a number between 1 and 32 (**Figure 4.21**).

Figure 4.20 Choose Edit > Undo to undo your last action.

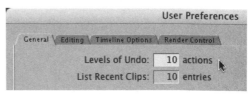

Figure 4.21 You can set the levels of undo actions to any number between 1 and 32 on the General tab of the User Preferences window.

FCE Protocol: Undoing Changes in Multiple Projects

FCE's Undo feature can track up to 32 changes across multiple projects, but it makes no distinction between projects.

If you are working with more than one sequence or project, check to be sure that you are in the correct one when you choose Undo. Even so, the change you undo may not occur in the current project, so take care when undoing multiple changes.

Reconnecting Offline Files

In Final Cut Express, the links between your clips and sequences in the Browser and the underlying media source files on disk are based on the media file's name and location. If you rename the source media files used in a project or sequence, you'll be greeted with the Offline Files window full of clips marked "missing" the next time you open your project. Don't panic. You can reconnect clips to media on your disk using the Reconnect Media command.

It's important to understand how Final Cut Express's protocols governing clip versions affect the reconnection process. Starting in FCE 2, sequence clips by default are affiliated with a master clip in the Browser. The offline/online status of the master clip and all affiliated clips is linked; make any one affiliated clip offline, and all its affiliated clips are taken offline automatically. Fortunately, the same principle applies to relinking. Remember, however, that any independent clips in your sequence are considered separate copies of the clips in the Browser. If an independent clip is used in a sequence, the sequence copy and the Browser copy must be reconnected separately. This is a little tricky, because the sequence icon in the Browser doesn't display the red diagonal offline indicator to warn you that it contains offline clips. Selecting the sequence when you are reconnecting allows you to locate files for all offline clips in the sequence.

✔ Tip

- You can use Final Cut Express's Find function to search for all the offline clips and sequences in a project (search the Offline Yes/No column for Yes) and then select and reconnect the offline clips and sequences right in the Find Results window.

FCE Protocol: Broken Links

How did your clips get thrown offline? Here's a list of things you might have done that severed the link between your FCE project and its source media files:

- You renamed your source media files.

- You renamed the folder containing your source media files.

- You moved your source media files to another disk.

- You deleted your source media on disk.

FCE is actually pretty good at tracking the "unofficial" relocation of source media folders (try it sometime), but forcing FCE to do so is not recommended procedure.

To reconnect offline files:

1. Select the file or files to be reconnected (**Figure 4.22**). You can select a clip or sequence in the Browser or clips in an open sequence in the Timeline.

2. *Do one of the following:*
   - ◆ Choose File > Reconnect Media.
   - ◆ Control-click the clip or sequence; then choose Reconnect Media from the shortcut menu (**Figure 4.23**).

3. In the Reconnect Options dialog box, Offline, Online, or Render file options may be available, depending on your current file selection. Check the box for each type of file you want to reconnect; then click OK (**Figure 4.24**).

   Final Cut Express searches your media drives for the first file in your selection. If FCE successfully locates the source media file for your first offline clip, the Reconnect dialog box appears with that source file listed in the file window (**Figure 4.25**). If FCE cannot locate the first source media file, a prompt at the top of the window displays the name of the clip and the first file you should locate.

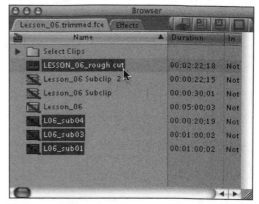

Figure 4.22 Select the clip you want to reconnect to its source media file.

Figure 4.23 Control-click the clip; then choose Reconnect Media from the shortcut menu.

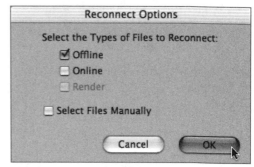

Figure 4.24 In the Reconnect Options window, check the box for each type of file you want to reconnect; then click OK.

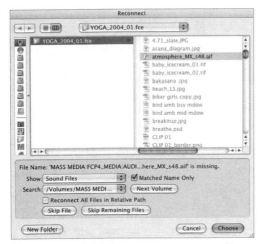

Figure 4.25 Final Cut Express searches your media drives for the first file in your selection and then opens the Reconnect dialog box with that source file displayed in the file window. Files that don't match are dimmed. You may have to scroll down through the list to see your file.

Figure 4.26 Click Choose to reconnect the file to the clip.

4. *Do any of the following:*

◆ Select a file type from the Show pop-up menu to limit the file list display to the selected file type.

◆ Check Matched Name Only to highlight only an exactly matching name in the file list display and dim all non-matching names. Disable this feature to have access to a complete list of the folder's contents.

◆ Select a drive or folder to search from the Search pop-up menu. Click the Next Volume button to move to the next media drive.

◆ Check Reconnect All Files in Relative Path to automatically reconnect any other clips in the sequence that are associated with files in the same folder. You must reconnect the first file manually by clicking Choose.

◆ Click Skip File to bypass the clip currently displayed in the File Name prompt.

◆ Click Skip Remaining Files to bypass all remaining clips that can't be located automatically.

◆ Click Choose to reconnect the clip and its source media (**Figure 4.26**).

5. The dialog box closes and then reopens, and the File Name prompt indicates the next file to locate. Continue until the dialog box closes.

continues on next page

✔ Tip

- The File Name prompt area in the Reconnect dialog box is often too small to display the full directory path for the clip you're searching for. When you search for many clips with similar names, the partial display is pretty useless. You can see the full directory path name for your stray clip by stretching the Reconnect dialog box horizontally (**Figure 4.27**). Stretching the dialog box doesn't widen the columns in this window, but if you pause the pointer over a name, FCE will display a tooltip with the full name of the file.

Reconnecting Online Files

The Reconnect Media feature offers an option to reconnect online as well as offline files. Reconnecting missing or offline clips is the most common use of the Reconnect Media command, but you could have occasion to reconnect online files, too—for example, when you want to replace the media in a clip you've used in a sequence with a revised version of the same media element or with another element entirely.

If you do want to relink a clip in your sequence to an entirely different source media file, the new source file must be at least long enough to cover the current marked duration of the clip you're relinking it to. If your new source file is too short, you'll see an error message.

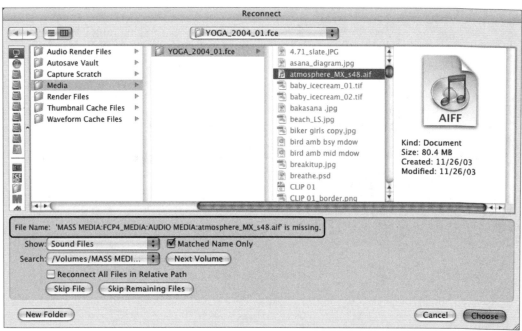

Figure 4.27 You can stretch the Reconnect dialog box horizontally to display the full directory path to the location of your files.

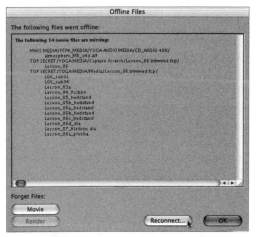

Figure 4.28 The Offline Files window contains a list of all media files missing from the current project and their most recent hard disk location.

Using the Offline Files window to reconnect

Final Cut Express displays the Offline Files window to alert you that media files have gone missing since the last time you saved a project. Any time you open a project or switch back to FCE from the Finder, Final Cut Express rechecks the status of your media files. If FCE detects missing files, the Offline Files window appears automatically to alert you and offer you options for restoring order to your FCE project.

To reconnect using the Offline Files window:

1. Final Cut Express displays the Offline Files window (**Figure 4.28**), which lists all media files missing from the current project and their most recent hard disk location. This list could include:

   ◆ Missing source media files

   ◆ Render files lost because they reference a missing media file

   ◆ QuickTime reference movies made invalid by a missing media file

   ◆ A segment of a spanned media file

continues on next page

RECONNECTING OFFLINE FILES

2. *Do any of the following:*

♦ Use the Forget Files buttons (**Figure 4.29**) if you want to change the status of all the files listed from "missing" to "offline" and remove them from this list of missing files. If you don't use the Forget Files option, Final Cut Express will continue to post alerts about missing media each time you launch the project, until you reconnect the media and clips or make the clips offline.

♦ Click the Movie button to change the status of all the source media files in the list from "missing" to "offline." All clips referencing these files will be marked as offline clips in your project, but you can still relink the files later.

♦ Click the Render button to remove all of the render files from this list. If you choose to forget render files, you won't have the opportunity to reconnect them later.

3. To finish the process, *choose one of the following options:*

♦ Click the Reconnect button (**Figure 4.30**) to access the Reconnect Media feature, and then try to locate and reconnect the missing files. The Reconnect Media operation is described earlier in this chapter.

♦ Click OK to exit the Offline Files window and leave all the files remaining in the list classified as missing or invalid. The next time you launch this project, FCE will display the Offline Files window again, and you can choose to reconnect or to take files offline at that time.

Figure 4.29 Use the Forget Files buttons to change the status of the files listed in the window from "missing" to "offline" and remove them from this list of missing files.

Figure 4.30 Click the Reconnect button to access the Reconnect Media feature and try to locate and reconnect the missing files.

FCE Protocol: Offline vs. Missing Clips

Missing clips and offline clips look the same in the Browser, Viewer, Timeline, and Canvas.

What's the difference?

Offline clips are listed as offline in your project's item tracking data, so Final Cut Express doesn't look for them the next time you open that project.

Missing clips are listed as online in your project's item tracking data, but FCE can't find the clips' underlying media files. FCE will search for missing files each time you open a project until you reconnect the files or make them official offline files by clicking Forget in the Offline Files window.

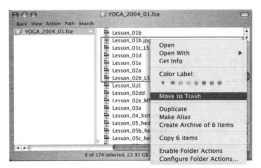

Figure 4.31 In the project's Capture Scratch folder, Control-click the media file you want to delete; then choose Move to Trash from the shortcut menu.

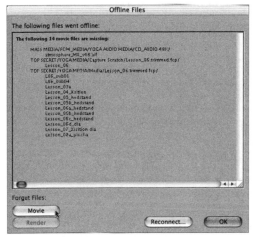

Figure 4.32 Clicking the Forget Files Movie button updates your FCE project's item tracking, removing the deleted file from the project's database.

✔ Tip

■ You can delete render files in the same way. With your Finder window in Column view, you can preview each media file in the QuickTime preview utility built right into the file window. Select the clip you want to preview, and the QuickTime preview appears automatically. This trick works only in the Finder, though—not within the Reconnect dialog box in FCE.

Deleting Media

To delete media files, you have to go outside Final Cut Express, locate the files in the project's Capture Scratch folder, and move them to the Trash.

You delete unused render files from disk in the same way. You'll find render files in folders labeled Audio Render Files and Video Render Files. If you render frequently, you would be surprised how much storage space your old render files can hog.

To delete a source media file from disk:

1. Save your project and quit Final Cut Express.

2. In the Finder, navigate to the project's Capture Scratch folder and select the media file you want to delete.

3. Control-click the selected media file; then choose Move to Trash from the shortcut menu (**Figure 4.31**).

   The source media file is moved to the Trash.

4. Relaunch FCE and open the project.

   If you have not previously deleted the clips that reference the source media file, you'll see the Offline Files window listing the media file you moved to the Trash.

5. Click the Forget Files Movie button to update your FCE project's item tracking (**Figure 4.32**).

   To finally delete the files, you'll need to empty the Trash manually. If you change your mind later, before you empty the Trash, and want to retrieve the files, drag them out of the Trash and reconnect them to your project by using the Reconnect Media command. If you empty the Trash, your files are finally deleted.

FCE Protocol: Deleting Media

How do you delete media files from Final Cut Express the right way?

Before you toss that folder full of source media files in the Trash, take a moment to review the way Final Cut Express tracks files. Remember that the Browser clips you use to construct sequences in your project are not actually media files; they are pointers to the actual media files on disk, and Final Cut Express's links to those underlying source media files are location dependent. If you open the Item Properties window for any clip in Final Cut Express, you'll see the directory path to the underlying source media (the clip's directory path also appears in the Browser's Source column). If you have created subclips, repeated the same clip in a sequence, divided a clip with the Razor tool, or created multiple versions of your sequence, you can have quite a few different clips all pointing to the same media file on disk.

If you delete a clip from the Browser folder or a Timeline sequence, you haven't thrown out the underlying media source file on disk. You can re-import the file to reconnect it to your project, or if you've already used that clip in a sequence, you can drag a copy of the sequence version of the clip back into the Browser. Dragging a clip from an open sequence in the Timeline back into the Browser places a copy of the sequence version of the clip in your project.

Your source media files stay on disk until you drag them to the Trash in the Finder. It's best not to delete media files linked to an open project while Final Cut Express is running.

You should save and close the project before you delete media files in the Finder. Determine your own comfort level here, but quitting Final Cut Express before you trash any media files would be the safest course.

Once you've deleted a source media file, all clips referring to that file are marked as offline. Final Cut Express warns you that the clips are offline each time you open the project until you delete the clip references, including any versions of the clips that appear in sequences, or tell FCE to "forget" the offline clips. See "Using the Offline Files window to reconnect" earlier in this chapter.

Figure 4.33 Enter a name for the new project version in the Save As field. This version of the project is the one you're going to clean up.

Figure 4.34 The new version of your project replaces the old one on the front tab of the Browser window.

Project Maintenance Tips

Even if you are not forced to reorganize your project's media elements because you have run out of disk space, it's a good idea to streamline a project as you go, especially if you're working on a long, complex project. As your project accumulates clips, sequences, edits, render files, multiple tracks of audio, and effects, more and more of your available RAM is needed just to open the project. At some point, you could experience a drop in Final Cut Express's speed or video playback performance.

✔ Tip

■ Do you really need to preserve every scrap of media and every old duped sequence in your project? Redundant copies of project items may seem valuable now, but will you remember why you saved them when you return to this project in a year? Consider some project streamlining before you pack up and move. Check out the "Deleting media" section earlier in this chapter for ideas.

To streamline a project in progress:

1. With the project open in the Browser, choose File > Save All.

   The current version of the project is saved.

2. Choose File > Save Project As.

   The Save dialog box appears.

3. Navigate to the folder where you want to store your project file, enter a name for the new project version in the Save As field (**Figure 4.33**), and then click Save.

   The new version of your project replaces the older one on the front tab of the Browser window (**Figure 4.34**).

continues on next page

PROJECT MAINTENANCE TIPS

4. Remove all but the most current versions of your sequences and delete any excess clips (**Figure 4.35**). If you are short of disk space, you could choose to delete the clips' source media files as well, but you don't need to delete the source media files to get the benefits of a streamlined project.

5. In the Finder, navigate to the Render Files and Audio Render Files folders. They're located inside the Final Cut Express Documents folder where your media files are stored. Delete any obsolete render files.

6. With the new, streamlined project open in the Browser, choose File > Save.

7. If you streamlined your project to improve Final Cut Express's performance, you'll need to close and then reopen the project to recapture the available RAM and start enjoying improved performance.

✔ Tip

■ Remember that the Render Files folder contains render files for all your projects, so be careful as you select the files you want to delete. Check each file's creation date and view any candidates for the Trash bin on the Finder's built-in QuickTime preview player (**Figure 4.36**).

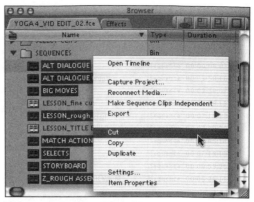

Figure 4.35 Remove all but the most current versions of your sequences and delete any excess clips. If you need the old versions later, you still have them in the project version you saved in step 1.

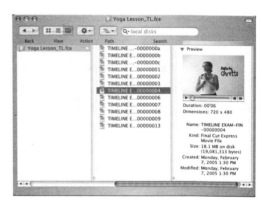

Figure 4.36 Be careful which render files you delete. The Finder's built-in QuickTime player can help you ID the files you want to trash.

Editing in stages

If you are trying to assemble a long project in Final Cut Express on a modest system, you may find that you have much more media than hard drive space to store it on.

The simplest approach to a staged editing process is to edit one sequence at a time, print the sequence to video, clear off the media, and then edit the next sequence.

Here's a checklist for taking a completed sequence offline and preparing your drives for the next sequence:

◆ After you have completed a sequence and printed it to tape, make sure you save the project file that contains the final version of your sequence.

◆ You should also save a backup copy of the project file on a Zip disk, CD, or some other form of removable media.

◆ Back up any media elements in your sequence, such as graphics files or digital audio from a CD, that won't be restored in a batch recapturing process.

◆ In the Browser, select all the clips and sequences that reference media files you no longer need. Use the method for deleting media files described earlier in this chapter to delete all the media source files you no longer need.

◆ The clips and sequences referring to the deleted media files will be marked offline, but the clip data will remain in your completed project file. This clip and sequence data takes up very little room, so you don't need to delete it; you can store it in a single Browser folder.

◆ Capture the next batch of media files and start work on your next sequence.

The Last Mile: Tips for Final Assembly of BIG Projects

You can tell when the size of your project is taxing the limits of FCE's performance. Everything takes longer—opening and saving the project, screen refreshes, even moving around the Timeline. If you have no choice but to press FCE's capacity to handle large amounts of media and multiple long sequences, try this:

◆ Split your show into a series of separate sequences and complete all rendering inside the individual sequences.

◆ Create a new project and drag just the finished individual sequences from your old projects into the new project; then close the old projects.

◆ Create the master sequence assembly of all your finished segment sequences in the brand-new project, including just the master sequence, and keep all other projects closed as much as possible.

◆ Back up your project file frequently.

Restoring a sequence

If you find that you need to go back and modify a sequence after you have deleted its underlying media files, you can use the sequence data you saved in the project file to batch recapture your footage and re-create the sequence.

All filters, motion paths, keyframes, transitions, nested sequences, and audio mixing are reconstituted when you batch recapture the media files for a sequence. Your render files will be gone, however, and you'll need to re-render any sequence material that requires them.

To restore a sequence:

1. Control-click the sequence in the Browser and choose File > Capture Project (**Figure 4.37**).

2. Follow the steps in "To batch capture selected clips" in Chapter 5 and batch recapture your footage from tape.

3. Restore to your hard disk any non-DV media elements in your sequence, such as graphics files or digital audio from CD, that won't be restored in the batch-recapturing process.

4. Follow the steps described in "To reconnect offline files" earlier in this chapter (**Figure 4.38**) and reconnect any non-DV media elements you restored.

5. To restore the render files, re-render any sequence material that requires rendering (**Figure 4.39**).

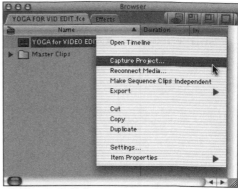

Figure 4.37 In the Browser, Control-click the sequence that you want to restore and choose File > Capture Project.

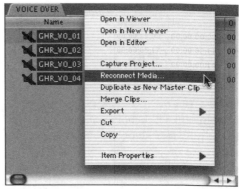

Figure 4.38 To restore non-DV media elements, follow the steps for reconnecting offline files.

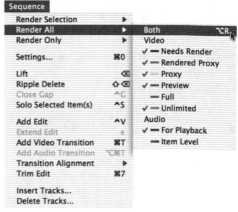

Figure 4.39 To restore the render files, you must re-render any sequence material that requires rendering.

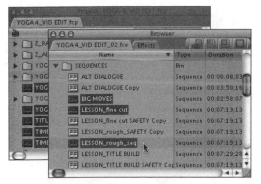

Figure 4.40 On each project's tab in the Browser, Command-click to select the sequences you want to include in your search.

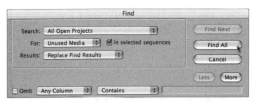

Figure 4.41 The Find dialog box, configured to find unused clips in selected sequences. Click Find All to perform the search.

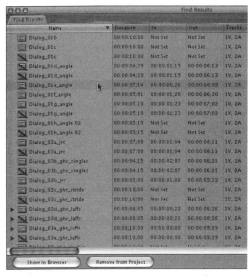

Figure 4.42 A list of clips that are unused in the sequences you searched appears in the Find Results window.

Tracking used and unused clips

If you just want to do a little housecleaning in your project's media file folder, it's handy to have an inventory of every clip that's currently being used in a sequence in your project and another list of every element in your project that remains unused. How can you create complete lists of used and unused elements in your project? It's simple. You can use the Find feature to assemble these lists—you can even inventory multiple projects in a single Find operation. Powerful stuff.

To get a complete list of unused clips in a group of sequences:

1. Open all the projects you want to search.

2. On each project's tab in the Browser, Command-click to select the sequences you want to include in your search (**Figure 4.40**).

3. Choose Edit > Find; or press Command-F.

4. In the Find dialog box, configure the options as follows:

   ◆ Choose All Open Projects from the Search pop-up menu.

   ◆ Choose Unused Media from the For pop-up menu and check the box next to In Selected Sequences.

   ◆ Choose Replace Find Results from the Results pop-up menu.

5. Click Find All (**Figure 4.41**).

   A list of all the clips that remain unused in the sequences you selected is displayed in the Find Results window (**Figure 4.42**).

   continues on next page

✔ Tips

■ Final Cut Express does not support text export; the best you can do is to take a screen shot of the Find Results window and print it.

■ If your clip's name is different from the name of the underlying media file, you can find the underlying media file (and its location) in the clip's Item Properties window or the Browser's Source column.

Removing a project from your drives

Final Cut Express doesn't generate separate preview or temporary files when you use the Print to Video function. The only files you need to clean up after a project are the project file, media files, render files, and thumbnail and waveform cache files (**Figure 4.43**).

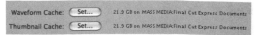

Figure 4.43 Looking for the Thumbnail and Waveform Cache folders? You'll find the directory path to their disk locations listed on the Scratch Disks tab in the System Settings window.

Figure 4.44 Creating a single user ID for all project collaborators can simplify file access on shared FCE projects.

Setting Up for Multiple Projects and Users

Mac OS X was designed as a multiuser environment. The operating system's hierarchy of users and file access privileges is built on the assumption that multiple people are sharing the data and applications stored on your computer. For Final Cut Express users, this has a few specific effects.

File access

How you choose to set up your file access depends on your individual circumstances.

◆ If you are a solo user running Final Cut Express on a computer that you own, you should already be set up as the computer's Owner-User. This gives you access to any file in the system that you created.

◆ If you are collaborating on a project with a small group of trusted colleagues sharing Final Cut Express, you'll need to decide how you want to handle access to Final Cut Express's project and media files. You can choose to administer the project in OS X's multiuser domain and allow multiple users access to the project files, or you might find it simpler to create a single user ID for the entire group (**Figure 4.44**). In the latter case, everyone in the group logs in as that Project User and has the same read/write privileges to the project and media files.

◆ If you are sharing a Final Cut Express system with many users working on different projects, you'll want to configure your file access for maximum privacy.

Creating and saving files

Solo users can save their project files in a public or private Documents folder (save in your private Documents folder if you have any security concerns); groups collaborating on an FCE project should save common project files in the Shared folder (**Figure 4.45**), located inside the Users folder, so that all users can access the shared documents.

In FCE, any time you create a new file—by saving a project file, capturing media, or creating graphics—that file's access privileges are set to the system default: Read & Write for the file's owner, and Read Only for all other users (**Figure 4.46**). You may occasionally need to modify file access privileges to allow other users access to your project and its media.

Figure 4.45 Groups collaborating on a Final Cut Express project should save common project files in the Shared folder so all group members have access to them.

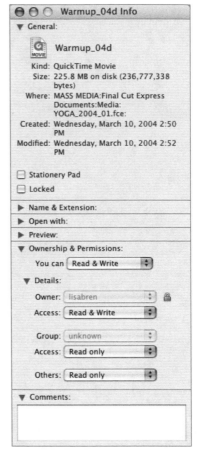

Figure 4.46 The Mac OS X default file access for new files is Read & Write for the file's owner and Read Only for all other users.

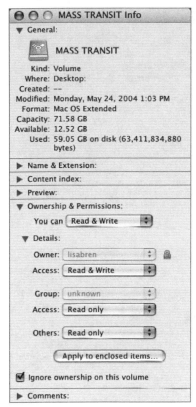

Figure 4.47 In the disk's Info window, check Ignore Ownership on This Volume to make all files on the volume accessible to all users.

✔ Tips

- A non-bootable hard disk may offer Read & Write privileges to all users by default, but that doesn't mean individual files and folders on that drive are accessible to all. To set open access for all files on a disk volume, check Ignore Ownership on This Volume in the drive's Info window (**Figure 4.47**).

- Mac OS X considers FireWire drives to be removable media (because they're hot-swappable) and offers Read & Write privileges to all users for the entire contents of the drive by default.

What's a Sequence?

A sequence is an edited assembly of audio and video clips. Sequences are the middle level of the Final Cut Express organizing framework. A sequence is always part of a project, and you can have multiple sequences in a project. Sequences can be exported independently as movies or clips, but they can't be saved separately from a project.

Once you've assembled a sequence, that sequence can be manipulated as if it were a single clip. You can open a sequence and play it in the Viewer, mark In and Out points, and insert all or part of that sequence into another sequence, just as if it were a clip. Inserting a sequence into another sequence creates what's known as a nested sequence. (See "Working with Multiple Sequences" later in this chapter.)

Creating a new sequence

A new project created in FCE automatically generates a new, untitled sequence in your default sequence format.

Note that you probably won't need to change Sequence presets unless you change your audio or video input device. Final Cut Express selects an Easy Setup with your default pre-set based on setup information you supplied when you installed the program. See "How to Choose an Easy Setup" in Chapter 3.

To add a new sequence to the current project:

1. Choose File > New > Sequence; or press Command-N.

   A new sequence with a default, high-lighted name appears at the top level of the current folder (**Figure 4.48**).

2. Type a new name for the sequence to rename it (**Figure 4.49**).

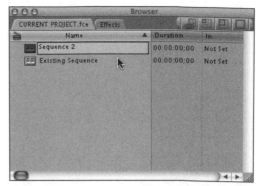

Figure 4.48 A new sequence with a default, highlighted name appears in the current folder.

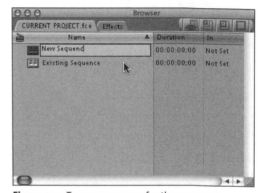

Figure 4.49 Type a new name for the sequence.

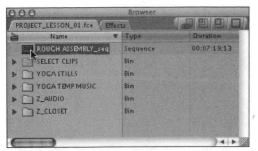

Figure 4.50 Double-click the sequence's icon in the Browser to open it for editing.

Figure 4.51 The sequence opens in the Canvas and the Timeline.

To open a sequence for editing:

Do one of the following:

◆ Double-click the sequence in the Browser (**Figure 4.50**).

◆ Control-click the sequence's icon; then choose Open Timeline from the shortcut menu.

◆ Select the sequence; then choose View > Sequence in Editor.

The sequence opens in both the Canvas and the Timeline (**Figure 4.51**).

Time Stamp for Sequences

The Last Modified column in the Browser makes it easy to find the most recently revised version of your sequence—a real lifesaver when you're returning to a project after a long absence.

To duplicate a sequence:

1. Select the sequence in the Browser (**Figure 4.52**).

2. Choose Edit > Duplicate (**Figure 4.53**); or press Option-D.

3. In the Browser, rename the sequence copy with a unique name (**Figure 4.54**).

✔ Tip

■ The copy procedure described here is a convenient way to "safety copy" a version of a sequence and associated media files after a long rendering process. With a safety copy of the rendered sequence, you can feel free to experiment with changes that could cause a re-render, because any changes you make to the duplicate sequence will not affect the original sequence or its render files.

To copy a sequence from one project to another:

1. Select the sequence in the Browser.

2. Choose File > Copy; or press Command-C.

3. Open the second project and select its tab in the Browser.

4. Choose File > Paste; or press Command-V. The sequence now appears in both projects. The two copies of the sequence reference the same source media files on disk, but you'll need to re-render any previously rendered sequence material in the new project location.

✔ Tip

■ You can also create a copy of a sequence by dragging it from a project window and dropping it on the destination project's Browser tab.

Figure 4.52 Select the sequence in the Browser.

Figure 4.53 Choose Edit > Duplicate.

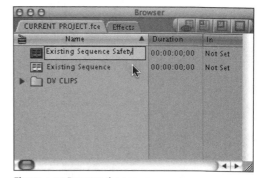
Figure 4.54 Rename the sequence copy.

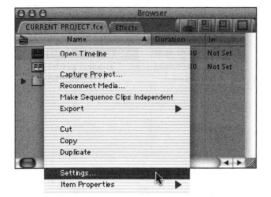

Figure 4.55 Control-click the sequence icon; then choose Settings from the shortcut menu.

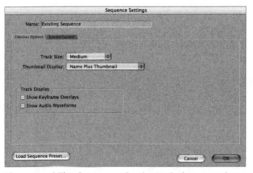

Figure 4.56 The Sequence Settings window contains the same options as the Timeline Options and Render Control tabs. Modifying a sequence's settings in the Sequence Settings window changes the settings for that sequence only.

Changing the Settings of an Existing Sequence

You can open and review or modify settings for an existing individual sequence in the Sequence Settings window. The Sequence Settings window contains the same main display options as the Timeline Options and Render Control tabs in the User Preferences window. When you modify any settings for an individual sequence, you are changing the settings for that sequence only.

You can use this window's Load Sequence Preset button to switch to a different Sequence preset, but unless you're sure that's what you need to do, it's not advisable.

To change the settings for an individual sequence:

1. Control-click the sequence's icon in the Browser.

2. Choose Settings from the shortcut menu (**Figure 4.55**).

3. Modify your Sequence settings (**Figure 4.56**); then click OK. (For more information about the Sequence Settings window, see "Customizing the Timeline Display" and "Specifying Render Control Settings" in Chapter 3.)

To switch a sequence's settings to a different Sequence preset:

1. Make the sequence active by selecting it in the Browser or Timeline.

2. Choose Sequence > Settings.
   The Sequence Settings window appears.

3. Click the Load Sequence Preset button at the bottom of the General tab.

4. Choose a different preset from the Select pop-up menu in the Select Sequence Preset dialog box (**Figure 4.57**); then click OK.

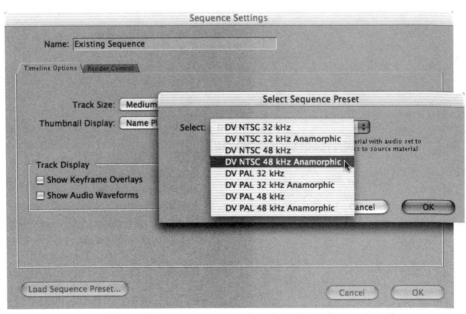

Figure 4.57 Choose a different Sequence preset to replace the settings of your selected sequence.

Working with Multiple Sequences

In Final Cut Express, you can edit a sequence into another sequence in the same way you would a clip: Drag the entire sequence from the Browser to another open sequence in the Timeline or Canvas. Alternatively, you can drag the sequence from the Browser and drop it on the Viewer's image area and then edit it into your open sequence as you would a clip.

Unlike clips, nested sequences are actually pointers or references to the original sequence, not copies. You can nest a sequence in multiple projects; then, if you change the original sequence, all the projects in which that sequence is nested will be updated.

Assembling multiple sequences into a master sequence is useful for a number of purposes, from reusing a previously edited and rendered segment such as a logo or a credit sequence to assembling a final master sequence from shorter segments produced by multiple editors.

Nesting and Sequences: A Glossary

What's the difference between a nested sequence and a sub-sequence? Here's a short glossary of terms related to nesting sequences as used in this book.

◆ **Main sequence:** A sequence containing one or more nested sequences. Sometimes referred to as a *parent sequence.*

◆ **Nested sequence:** Any sequence that has been nested within another sequence. Sometimes referred to as a *child sequence.* A nested sequence can range from a clip on a single track to an entire sequence. What designates a sequence as nested is its placement in a parent sequence. The word *nest* can also be used as a verb, as in "nest a sequence," which refers to editing all or a portion of an existing sequence into another sequence.

◆ **Sub-sequence:** Can be used interchangeably with the term *nested sequence.* Nested sequences function as sub-sequences in their parent sequences.

Creating nested sequences

You can select a group of sequence clips or a portion of a Final Cut Express sequence and convert that selection to a self-contained sub-sequence. There's no simple "Nest Items" command—that's reserved for Final Cut Pro users—but you can achieve the same effect with a little more trouble by cutting and pasting your selected clips into a new, empty sequence that you place in the clips' former location in the master sequence.

Converting a group of clips to a nested sequence has several advantages:

◆ Nesting a group of clips can simplify the process of moving them around within a sequence or placing them in another sequence.

◆ Converting a series of edited clips into a single nested sequence allows you to create a single motion path for the nested sequence rather than having to create a separate motion path for each clip.

◆ Nesting a group of clips allows you to apply and adjust a single copy of a filter to a series of clips, rather than having to apply and adjust filters for each individual clip.

◆ You can nest clips that are stacked on multiple tracks (such as layered title elements) and animate them as a single sub-sequence.

◆ You can nest a clip containing an element you want to blur. By increasing the frame size when you nest, you can create a roomier bounding box that will accommodate the larger size of your blurred element.

◆ Nested sequences can help preserve your render files—most render files associated with the nested sequence are preserved within the nested sequence, even if you move it around or change its duration. For more information on nested sequences and rendering protocol, see "Using nested sequences to preserve render files" in Chapter 18.

◆ In a sequence with multiple effects applied, nesting a clip can force a change in the rendering order.

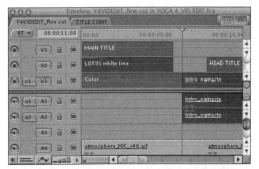

Figure 4.58 In the Timeline, select the clips you want to cut or copy. In this example, the selected clips are on Tracks V1, V2, and V3.

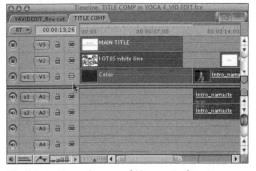

Figure 4.59 Press Command-V to paste the sequence tracks into your destination sequence. As long as you make no change to the Auto Select controls between cutting and pasting commands, the pasted clips are assigned to the same tracks they occupied in the source sequence. In this example, Auto Select control settings have been overridden and the clips are pasted into the destination sequence on Tracks V1, V2, and V3.

Copying and pasting from sequence to sequence

Moving selected clips into a new, separate sequence is the first step in nesting a selection of clips inside your master sequence. Moving material from sequence to sequence is easy; simply copy (or cut) material from one sequence and paste it into another sequence. You can copy and paste the entire contents of a sequence, or you can select a single clip.

Copying and pasting between sequences is governed by the same rules that govern copy and paste within the same sequence: When you paste, the clips paste themselves into the destination sequence on the same tracks you cut them from *unless you make a change to the Auto Select controls of the destination sequence after you cut (or copy) but before you paste.* If you do, then the Auto Select controls determine the track destination of pasted tracks. Clips will be pasted starting at the lowest-numbered Auto Select–enabled track.

To copy and paste clips between sequences:

1. In the Timeline, select the clips you want to copy into the destination sequence (**Figure 4.58**) and then *do one of the following*:
   - ◆ To copy the selected clips, press Command-C.
   - ◆ To cut the selected clips, press Command-X.

2. In the destination sequence, position the playhead where you want to paste the clips; then press Command-V.

   The clips are pasted into your destination sequence according to the protocols described above (**Figure 4.59**).

✔ Tip

- ■ You can also select and then Option-drag items from one sequence to another.

Editing a sequence into another sequence

You can use sequences as source clips and edit them into another sequence. Your source clip sequence could be a preexisting sequence you drag into the Viewer or Timeline from the Browser, or it could be a nested sequence located inside a parent sequence in the Timeline. Opening a sequence in the Viewer is not quite as easy as opening a clip. Once you've loaded a sequence into the Viewer, however, you can edit it into a sequence just as you would a clip.

If you need more information on how to perform edits in Final Cut Express, see Chapter 9, "Basic Editing."

To load a sequence into the Viewer:

In the Browser, select the sequence you want to edit into your main sequence; then *do one of the following:*

◆ Choose View > Sequence.

◆ Drag the sequence's icon from the Browser and drop it on the image area in the Viewer window (**Figure 4.60**).

Your edited sequence opens in the Viewer, ready to be used as source media (**Figure 4.61**). If the sequence you select is open in the Timeline and the Canvas, it closes automatically when you load it into the Viewer.

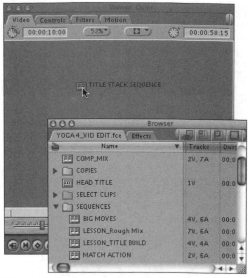

Figure 4.60 To open a sequence in the Viewer, drag the sequence's icon from the Browser and drop it on the image area in the Viewer window.

Figure 4.61 Your edited sequence opens in the Viewer window. You can edit the sequence into an open sequence in the Timeline, just as you would a clip.

Figure 4.62 In the Timeline, Control-click the nested sequence and then choose Open in Viewer from the shortcut menu.

To load a nested sub-sequence into the Viewer:

In the Timeline, *do one of the following:*

◆ Control-click the nested sequence and then choose Open in Viewer from the shortcut menu (**Figure 4.62**).

◆ Double-click the nested sequence while holding down the Option key.

Your nested sequence opens in the Viewer window, ready to be used as a source clip.

✔ Tips

■ When you load a nested sequence from the Timeline and edit it back into your main sequence, you are creating a duplicate of the nested sequence—an independent copy of the original sequence that will not reflect changes you make to the original. If you want all copies of your nested sequence to update when you make changes, use the Browser version of your nested sequence as your source clip instead.

■ All nested audio appears as stereo pairs on two tracks, even if the sub-sequence contains only a single channel of audio.

WORKING WITH MULTIPLE SEQUENCES

Making changes to a nested sequence

You can open a nested sequence and add, remove, or trim clips. When you return to your main sequence, you'll see that the duration of the nested sequence has been adjusted to reflect your changes. Clips to the right of the nested sequence will be rippled to accommodate the change to your nested sequence duration. You'll still need to open the nested sequence to make changes to the clips inside.

To make changes to a nested sequence:

Do one of the following:

- In the main sequence in the Timeline, double-click the nested sequence (**Figure 4.63**).

- In the Browser, double-click the icon for the nested sequence.

  The nested sequence opens as the front tab of the Timeline (**Figure 4.64**). If you opened the nested sequence from inside the main sequence, the main sequence is still open on the rear tab (**Figure 4.65**).

To "un-nest" a sequence:

- There's no "Un-nest" command in Final Cut Express. If you want to replace a nested sequence that you have placed in your main sequence with the clips contained in that nest, you should first open the nest in the Timeline and then copy the clips from the open nest and paste them back over the nested sequence's original location in the main sequence. For more information, see "Copying and pasting from sequence to sequence" earlier in this chapter.

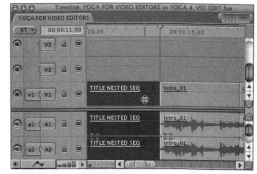

Figure 4.63 In the main sequence in the Timeline, double-click the nested sequence.

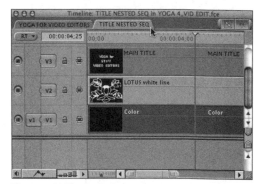

Figure 4.64 The nested sequence opens as the front tab of the Timeline.

Figure 4.65 The main sequence is still open on the rear tab of the Timeline.

FCE Protocol: Updating Nested Sequences

When you insert a clip from the Browser into a sequence, the clip is copied into the sequence. The copy of the clip you placed in the sequence refers directly to the actual media file on the disk and is not a reference to the clip in the project file. Changes you make to the sequence version of the clip will not be reflected in the Browser version.

Nested sequences update globally

The protocol governing sequence versions is different, and it is also central to understanding Final Cut Express. Unlike clips, sequences nested inside another sequence are actually pointers, or references, to the original sequence, not copies. *If you make changes to a sequence after you've edited it into a number of other master sequences, any changes you make to the original **will be reflected** every place you have used it. You'll need to make a duplicate of the sequence and make changes to the copy if you want to avoid a global update.*

For example, you could create a standard credit sequence and edit that sequence into every program in your series. If your credits require any last-minute changes, you can make the changes in the original sequence, and all the projects in which that sequence is nested will be updated.

But duplicate sequences are independent copies

Keep a close watch on nested sequences that you're using in multiple locations.

Multiple nested copies of the same sequence point to the original sequence IF (that's a big *if*) you always use the original Browser version of your sequence as your source when you nest the sequence in multiple locations.

*If you duplicate the original sequence in the Browser, the duplicate sequence you create is an independent copy of the original sequence that **will not reflect** changes you make to the original.* Duping a sequence is a good way to preserve render files, but it's bad news if you want to nest an identical sequence in multiple locations and take advantage of the global updating feature.

Copying and pasting a nested sequence to multiple locations within the master sequence in the Timeline produces the same result: independent duplicates of the original that don't update.

If you need to place multiple copies of a nested sequence you created in the Timeline, always use the Browser version of your nested sequence (it appeared when you performed the Nest Items command) to place the sequence in multiple locations.

Assembling Nested Sequences with Transitions

Building your program as a series of separate sequences and then assembling your sequence "scenes" into a final master sequence is a common post-production strategy. If you want to use transitions to join your scenes together, you'll need to allow extra media handles at the start and end of your nested sequences. When you're ready to assemble your master sequence, load each sub-sequence into the Viewer. Mark the frames you want to appear as the center point of your scene-to-scene transition as the sub-sequence's In and Out points before you edit them into the final master sequence (**Figure 4.66**).

Figure 4.66 If you want to use a transition to join two sub-sequences, mark In and Out points that allow handles on your sub-sequences, to establish the extra frames your transition will require.

About Clips

Final Cut Express has always used clip types—audio, video, graphic, and generated—to identify clips that reference different types of source media. FCE uses a different class of clip types—subclip, merged clip, and sequence—to identify clips that reference a portion of another clip (like a subclip) or multiple clips (like merged clips and sequences).

FCE 2 introduced three new clip types—master, affiliate, and independent—to identify clips that are linked by shared properties (like master and affiliate clips) or clips whose properties and behavior are independent of other clips (like independent clips). The new clip type classifications and behavior are designed to ease project management by automatically updating all affiliated clips when you make a change to a shared property on any of the individual affiliates anywhere in the project. The master/affiliate clips' shared properties are all related to media management; clip properties that remain independent—In and Out points, markers, and applied effects—are all modified during the normal course of editing and must remain independent in each clip copy you use.

Here's an example: You have a master clip in the Browser, and you edit it into your sequence. An affiliate copy of that master clip appears in the sequence. Rename the affiliate copy, and the name of its master clip is also renamed. Change the reel name of the master clip, and the reel name of the affiliate clip in the sequence reflects the same change.

The master/affiliate clip-handling scheme keeps your clip duplicates in sync, which can simplify your life when you're media-managing certain types of projects. Projects best suited to master/affiliate clip handling are well logged, with discrete clips that you don't plan on subdividing much.

If your preferred editing method is to capture large chunks of media and then subdivide and rename the clips post-capture, consider converting your master clips to independent-type clips before you start dicing them up. It could save you from the headache and confusion of converting (and tracking) each clip's type separately. For more information on clip affiliation protocols, see "About Clip Affiliations" in Chapter 7 of Apple's *Final Cut Express Help* PDF.

continues on next page

Here's a rundown of FCE's clip types.

Format-based clip types

◆ **Audio, Video, and Graphics clips:** These clip types are determined by the type of source media the clip is referencing.

◆ **Generated clip:** Create a generated clip by opening a generator from the Viewer's Generators pop-up menu. Generated clips are created as master-type clips. For more information, see Chapter 17, "Titles and Generators."

Relationship-based clip types

◆ **Master clip (Figure 4.67):** Any clip that can generate affiliate clip copies is a master clip. See **Table 4.1** for a complete list of ways to create one.

◆ **Affiliate clip (Figure 4.68):** An affiliate clip is a copy of a master clip that is created by inserting the master clip into a sequence or duplicating the master clip in the Browser. Copies of affiliate clips remain linked to their master clip originals; the linked relationship extends to the clip name, reel name, source timecode, labels, subclip limits, and online/offline state of all affiliate clips. Change one of these shared properties in any one of the affiliated clips, and the change will appear in all the affiliated clips. Markers, In and Out points, and applied effects or motion properties remain independent in master/affiliate clips. See Table 4.1 for a complete list of ways to create an affiliate clip.

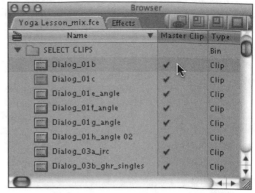

Figure 4.67 It's not easy to identify master, affiliate, and independent clips in the FCE interface. Master clips are easiest to spot; a check mark in the Master Clip column identifies a master clip in the Browser. Master clips never appear in a sequence.

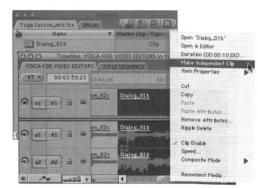

Figure 4.68 Affiliate clips have no check mark in the Browser's Master Clip column. In a sequence, the only way to identify an affiliate clip is to open the clip's shortcut menu. If the Make Independent Clip command is available and not dimmed, the clip is an affiliate clip.

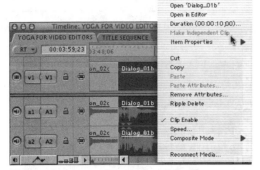

Open 'Dialog_01b'
Open in Editor
Duration (00:00:10;00)...
Make Independent Clip
Item Properties

Cut
Copy
Paste
Paste Attributes...
Remove Attributes...
Ripple Delete

✓ Clip Enable
Speed...
Composite Mode

Reconnect Media...

Figure 4.69 In a sequence, you can identify an independent clip by opening the clip's shortcut menu. If the Make Independent Clip command is dimmed, the clip is already an independent clip. Independent clips appear in the Browser only when you open a pre-FCE 2 project file.

- ◆ **Independent clip (Figure 4.69):** Each copy of an independent clip refers directly back to its source media and does not synchronize clip naming or any other properties with any other independent clip copy. All clips in pre-FCE 2 projects are independent clips. See Table 4.1 for a complete list of ways to create an independent clip.

- ◆ **Subclip:** Subclips are shorter clips you create from a section of a longer master clip. A subclip is always created as a new master-type clip, with no affiliate relationship to the clip it was created from. For information on subclips, see Chapter 8, "Working with Clips in the Viewer."

Table 4.1

FCE Clip Type Relationships

TYPE	MASTER?	HOW TO CREATE	BEHAVIOR
Master clip	yes	Capture new video or audio. Import video or audio. Create a subclip. Create a freeze-frame. Create a merged clip. Drag a merged clip from the sequence back to the Browser. Use the Duplicate as New Master clip command. Use Modify > Make Master Clip on an affiliate or independent sequence clip. Delete an affiliate's master clip. Affiliate clips in the Browser are converted to master clips.	Synchronizes clip name, reel name, source timecode, subclip limits, and online/offline state with all affiliated clips and the master clip. Does not synchronize markers, In and Out points, applied effects, or motion properties. Master clips appear only in the Browser.
Affiliate clip	no	Edit a master clip into a sequence. Duplicate a clip in the Browser or in a sequence. Copy and paste a clip in the Browser or in a sequence. Drag a sequence clip back into the Browser.	Synchronizes clip name, reel name, source timecode, subclip limits, and online/offline state with all affiliated clips and the master clip. Does not synchronize markers, In and Out points, applied effects, or motion properties. Affiliate clips can appear in the Browser or Timeline.
Independent clip	no	Delete an affiliate's master clip. Use the Make Independent Clip command on a sequence clip. Copy a sequence from Project A to Project B; sequence clips become independent in Project B. Edit a clip opened outside the project directly into a sequence. Open an FCE 1 (or an FCP 1, 2, or 3) project in FCE 2; all project clips will be independent.	Maintains independent clip name, reel name, source timecode, remove subclip limits, online/offline state, markers, In and Out points, and applied effects or motion properties. Independent clips appear only in the Timeline, except when a pre-FCE 2 project is opened.

ABOUT CLIPS

FCE Protocol: Clips and Sequences

A clip is the basic unit of media in Final Cut Express.

A clip can represent a movie, still image, nested sequence, generator, or audio file.

A clip is a reference to the actual media file stored on your hard disk. But a clip can also reference material that is not currently online. If you delete the original media file, the clip will still appear in the Browser and Timeline, but you won't see its frames and you won't be able to play it.

When you apply special effects and perform edits on clips, you are *not* affecting the media file on disk.

Before FCE 2, all clips were governed by the same clip-handling protocols. FCE 2 and HD use three clip types: master, affiliate, and independent. Master and affiliate clips use one set of behavior protocols; independent clip behavior is governed by a different set of rules.

Using Master and Affiliate Clips in Sequences

When you insert a master clip from a project into a sequence, FCE inserts a copy of the master clip, known as an *affiliate clip.* That affiliate copy in the sequence shares certain properties with the master clip but maintains independent control over other properties.

This protocol is important to understand because it affects how and where you should make changes to master/affiliate clips, and it illuminates what's different about independent clip behavior. So let's lay out the rules.

When you modify a master or affiliate clip's name, reel name, source timecode, or labels; remove its subclip limits; or change its online/offline state:

* The change you make is applied to all affiliated clips in the project. It doesn't matter if you make the change to the master clip or its affiliate; the result is the same.

* Master and affiliate clips' shared property behavior applies only within a single project; your changes will not be applied to other projects.

continues on next page

ABOUT CLIPS

FCE Protocol: Clips and Sequences *continued*

When you apply markers, In and Out points, effects, or motion properties to a master clip or its affiliate clip copy:

◆ You can open the clip from the Browser (outside a sequence) or from the Timeline (within a sequence).

◆ If you make changes to the clip in the Browser and then insert that clip into a sequence, the clip copy that is placed in the sequence *includes* the changes that have been made in the Browser.

◆ Any changes you make to a clip from within a sequence are *not* made to the clip in the Browser.

◆ After you've inserted a clip into a sequence, any further changes you make to that clip from the Browser will not be reflected in any sequence where the clip is used.

◆ Clips that appear in multiple sequences are independent of one another. Changes to one will not affect the others.

◆ If you want to make further revisions to a clip that's already in a sequence, open the clip from the Timeline and then make the changes.

◆ If you want to make changes to a clip and have the changes show up in all the sequences in which that clip is used, open the clip from the Browser and make the changes. Then reinsert the revised clip into each sequence in which you want the updated clip to appear.

◆ Final Cut Express identifies clips that have been opened from the Timeline by displaying two lines of dots in the Scrubber bar. No dots appear in the Scrubber bar of clips that have been opened from the Browser.

Using Independent Clips in Sequences

When you convert an affiliate-type sequence clip to an independent-type clip, that independent clip refers directly back to the source media file on the disk, and any clip property can be modified independently from any master or affiliate clip referencing the same source media file.

Because each independent clip copy maintains independent control over all its properties, the same rules that apply to the In and Out points of master and affiliate clips (listed above) apply to all properties of independent clips.

Figure 4.70 Control-click the Browser clip and then choose Duplicate as New Master Clip from the clip's shortcut menu.

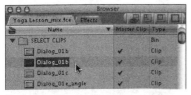

Figure 4.71 The duplicate master clip appears in the Browser.

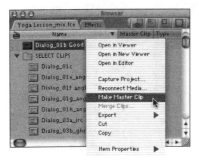

Figure 4.72 Choose Make Master Clip from the clip's shortcut menu.

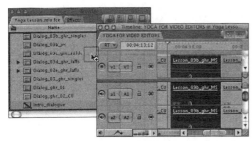

Figure 4.73 A special pointer (with an M for master) appears when both the Command and Option keys are held down, alerting you that you're creating a duplicate master clip.

To duplicate a Browser clip as a new master clip:

Select the clip in the Browser and then *do one of the following:*

◆ Control-click the clip and then choose Duplicate as New Master Clip from the shortcut menu (**Figure 4.70**).

◆ Choose Modify > Duplicate as New Master Clip.

The duplicate of the clip appears as a new master clip in the Browser (**Figure 4.71**).

To convert an independent or affiliate clip into a master clip:

Select the clip in the Browser and then *do one of the following:*

◆ Control-click the clip; then choose Make Master Clip from the shortcut menu (**Figure 4.72**).

◆ Choose Modify > Make Master Clip.

✔ Tips

■ After you're done hacking, renaming, and subdividing, and the independent clips in your sequence finally settle down enough to get hitched, you can create master clips for every sequence clip simply by selecting the entire contents of the sequence and dragging it to the Browser. Your independent sequence clips become affiliates of the newly created master clips in the Browser.

■ Create a duplicate master clip for a sequence clip by pressing Option as you drag the sequence clip out of the Timeline and then adding the Command key as you drop the clip in the Browser (**Figure 4.73**). "Voilà!" is so overused these days, but still...

To locate an affiliate clip's master clip:

◆ Select the affiliate clip in the Timeline or Browser; then choose View > Reveal Master Clip.

The master clip is revealed in the Browser.

To make a sequence clip independent:

◆ In the Timeline, Control-click the sequence clip; then choose Make Independent Clip from the shortcut menu (**Figure 4.74**).

The affiliate sequence clip is converted to an independent-type clip.

To make all clips in a sequence independent:

◆ Select the sequence icon in the Browser; then choose Make Sequence Clips Independent from the shortcut menu (**Figure 4.75**).

To break an affiliate clip's relationship with its master:

Do one of the following:

◆ In the Browser, delete the master clip associated with that affiliate clip.

◆ Copy the sequence containing the affiliate clip into another project.

◆ In the Timeline, use the Make Independent Clip command to convert the affiliate clip into an independent clip.

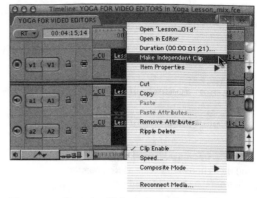

Figure 4.74 Choosing Make Independent Clip from the sequence clip's shortcut menu converts an affiliate-type clip to an independent-type clip.

Figure 4.75 Control-click a sequence's icon in the Browser and choose Make Sequence Clips Independent, and you convert all the clips in that sequence to independent clips with a single command.

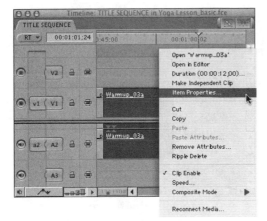

Figure 4.76 Choose Item Properties from the clip's shortcut menu.

Viewing and Setting Item Properties

The Item Properties window is the central location for information about an individual clip. The settings on three tabs in the Item Properties window allow you to view or change the properties of a clip. Besides the general clip information column in the far left of the window, you'll see a column for the clip's video track and separate columns for each audio track in the clip. This expansion of the Item Properties window makes it possible to combine one video track with up to 24 tracks of audio from different sources and track each audio channel separately.

To open a clip's Item Properties window:

1. Select the clip in the Browser or Timeline or open it in the Viewer.

2. *Do one of the following:*
   ◆ Choose Edit > Item Properties.
   ◆ Control-click the item; then choose Item Properties from the shortcut menu (**Figure 4.76**).
   ◆ Press Command-9.

✔ Tips

■ Want to view item properties for multiple clips in a single window? Just select the clips in the Browser or Timeline before you use the Edit > Item Properties command.

■ What if you have changed the name of a clip and removed all traces of the original source media file it references? You can consult the Item Properties window for the renamed clip to trace the underlying source media filename and location.

To get information about the format of a clip:

1. Open the clip's Item Properties window using one of the methods described on the previous page.

   The Item Properties window opens, displaying the Format tab. This tab displays data on the location of the source media file, file size, and format characteristics for each track of the clip (**Figure 4.77**).

2. Control-click the item's setting in the Clip column to modify the following Format properties:

   ◆ **Name:** Enter a new name for the clip.

   ◆ **Pixel Aspect Ratio:** Select a pixel aspect ratio for the clip.

◆ **Anamorphic 16:9:** If your clip's source media is 16:9, enabling this option ensures that FCE will interpret and display the clip's pixel aspect ratio properly.

◆ **Field Dominance:** Specify the dominant field by making a selection from the shortcut menu.

   ◆ **Alpha Type:** Select an alpha channel type for the video clip.

   ◆ **Reverse Alpha:** Reverse the alpha channel of the video clip.

   ◆ **Composite Mode:** Select the mode to be used when compositing the video clip.

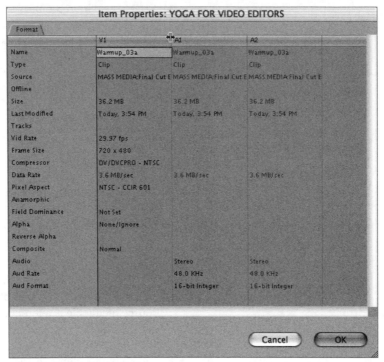

Figure 4.77 The Format tab of the Item Properties window displays format information about an individual clip or sequence.

CAPTURING VIDEO

Final Cut Express offers three DV video capture options, which use FireWire to transfer DV-format video and audio from a qualified DV camcorder, deck, or qualified analog-to-digital converter box.

- ◆ **Capture Clip:** Capture clips one at a time. Set In and Out points to define the portion of the tape you want to capture, enter identifying information in the Logging tab, and capture the clip.

- ◆ **Capture Now:** Capture single clips without setting In and Out points. Use Capture Now to capture DV with or without device control, or to capture live video.

- ◆ **Capture Project:** A single, automated batch recapture process recaptures selected clips, or all the DV clips in a project. You need a device-controllable DV camcorder or deck to perform a Capture Project operation.

All three capture methods store the original DV timecode with the captured clip, but Final Cut Express assigns the same starting timecode (00:00:00:00) to all clips you are working with inside the program.

You will not be able to use FCE's automated capture and output features unless your external video hardware supports device control. You still can capture clips that are logged and manually captured while the tape is playing, but you won't be able to perform automated project recapture.

FCE's new HDV capture process converts your HDV compressed format video to the more edit-friendly AIC format as you capture, so HDV capture operates a little differently from the DV format capture options. HDV capture is described later in this chapter.

Capturing video is probably the first thing you'll want to do, but a little general knowledge of the FCE interface will make your first few captures go more smoothly.

If you are new to Final Cut Express, take a moment to read Chapters 7 and 8, which contain details on Browser and Viewer operation, before you start a capture process. You may also need to review Chapter 2, "Installing and Setting Up," for details on preference and preset settings.

Anatomy of the Capture Window

Use the Capture window to capture video and audio media in Final Cut Express. This window supports a range of capture options, from live video capture on the fly to automated project recapture with full device control.

To open the Capture window:

◆ Choose File > Capture (**Figure 5.1**); or press Command-8.

✔ Tips

■ The size of your Capture window is determined by the zoom level of the Canvas and Viewer windows in your workspace arrangement. If you're using a high zoom level for the Canvas and the Viewer, your Capture window will be large as well. Small Canvas and Viewer windows will result in a small Capture window. If you're using different sizes in the Viewer and Canvas windows, the Capture window appears at the size of the smaller one.

■ When you open the Capture window for the first time after launching FCE, the screen reads "Preview Disabled." Don't freak out. That's standard operating procedure—the warning disappears when you click Play.

■ For best performance, the Capture window should be completely visible on your computer monitor, with nothing overlapping the window, not even the cursor.

■ If you have been capturing clips, FCE will not play back clips in your external monitor until you close the Capture window.

Figure 5.1 To open the Capture window, choose File > Capture.

DV Timecode vs. FCE Timecode: What's the Difference?

On your original DV tape, each frame of the tape is assigned a unique number, called a *timecode number*. This system of timecode numbers has been the basis of video editing systems for over 30 years. In Final Cut Express, all captured clips are assigned the same starting timecode: 00:00:00:00. Each FCE clip, however, preserves the original DV tape timecode start and end numbers with the clip's media file. FCE accesses the original timecode numbers when you go back to the original DV tapes and recapture a project. If you open an FCE project in Final Cut Pro (FCE's big brother application), you'll have full access to the original DV timecode. In FCE, that DV timecode information is hidden.

Preview section

Many of the controls in the Preview section of the Capture window also appear in the Viewer window. For more information, review "Anatomy of the Viewer" in Chapter 8.

Figure 5.2 shows an overview of the Capture window.

◆ **Current Timecode field:** This field displays the current timecode location of your source tape. Enter a timecode number in this field to shuttle the source tape to that timecode location.

◆ **Timecode Duration field:** This field displays the duration of the currently marked clip.

◆ **Free Space status display:** This display shows the amount of available hard disk space remaining.

◆ **Transport controls:** Use these buttons to control your deck or camcorder transport if you have device control enabled. Transport control operation is described in more detail in Chapter 8, "Working with Clips in the Viewer."

continues on next page

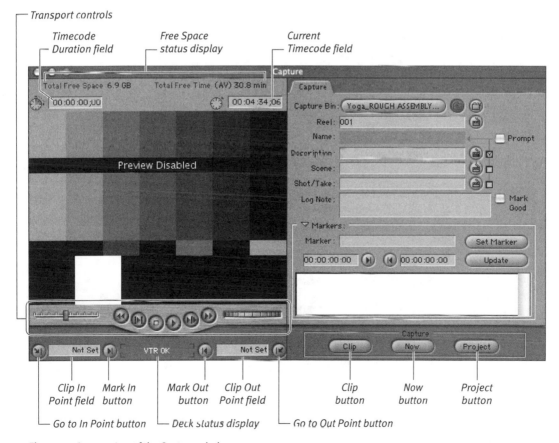

Figure 5.2 An overview of the Capture window.

◆ **Deck status display:** This display shows the status of communication between your deck or camcorder and Final Cut Express.

◆ **Go to In Point button:** Click to shuttle tape to the currently marked clip's In point.

◆ **Clip In Point field:** This field displays the timecode location of the currently marked clip's In point.

◆ **Mark In button:** Click to mark an In point for your capture.

◆ **Mark Out button:** Click to mark an Out point for your capture.

◆ **Clip Out Point field:** This field displays the timecode location of the currently marked clip's Out point.

◆ **Go to Out Point button:** Click to shuttle tape to the currently marked clip's Out point.

✔ **Tip**

■ Not only can you copy and paste timecodes from one field to another; you can Option-click and then drag and drop a timecode to copy it into another timecode field—a useful procedure while you're logging.

Capture controls

The Capture control buttons appear below the tabbed portion of the window. Each of the three buttons performs a different kind of capture operation.

◆ **Capture Clip button:** Click this button to capture a single clip immediately. Capture Clip requires that you enter identifying information on the Capture tab and set In and Out points before capturing the clip. For more information, see "Capture Clip: Capturing Video with Device Control" later in this chapter.

◆ **Capture Now button:** Click this button to capture without setting In or Out points. Capture Now is useful if your camcorder or deck doesn't have device control, or if you want to capture long clips without setting the Out point in advance. For more information, see "Capture Now: Capturing Video without Device Control" later in this chapter.

◆ **Capture Project button:** Click this button to batch recapture multiple DV clips in your project. For more information on batch recapturing, see "Capture Project: Batch Recapturing" later in this chapter.

Capture tab

The Capture tab (**Figure 5.3**) contains fields and shortcut tools you use to enter the information you need to log a clip. Try to get into the habit of recording log information—you'll thank yourself when you need to sort through hundreds of clips to find a frame or short sequence.

◆ **Capture Bin button:** Click to open the current capture folder (the Browser folder where captured clips are stored).

◆ **Up button:** Click to move the capture bin selection up a level from the currently selected capture bin.

◆ **New Folder button:** Click to create a new capture folder inside the currently selected capture folder.

◆ **Reel field:** Enter the name of your current source tape in this field. Control-click the text field to select from a list of recent reel names.

◆ **Reel Slate button:** Click to add a number at the end of the name for incremental labeling. Click again to increment the number by one. Option-click to clear the contents of the field. All the Slate buttons on the Capture tab perform the same functions for their respective fields.

continues on next page

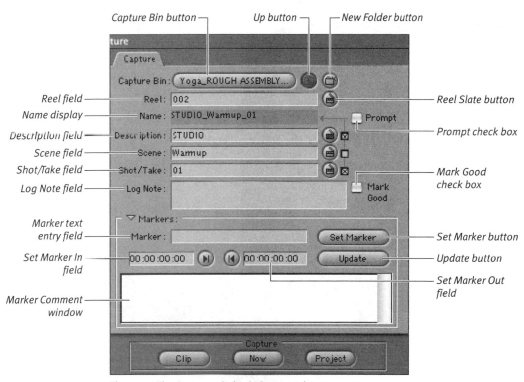

Figure 5.3 The Capture window's Capture tab.

◆ **Name display:** The name in this field is compiled from information entered in the Description, Scene, and Shot/Take fields. This is the name that appears in the Browser's Name column.

◆ **Prompt check box:** Check this box for a prompt to name a clip when you click the Capture Clip button.

◆ **Description field:** Enter descriptive text in this field. Check the box at the right to include this description in the Name display.

◆ **Scene field:** Enter descriptive text in this field. Check the box at the right to include this description in the Name display.

◆ **Shot/Take field:** Enter descriptive text in this field. Check the box at the right to include this description in the Name display.

◆ **Log Note field:** Enter descriptive text in this field. Control-click the text field to select from a list of recent log notes.

◆ **Mark Good check box:** Check this box to place a marker in the Browser's Good column. When you're done capturing, you can use the Browser's sort function to group all the clips you've marked "Good."

◆ **Marker text entry field:** Enter a marker name or remarks in this field. For more information, see "Using Markers" in Chapter 8.

◆ **Set Marker In field:** Click to set a Marker In point, or enter a timecode in the field.

◆ **Set Marker Out field:** Click to set a Marker Out point, or enter a timecode in the field.

◆ **Set Marker button:** Click to log the marker.

◆ **Update button:** Click to modify a previously entered marker.

◆ **Marker Comment window:** This window displays marker information for the current clip.

Setting Up for Capture

Apple's FireWire capture system has simplified video capture, but capturing still requires some preparation, because it puts your entire editing system through its paces.

Capturing is important, and you should set up for it correctly. Here's an overview of the setup procedure and your objectives in each step:

◆ **Review your selected Easy Setup.** You want to be sure that you've selected an Easy Setup that uses the proper combination of presets for this capture operation. Select an Easy Setup that uses the correct audio sample rate to match the media you want to capture. Your capture settings should match the video hardware and tape format you're using. Your device control settings should be compatible with your camcorder or deck.

◆ **Check scratch disk preferences.** You want to ensure that any media you capture will be written to the correct hard disk or folder, that your designated scratch disk is fast enough to handle the data transfer, and that you have enough space to accommodate the media files you want to capture.

◆ **Review the Abort Capture on Dropped Frames option on the General tab of the User Preferences window.** Abort Capture on Dropped Frames automatically stops the capture process if dropped frames are detected. If your system and source tapes are in perfect condition, you should leave this safeguard option checked. However, if you're unable to complete a capture because FCE is reporting trouble (and you're willing to risk some uncertainty about timecode or frame integrity), you should uncheck this option.

◆ **Test device control settings.** You want to ensure that the video, audio, timecode, and device control connections between your deck or camcorder and Final Cut Express are operational.

✔ Tips

■ FCE 2 introduced a new capture feature that can salvage DV tapes with timecode breaks. If the program detects a timecode break during a capture process, it will save a media file containing all video captured up to the break, setting the frame before the break as that file's Out point. FCE continues capturing video after the break as a second media file.

■ If you want to capture video by using a non-controllable device such as an analog-to-DV converter, switch to one of the two Easy Setups that support capture from converter boxes: DV NTSC DV Converter or DV PAL DV Converter.

■ Before you start capturing footage, you should use color bars to check the image quality on your external video monitor as well. Your monitor is a critical tool for evaluating your footage, so set it up right—once you've calibrated it, leave the monitor's image settings alone. See Apple's online Knowledge Base article "Final Cut Pro 3: How to Calibrate Your Broadcast Monitor" (article ID 36550) for instructions.

■ If your DV clips need image-quality adjustments, you can fix them post-capture by applying the appropriate image control filters. To learn how to use FCE's filters, see Chapter 14, "Compositing and Effects Overview."

Is Your System Capture-Ready?

Capturing video puts your entire FCE system—including external hardware—to the test. Any conditions that impair its performance can show up as dropped frames, audio sync drift, or error messages—not a good start for your project.

Apple's Knowledge Base has a good article on the subject: "Final Cut Pro: Dropped Frames and Loss of Audio Sync" (article ID 58640).

Here's a checklist, summarized from the article, that you can use to avoid the most common causes of capture troubles:

◆ The Canvas size should be set to Fit to Window or smaller. If you can see scroll bars in the Canvas, you have a problem.

◆ Your computer monitor's refresh rate should be set to 75 Hz or higher in the Displays pane in your System Preferences.

◆ On PowerBook FCE systems, turn off processor cycling on the Options tab of the Energy Saver preferences pane.

◆ You should be using FCE-qualified drives. If your drives are overly full, or if the data is too fragmented, drive performance can be impaired.

See "Optimizing Performance" in Chapter 2 and "Troubleshooting Capture Problems" later in this chapter for more tips on improving performance in Final Cut Express.

Entering Information on the Capture Tab

Logging is the process of reviewing your source video tapes and labeling and marking the In and Out points of usable clips. Other logging data could include shot and take numbers, added markers at specific points in the action, and production notes. You can also mark clips as "Good," so that you can easily sort out the most promising takes.

In Final Cut Express, you cannot store logging information for a clip without capturing it immediately. You must enter log information and then capture each clip in a single operation.

This section explains how to use all the logging features on the Capture window's Capture tab. You use these features the same way in all three types of video capture. You'll also learn how to select a *capture folder*—the folder your clips will be stored in after capture.

To use all the logging options in Final Cut Express, you need device control over your video deck or camcorder. If you don't have a controllable video device, you can log only the duration and In and Out points for individual clips, and you must enter the data manually.

FCE Protocol: What Are Offline Clips?

An offline clip is a clip reference to a media file that has been deleted, moved, or renamed. If you log and capture a clip and then delete the clip's media file from disk, the clip "goes offline" and a red slash appears through the clip icon.

The offline clips appear in the Browser; you can even edit them, but you won't see or hear anything on the screen while you're editing. The only difference is that online clips are linked to captured media files on disk.

You can restore offline clips that reference deleted media by using the Capture Project feature, detailed later in this chapter, to recapture the media from tape.

You can use the Reconnect Media command to restore an offline clip's link to a moved or renamed media file.

Or you can delete a clip's media file deliberately to recapture some disk space, and recapture the clip's media only when you want to use it.

The Art of File Naming

When you capture or import media into Final Cut Express, you name each file as a part of the process. You'll be living with these file names for a long time. Since it's not a trivial matter to change file names once you've assigned them, you should develop a file naming system before you start your project. Write it down, distribute it to your production team, and stick to it.

Much of the logic behind file naming schemes involves constructing file names in a way that allows you to make use of FCE's Sort and Find functions and to identify the file's content, file type, and version number. In Final Cut Express, an added level of flexibility is available to you because clips and their underlying media files do not need to have the same name.

A directory structure is the planned organization of folders you use to store your project's media elements. A complete file naming system should also be extended to the naming and organization of your files into folders. If you can, create your folder structure before you start acquiring your media elements. This will make it easier to file your elements correctly after the pace of production heats up.

Final Cut Express imposes an automated directory structure for captured media files, automatically generating folders named after your current project inside the Capture Scratch folder. This complicates the process of filing media elements according to your own system, but if you're organized, you can work around it. After you capture, you can move your captured clips into your own folder system and then import them into a project before you start assembling sequences.

Here are a few guidelines to help you develop file names that will remain useful throughout the life of your project:

◆ Incorporate file names into your shooting scripts, voice-over scripts, and storyboards early in production. Some projects actually enter the entire script into a database and use that script/database to track media elements.

◆ File names should contain the shot's scene and take numbers, if appropriate.

◆ Avoid duplicate file names.

◆ File suffixes are traditionally used as file type indicators. There are some standard file suffixes in use, but don't be shy about making up your own system of file type abbreviations. Be sure to document them.

◆ Audio file names should incorporate a code that indicates sample rate, file format, and whether the files are stereo or mono files.

◆ Your file naming system should include a code for version control. Don't rely on a file's creation or modification date as your only means of identifying the latest version of a file.

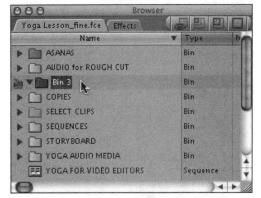

Figure 5.4 Click the New Folder button on the Capture tab to create a new folder inside the current capture bin and select it as the current capture bin.

Figure 5.5 The new capture bin in the Browser. The clapstick icon indicates the current capture bin.

Figure 5.6 Control-click the bin; then select Set Capture Bin from the bin's shortcut menu.

Selecting a capture folder

A *capture folder* (or *capture bin)* is the Browser folder where your clips are stored after capture. The default location for a new capture folder is the top level of a project tab in the Browser window. You can set the capture bin using the buttons in the Capture window or from a Browser window shortcut menu. Your choice of capture folder does not affect the location of the captured media files on your hard disk; instead, it specifies where in the Browser the clips referencing those media files appear.

To set a capture bin in the Capture window:

1. On the Capture tab of the Capture window, *do one of the following*:
   - Click the New Folder button (**Figure 5.4**) to create a new folder inside the current capture bin and select it as the current capture bin (**Figure 5.5**).
   - Click the Up button to set the bin hierarchically above the current capture bin as the new capture bin.

2. Click the Capture Bin button to switch to the Browser and open the new capture bin you created.

   A little clapstick icon appears in the Browser next to the current capture bin.

To set a capture bin in the Browser:

1. In the Browser, select the bin that you want to set as the capture bin.

2. Control-click the bin; then select Set Capture Bin from the bin's shortcut menu (**Figure 5.6**).

   A little clapstick icon appears next to the current capture bin.

Entering clip information on the Capture tab

Final Cut Express allows you to store quite a bit of information along with your media. You can enter the bare minimum—a reel number and a clip name—or you can take full advantage of FCE's auto-incrementing log fields and marker notes.

To enter log information:

1. Load the source tape you want to capture into your camcorder or deck.

2. Choose File > Capture; or press Command-8.

3. In the Capture window, specify a Capture bin using one of the methods described in the previous task.

4. In the Reel field, *do any of the following:*

   ◆ Enter a name for the reel (the tape or other video source you are currently logging).

   ◆ Click the Reel Slate button to add a numeric reel name.

   ◆ Control-click the Reel field; then choose from a pop-up list of recent reel names (**Figure 5.7**).

5. In the Description field, *do any of the following:*

   ◆ Enter a name for the clip.

   ◆ Select the Prompt check box if you want to name each clip as you log it (**Figure 5.8**).

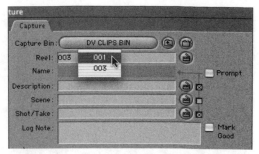

Figure 5.7 Control-click the Reel field; then select from a list of recent reel names.

Figure 5.8 Check Prompt if you want to name each clip as you log it.

ENTERING INFORMATION ON THE CAPTURE TAB

Figure 5.9 Click a Slate button to add an incremented numeral to its associated text field.

Figure 5.10 Click the Mark Out button to set an Out point for the capture.

Figure 5.11 Capture the clip using the Capture Clip or the Capture Now button.

6. In the Description, Scene, and Shot/Take fields, *do any of the following:*

   ◆ Click the check boxes next to the fields you want to incorporate into the clip's name.

   ◆ Enter any identifying text you want to use in the text field.

   ◆ Click the Slate button to automatically increment the corresponding text field's numeral (**Figure 5.9**).

   The automatic naming function in Final Cut Express creates clip names by combining the fields you selected, such as Description_Scene01_01, in the Name field. This is the name that appears in the Browser's Name column, and it is the name of your source media file on disk.

7. Use the transport controls in the Capture window to control your source device and locate the footage to capture. If you have full device control enabled, you can also navigate to a specific timecode location on your source tape by entering a timecode value in the Current Timecode field.

8. Mark media In and Out points for a clip *by doing one of the following:*

   ◆ Click the Mark In and Mark Out buttons (**Figure 5.10**); or press I (the letter *i*) to set the In point, and press O (the letter *o*) to set the Out point.

   ◆ Enter specific timecodes in the timecode fields at the bottom of the Capture window. Enter the In point in the left timecode field and the Out point in the right timecode field.

9. Capture the clip using either the Capture Clip or the Capture Now button (**Figure 5.11**). Step-by-step instructions for each type of capture appear in the following sections of this chapter.

ENTERING INFORMATION ON THE CAPTURE TAB

129

To add a marker to a clip while logging:

1. To access the marking controls, click the expansion triangle next to Markers at the bottom of the Capture tab.

2. Enter a marker name or comment in the Marker field.

3. To set the In and Out points of the marker, *do one of the following:*

   ◆ Enter timecode values in the In and Out timecode fields. You can Option-drag values from any timecode fields in the Capture window to copy them into these fields.

   ◆ Click the Mark In and Mark Out buttons.

4. Click Set Marker (**Figure 5.12**).

   The marker In and Out points and any information entered in the Marker field appear in the Marker Comment window (**Figure 5.13**).

   These markers appear as subclips in the Browser once a clip is captured.

✔ Tip

■ If you need to modify your marker data after you've set the marker, enter the revisions in the Marker fields and then click the Update button to save your changes.

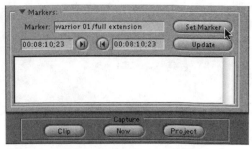

Figure 5.12 Click Set Marker to enter the marker's In and Out points as well as any information entered in the Marker field.

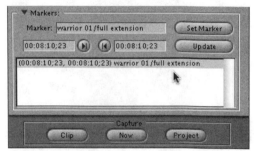

Figure 5.13 The marker information appears within the Marker Comment window and is saved with the captured clip.

ENTERING INFORMATION ON THE CAPTURE TAB

FCE Protocol: Auto-Incrementing on the Capture Tab

The rules governing the behavior of the Description, Scene, and Shot/Take fields on the Capture tab are too many to list in this sidebar. Here, however, are a few handy rules that should help you get more efficiency out of the auto-entry features built into the Capture tab:

◆ The check box to the right of a field's name controls whether the field will be included in the clip's name.

◆ The last-checked field is the one that will increment automatically. Here are some examples:

   ◆ If you check only the Description field, just the Description field will increment.

   ◆ If Scene is the last-checked field, the scene number automatically increments, even if you entered a number in the Shot/Take field but left it unchecked.

   ◆ If Shot/Take is the last-checked field, the Shot/Take field increments, and the scene number remains unchanged until you click its Slate button to increment it. Clicking the Scene field's Slate button resets the Shot/Take field to 01 (FCE assumes that your new scenes start with Take 01).

◆ You can include a Shot/Take number only if you include a scene number.

Logging Tips

◆ Click the Capture Bin button to display the selected capture bin on the front tab of the Browser.

◆ Control-click the Reel field to access a pop-up menu displaying all the reel names you've used in the current project. Selecting your reel name from the pop-up list helps you ensure you're entering exactly the same name each time. That's critical to successful batch capture.

◆ Clear text from a field by Option-clicking the Slate button next to it.

◆ Use the Mark Good check box to mark your best stuff. You can use the Find feature to search the Browser's Good column and select only the clips you've marked "Good" for your first rough cut.

Capture Clip: Capturing Video with Device Control

Capture Clip combines logging tasks (marking In and Out points, naming the clip, entering comments) and capturing a single clip. Using a controllable DV camcorder or deck allows you to mark In and Out points at specific timecodes and capture exactly the section you marked. Later, you'll be able to recapture the exact same clip by using the Capture Project feature.

To capture a clip with device control:

1. Make sure your video device is properly connected and device control is operational. If you're using a camcorder, make sure it's switched to Play (VCR) mode; similarly, if you're using a deck with a Local/Remote switch, make sure the switch is set to Remote.

2. Choose File > Capture (**Figure 5.14**).

Figure 5.14 Choose File > Capture.

Capture Strategies to Manage Project Media

It's tempting to skip the time-consuming process of logging and capturing individual DV clips and just hit the Capture Now button. Final Cut Express offers DV Start/Stop Detection and subclipping to handle extra-long clips (see the next section for details). So why not capture whole tapes and log them after you've captured?

The primary reason to go to the extra trouble of capturing shorter individual clips is because once you've captured a large clip, you can't easily delete the unused portions of its huge media file.

FCE's media management options are limited, allowing you only to manually delete whole clips and their associated media files, and to recapture all DV project clips with the Capture Project feature. Neither of these options allows you to discard unused portions of the media file.

If you're desperate to reclaim some drive space, you can shed unused portions of a media file by exporting a clip that contains just the part of the media you want to keep, but you'll have to re-import the trimmed clip and then re-edit into your sequence. For more information on exporting a clip, see Chapter 19, "Creating Final Output."

Figure 5.15 Use the transport controls in the Capture window to control your video deck and locate the footage that you want to capture.

Figure 5.16 Click the Mark Out button to set an Out point for the capture. You could also enter a timecode value in the Out point timecode field.

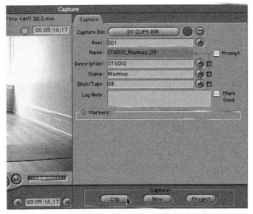

Figure 5.17 Click the Capture Clip button located at the bottom of the Capture tab.

3. Use the transport controls in the Capture window to control the source device and locate the footage that you want to capture (**Figure 5.15**). If you have full device control enabled, you can also navigate to a specific timecode location on your source tape by entering a timecode value in the Current Timecode field.

4. In the Capture window, specify a capture bin using one of the methods described in the previous task.

5. Enter logging information for your clip (follow steps 4 through 6 in "To enter log information" earlier in this chapter).

6. To mark a clip, *do one of the following:*
   - Click the Mark In and Mark Out buttons (**Figure 5.16**); or press I to set the In point and press O to set the Out point.
   - Enter specific timecodes in the timecode fields at the bottom of the Capture window. Enter the In point in the left timecode field and the Out point in the right timecode field.

7. Click the Capture Clip button located at the bottom of the window (**Figure 5.17**). Final Cut Express captures the clip, and the captured clip appears in a new Viewer window. Your captured clip is saved in the current project's designated capture bin.

Capture Now: Capturing Video without Device Control

If you don't have a video device that your computer can control, you can still capture video in Final Cut Express by using the controls on your video deck or camcorder to search and play your source tape.

To log clips without the benefits of device control, you need to manually enter the clip's starting and ending timecodes and other information in the appropriate fields in the Capture window. That clip information is used to identify the clip when you save it.

If you enter log information before a Capture Now operation, the captured clip will be saved in your designated capture bin.

If you do not enter log information, the captured clip will be saved as an untitled clip in your designated capture bin.

✔ Tips

■ Before you start capturing, check your Capture Now time-limit setting on the Scratch Disks tab of the System Settings window in FCE. The default limit is 30 minutes. Very long Capture Now time limits can increase the lag between the time you click the Capture Now button and the time that capture begins, so specify a time limit not much longer than the longest clip you're planning to capture.

■ Analog-to-digital video converter boxes are handy for resurrecting treasured analog video footage, but if you're using a converter box with FCE to capture video, you must use an Easy Setup configured specifically for that purpose: DV-NTSC (or PAL) 48 kHz - DV Converter.

To capture a clip without device control:

1. Make sure your DV camcorder or deck is properly connected.

2. Choose File > Capture; or press Command-8.

3. In the Capture window, specify a capture bin by one of the methods described earlier.

4. To enter logging information for your clip, follow steps 4 through 6 in "To enter log information" earlier in this chapter.

5. Use your device's controls to locate the footage you want to capture, rewind 7 to 10 seconds, and then press the device's Play button.

6. Click the Capture Now button at the bottom of the Capture window 1 to 5 seconds before the device reaches the first frame in your clip (**Figure 5.18**).

   There's a slight delay after you click the button before capture begins—how long a delay depends on your Capture Now time limit and the number of scratch disks you have assigned to FCE.

continues on next page

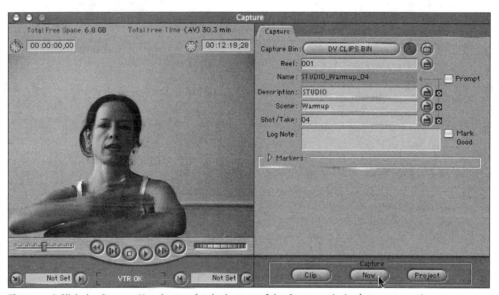

Figure 5.18 Click the Capture Now button (at the bottom of the Capture window) 1 to 5 seconds before the first frame in your clip appears.

7. To stop capturing, press the Escape key (**Figure 5.19**); then stop playback on your device.

   The captured clip appears in the designated capture bin on the project's tab in the Browser (**Figure 5.20**).

8. Play the clip to make sure it contains the video you want. You may need to close the Capture window—some video capture hardware won't play the captured clip while this window is open.

✔ Tip

■ If you're using a camcorder, you can use Capture Now to capture live footage. On most consumer DV models, your camcorder must be recording to tape as you capture the live footage in Final Cut Express.

Capturing analog audio

You can use FCE's Voice Over tool to digitize analog audio from a cassette player, TV, or other source and capture it in Final Cut Express. This can be a great convenience if you want to capture temporary, rough voice-over or music. For more information, see "Recording Audio with the Voice Over Tool" in Chapter 12.

Figure 5.19 To stop capturing, press the Escape key.

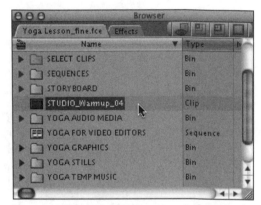

Figure 5.20 The captured clip appears in the project's capture bin in the Browser.

Capturing HDV Video

The HDV capture scheme in Final Cut Express HD is Apple's first pass at devising a simple capture process for HDV. HDV uses MPEG-2—that's the same compression used in iDVD—to squeeze the extra-large HD datastream down to a size that can be handled without an additional video card. MPEG-2 compression reduces the size of the HDV datastream by reducing the number of frames that contain complete picture information. One of these complete frames (called I-frames) is followed by a sequence of reduced-image-data frames (called B-frames and P-frames).

As you capture, FCE converts the HDV footage to Apple Intermediate Codec (AIC) format. AIC generates complete image and audio information for each frame. FCE attempts to perform this format conversion in real time, but unless you are running a top-of-the-line G5, the conversion will probably lag behind capture. The HDV capture process is similar to Capture Now—you must manually cue up the footage you want to capture using your HDV camcorder's controls. For more information, see Apple's *New Features in Final Cut Express HD* PDF.

HDV Capture Setup Checklist

Here's a pre-capture checklist to help make your HDV capture go smoothly:

◆ Is your HDV camcorder properly connected and powered on?

◆ Have you selected the correct Easy Setup? You should select the setup that matches the frame size and frame rate of the HDV footage you want to capture.

◆ Does your selected scratch disk have enough room to accommodate your captured footage? 1080i60 HDV can require up to 46 gigabytes of storage per hour of captured footage—that's nearly four times the space required to store an hour of captured DV. **Table 5.1** lists storage requirements for DV and HDV. Note that AIC file sizes are approximate; more detail and motion in your HDV images will generate larger AIC-processed files. Static shots with large blocks of plain surface will generate smaller files.

◆ Is your Capture Now time-limit set properly? The Capture Now time-limit setting on the Scratch Disks tab of the System Settings window should specify a time limit not much longer than the longest clip you're planning to capture.

◆ Have you set a capture folder for your captured HDV clips? The project tab in the Browser is the default capture folder destination. If you want to create a separate capture folder in your project, control-click a folder in the Browser window, then choose Set Capture Folder from the shortcut menu.

Table 5.1

DV and HDV Storage Requirements

FORMAT	FRAME SIZE	STORAGE REQUIREMENT
DV NTSC	720:480	12 GB per hour
DV PAL	720:576	12 GB per hour
720p30 HDV (processed as AIC)	1280:720	23 GB per hour
1080i60 HDV (processed as AIC)	1440:1080	46 GB per hour
1080i50 HDV (processed as AIC)	1440:1080	38 GB per hour

To capture an HDV clip:

1. Read and follow the setup process described in "Setting Up for Capture" earlier in this chapter.

2. Use your HDV camcorder's controls to locate the HDV footage you want to capture in this clip, and then rewind 5-7 seconds and pause the tape.

3. Choose File > Capture, or press Command-8.

   The HDV Capture dialog box appears.

4. In the HDV Capture dialog box, enter a name for the clip you're about to capture, then click Capture (**Figure 5.21**).

   The capture preview window appears as FCE starts videotape playback of your cued tape (**Figure 5.22**). During capture, FCE converts the HDV datastream to AIC format. The capture preview window displays the AIC-encoded video. FCE attempts to process in real time, but the speed of the conversion process depends on your Mac's processor speed and available RAM. A status message at the bottom of the capture preview window indicates whether the conversion process is occurring in real time (**Figure 5.23**), or is lagging behind capture.

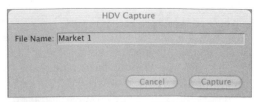

Figure 5.21 Enter a name for the HDV clip, and then click Capture.

Figure 5.22 The HDV capture preview window displays video as it's encoded to Apple Intermediate Codec (AIC) format.

Figure 5.23 The capture preview window's status message indicates this capture is being converted to AIC in real time.

CAPTURING HDV VIDEO

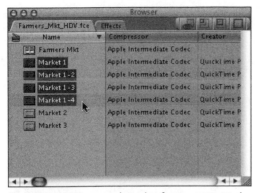

Figure 5.24 FCE's scene detection feature generated these four discrete Browser clips from a single capture. Each clip references a discrete AIC format media file on disc.

5. To stop capturing, press the Escape key; then, stop playback on your camcorder.

   The captured clip appears in the designated capture folder on the project's tab in the Browser.

6. Play the clip to make sure it contains the video you want.

✔ Tips

■ To abort an HDV capture, press the Escape key twice.

■ FCE's HDV capture includes a scene detection feature that works just like iMovie's. During the AIC-encoding process, FCE automatically creates a separate clip (and a separate media file on disk) each time it detects a Start/Stop (Record/Pause) signal in captured HDV datastream (**Figure 5.24**).

■ Apple warns users that FCE HD cannot capture reliably from a tape that has been recorded initially in one format (such as an HDV format), and then recorded over in another video format (such as DV). This caution extends to material recorded in two different formats of HDV, such as 720p30 followed by 1080i60. Try to capture from mixed format tapes and you could see dropped and frozen frames galore. Take Apple's advice and black and code (completely re-record) any tape before trying to record over it in another format. Or better yet, crack open a fresh tape.

CAPTURING HDV VIDEO

Capture Project: Batch Recapturing

Use Capture Project to batch recapture DV clips and sequences you've previously captured with Final Cut Express. Capture Project captures selected DV clips, all DV clips, or just the offline clips in your project. Capture Project requires a camcorder or deck with device control.

This command is useful if you want to recapture several clips or an entire sequence in one automated batch recapture process— for example, when restoring a project you've removed from your hard disk. If you've accidentally deleted a few media files in the course of a project, you can use the Select Offline Items Only option to recapture just the footage you deleted.

Capture Project can recapture only DV clips from a source video tape. To restore an entire project, you must also restore all graphics, music, and any digital video that did not originate on a DV tape. For information on archiving and restoring FCE projects, see "Project Maintenance Tips" in Chapter 20.

Automated, unattended batch capture is limited to clips from one tape. You can set up an automated batch capture that involves clips from several reels, but you'll have to hang around and feed new tapes to your video deck during the process.

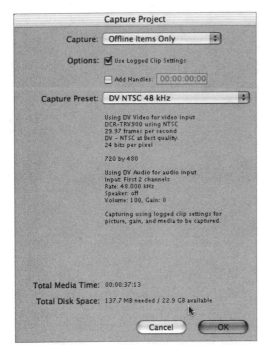

Figure 5.25 Total Disk Space, calculated at the bottom of the Capture Project window, compares estimated space needed to storage space available for this batch capture operation.

Preparing to recapture a project

Capture Project is an automated process. It's worthwhile to prepare carefully before you kick off an automated capture because, well, things can happen while your back is turned. Here are some suggestions:

◆ Check your currently selected Easy Setup and scratch disk preferences. Make any changes you want applied to this batch capture; you won't be able to change these settings after you open the Capture Project dialog box.

◆ Answer these questions: Are your capture settings correct for this batch capture, or are you capturing tapes in a different format? Is the estimated space available on your designated scratch disk sufficient to contain your incoming media files?

◆ Make a note of the available space estimate compared to the estimate of space needed in the Capture Project dialog box (**Figure 5.25**). This comparison can yield clues that can help you debug your batch capture list. For example, a 10-second subclip from a 20-minute master clip can throw your whole capture scheme out of whack; Final Cut Express would capture the entire 20-minute master clip.

◆ If you suspect that your tape contains timecode breaks, you should be aware that each time it encounters a timecode break during capture, FCE will automatically create a new clip that starts at the first frame of timecode after the break. (Timecode breaks can be caused by shutting down the camera or ejecting your tape in mid-reel and not re-cueing on the last bit of previously recorded timecode.)

To batch recapture selected clips:

1. In the Browser, select the clips and sequences you want to recapture; then control-click and choose Capture Project from the shortcut menu (**Figure 5.26**).

2. In the Capture Project window's Capture pop-up menu, *do one of the following:*

   ◆ Choose All Selected Items to recapture all selected offline and online DV clips in the project (**Figure 5.27**).

   ◆ Choose Offline Items Only to recapture just the offline DV clips in the project.

3. Enter a duration to set the handle size of offline clips (this is optional).

   Handles add extra frames beyond the In and Out points of a captured clip.

4. Select a capture preset option from the Capture Preset pop-up menu. This setting should match the video format and audio sample rate of the source tape you are recapturing.

5. Click OK.

   The Insert Reel dialog box appears, displaying a list of all the reels (tapes) required for this batch capture operation.

6. Load the first tape you want to capture into your camcorder or deck, select it from the list, and click Continue (**Figure 5.28**).

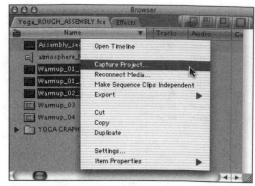

Figure 5.26 Select the clips and sequences you want to recapture; then choose Capture Project from the Browser's shortcut menu.

Figure 5.27 Select All Selected Items to recapture the entire length of all selected offline and online DV clips in the project.

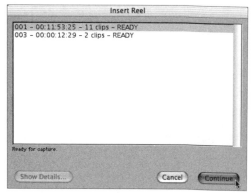

Figure 5.28 Load the reel you want to capture into your deck, select it from the list, and click Continue. When it's finished capturing all the clips from that reel, FCE will prompt you to select the next reel.

CAPTURE PROJECT: BATCH RECAPTURING

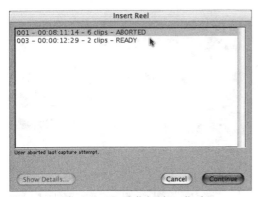

Figure 5.29 The Insert Reel dialog box displays a count of "aborted" clips—project clips that remain uncaptured.

Figure 5.30 To recapture all the DV clips in the project, start by deselecting everything in the Browser window; then choose File > Capture Project.

Figure 5.31 Choose All Selected Items from the Capture Project window's Capture pop-up menu.

7. To interrupt batch capture, press Escape or click the mouse button.

   If you interrupt batch capture, Final Cut Express displays the Insert Reel dialog box again with a count of "aborted" clips—project clips that remain uncaptured (**Figure 5.29**).

8. Click Cancel to abort the Capture Project recapture, or click Continue to resume capture. If you cancel the process, you'll have to recapture all the clips in the current reel if you retry the Capture Project operation.

✔ Tip

- If you recapture online clips into the same scratch disk folder where the original clips' media files are stored, the original media files are overwritten. If you recapture into a different folder, the original media files are preserved.

To recapture all DV clips in a project:

1. With the Browser window active, make sure no clips, sequences, or bins are selected in the Browser window.

2. Choose File > Capture Project (**Figure 5.30**).

3. In the Capture Project window's Capture pop-up menu, choose All Selected Items (**Figure 5.31**).

4. Follow steps 3 through 8 in "To batch recapture selected clips" earlier in this chapter.

Using DV Start/Stop Detection

The DV Start/Stop Detection feature automatically sets markers in a previously captured DV clip each time it detects a Start/Stop (Record/Pause) signal in that clip. Because FCE can use markers to break a clip into individual subclips, you can use the technique outlined here to capture long sections of DV tape and break it into usable subclip chunks.

If you're accustomed to working in iMovie, DVD Start/Stop Detection is the closest thing to using iMovie's Import button with automatic scene detection enabled. Instead of getting a collection of separate clips, however, in Final Cut Express you end up with one large clip containing many markers, which can be converted to subclips. For more information, see "About Subclips" in Chapter 8.

To divide a captured DV clip into subclips based on starts and stops:

1. Open your previously captured DV clip in the Viewer.

2. With the Viewer active, choose Mark > DV Start/Stop Detection (**Figure 5.32**).

   Final Cut Express places a marker at every point where it detects a Stop/Start signal in the clip's media file (**Figure 5.33**).

Figure 5.32 Choose Mark > DV Start/Stop Detection.

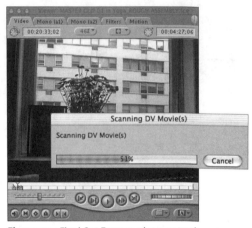

Figure 5.33 Final Cut Express places a marker at every point where it detects a Stop/Start signal in your clip's media file.

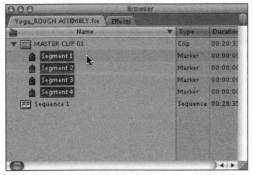

Figure 5.34 Click the expansion triangle next to the clip to view the new markers. Select the markers you want to convert to subclips.

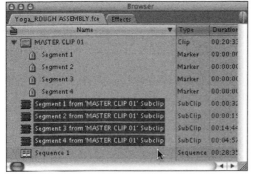

Figure 5.35 New subclips, derived from the markers in your marked clip, appear in the Browser.

3. If you want, add more markers at any point in the clip where you want to create a subclip.

4. Locate your clip's icon in the Browser; then click its expansion triangle to view the markers you just added to the clip (**Figure 5.34**).

5. If you want, rename markers with the names you want your subclips to have.

6. Select all of the markers; then choose Modify > Make Subclip.

New subclips, derived from your marked clip, appear in the Browser (**Figure 5.35**). If you renamed your markers, your new subclips use those names.

7. Review your new subclips and delete any with material you don't need.

✔ Tip

■ This DV Start/Stop technique is handy for converting a long clip into a group of smaller subclips, but when you're done, you still have a batch of subclips on your hands, and all of those subclips are still referencing the full length of your original media file.

USING DV START/STOP DETECTION

Troubleshooting Capture Problems

If you experience problems during video capture, you may see an error message. Final Cut Express monitors the state of controlled devices and reports an error if the problem is due to a camcorder or deck malfunction. Cancel the operation before proceeding and consult your camcorder or deck manual for troubleshooting information. Here are some basic troubleshooting tips that may help you get back on the road.

If a "No Communication" message appears in the Deck Status area of the Capture window (Figure 5.36):

◆ Check that your device is plugged in, switched on, and properly connected to your computer.

◆ Turn on the device and restart the computer. If your device's power was not switched on when you started your computer, the device may not have been recognized.

◆ Reconnect the FireWire cable and restart the computer. If the cable was not connected properly when you started your computer, the device may not have been recognized.

Figure 5.36 The "No Communication" message appears in the Deck Status area of the Capture window if device control is disabled.

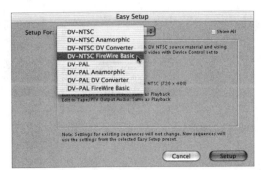

Figure 5.37 If Apple FireWire doesn't provide reliable device control, switch to the Apple FireWire Basic protocol by switching to an Easy Setup that uses FireWire Basic.

If you experience problems controlling your camcorder or deck:

◆ If your deck has a Local/Remote switch, be sure it's set to Remote.

◆ If you're using the Apple FireWire protocol, try Apple FireWire Basic instead. Switch to an Easy Setup that includes FireWire Basic (**Figure 5.37**).

◆ Check Apple's Final Cut Pro web site to download Apple's Final Cut Express Device Qualification PDF. This document lists all qualified cameras and their recommended device control settings (**Figure 5.38**). Here's the URL for the Final Cut Express Device Qualification page: www.apple.com/finalcutexpress/qualification.html

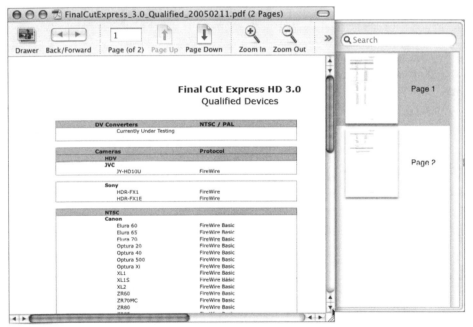

Figure 5.38 Check Apple's Final Cut Express web site to download the latest Final Cut Express Device Qualification PDF.

If you encounter a "Bus Error" message when you try to capture:

◆ Something went wrong when your captured data crossed the bus, the data delivery interface between your computer and the outside world. Bus errors can be caused by a number of things, but you can try making sure that your cables are hooked up completely and that any hardware cards in your computer are seated properly.

If you encounter a "Time Code Break" error message when you try to capture:

◆ FCE does offer automatic capture across timecode breaks, but if your tape's time-code track contains a lot of breaks, reliable recapture becomes more difficult. Is there anything you can do to salvage a tape with timecode breaks? Certainly. You can dub the entire tape onto a tape with continuous timecode and start your logging and capturing process with the dubbed copy.

If your captured audio and video play back out of sync:

◆ The video displayed in the Viewer and the Canvas will not appear to play back in sync if you are monitoring your audio through external speakers connected to your camcorder or deck. The audio from the external speakers will be synchronized with video displayed on the video monitor.

◆ The audio sample rate of your original source tape must match the audio sample rate of your capture settings. Check the source tape's audio sample rate against your capture settings.

◆ Your FCE system may be dropping frames during capture or playback. See "Is Your System Capture-Ready?" earlier in this chapter for a list of possible causes for dropped frames.

IMPORTING
DIGITAL MEDIA

One of the most enchanting aspects of the DV revolution is the world of digital media elements that you can mix, match, and manipulate freely to spice up your video. Final Cut Express is exceptional in the wide latitude of digital file formats it accepts. You can import most types of QuickTime-compatible files into an FCE project, including video clips, still images, and sound files.

Apple's QuickTime web site contains a complete list of supported file formats at `www.apple.com/quicktime/products/qt/specifications.html`.

Here's a list of common FCE-supported QuickTime formats:

♦ **Graphics:** BMP, FlashPix, GIF, JPEG/JFIF, Photoshop (PSD), PICS, PICT, PNG, QuickTime Image File (QTIF), SGI, TARGA (TGA), and TIFF

♦ **Video:** AVI, QuickTime Movie

♦ **Audio:** AIFF, Audio CD Data (Macintosh), Sound, and Wave

♦ **Other:** Macromedia Flash (video only)

You can import an entire folder or an organization of multiple folders in a single operation. When you import a folder, Final Cut Express imports all files it recognizes in the folder, as well as all recognized files in any subfolders. Folders are imported with their internal hierarchies intact.

To import files or a folder:

1. Copy or move the file (or folder) that you want to import into the desired media folder in your project (**Figure 6.1**).

2. In the Browser, select a destination for your incoming file *by doing one of the following*:

   ◆ To import files or folders into the top level of a project, click the project's Browser tab.

   ◆ To import files into a bin within a project, double-click the bin to open it.

3. *Do one of the following*:

   ◆ Choose File > Import; then choose Files (or Folder) from the submenu, select the items, and click Open.

   ◆ In the Browser or any Browser bin window, Control-click and then choose Import File (or Import Folder) from the shortcut menu.

   ◆ Drag the desired files or folders directly from your Desktop (**Figure 6.2**) to a project tab or a bin within the Browser (**Figure 6.3**).

   ◆ Drag the desired files or folders from your Desktop to an open sequence in the Timeline. This places a clip reference to the media in the Timeline but does not place a reference in the Browser.

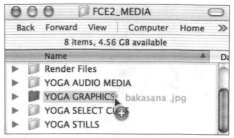

Figure 6.1 Before you import a file, copy or move it to the correct asset folder in your project.

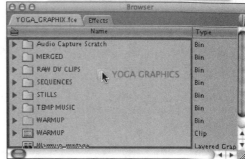

Figure 6.2 Drag the desired files or folders directly from your Desktop into Final Cut Express.

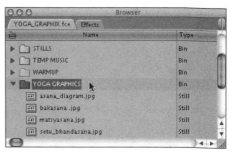

Figure 6.3 Drop the files or folder on a project tab or in a bin within the Browser.

IMPORTING DIGITAL MEDIA

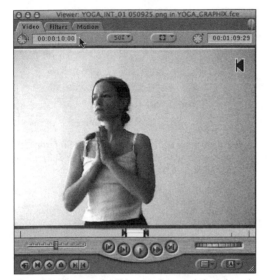

Figure 6.4 Imported still images have a default length of 2 minutes of identical video frames, with a duration of 10 seconds between In and Out points. The source media files for still-image clips don't occupy 2 minutes' worth of drive space; you generate media only for the portions you render.

Importing Still Images

The default format for imported still images is a clip containing 2 minutes of identical video frames, with a duration of 10 seconds between In and Out points (**Figure 6.4**). If you edit still images into a sequence, they won't be visible on your NTSC external monitor until they are rendered.

Final Cut Express supports all QuickTime-compatible graphics file formats. Check the QuickTime readme file or Apple's QuickTime web site for a complete list of compatible file formats.

✔ Tips

- Final Cut Express does not import EPS files.

- Large images take longer to insert and longer to open in projects because FCE must scale them before displaying them. Really large images should be scaled in a graphics program prior to importing.

FCE Protocol: File Location Is Critical

When you import a file into a Final Cut Express project, that file is not copied into the FCE project file. Importing a file places a clip in your Browser, but that clip is a reference to the current hard disk location of your imported media file at the time you import it.

In Final Cut Express, any clip's link to its underlying media file is entirely location based. If you move media files to another disk location after you've used them in a project, you break their links to the clip references in your FCE projects. You can use the Reconnect Media command to restore those clip-to-media file links, but a little forethought before you import files can save you a lot of hassle later. (The Reconnect Media function is discussed in Chapter 4, "Projects, Sequences, and Clips.")

Before you import a file into FCE, be sure to copy it to its permanent folder location in your project's media assets directory structure. Importing files directly from a removable media storage device (such as a Zip disk) will cause your file to be marked "Offline" in your project once you remove that disk from your system. The same principle applies to audio imported from a CD.

Setting the default duration for stills

Still images and generators are assigned a duration at the time they're imported into Final Cut Express. You specify the default duration for still images on the Editing tab of the User Preferences window.

No matter what duration you set, your Final Cut Express clip references a single still image, so you won't create large, full-length video files until you render or export your stills at their edited lengths.

The default still duration is applied at the time you import the still into Final Cut Express. If you have imported a still image and want the duration to be longer, you must modify the preference setting and then re-import the still.

To change the default still duration:

1. Choose Final Cut Express > User Preferences; or press Option-Q.

2. On the Editing tab of the User Preferences window, enter a new default duration in the Still/Freeze Duration field (**Figure 6.5**).

3. Click OK.

✔ Tip

- Modify the default still duration any time you're importing a large number of stills that you plan to cut to the same length. The stills will be imported at the final edited length, and you can drop them directly into your sequence. *Molto bene.*

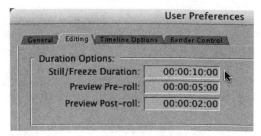

Figure 6.5 On the Editing tab of the User Preferences window, type a new default duration in the Still/Freeze Duration field.

Working with Adobe Photoshop Files

Adobe Photoshop is the industry-standard tool for creating graphics elements for use in Final Cut Express. Its file format compatibility with Final Cut Express makes importing your artwork's layers and alpha channels easy.

When you're creating graphics for use in a video program, keep your final format's requirements in mind. Remember that video has title-safe requirements, a different pixel aspect ratio, and a different tolerance for color and contrast levels than still graphics do.

Images that look beautiful in print or on a computer screen may not display well on a television monitor. The NTSC broadcast video standard cannot tolerate extreme contrast shifts on many of the colors that you can create and display in Photoshop.

Photoshop comes with an NTSC Colors filter that you can apply to your artwork to make it color safe for TV sets, and FCE has a Broadcast Safe filter that performs a similar function.

✔ Tip

- Photoshop's NTSC Colors filter is a fine tool, but it's easier to use the Broadcast Safe filter in Final Cut Express once you've incorporated the Photoshop files into your sequence. For more information, see Chapter 16, "Filters and Compositing."

Preparing a Photoshop file for use in FCE

The best way to preserve image quality in digital image formats is to maintain the same frame size and resolution from beginning to end. You will get best results by creating your art with the required pixel dimensions in mind, but if you create artwork on a computer for display on broadcast television, you'll find that you must jump through a few hoops.

The native frame size of DV is 720 by 480 pixels. However, if you create your artwork in Photoshop at that size, your image looks squeezed when it is displayed on a TV monitor after printing to video. This is because pixel aspect ratios in the computer world and the broadcast television world are different.

Computer monitors use square pixels, where each pixel's height equals its width. NTSC television monitors use a system that has a non-square pixel aspect ratio of 1.33:1, where the height is just a little bit greater than the width.

To accommodate the difference between these two frame sizes, you must create your full-frame graphics elements at a slightly larger size than your target resolution and then size them down to the target resolution in Photoshop before you import them into Final Cut Express. (*Target resolution* refers to the actual pixel count of an image's frame size in its final delivery, or target, format.)

To create a Photoshop file at DV-NTSC target resolution:

1. In Photoshop, choose File > New; or press Command-N.

2. Enter a width of 720 pixels, a height of 534 pixels, and a resolution of 72 pixels per inch (**Figure 6.6**).

   This ratio of 720:534, or 1.33:1, is the proper proportion for creating text and graphics that will look the same on your NTSC monitor as on your computer monitor.

3. Create your image file (**Figure 6.7**).

4. Save the file as your original image file. Use this original graphics file to make any subsequent changes to the artwork.

5. Choose Image > Image Size (**Figure 6.8**).

6. In the Image Size dialog box, uncheck Constrain Proportions.

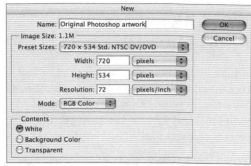

Figure 6.6 In the New dialog box, enter a width of 720 pixels, a height of 534 pixels, and a resolution of 72 pixels per inch.

Figure 6.7 The original Photoshop image before resizing, at 720 by 534 pixels.

Figure 6.8 Choose Image > Image Size.

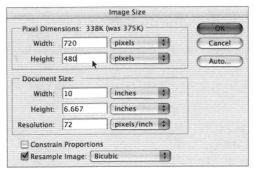

Figure 6.9 In the Image Size dialog box, specify a width of 720 pixels and a height of 480 pixels.

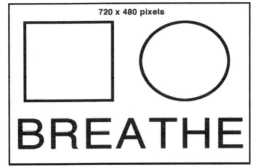

Figure 6.10 The "squashed" Photoshop image after resizing, at 720 by 480 pixels.

7. In the Pixel Dimensions section, enter a width of 720 pixels and a height of 480 pixels (**Figure 6.9**).

8. Click OK.

   The vertical aspect of the image shrinks, which makes it look squashed (**Figure 6.10**).

9. Save the file as your production graphics file. Use this production graphics file in your project.

10. If you need to make changes to the artwork, use the original graphics file, which has the unaltered aspect ratio; then, when you're ready to save, repeat steps 4 through 9.

✔ Tips

- You don't have to import an entire full-screen image if your image uses only a small portion of the frame. Position your elements in full-screen format, resize for the pixel aspect ratio difference, and then crop the artwork.

- If you're planning to zoom in on the image you're preparing, you should import a file with pixel dimensions that will allow the tightest framing to fill the entire video frame without scaling the image above 100 percent.

- You can import a variety of file formats, but the most common are the native Photoshop format (for images with multiple layers) and the standard PICT format (for single-layer images with alpha channels).

- You can also resize imported graphics clips and sequences in Final Cut Express, but you'll get better results using Photoshop's bicubic scaling for resizing because it uses a better resampling algorithm.

WORKING WITH ADOBE PHOTOSHOP FILES

FCE Protocol: Updating Photoshop Files in FCE

It's easy to import Adobe Photoshop files into FCE, but if you need to change to a Photoshop file you've already used in a sequence, there are some hoops to jump through. Get ready to jump...

When you import a multilayer Photoshop file into your project for the first time, Final Cut Express constructs a description of this file that includes the number of layers and the frame size of each layer.

First hoop: It's not always easy to get Final Cut Express to update its description data of your Photoshop file. If you revise your existing image in Photoshop and save changes in the original file, you may not see the changes reflected when you return to Final Cut Express. FCE protocol dictates that the original proxy description of your Photoshop file is used.

How do you get FCE to refresh its memory and update your Photoshop file's description? Here are some suggested workarounds:

◆ After you've revised your Photoshop file, rename the file when you save your changes and then re-import it into FCE. Because you're re-importing the file with a new name, FCE will create a new description for it. The good news? Your Photoshop file revisions show up in FCE. The bad news? Now you have to manually replace the file with the revised file everywhere you've used it.

◆ If your file has the same number of layers and those layers have the same frame size, you should be able to select the Photoshop clip wherever you've used it in your sequence and then use the Reconnect Media command to manually re-introduce the clip and the Photoshop source media file.

Second hoop: FCE uses the frame size data it recorded when you first imported your Photoshop file in all effect calculations that use x, y coordinates—motion paths, scaling, warp filters, and so on. However (get ready to jump...), FCE does not include transparent pixels when it calculates a Photoshop layer's frame size. Say you've created text on a transparent background in Photoshop, imported your file into FCE, and then applied effects. Should you need to revise your text, when you return to it, you'll find that the frame size of your text layer has changed. Even if you successfully reconnect your revised Photoshop file to your FCE sequence, FCE will use the data description from the original import (with the old frame size) to calculate your effects. The result? Your text effects will look distorted, and you'll briefly consider quitting the business.

There's a workaround for this dilemma. It's not pretty, but you can save yourself some headaches down the road by anticipating changes to your text. Again, get ready to jump...

◆ When you build your original Photoshop file, place a single nontransparent pixel in each corner of the frame (**Figure 6.11**). You'll need to do this for each and every layer. FCE will use the rectangle created by those four placeholder pixels to calculate the frame size. You can change text to your heart's content inside the bounding box created by the four corner pixels, and your FCE frame size will not change. So if you can reconnect your Photoshop file, your effects will be calculated with the correct frame size data.

continues on next page

FCE Protocol: Updating Photoshop Files in FCE *continued*

Final warning: Once you've imported a layered Photoshop file into FCE, you should avoid adding or subtracting layers in the file.

FCE identifies a Photoshop layer by its position relative to the file's bottom layer. Increase the total number of layers in the Photoshop file, and FCE will ignore any layers numbered above the previously topmost layer. Deleting a layer from a Photoshop file that you've already imported could yield a variety of unpleasant results, so you should re-import any file with changes to the layer count.

The best workaround? Once you've imported your Photoshop graphics, don't change your mind. Or get ready to jump...

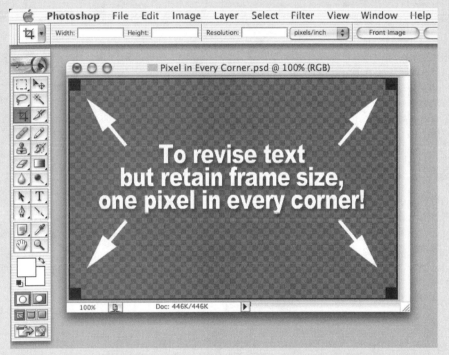

Figure 6.11 Place a single nontransparent pixel in each corner of each layer of your Photoshop composition. If you revise your Photoshop text later, those corner pixels will maintain a constant frame size, and when you re-import or reconnect your revised Photoshop file, FCE will recalculate your previously applied effects with the correct frame size. Hey—it's a workaround.

WORKING WITH ADOBE PHOTOSHOP FILES

Importing a layered Photoshop file into Final Cut Express

Final Cut Express preserves the layers in a layered Photoshop file, importing the file as a special type of sequence, known as a *layered graphic* sequence. Each Photoshop layer is represented by a clip on a track in that sequence.

Double-click a Photoshop file sequence to open it in the Timeline, where you can choose individual layers to manipulate. Each layer is found on its own video track.

When you place a layered Photoshop file into your FCE sequence, you're actually *nesting* it: placing a sequence within another sequence. Sequence nesting is a powerful tool, and knowing the rules that govern the behavior of nested sequences will help you plan your work better. See "Working with Multiple Sequences" in Chapter 4.

To view individual layers in imported Photoshop files:

◆ In the Browser, double-click the Photoshop file, which appears as a sequence (**Figure 6.12**).

The Photoshop file opens as a sequence in the Timeline. Individual layers appear as clips aligned on separate video tracks (**Figure 6.13**).

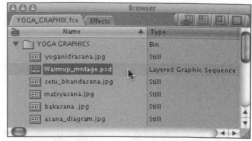

Figure 6.12 A layered Photoshop file appears as a sequence when it's imported into Final Cut Express. Double-click the sequence icon to open the file.

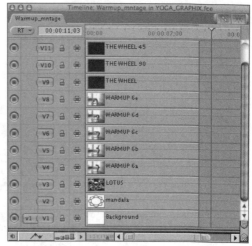

Figure 6.13 The Photoshop file opens in the Timeline as a sequence. Individual layers appear as clips.

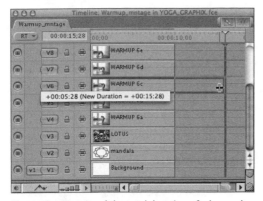

Figure 6.14 To extend the total duration of a layered Photoshop file, open it as a sequence in the Timeline and adjust the length of the individual layers.

✔ Tips

- Once you've opened your multilayer Photoshop file as an FCE sequence, you can drag individual layer "clips" out of the sequence and drop them in the Browser. You can then use the individual layers as independent graphics clips.

- To import a layered Photoshop file as a clip instead of a sequence, flatten the image in Photoshop before importing it.

- Because imported layered Photoshop files appear in FCE as sequences, your Still/Freeze Image Duration preference will set the total length of the imported file, with no allowance for handles. If you want to increase the file's length after you import, you'll have to open the Photoshop file sequence and extend the length of the individual layers inside (**Figure 6.14**). Extending the length of multiple-layer clips in one operation is a terrific use for the Extend edit. See "To perform an Extend edit in the Timeline" in Chapter 11.

FCE Protocol: Layered Photoshop Files

- A layered Adobe Photoshop file imported into a Final Cut Express project retains its transparency information, visibility, and composite mode.

- Layer opacity settings and layer modes are preserved, but layer masks and layer effects are not.

- If a Photoshop layer mode has no corresponding compositing mode in Final Cut Express, the layer mode is ignored.

Importing Audio Files

You import digital audio files into Final Cut Express just as you do any other digital media. You can import files in any QuickTime-supported audio format.

You can capture audio at its originally recorded sample rate and use it in the same sequence with audio recorded at other sample rates. When you play back the sequence, Final Cut Express converts the sample rate in real time for any audio clips whose sample rates do not match the sequence settings.

Letting Final Cut Express convert the sample rates in real time is not always the best solution, however, as real-time sample-rate conversion is optimized for speed, not audio quality. You can convert the sample rate of your nonconforming audio by using the Export feature in Final Cut Express to make a copy of your audio file at the correct sample rate, or you can wait until you're ready to export your final product. FCE will sample-rate-convert your nonconforming audio tracks using a higher quality, non-real-time conversion during the audio mixdown rendering process. See Chapter 19, "Creating Final Output."

To import an audio CD track into an FCE project:

1. In the Finder, double-click the audio CD icon to open it; then drag the desired .aif audio files into your project's media folder (**Figure 6.15**).

2. Rename the files so you can remember where they came from.

3. Follow the steps outlined in "To import files or a folder" earlier in this chapter (**Figure 6.16**).

Figure 6.15 Drag the .aif audio files you want to import into your project's media folder.

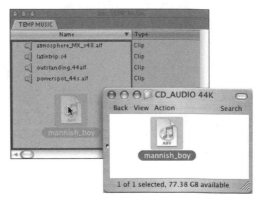

Figure 6.16 Rename the file; then drag it directly into your FCE project.

✔ Tip

■ FCE does not support playback of compressed audio formats (such as MP3 or AAC) in the Timeline, and rendering will not make them compatible. Convert your compressed audio files to AIFF before import.

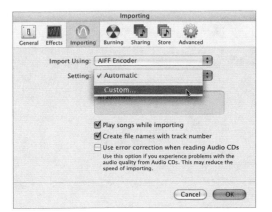

Figure 6.17 Specify your file conversion settings in the Importing pane of the iTunes Preferences window.

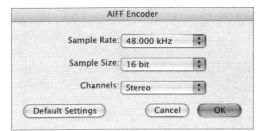

Figure 6.18 In the AIFF Encoder window, make your settings match these.

Converting Audio to 48 kHz on Import with iTunes

If you are using a lot of material from audio CDs in your FCE projects, consider using Apple's free iTunes, an audio jukebox application. Here's how to set your preferences in iTunes to convert 44.1-kHz audio to 48 kHz as the application imports the CD audio track directly to your project's media folder.

To convert audio in iTunes:

1. Open iTunes; then choose iTunes > Preferences and click the Importing icon.

2. In the Importing pane, choose AIFF Encoder from the Import Using pop-up menu and Custom from the Setting pop-up menu (**Figure 6.17**).

3. In the AIFF Encoder window, specify the following (**Figure 6.18**); then click OK.
   - Sample Rate: 48.000 kHz
   - Sample Size: 16 bit
   - Channels: Stereo (or Auto)

4. Back in the Preferences window, click the Advanced icon.

continues on next page

CONVERTING AUDIO ON IMPORT WITH iTUNES

5. In the Advanced pane, the iTunes Music Folder Location field shows the currently selected destination folder for the CD audio you're about to import. Click the Change button (**Figure 6.19**) and navigate to your project's audio media folder. Click Choose and then click OK.

6. In the iTunes playlist window, choose the tracks you want to import by ensuring that their check boxes are marked; then click the Import button (**Figure 6.20**).

The CD audio tracks are converted to 48-kHz AIFF files and appear in the destination folder you specified in step 5, ready to be imported into your FCE project (**Figure 6.21**).

✔ Tip

■ It is not recommended that you import audio tracks by dragging directly from an audio CD to the Browser window in Final Cut Express, because once you remove the CD from your computer, your project will no longer have access to the audio file.

Figure 6.19 Select your project's audio media folder as the destination folder for your sample-rate-converted audio files.

Figure 6.20 In the iTunes playlist window, check the tracks you want and click the Import button.

Figure 6.21 iTunes converts your CD audio tracks into 48-kHz AIFF files and places them in the specified folder.

CONVERTING AUDIO ON IMPORT WITH ITUNES

Figure 6.22 Choose File > Open; then select the iMovie project file you want to open.

Importing an iMovie Project

Final Cut Express HD can import, open, and edit movies created in iMovie 3, 4, or 5. When you import an iMovie project, the clips in the Browser are linked to the original source media files you captured in iMovie.

iMovie uses a different DV encoding method, which produces files in DV Stream format. DV Stream differs from FCE's DV-NTSC (or DV-PAL) format, so you'll encounter a little extra work and a couple of limitations as you continue to work on a project that originated in iMovie 3, 4, or 5:

◆ Once you've imported the project, you must render all its media to convert it to an FCE-compatible DV format.

◆ Your DV Stream iMovie files do not have timecode tracks, so you cannot recapture any media that originated in iMovie. Don't throw away your iMovie media files once you've rendered; you'll need them if you plan to continue editing.

◆ Final Cut Express may not play back your iMovie DV files in real time unless you render them first.

◆ Your imported iMovie project won't include any iMovie sound effects, titles, transitions, effects, or iDVD chapter markers.

To open an iMovie project:

1. Choose File > Open.

2. Select the iMovie project you want to open (**Figure 6.22**).

   The iMovie project appears on a project tab in the Browser. The project contains the iMovie sequence plus the individual clips from iMovie's clips shelf.

continues on next page

IMPORTING AN iMOVIE PROJECT

3. Double-click the sequence to open the iMovie project sequence in the Timeline.

4. Choose File > Save Project As and save your imported iMovie project as a Final Cut Express project (**Figure 6.23**).

5. Render the sequence if necessary.

✔ Tips

■ Final Cut Express versions 1 and 2 do not support iMovie HD projects. If you try to open an iMovie HD project in these earlier versions of FCE, you see a file error message.

■ Final Cut Express will not allow import of an iMovie project unless iMovie is also installed on your computer. If you try to import an iMovie project and FCE does not find iMovie installed, you'll see an "Unrecognized file" error message.

Figure 6.23 Once you've opened your iMovie project in FCE and checked that your media and sequence information have been imported successfully, choose File > Save Project As and save a new version of the project as a Final Cut Express project.

IMPORTING AN iMOVIE PROJECT

ORGANIZING CLIPS IN THE BROWSER

The Browser is the window you use to organize and access clips, audio files, graphics, and offline clips—all the media elements you use in your project. It also includes the project's sequences—Final Cut Express objects that contain your edits.

The Browser performs these organizing tasks on your project's virtual clips and sequences—although Browser items look like files on your computer Desktop, Browser items are *references* to media files, not the files themselves. It's very important to remember that copying, moving, or deleting a clip in the Browser does not affect that clip's source media file on disk. Moving a batch of clips from one folder to another in the Browser does not change the location of the clips' corresponding files on your hard drive. File storage is independent of Browser organization, so you can place the same clip in several Browser projects, and each instance of the clip will include a reference to the same media file on your hard drive.

See "What Is Nonlinear, Nondestructive Editing?" in Chapter 1 for more background on nonlinear editing technology.

Anatomy of the Browser

When you open Final Cut Express for the first time, the Browser contains just two tabs:

◆ A new, Untitled Project tab with a single empty sequence.

◆ The Effects tab, which contains default copies of FCE's effects, filters, and generators, including the text generators.

For information on using FCE's effects features, see Chapter 14, "Compositing and Effects Overview."

If you have multiple projects open, the Browser displays a tab for each open project. You can also open a Browser folder in a separate window and then drag the folder's tab from that window into the main Browser window to display the folder as a tab.

Figure 7.1 shows the Browser window in List view. Note that FCE opens projects with the Browser in Icon view by default. Icon view is useful for organizing a storyboard, but doesn't provide the wealth of clip data available from the Browser columns in List view. To learn how to switch between List and Icon views, see "Customizing the Browser Display" later in this chapter.

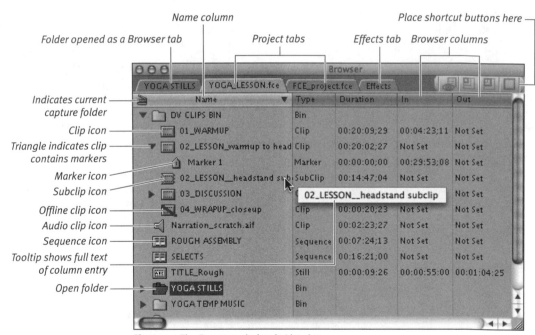

Figure 7.1 The Browser window in List view.

Browser columns

The Browser window can display up to 42 columns of data, but you can customize the Browser to display only the columns you are using and hide the rest. Some columns accommodate remarks and other types of information that help you track and sort information about your clips.

Table 7.1 provides a complete list of the columns available for use in the Browser.

Table 7.1

Browser Columns and Functions

COLUMN	FUNCTION	COLUMN	FUNCTION
Alpha	Alpha channel present	Master Clip	A check mark indicates that this clip is a master clip
Anamorphic	Indicates whether a clip is flagged to be displayed in anamorphic (16:9) aspect ratio	Master Comment 1–4	Four columns for displaying clip comments; column names can be edited
Aud Format	File format of audio clip	Name	Name of the media element; rename clips and sequences here
Aud Rate	Frequency and bit rate of audio clip		
Audio	Indicates the number of audio channels for clips that include audio	Offline	Indicates that the clip's source media has not yet been captured, is missing, or has been deleted from disk
Aux Reel 1-2	Lists reel numbers for Aux TC 1 and 2	Out	Out point specified on a clip
Capture	Capture state of a clip in the Batch Capture list	Pixel Aspect	Pixel aspect ratio
Comment A-B	Used for logging information	Reel	Lists the reel number entered at the time of capture; changing the reel number in the Browser changes the identifying reel number of the clip's source media file on disk
Composite	Composite mode that this clip uses		
Compressor	Indicates the compression codec that this clip uses		
Creator	Application used to create the media file referenced by this clip	Reverse Alpha	Choose Yes to reverse opaque and transparent area interpretation in a clip's alpha channel
Data Rate	Rate of data flow per second	Scene	Displays information entered in the Logging tab's Scene field
Duration	Duration between a clip's In and Out points		
Field Dominance	Interlaced video breaks each frame into two fields; the dominant field will be played first; DV-NTSC and PAL should be set to Lower (Even)	Shot/Take	Displays information entered in the Logging tab's Shot/Take field
		Size	Source media file size, in megabytes
		Source	Directory path name of the media file on disk
Frame Blending	Indicates whether a speed-modified clip has frame blending enabled	Speed	Displays the adjusted speed of speed-modified clips as a percentage.
Frame Size	Video frame size, in pixels	Thumbnail	Displays the poster (or first) frame of the clip; drag a thumbnail to scrub through the clip
Good	Indicates whether a clip was marked "Good" in the Capture window or Browser		
In	In point specified on a clip	Tracks	Number of video and audio tracks in the item
Last Modified	Indicates the time and date of an item's last modification	Type	The type of each item; possible types are sequence, clip, subclip, folder, effect
Length	Length of the source media file on disk	Vid Rate	Video frame rate; the clip frame rate is written to the source media file, and the sequence frame rate is based on that sequence's settings
Log Note	Displays notes entered in the Capture window's Log Note field		

Browser window icons

Along the left side of the window, you'll notice icons that accompany each item listed in the Browser. These icons represent file types in FCE.

 Sequence: An edited assembly of video and audio clips; open sequences are displayed in the Timeline.

 Folder: Folders are used to organize groups of clips, sequences, or other Browser items. A folder can also contain other folders.

 Open Folder: A folder that is currently open in a separate Browser window.

 Clip: A media file; can represent audio, video, graphics, or other media imported into FCE.

 Subclip: A portion of a clip defined by In and Out points; any number of subclips can be created from a single master clip.

 Offline Clip: A placeholder clip referencing media not currently on the local hard drive.

 Audio Clip: A media clip composed of audio samples.

 Graphic: A clip in a single-layer graphic file format (multilayer Photoshop files appear with a sequence icon).

 Layered Graphic Sequence: A multilayer graphic clip (such as a layered Photoshop file) appears with a sequence icon, but is listed as a Layered Graphic Sequence in the Browser's Type column.

 Marker: Reference point in a clip.

 Video Transition: Transition effect; can be applied to a video track.

 Audio Transition: Transition effect; can be applied to an audio track.

 Video Filter: Effects filter; can be applied to a video clip.

 Audio Filter: Effects filter; can be applied to an audio clip.

 Generator: Effects utility that generates screens, tones, and text for program transitions.

What Does "Not Set" Mean?

When you see "Not Set" displayed in the In (or Out) Browser column, it simply means that you haven't set an In (or Out) point in that clip. For instance, you could have inserted the full length of your clip into a sequence and then set In and Out points in the sequence version of the clip, or you could be using every captured frame of your clip in the sequence.

"Not Set" does not mean that you've somehow lost your source media file or that the clip has lost its timecode.

ANATOMY OF THE BROWSER

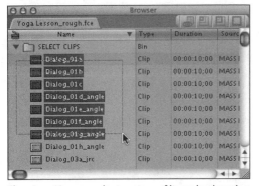

Figure 7.2 You can select a group of items by dragging a bounding box around them.

Using the Browser to Organize Your Project

The Browser is a powerful tool for organizing all your program elements in a way that makes sense to you. You could construct a multilevel folders-within-folders structure by organizing your material in multiple folders, or you could use one long list containing every element in the same display. You might want to keep separate folders for your live-action footage, graphics, and music files; or you might use folders to organize stock footage from multiple sources. You can search for your clips based on any clip property and sort from most Browser columns. Any markers you've placed in a clip will be noted in the Browser. You can use the Browser shortcut menu to modify some clip and sequence properties, or you can add or modify most clip information directly by double-clicking a Browser column entry.

To select an item in the Browser:

Do one of the following:

◆ Click the item that you want to select.

◆ Use the arrow keys to step through the item list until you arrive at the item you want.

◆ Use the Tab key to move between items alphabetically from A to Z.

◆ Type the first few letters of an item's name, and the corresponding item will be highlighted.

✔ Tip

■ Multiple-item selection in FCE's Browser works in the same way as it does in the Mac OS X Finder: Command-click to select multiple items individually; Shift-click to select a range of items; or drag a bounding box around a group of list items or icons (**Figure 7.2**).

Sorting items

FCE allows you to sort by almost every column you see in the Browser. You can use a series of secondary sorts (up to eight) to further refine your list order.

To sort items in the Browser:

1. Select the primary sort column *by doing one of the following:*

   ◆ Click a column header.

      A black arrow in the column header indicates the primary sort column (**Figure 7.3**).

   ◆ To reverse the sort order, click again (**Figure 7.4**).

2. Select secondary sort columns *by doing one of the following:*

   ◆ Shift-click additional headers.

      A gray arrow in the column header indicates a secondary sort column (**Figure 7.5**).

   ◆ To reverse the sort order, Shift-click again.

✔ Tip

■ If you've defined secondary sort columns by Shift-clicking, you'll need to click a deselected column to clear the current sort before you can select a new primary sort column.

Figure 7.3 Click the column header to sort by name; the direction of the arrow to the right of the column name here indicates ascending order.

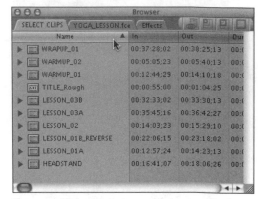

Figure 7.4 Click again to reverse the sort order; the arrow's direction now indicates a descending order.

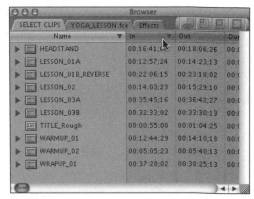

Figure 7.5 Shift-click another column header to select a secondary sort column.

Figure 7.6 The Browser in Large Icon display mode. You can also select Medium Icon, Small Icon, or List view.

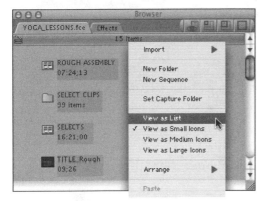

Figure 7.7 Control-click inside the Browser window and choose a display option from the shortcut menu.

Figure 7.8 The shortcut buttons at the top of the Browser offer another way to choose a display option.

Customizing the Browser Display

Different Browser display modes offer different functionality. List view, for example, offers a multitude of data, arranged in sortable columns, plus sexy scrubbable Thumbnail clips. Large Icon view allows you to drag your clips into any order you choose. FCE will save your custom Browser arrangement between sessions, and you can save multiple custom Browser layouts with the Save Column Layout feature described later in this chapter. You can customize the Browser in the following ways:

◆ Make items appear as icons (**Figure 7.6**) or in a text list.

◆ In List view, rearrange, resize, hide, or show as many columns as you like. (Note: You can't hide the Name column.)

◆ Sort by most columns.

◆ Set a standard arrangement of columns and switch between that preset and another preset column arrangement for logging clips. Both presets can be selected from the column header's shortcut menu.

◆ Change the Comment column headers.

To display items as a list or as icons:

Do one of the following:

◆ If you're in Icon view, Control-click the Browser window; if you're in List view, Control-click the Name column. Then choose a display option from the shortcut menu (**Figure 7.7**).

◆ Choose a different Browser view by clicking the corresponding shortcut button at the top of the Browser window (**Figure 7.8**).

◆ Choose View > Browser Items and select a display option from the submenu: As List, As Small Icons, As Medium Icons, or As Large Icons.

171

To display thumbnails in List view:

1. In the Browser window, Control-click any Browser column header except Name.

2. From the shortcut menu, choose Show Thumbnail (**Figure 7.9**).

✔ Tip

■ You can scrub through a clip's thumbnail in the Browser by clicking the thumbnail and then dragging in the direction you want to scrub (**Figure 7.10**). Initially, your thumbnail will display the clip's first frame, but you can select another poster frame by scrubbing through the clip until you locate the frame you want and then pressing the Control key before you release the mouse button. Very slick.

To hide a column:

1. In the Browser window, Control-click the column header of the column that you want to hide.

2. From the shortcut menu, choose Hide Column (**Figure 7.11**).

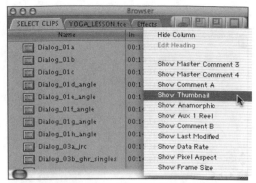

Figure 7.9 Choose Show Thumbnail from the shortcut menu.

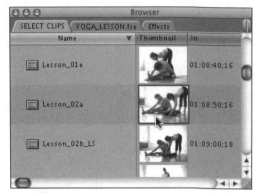

Figure 7.10 Drag your pointer across a thumbnail in the Browser; the thumbnail scrubs through the action in that clip.

Figure 7.11 Choose Hide Column from the shortcut menu; the selected column disappears from view.

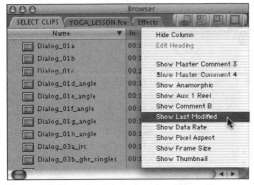

Figure 7.12 From the shortcut menu, choose the name of the column that you want to display.

Bin: SELECT CLIPS			
cts	YOGA_LESSON.fce		
▼	Type	In ▢	Reel
	Clip	00:12:57;24	001
REVERSE	Clip	00:22:06;15	001
	Clip	00:14:03;23	001

Figure 7.13 Drag a column to a new location.

To display a hidden column:

1. In the Browser window, Control-click the column header to the right of the place where you want the hidden column to be displayed.

2. From the shortcut menu, choose the name of the column you want to display (**Figure 7.12**).

   The column appears in the place you designated.

✔ Tips

■ FCE initially hides some Browser columns by default. Control-click the Browser's column header to see a complete list of available columns.

■ You can keep your Browser columns narrow and still see the full-length entry in every column. Pause your pointer over a column entry; a tooltip appears displaying the complete contents of the column.

■ When you want to move a column to the other end of the Browser column layout, use the column hide/display feature. This method can be easier than dragging the column to its new location.

To rearrange columns:

◆ Drag the column header to the new location (**Figure 7.13**).

To resize columns:

◆ Drag the right edge of the column header to the new width.

CUSTOMIZING THE BROWSER DISPLAY

To edit the Comment column name:

1. In the Browser window, Control-click the Comment column header.

2. From the shortcut menu, choose Edit Heading (**Figure 7.14**).

3. Type the new column name (**Figure 7.15**).

4. Press Enter.

Or do this:

1. Choose Edit > Project Properties.

2. Type the new column name in the Comment text box and click OK.

✔ Tip

■ Try double-clicking or Control-clicking clip information right in its Browser column. You will find that you can modify lots of clip settings without bothering to open the clip's Item Properties window. You can also modify clip settings for multiple clips in a single operation: Select the clips and then adjust the settings of just one of the selected clips.

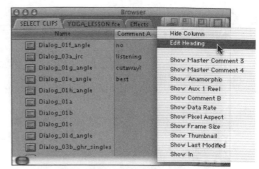

Figure 7.14 Control-click the Comment column heading and choose Edit Heading from the shortcut menu.

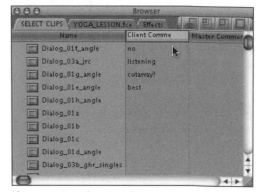

Figure 7.15 Type the new column name and press Enter.

Figure 7.16 Choose Find from the Edit menu.

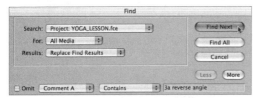

Figure 7.17 You can search for a clip by comment.

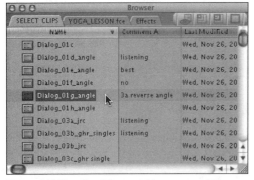

Figure 7.18 The clip with a matching comment is highlighted in the Browser.

Searching for Items in the Browser

FCE has a powerful search engine in its Find function. You can perform a simple name search, but you can also search for single or multiple items by timecode, by file type, or by comment, or you can search your project for unused clips—clips you have not yet used in any sequence. Take a moment to explore the search options available in the Browser and imagine how you might plan your project to make use of them.

To search for a single item:

1. Start in the Browser window. Choose Edit > Find (**Figure 7.16**); or press Command-F.

2. In the Find dialog box, type your search criteria or choose from the search criteria options available from the pop-up menus along the bottom of the dialog box (**Figure 7.17**).

3. Click Find Next.

   FCE highlights the found item in the Browser (**Figure 7.18**).

To search for multiple items:

1. In the Browser window, choose Edit > Find; or press Command-F.

2. In the Find dialog box, type your search criteria, or select from the search criteria options available from the pop-up menus along the bottom of the dialog box (**Figure 7.19**).

3. Select an option from the Results pop-up menu. You can choose to replace the results of your previous Find command or add the new results to your previous list of found items (**Figure 7.20**).

4. Click Find All.

   The list of found items that match your search criteria appears in the Find Results window (**Figure 7.21**).

✔ Tip

- Searching by the Name column in the Browser will return clips whose current name matches the search criteria. But if you renamed your clips after capture, searching by both the Source and Name columns will track down all of the clips (including those pesky renamed clips) associated with a source media file.

Figure 7.19 This example searches for all clips with names that contain *ghr* and that have a check mark in the Good column.

Figure 7.20 You can set the Results option to replace or add to the existing Find results.

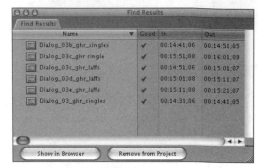

Figure 7.21 The Find Results window with the list of clips that match your search criteria; note the two shortcut buttons at the bottom of the window.

SEARCHING FOR ITEMS IN THE BROWSER

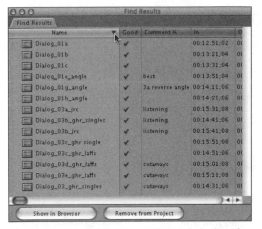

Figure 7.22 The Find Results window with the list of found clips; columns can be sorted just like in the Browser window.

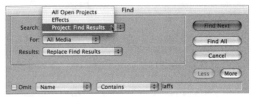

Figure 7.23 Performing a search of the Find Results window.

Using the Find Results window

The Find Results window displays a list of found items that match your search criteria (**Figure 7.22**). This window displays the same clip information as the Browser, and it offers the same flexible sorting and display options, including custom column layouts. You can perform multiple searches in the Find dialog box and assemble a collection of items in the Find Results window to do any of the following:

◆ Copy or move found items to a single folder for assembly into an edited sequence.

◆ Delete found items from a project.

✔ Tips

■ You can search within the Find Results window. If you've assembled a large group of items in the Find Results window and you want to refine your list or perform an additional search, you can choose Project: Find Results from the Search pop-up menu (**Figure 7.23**).

■ Can't remember the name of a clip, but you know what it looks like? In Icon mode, the Find Results window displays thumbnail images, just like the Browser. What a relief.

SEARCHING FOR ITEMS IN THE BROWSER

Search the Project or Search the Sequence?

You can perform two types of searches in FCE:

◆ Choose Edit > Find with the Browser window selected, and FCE will search all open projects for clips, sequences, graphics, and effects, but will not search for items located inside sequences.

◆ Choose Edit > Find with the Timeline selected, and your search will be limited to the currently open sequence. You'll want to search in the sequence if you are looking for the sequence version of a particular clip—a clip you applied effects to after you inserted it into a sequence, for example. Searching for items in the Timeline is discussed in Chapter 10, "Editing in the Timeline and the Canvas."

Working with Folders

FCE's Browser folders are similar to the folders you use to organize your Mac Desktop—with one crucial difference. When you make changes to the contents of a Browser folder, such as moving, renaming, or deleting clips, the changes will not affect the disk files or the folders in which your source material is stored. If you delete a clip from the folder, it is not deleted from the disk. Creating a new Browser folder does not create a corresponding folder on your hard drive. The Browser folder exists only within your project file. (See "What Is Nonlinear, Nondestructive Editing?" in Chapter 1 for more information.)

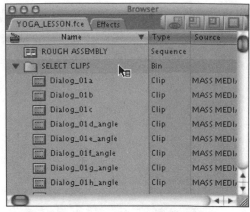

Figure 7.24 Control-click to open the shortcut menu.

To add a new folder to a project:

In the Browser window, *do one of the following:*

◆ Control-click an empty portion of the Name column (**Figure 7.24**). Then, from the shortcut menu, choose New Folder (**Figure 7.25**).

◆ Choose File > New > Folder.

Figure 7.25 Select New Folder from the shortcut menu.

What's That Little Doodad?

The tiny clapstick icon (**Figure 7.26**) indicates that the current folder is set as the *capture folder*, the Browser folder where your captured clips will be stored. For details, see "Selecting a capture folder" in Chapter 5.

Figure 7.26 The current capture folder indicator is located at the left edge of the folder's Name column.

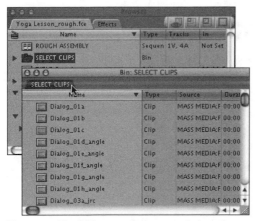

Figure 7.27 The folder opens as a new window; drag the tab to the Browser window.

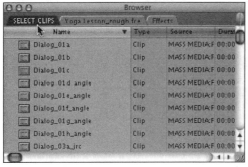

Figure 7.28 The folder is now accessible from its own tab in the Browser window.

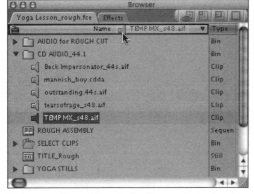

Figure 7.29 Drag an item to the Name column header to move it to the top level of a project.

To open a folder and create a Browser tab for it:

1. In the Browser window, double-click a folder name.

2. In the newly opened Bin window, drag the tab from the bin header into the area above the Name column in the Browser window (**Figure 7.27**).

   The folder appears as a tab in the Browser window (**Figure 7.28**).

To move items between folders in List view:

◆ Drag the items that you want to move onto your destination folder; then drop the items into the folder.

✔ Tip

■ To move any item to the top level of a project, drag the item to the Name column header in the Browser window (**Figure 7.29**).

Working with Browser Items

Copying, pasting, and moving items in FCE's Browser is very much like working with items in the Mac Finder, with one important exception: When you delete a Browser clip, you're not actually deleting its underlying source media file, just the clip reference. Delete a sequence, though, and your edits are really gone for good.

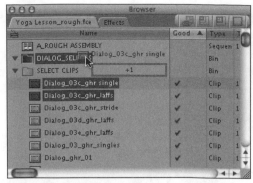

Figure 7.30 Hold down the Option key as you drag a selection to copy it to a new location.

To make a copy of a Browser item:

1. Hold down the Option key as you drag the item (or items) that you want to copy (**Figure 7.30**).

2. In the new location, release the mouse button.

   The item is copied and appears in both locations (**Figure 7.31**).

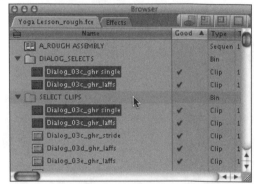

Figure 7.31 The items are copied and now appear in both locations.

Figure 7.32 Control-click the item that you want to delete; then choose Cut from the shortcut menu.

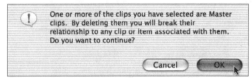

Figure 7.33 FCE will warn you if you're about to delete a master clip with links to other clips in your project.

Figure 7.34 Control-clicking an item is the quickest way to access a specified tab in the Item Properties window.

To remove a Browser item from a project:

Do one of the following:

◆ Select the item and press Delete.

◆ Control-click the item you want to delete; then, from the shortcut menu, choose Cut (**Figure 7.32**).

✔ Tips

■ Remember: when you cut a clip from the Browser, you're not deleting the media file on disk, just the virtual reference that points to the file on disk. See Chapter 4, "Projects, Sequences, and Clips," for details on how to delete media files on disk.

■ If you try to delete a master clip from a project, FCE warns you that you're about to break that master clip's relationship to any affiliated clips you've used elsewhere in the project (**Figure 7.33**). If you're new to FCE's lexicon of clip types and their relationships, see "About Clips" in Chapter 4 for more information.

To modify clip properties in the Browser:

1. Control-click the clip that you want to modify.

2. From the shortcut menu, choose Item Properties (**Figure 7.34**).

   The Item Properties window opens with the clip's name highlighted.

✔ Tip

■ Try selecting the clip and pressing Command-9—that's the keyboard shortcut that opens the Item Properties window.

WORKING WITH BROWSER ITEMS

181

To make changes to multiple Browser items or entries:

1. Command-click to select the items or entries that you want to modify (**Figure 7.35**).

2. Control-click one of the selected items.

3. From the shortcut menu, specify the change you want to make (**Figure 7.36**).

To rename clips, sequences, and folders:

1. Click to select the item that you want to rename (**Figure 7.37**).

2. Press Enter.

3. Type a new name (**Figure 7.38**).

✔ Tips

- Heads up: If you rename a master clip after multiple sections have been edited into the Timeline, those Timeline clips will be renamed as well, unless you change the sequence clips to independent-type clips.

- To meet the whole family of FCE clip types and learn about their quaint customs, see "About Clips" in Chapter 4.

Figure 7.35 Command-click to select multiple items to modify.

Figure 7.36 Use the shortcut menu to specify a change you want to make.

Figure 7.37 First, select the item you want to rename.

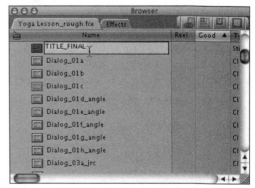

Figure 7.38 Click the item's name again to open the field for editing; then type a new name.

Working with Clips in the Viewer

8

You'll be spending a lot of time in the Viewer window. Not only do you use the Viewer to play clips and mark edit points and keyframes, you also work in the Viewer to sculpt audio and video with effects and filters.

The Viewer window interface uses tabs to organize and display the clip controls. You'll see only the tabs that are relevant to the clip that's currently open; not all tabs are open by default. Following are summaries of the functions available on each tab:

◆ **Video tab:** View video frames and set In and Out points and keyframes. This is the default playback window for a video clip.

◆ **Audio tab:** Audition and mark edit points in audio-only clips. This is where you can set the level and pan or spread. The Audio tab will display the audio portion of an audio+video clip. Clips with two channels of audio will display two Audio tabs: one for each audio channel. To learn more about working in the Audio tab, see Chapter 12, "Audio Tools and Techniques."

◆ **Filters tab:** Adjust the settings for any video or audio filter effects you have applied to a clip.

◆ **Motion tab:** Apply and modify motion effects. You can create animated effects by using a combination of keyframes and changes to motion settings. For more on creating motion effects, see Chapter 15, "Motion."

◆ **Controls tab:** Adjust the settings for a generator you have opened. A text entry field for a text generator appears on this tab.

◆ **Color Corrector tab:** Use the onscreen controls for FCE's color correction filters. The Color Corrector tab appears only on clips with a color correction filter applied. To learn about applying filters and effects, see Chapter 16, "Filters and Compositing."

Anatomy of the Viewer

The Final Cut Express Viewer has a wide variety of tools for navigating and marking your clips: transport controls, clip-marking controls, pop-up selectors, view selectors, and timecode navigation displays (**Figure 8.1**).

All the Viewer controls listed here, except the pop-up selectors, appear in the Canvas window as well. The controls operate in the same way in the Canvas window that they do in the Viewer.

The next few sections discuss the onscreen controls you'll encounter in the Viewer.

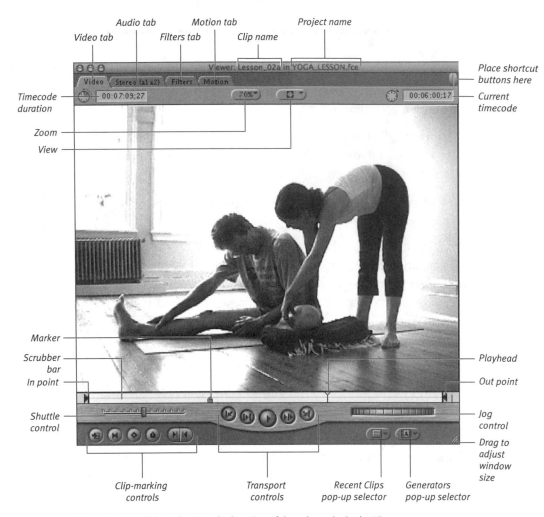

Figure 8.1 The Video tab. Note the location of the other tabs in the Viewer.

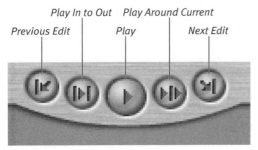

Previous Edit   Play In to Out   Play Around Current   Play   Next Edit

Figure 8.2 The Viewer's transport control buttons.

Figure 8.3 The Shuttle control.

Figure 8.4 The Jog control.

Figure 8.5 The Scrubber and playhead.

Transport controls

Figure 8.2 shows the transport controls, which are located in the middle of the bottom section of the Viewer:

◆ **Previous Edit button:** Click to jump the playhead back to the previous edit (if the open clip is a sequence clip).

◆ **Play In to Out button:** Click to play the clip from the In point to the Out point.

◆ **Play button:** Click to play the clip from the current position of the playhead. Click again to stop playback.

◆ **Play Around Current Frame button:** Click to play the part of the clip immediately before and after the current position of the playhead. The pre-roll and post-roll settings (in the Preferences window) determine the duration of the playback.

◆ **Next Edit button:** Click to move the playhead to the next edit in a sequence clip.

◆ **Shuttle control:** Drag the control tab away from the center to fast forward or rewind (**Figure 8.3**). Speeds vary depending on the control tab's distance from the center. A green control tab indicates normal playback speed.

◆ **Jog control:** Drag to the left or right (**Figure 8.4**) to step through your clip one frame at a time.

◆ **Scrubber and playhead:** The Scrubber is the strip that stretches horizontally below the image window. Move through a clip by dragging the playhead, or click the Scrubber to jump the playhead to a new location (**Figure 8.5**).

✔ Tip

■ The Viewer's transport and clip-marking controls all have keyboard shortcut equivalents. Use the ToolTips feature to learn keyboard shortcuts for onscreen controls you use regularly.

ANATOMY OF THE VIEWER

185

Clip-marking controls

All the onscreen controls you use to mark clips are grouped in the lower-left corner of the Viewer (**Figure 8.6**):

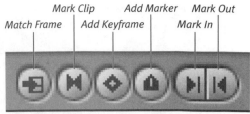

Figure 8.6 The Viewer's clip-marking controls.

- **Match Frame:** Click to match the frame currently showing in the Viewer with the same frame as it appears in your sequence. The sequence frame appears in the Canvas window. Match Frame is useful for synchronizing action.

- **Mark Clip:** Click to set In and Out points in the sequence. Edit points will be set at the outer boundaries of the clip at the position of the playhead in the target track.

- **Add Keyframe:** Click to add a keyframe to the clip at the current playhead position.

- **Add Marker:** Click to add a marker to the clip at the current playhead position.

- **Mark In (left) and Mark Out (right):** Click to set the In point or the Out point for the clip at the current playhead position.

ANATOMY OF THE VIEWER

Recent Clips

Generators

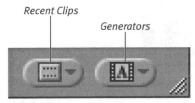

Figure 8.7 Pop-up selectors.

Figure 8.8 The Zoom selector.

Figure 8.9 The View selector.

Pop-up selectors

Two buttons at the lower right of the Viewer window provide convenient access to source materials (**Figure 8.7**):

◆ **Recent Clips:** Select recently used clips directly from this pop-up menu.

◆ **Generators:** Select a generator effect from this pop-up menu. (To read about generators, see Chapter 17, "Titles and Generators.")

View selectors

The selectors directly above the Viewer's image area allow you to adjust the window's view.

◆ **Zoom:** Adjust the Viewer's image display size (**Figure 8.8**). This pop-up selector does not affect the actual frame size of the image.

◆ **View:** Select a viewing format (**Figure 8.9**). Title Safe and Wireframe modes are accessible from this pop-up menu. (For more information, see "Viewing Overlays" later in this chapter.)

Timecode navigation and display

Two timecode displays appear in the upper corners of the Viewer window. They are useful for precisely navigating to specific timecode locations.

Figure 8.10 The Timecode Duration display.

Figure 8.11 The Current Timecode display and shortcut menu. The shortcut menu offers a choice between Source Time or Clip Time.

- ◆ **Timecode Duration:** This field displays the elapsed time between the In and Out points of a clip. If no edit points are set, the beginning and end of the clip serve as the In and Out points (**Figure 8.10**). Control-click the Timecode Duration display to switch the elapsed time view among Drop Frame, Non-drop Frame, and Frames views.

- ◆ **Current Timecode:** This field displays the timecode at the current position of the playhead. You can enter a time in the display to jump the playhead to that point in the clip.

- ◆ **Current Timecode display shortcut menu:** Control-click the display to switch the elapsed-time view between Source Time (which matches the timecode rate of the clip's source media file) or Clip Time (which starts with the timecode value of the first frame in the clip, then calculates and displays timecode based on the current frame rate assigned to the clip) (**Figure 8.11**).

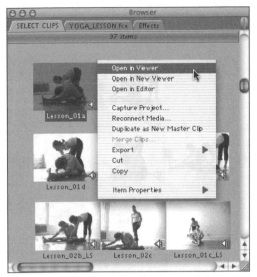

Figure 8.12 Control-click the clip's icon and choose Open in Viewer from the shortcut menu.

Figure 8.13 Open a clip by dragging it from the Browser and dropping it in the image area of the Viewer

Working with Clips in the Viewer

You can open clips from the Browser or from the Timeline. You can open single and multiple clips or clips you have viewed recently. You can also open clips from outside an open project.

When you open an audio+video clip, it appears in a Viewer window with the Video tab selected.

To open a clip in the Viewer:

Do one of the following:

◆ Double-click the clip's icon in the Browser or Timeline.

◆ Control-click the clip's icon and choose Open in Viewer from the shortcut menu (**Figure 8.12**).

◆ Select the clip's icon and press Enter.

◆ Drag the clip's icon from the Browser and drop it in the image area of the Viewer (**Figure 8.13**).

To open a clip in a new window:

1. Select the clip in the Browser or Timeline.

2. Choose View > Clip in New Window.

✔ Tips

■ It's common practice in Final Cut Express to load an entire sequence into the Viewer and edit it into another sequence, just as if it were a clip. To do this, select the sequence in the Browser; then choose View > Sequence or drag the sequence's icon from the Browser and drop it in the image area of the Viewer.

■ If loading a sequence into the Viewer causes the Canvas and Timeline to disappear, you have loaded a sequence that was currently open in the Timeline. The Timeline closes because FCE protocol dictates that you cannot edit a sequence into itself.

189

To open multiple clips:

1. Command-click to select multiple clips in the Browser.

2. Drag the clips to the Viewer (**Figure 8.14**). The first clip opens in the Viewer, and the other selected clips are listed in the Recent Clips control (**Figure 8.15**).

To open a recently viewed clip:

◆ Select the clip name from the Recent Clips control's pop-up list (**Figure 8.16**).

✔ Tip

■ You can load an entire Browser folder of clips into the Viewer in one move by dragging the folder from the Browser and dropping it in the image area of the Viewer. The clips in the folder will show up in the Recent Clips control (as long as your List Recent Clips preference is set high enough to cover the folder's item count).

Figure 8.14 Drag the clips to the Viewer and then drop them on the image area.

Figure 8.15 The first clip is opened in the Viewer; the rest are listed in the Recent Clips pop-up list.

Figure 8.16 Select a clip from the Recent Clips control's pop-up list.

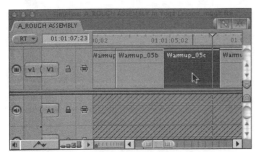

Figure 8.17 Double-click a sequence clip in the Timeline to open it in the Viewer.

To open a clip from the Timeline or Canvas:

◆ Double-click the clip in the Timeline (**Figure 8.17**).

The clip opens in the Viewer. If you positioned the Timeline's playhead over a frame in the clip, the clip opens with the Viewer's playhead located at the same frame (**Figure 8.18**). The two lines of dots in the Scrubber indicate that you've opened a sequence clip.

Figure 8.18 The clip opens with the Viewer's playhead located at the same frame. Two lines of dots in the Scrubber indicate that you've opened a sequence clip.

To open an imported clip in its original application:

1. Open the clip in the Viewer or Canvas window.

2. Choose View > Clip in Editor (**Figure 8.19**).

   Clips created in an application other than Final Cut Express will open in that application (**Figure 8.20**). If the application used to create the clip is not installed on your computer, a dialog box opens that allows you to choose an application in which to edit the clip.

✔ Tip

■ You can specify default applications for editing imported graphics, video, and audio files on the External Editors tab of the System Settings window. For more information, see "Setting External Editors Preferences" in Chapter 3.

Figure 8.19 Choose View > Clip in Editor to open a clip in the application you used to create it.

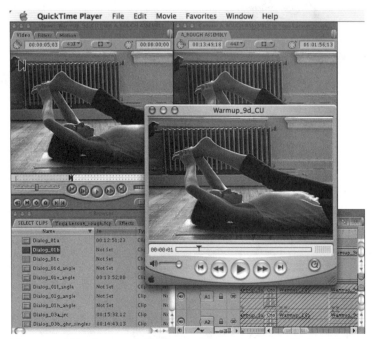

Figure 8.20 This clip, captured in Final Cut Express, has opened in QuickTime Player, the application that was specified on the External Editors preference tab.

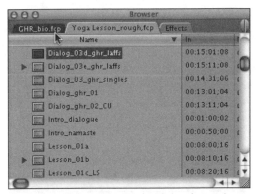

Figure 8.21 Click a project's tab to bring that project to the front of the Browser window.

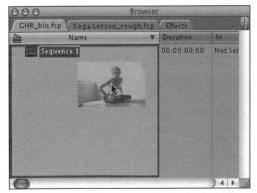

Figure 8.22 Drag a clip into a project in the Browser window. Clip changes will be saved with the project.

To open a clip outside the current project:

1. Choose File > Open.

2. Locate the clip's media file on disk.

3. Select the file and click Choose.

To save changes in a clip outside the current project:

1. In the Browser window, select a project in which to save your modified clip by clicking the tab of that project.

   This brings your selected project to the front of the Browser window (**Figure 8.21**).

2. Drag from the image area in the Viewer to the project's tab in the Browser.

   Your clip is now inserted in that project, and your changes will be saved with that project (**Figure 8.22**).

FCE Protocol: Saving Clip Changes

Say you have marked edit points and placed some other markers in a clip you opened outside of your project. To save the changes you made to that clip, *you'll need to do the following*:

◆ Insert the modified clip into a project that's currently open.

   or

◆ Export the clip.

Remember that FCE will save the changes you make only if the clip has been placed in a project or exported as a new file. If you mark changes and close the Viewer window without taking the steps listed here ... bye-bye changes. There's no warning dialog box, so take care. One exception to this rule: Any modification of a clip's reel number will be written to the clip's media file immediately.

To open a generator effect in the Viewer:

1. Start in the Browser window with the Effects tab selected.

2. *Do one of the following:*

   ◆ Double-click the generator icon in the Browser (**Figure 8.23**) or Timeline.

   ◆ Select a generator icon and press Enter.

✔ Tip

■ You can select generator effects directly from the Generators pop-up menu in the Viewer window (**Figure 8.24**).

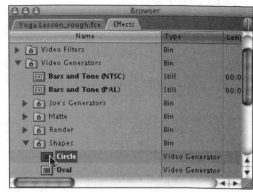

Figure 8.23 Double-click a generator icon to open the generator effect in the Viewer.

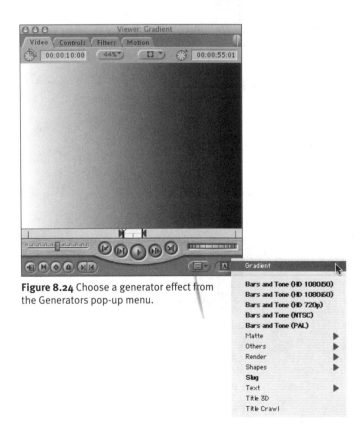

Figure 8.24 Choose a generator effect from the Generators pop-up menu.

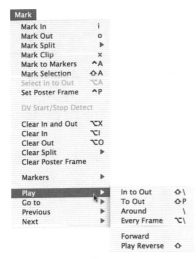

Figure 8.25 FCE offers so many ways to play.

Playing clips

Check out the Play submenu of the Mark menu (**Figure 8.25**), and you'll see a cadre of playback options. You can also select a playback option from the Viewer's transport controls (see Figure 8.2 earlier in this chapter), or use one of the keyboard shortcuts that controls playback.

For all the play operations described in this section, start with an open clip and the Viewer window active.

To play a clip in the Viewer:

1. Click the Play button (**Figure 8.26**); or press the spacebar; or press L.

2. To stop playback, click the Play button; or press the spacebar; or press K.

To play a clip in reverse:

◆ Shift-click the Play button; or press Shift-spacebar; or press J.

To play a clip between In and Out points:

◆ Click the Play In to Out button (**Figure 8.27**); or press Shift-\ (backslash).

To play a clip from the current playhead position to the Out point:

◆ Command-click the Play button.

Figure 8.26 Click the Play button to start clip playback. Click Play again to stop playback.

Figure 8.27 Click the Play In to Out button to play the section of the clip between the In and Out points.

To play a clip before and after the current playhead position:

◆ Click the Play Around Current Frame button (**Figure 8.28**); or press the back-slash (\) key.

The clip plays back the specified pre-roll duration before the playhead location, and it plays back the post-roll duration after the playhead location.

Figure 8.28 Click the Play Around Current Frame button to play a section of the clip before and after the current playhead position.

✔ Tip

■ You can set the duration of video play-back using the pre-roll and post-roll settings on the General tab of FCE's User Preferences window.

JKL Keys: The Way to Move

JKL Keys, a swift and efficient system for controlling variable-speed playback from your keyboard, is an import from expensive, pro digital editing systems. Learn it, and you'll be whipping through your footage like the pros do. Here's how it works.

The J, K, and L keys are in a row on your keyboard, and you use them to control playback speed and direction. The I and O keys, which you use for setting In and Out points, are located just above JKL. The comma (,) and period (.) keys, which you can use to trim edits, are located below JKL. The semicolon (;) and apostrophe (') keys control Previous and Next Edit. This arrangement makes editing easy because it places the most commonly used keyboard shortcuts under one hand. It's easy to see how editors get attached to this system.

Here's the rundown on J, K, and L keyboard command functions:

Press J to play in reverse. Tap J twice to double the reverse shuttle speed. Tap J three times for 4x reverse shuttle speed. Tap J four times for 8x reverse shuttle speed.

Press K to stop or pause.

Press L to play forward. Tap L twice to double the forward shuttle speed. Tap L three times for 4x forward shuttle speed. Tap L four times for 8x forward shuttle speed.

Hold down K and tap J or L to get slow-motion shuttling in either direction. A single J or L tap, with K held down, steps you forward or backward one frame at a time.

Figure 8.29 Choose View > Loop Playback to loop clip playback. Choose View > Loop Playback again to toggle looping off.

To play every frame:

◆ Choose Mark > Play > Every Frame; or press Option-P.

✔ Tip

■ If you've applied complex effects to a clip, use the Play Every Frame command to preview the clip without rendering it first. Playback is slower than normal, but you'll get a rough idea.

To loop playback in all playback modes:

1. Choose View > Loop Playback (**Figure 8.29**).

2. Choose View > Loop Playback again to turn off looping.

✔ Tip

■ You can toggle looped playback on and off from your keyboard by pressing Control-L.

Other ways to move: Jogging, scrubbing, and shuttling

While editing, you may find yourself spending more time playing your material at fast and slow speeds than at normal speed. Use the following tools for high- and low-speed navigation:

◆ To scrub through a clip, drag the playhead along the Scrubber bar above the transport controls (**Figure 8.30**).

◆ To jump the playhead to a location within the clip, click in the Scrubber bar.

◆ To move the playhead frame by frame, use the arrow keys.

◆ To jump the playhead in one-second increments, press Shift as you use the arrow keys.

◆ To jog one frame at a time, drag the Jog control (**Figure 8.31**). You can drag off the control area if you continue to hold down the mouse button.

◆ To play a clip at various speeds, drag the Shuttle control (**Figure 8.32**). Drag farther from the center to increase the playback speed. Drag right to play forward; drag left to play in reverse.

Figure 8.30 Drag the playhead across the Scrubber to scrub through a clip.

Figure 8.31 Drag the Jog control to step through a clip one frame at a time.

Figure 8.32 Drag the Shuttle control to play a clip in either direction at a range of speeds from slow to fast.

FCE Protocol: Entering Timecode Numbers

Final Cut Express uses the standard time-code format of Hours:Minutes:Seconds:Frames and employs a number of convenient shortcuts for timecode navigation.

For example, typing 01241315 sets the timecode to 01:24:13:15. You don't need to include the colons when you type.

You need to type only the numbers that change. Numbers that don't change, such as the hour or minute, don't need to be entered. Let's look at some examples.

Example 1

1. Start at timecode location 01:24:13:15.

2. To jump to timecode 01:24:18:25, type 1825 (for 18 seconds, 25 frames) and press Enter.

The playhead jumps to timecode location 01:24:18:25. The hour and minute don't change for the new timecode location, so you don't need to reenter the hour or minute.

Example 2

The same idea applies to a new timecode minutes away from your current location.

1. Again start at timecode location 01:24:13:15.

2. To jump to timecode 01:27:18:25, type 271825 (for 27 minutes, 18 seconds, 25 frames) and press Enter.

The playhead jumps to timecode location 01:27:18:25.

Entering Durations

Say you want to move 12 seconds, 27 frames back in your clip. You don't need to calculate the new timecode number yourself.

Type −1227, and your clip jumps back 12 seconds and 27 frames. You can enter the timecode value preceded by a plus (+) or minus (−) sign, and FCE will change the current time by that amount.

You can jump to a new location using the plus (+) and minus (−) keys in two ways: using time (Hours:Minutes:Seconds:Frames) or using the total number of frames, which Final Cut Express converts into time plus frames. Here are some examples using time:

♦ Typing −3723 jumps back 37 seconds and 23 frames.

♦ Typing +161408 moves ahead 16 minutes, 14 seconds, and 8 frames.

In the Frames position in the timecode, any two-digit value between 30 and 99 is converted to the correct number of seconds (30 frames = 1 second). Here are some examples using the frame count:

♦ Entering −69 frames jumps back 69 frames, which is 2 seconds and 9 frames.

♦ Entering +36 frames jumps ahead 36 frames, which is 1 second and 6 frames.

One More Shortcut

There's one other keyboard shortcut: You can substitute a period (.) for zeros in a timecode value. Each period replaces a pair of zeros in a timecode number. Here's an example:

♦ To jump to timecode location 00:07:00:00, type 8.. (7 and two periods). The periods insert 00 in the Frames and Seconds fields.

♦ Type 11... to move to 11:00:00:00.

Sure beats typing all those colons, huh?

Navigating with Timecode

Moving around using timecode values can be the most efficient way to work, especially if your sense of timing is tuned to "frames per second." Final Cut Express's timecode input functionality is quite flexible. If you know exactly where you want to go, this is the way to get there. Timecode navigation works the same way in both the Viewer and Canvas.

To navigate using timecode values:

1. Start with your clip open and the Viewer window selected. **Figure 8.33** shows the timecode location before repositioning.

2. Enter a new timecode number (or use the shorthand methods detailed in the nearby Tips and sidebar) (**Figure 8.34**) and then press Enter.

   The playhead moves to the location that matches the new timecode value, and the new timecode position is displayed in the Current Timecode field in the upper-right corner of the Viewer (**Figure 8.35**).

To change the Out point using timecode:

◆ To change the Out point for a clip or sequence, enter a new timecode value in the Duration field, in the upper-left corner of the Viewer; then press Enter (**Figures 8.36–8.38**).

✔ Tips

■ In the Viewer or Canvas, press Tab once to select the Duration field or twice to select the Current Timecode field.

■ You can copy the timecode from one field and paste it into another if the timecode is valid in the location where it is being pasted. You can also drag a timecode from one field to another by pressing Option while dragging.

Figure 8.33 Current Timecode display in the Viewer window.

Figure 8.34 Adding 1 second, 15 frames (45 frames) to the current timecode position using a timecode entry shortcut.

Figure 8.35 The playhead is repositioned 1 second, 15 frames later, and the Current Timecode display is updated.

Figure 8.36 Timecode Duration display in the Viewer window. The current clip duration is 10 seconds.

Figure 8.37 Adding 1 second (30 frames) to the current clip duration using a timecode entry shortcut.

Figure 8.38 The Out point is extended by 1 second, and the Timecode Duration display is updated.

Figure 8.39 Set an In point by clicking the Mark In button.

Figure 8.40 Set an Out point by clicking the Mark Out button.

Figure 8.41 Click the Play In to Out button to review the edit points you have marked.

Working with In and Out Points

The In and Out points determine the start and end frames of the clip portion that is used when the clip is edited into a sequence. Determining the usable part of a clip and setting In and Out points is the first step in assembling your edit. Many editing functions are performed by adjusting these points, either within the clip itself or from within a sequence.

To set In and Out points for a clip in the Viewer:

1. In the Browser, double-click the clip to open it in the Viewer.

2. Press the Home key to position the playhead at the beginning of the clip.

3. Use the Play button or the spacebar to start playing the clip from the beginning.

4. Click the Mark In button (**Figure 8.39**), or press I, when you see (or hear) the beginning of the part you want to use.

5. Click the Mark Out button (**Figure 8.40**), or press O, when you see (or hear) the end of the part you want to use.

6. To check your In and Out points, click the Play In to Out button, or press the vertical bar key (|, or Shift-\) (**Figure 8.41**).

✔ Tip

■ You don't need to have the clip playing to set its In and Out points. You can drag the playhead to locate a particular frame and then set the edit point.

To change In and Out points in the Viewer:

Do one of the following:

◆ Play the clip again and click Mark In or Mark Out at the new spot.

◆ Drag the In or Out point icon along the Scrubber bar to change the point's location.

◆ Drag the In or Out point icon above or below the Scrubber to remove the point.

✔ Tip

■ You can use the shortcut menu to set and clear edit points. Control-click in the Scrubber and choose an option from the shortcut menu (**Figure 8.42**).

To move the In and Out points simultaneously:

1. Start in the Viewer.

2. Hold down Shift while dragging either edit point indicator (**Figure 8.43**) with the pointer.

   The marked duration of the clip does not change, but the frames included in the marked clip shift forward or backward. Modifying an edit in this way is called *slipping*.

Figure 8.42 Use the Scrubber bar's shortcut menu to set and clear edit points.

Figure 8.43 Pressing Shift while dragging an edit point slides both the In and Out points.

Other Ways to Set In and Out Points

If you open FCE's Mark menu, you'll see a number of additional ways to set and clear In and Out points. Most of the marking shortcuts work only in the Timeline, but they'll come in handy after your sequence is assembled.

◆ **Mark Clip:** Sets In and Out points at the boundaries of a selected Timeline clip. You can also use Mark Clip to mark a Timeline gap. Place the Timeline playhead over the gap; then press X.

◆ **Mark to Markers:** Place your Timeline playhead between two markers, and FCE will use the markers' locations to set In and Out points.

◆ **Mark Selection:** Sets In and Out points at the boundaries of a selected area of the Timeline.

WORKING WITH IN AND OUT POINTS

About Subclips

Subclips are shorter clips you create from a longer master clip. You can create multiple subclips from a single master clip. For example, you can open a 15-minute clip in the Viewer and subdivide it into as many subclips as you need. As you create subclips, the master clip remains open in the Viewer.

Once you've created a subclip, you can open it in the Viewer and work with it in the same way as any other clip. Changes you make to a subclip won't affect the master clip.

Final Cut Express places new subclips in the same project folder as the master clip, automatically naming each clip as you create it. For example, if the master clip is named "Whole Thing," the first subclip is named "Whole Thing Subclip," the second is "Whole Thing Subclip 2," and so on.

Once you create a subclip, you can rename it and trim the edit points, but you cannot extend the subclip's In and Out points beyond the In and Out points of its master clip.

✔ Tip

■ If you need to extend a subclip's edit points beyond its current duration, you must remove the subclip's limits, restoring your subclip to the full length of the master clip, and then set new In and Out points.

FCE Protocol: Subclips Are Master Clips, Too

Final Cut Express 2 introduced new clip-handling behavior, classifying clips as Master, Affiliate, or Independent. Each clip type has protocols that govern its actions. You can get the gory details on FCE's new clip-handling behavior in Chapter 4, "Projects, Sequences, and Clips."

What's important to note here is that any new subclip you create starts out life as a separate master clip, with no affiliate ties to the master clip you created it from.

To create a subclip:

1. Double-click a clip in the Browser or Timeline to open it in the Viewer window.

2. Mark the clip's In and Out points (**Figure 8.44**).

3. Choose Modify > Make Subclip (**Figure 8.45**); or press Command-U.

   A new, automatically named subclip appears in the Browser, below the master clip (**Figure 8.46**).

Figure 8.44 Mark an Out point for your subclip.

Figure 8.45 Choose Modify > Make Subclip.

Figure 8.46 A new subclip appears in the Browser, below the master clip. The subclip's Name field is already highlighted; to rename the subclip, just start typing the new name.

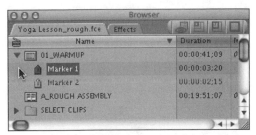

Figure 8.47 Click the clip's expansion triangle; then select the desired marker from the list.

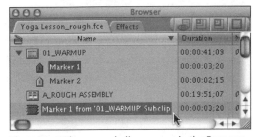

Figure 8.48 The new subclip appears in the Browser. Note that the subclip's duration is equal to the extended marker's duration.

✔ **Tip**

- A word of caution: If you choose to recapture a project containing a subclip, Final Cut Express will recapture the entire length of the master media file containing the subclip. For tips on project recapture, see Chapter 20, "Managing Complex Projects."

To create a subclip from a marker:

1. In the Browser, click the marked clip's expansion triangle to reveal a list of its markers; then select the marker you want (**Figure 8.47**).

2. Choose Modify > Make Subclip; or press Command-U.

   The new subclip appears in the Browser. The subclip has a duration equal to the extended marker's duration (**Figure 8.48**). If the marker has no extended duration, the subclip will extend to the next marker in the clip.

✔ **Tip**

- DV Start/Stop Detection is akin to the popular scene detection feature in iMovie. FCE will automatically set markers in your captured clip each time it detects a Start/Stop (Record/Pause). Because FCE can use markers to break a clip into individual subclips, you can use the technique outlined here to capture long sections of DV tape and break them into usable subclip chunks. To learn how, see "Using DV Start/Stop Detection" in Chapter 5.

To adjust a subclip's length:

1. Select a subclip in the Browser or a sequence subclip in the Timeline.

2. Choose Modify > Remove Subclip Limits.

3. Open the subclip in the Viewer.

   The full length of the master clip appears. If you have selected a Timeline subclip, the current In and Out points will still be displayed.

4. Set new In and Out points for the subclip.

Using Markers

Markers are reference pointers in a clip or sequence, and they have a variety of uses. You can:

◆ Quickly jump the playhead to markers in clips or sequences.

◆ Align the clip marker to a marker in the sequence.

◆ Align a filter or motion keyframe to the marker.

◆ Mark a range of the clip to use as you might a subclip.

◆ Align other clip markers, clip boundaries, or transition boundaries to a marker in the Timeline.

To learn more about using markers in sequences, see Chapter 10, "Editing in the Timeline and the Canvas."

To add markers to a clip or sequence in the Viewer:

1. Open the clip in the Viewer.

2. Play the clip or sequence.

3. When playback reaches the place where you want to set a marker, click the Add Marker button (**Figure 8.49**); or press M.

4. To add a custom label or comments to the marker, click Add Marker (or press M) a second time to display the Edit Marker dialog box (**Figure 8.50**).

✔ Tip

■ Save keystrokes! Shift-click the Add Marker button to set a marker and open the Edit Marker dialog box in one move.

Figure 8.49 Click the Add Marker button to set a marker in your clip.

Figure 8.50 Click Add Marker again to call up the Edit Marker dialog box.

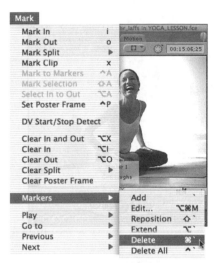

Figure 8.51 Choose Mark > Markers > Delete to remove a marker from your clip.

Figure 8.52 Drag the playhead to the marker location.

Figure 8.53 Rename a marker or add comments in the Edit Marker dialog box; then click OK.

To delete a marker:

1. Move the playhead to the marker.

2. *Do one of the following:*
   - Choose Mark > Markers > Delete (**Figure 8.51**).
   - Press Command-` (accent grave, which shares a key with the tilde [~]).
   - Option-click the Marker button.

To move the playhead to a marker:

Do one of the following:

- Press Shift-M to jump to the next marker, or Option-M to jump to the previous marker.
- Drag the playhead in the Scrubber bar to the marker location (**Figure 8.52**).
- Choose Mark > Previous > Marker (or Mark > Next > Marker).

To rename a marker or add comments:

1. Move the playhead to the marker.

2. Press M to open the Edit Marker dialog box.

3. Type a new name or comment in the corresponding text box (**Figure 8.53**); then click OK.

USING MARKERS

To extend the duration of a marker:

1. Move the playhead to the marker.

2. Press M to open the Edit Marker dialog box.

3. Extend the marker's duration by entering a duration value (**Figure 8.54**).

   An extended duration marker appears as a marker icon with a bar extending along the Scrubber bar (**Figure 8.55**).

✔ Tip

■ You can place extended duration markers on audio tracks to visually mark the location and duration of key dialogue or a specific passage in a music track.

To extend the marker duration to the playhead location:

1. Position the playhead where you want the endpoint of your extended marker to go.

2. Choose Mark > Markers > Extend (**Figure 8.56**); or press Option-` (accent grave, which shares a key with the tilde [~]).

   The marker's duration will extend from the original location of the marker to the location of the playhead (**Figure 8.57**).

Figure 8.54 Extend a marker's duration by entering a value in the Duration field of the Edit Marker dialog box.

Figure 8.55 The marker icon displays its duration on the Scrubber bar.

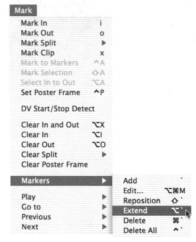

Figure 8.56 Choose Mark > Markers > Extend.

Figure 8.57 The marker's duration now extends to the playhead position.

Figure 8.58 Move the playhead to the new desired location for your marker.

To move a marker forward in time:

1. Move the playhead to where you want to reposition the marker (**Figure 8.58**). You can move a marker only forward.

2. Choose Mark > Markers > Reposition; or press Shift-` (accent grave).

✔ Tip

- To extend or reposition a marker on the fly during playback, use the keyboard shortcuts listed in the previous sections. Tap the keys when you see the frame you want to make your new marker location.

Marking Shortcuts

FCE offers lots of ways to mark In and Out points. This is something editors do all day long, so it may be worthwhile to try these shortcuts and see which ones work best for you.

To mark the In point:

Do one of the following:

- Press I on the keyboard.
- Click the Mark In button in the Viewer.
- Press the slash (/) key on the numeric keypad.
- From the Mark menu, choose Mark In.

To mark the Out point:

Do one of the following:

- Press O on the keyboard.
- Click the Mark Out button in the Viewer.
- Press the asterisk (*) key on the numeric keypad.
- From the Mark menu, choose Mark Out.

To delete edit points:

Do one of the following:

- To clear both In and Out points, press Option-X; or Option-click the Mark Clip button.
- To clear an In point, press Option-I; or Option-click the Mark In button.
- To clear an Out point, press Option-O; or Option-click the Mark Out button.

To jump the playhead to edit points:

Do one of the following:

- To go to the In point, press Shift-I; or Shift-click the Mark In button.
- To go to the Out point, press Shift-O; or Shift-click the Mark Out button.

Adjusting the Viewer Display

You can set up the Viewer to show your clips in a variety of display formats and magnifications. Final Cut Express can also overlay an array of useful information on your clip image, but you can turn off the overlay. View settings are clip specific and are stored with each clip.

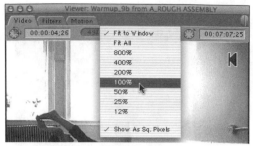

Figure 8.59 Choose a magnification level from the Zoom pop-up menu.

Changing magnification and window size in the Viewer or Canvas

Final Cut Express has an ambitious interface. Unless you work with a dual-monitor setup, you'll occasionally want to juggle window sizes to get a closer look at your work.

To zoom in:

Do one of the following:

◆ Choose a higher magnification level from the Zoom pop-up menu at the top of the Viewer or Canvas (**Figure 8.59**).

◆ Select the Zoom In tool from the Tool palette and click inside the Viewer or Canvas.

◆ From the View menu, choose a zoom-in amount from the Level submenu.

◆ Select the Zoom In tool from the Tool palette (**Figure 8.60**). Click the image area and drag a marquee to zoom in on the desired area of the image (**Figure 8.61**).

Note that clips will not play smoothly when you have zoomed in on a clip in the Viewer.

Figure 8.60 Select the Zoom In tool from the Tool palette.

Figure 8.61 Drag a marquee around the area you want to zoom in on.

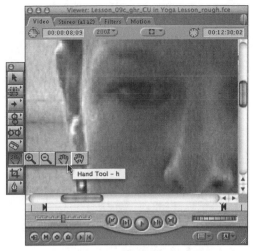

Figure 8.62 Drag the Hand tool over a magnified image to move it in the Viewer window.

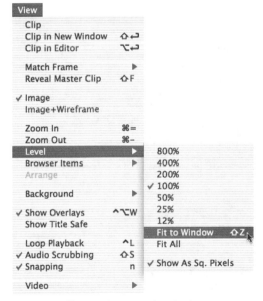

Figure 8.63 Choose View > Level and select a zoom-out level.

To view different parts of a magnified image:

Do one of the following:

◆ Select the Hand tool from the Tool palette and drag it over the image to move the view (**Figure 8.62**).

◆ Use the scroll bars to move around the image.

To zoom out:

Do one of the following:

◆ Choose a lower magnification level from the Zoom pop-up menu at the top of the Viewer.

◆ Select the Zoom Out tool from the Tool palette and click inside the Viewer or Canvas.

◆ From the View menu, select a zoom-out amount from the Level submenu (**Figure 8.63**).

ADJUSTING THE VIEWER DISPLAY

To fit a clip into the window size:

◆ From the Zoom pop-up menu at the top of the Viewer, choose Fit to Window; or press Shift-Z.

✔ Tip

■ Shift-Z is one of FCE's best-beloved keyboard shortcuts. In the Viewer's video tab, Shift-Z zooms your image to fit the window size. In the Viewer's audio tabs, the same shortcut scales the clip's waveform to fit into the window. In the Timeline, Shift-Z scales your sequence view to fit the entire sequence inside the Timeline window.

To fit all items into the view plus a 10 percent margin:

Do one of the following:

◆ From the Zoom pop-up menu at the top of the Viewer, choose Fit All (**Figure 8.64**).

◆ Choose View > Level > Fit All.

✔ Tip

■ Choosing Fit All causes FCE to zoom out enough to show all objects in a multilayered composited sequence, including those outside the screen area (**Figure 8.65**).

Figure 8.64 Select Fit All from the Zoom pop-up menu.

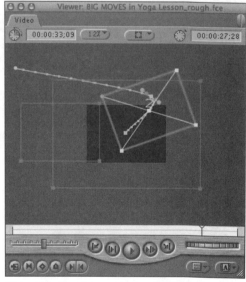

Figure 8.65 The Viewer showing all of the objects in a multilayered composited sequence. Selecting Fit All is the only way to get the Viewer zoom level to go below 12.5 percent.

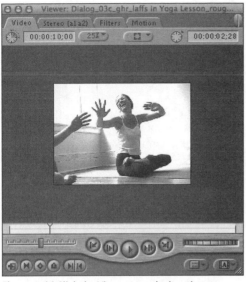

Figure 8.66 Click the Viewer to make it active.

To view at actual size:

◆ From the Zoom pop-up menu at the top of the Viewer, choose 100%.

To fit the window to the current clip size:

1. Make the Viewer active (**Figure 8.66**).

2. Double-click the Zoom In tool on the Tool palette (**Figure 8.67**).

   The Viewer window will adjust to fit the current clip size (**Figure 8.68**).

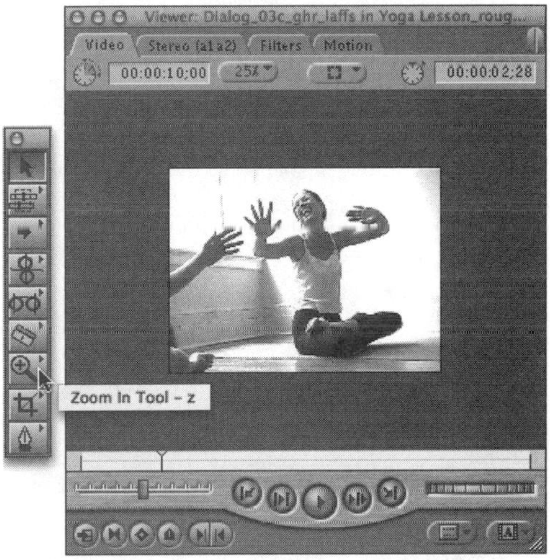

Figure 8.67 Double-click the Zoom In tool on the Tool palette.

Figure 8.68 The Viewer adjusts to fit the current clip image size.

Viewing overlays

Overlays are icons or text displayed on top of the video when the playhead is parked on a particular frame. Overlays indicate significant points, such as In and Out points, in a clip or sequence. Overlays appear only when the Viewer and Canvas are in Pause mode and are not rendered to output. Final Cut Express displays the following overlays by default (**Figure 8.69**):

◆ **In and Out Points:** These icons appear when the playhead is positioned on the In or Out point frame.

◆ **Start and End of Media:** The filmstrip symbol along the left or right side of the video frame indicates the start or end of the video media.

◆ **Start and End of Edits (not shown):** An L shape at the lower left indicates the start of an edit, and a backward L shape at the lower right indicates the end of an edit. These icons appear only in the Canvas.

◆ **Marker:** A marker overlay appears as a translucent box displaying the marker's name and comment text.

The Title Safe and Action Safe overlays are not displayed by default, and they have their own display controls in the View menu:

◆ **Title Safe and Action Safe:** Title Safe and Action Safe boundaries are rectangular boxes around the edges of the video.

In Point overlay

Out Point overlay

Title Safe overlay

Start of Media overlay

Action Safe overlay

Marker overlay

Figure 8.69 Viewer overlays.

Figure 8.70 Turn off all overlay displays in the Viewer by unchecking Show Overlays in the View pop-up menu.

Figure 8.71 Choose Show Title Safe from the View pop-up menu to display the Title Safe overlay.

To view or hide overlays:

◆ Choose Show Overlays from the View pop-up menu at the top of the Viewer or Canvas to toggle the display of all overlays (**Figure 8.70**).

Viewing Title Safe and Action Safe boundaries

Most NTSC (National Television Standards Committee) television sets don't display the full video image on their screens. Use the Title Safe and Action Safe overlays to be sure that crucial parts of your composition or titles are not cut off at the edges when displayed on a television screen.

✔ Tip

■ Consumer TV sets may trim the edges of your video, but video for the Web displays the whole frame—so if you are aiming your show at both the Web and TV, you'll need to watch the edges of your frame.

To view or hide Title Safe and Action Safe boundaries:

Do one of the following:

◆ Choose View > Show Title Safe.

◆ From the View pop-up menu at the top of the Viewer, choose Show Title Safe (**Figure 8.71**).

◆ Choose Show Title Safe again to toggle off the overlay.

Viewing with different backgrounds

If you are working with a clip that has an alpha channel—say some black generated text that you want to superimpose over video—you can change the default black background of your black text to white, to make the text more visible while you work with it. Translucent clips will be more visible if you choose a background that emphasizes them. When a clip is rendered, the background is always set to black.

To choose a background for viewing a clip:

◆ From the View menu, select a background from the Background submenu (**Figure 8.72**).

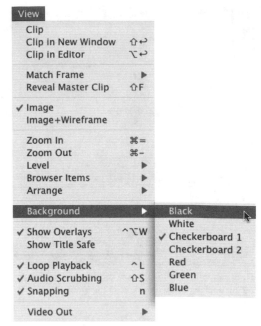

Figure 8.72 Select a black background by choosing View > Background > Black.

BASIC EDITING

Everything up to this point has been preamble—by now you're familiar enough with Final Cut Express that you can jump in and start the actual work of editing. But there's more to it than just slicing and rearranging clips.

In this chapter, you'll learn not only basic procedures for performing edits in FCE, including how to use the seven edit types available, but also the underlying concepts and protocols that govern editing: sequences, three-point editing, and multiple media tracks.

You assemble an edited sequence in the Timeline window, which displays a chronological view of a sequence. All the media elements you've assembled to create a sequence appear in the Timeline as elements that diagram the sequencing and layering of audio and video tracks. As you drag the playhead along the Timeline ruler, the current frame of the sequence updates in the Canvas window. The Canvas window is the viewer you use to play back the edited sequence you've assembled in the Timeline. (A more detailed discussion of Timeline and Canvas window operations appears in Chapter 10, "Editing in the Timeline and the Canvas.")

Once you've assembled a first draft of an edited sequence, known as a *rough cut* (isn't that a great expression?), you'll probably want to go back and *trim* (fine-tune) your edits. Final Cut Express's edit trimming tools and techniques are outlined in Chapter 11, "Fine Cut: Trimming Edits."

If you need a review of FCE's project structure and media elements basics before the clips start flying, see Chapter 4, "Projects, Sequences, and Clips."

Basic Editing Overview

Figure 9.1 summarizes the steps for performing a drag-and-drop-style edit that uses the Canvas overlay. The next section offers a step-by-step breakdown of the same edit.

3. Set In and Out points
- Press I to set In point
- Press O to set Out point

4. Drag clip from Viewer to Canvas
- Canvas edit overlay will appear
- Drop clip on the Overwrite edit area

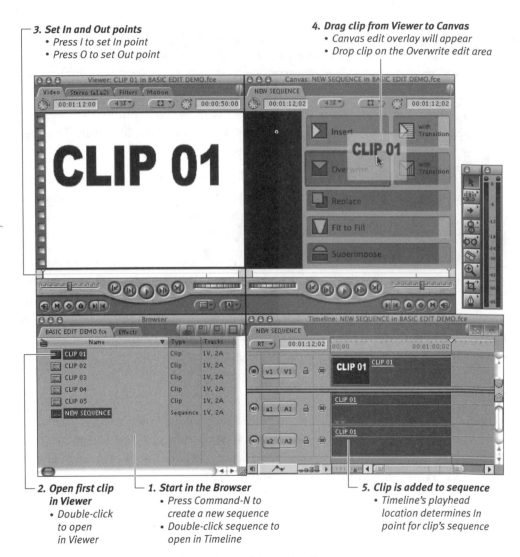

2. Open first clip in Viewer
- Double-click to open in Viewer

1. Start in the Browser
- Press Command-N to create a new sequence
- Double-click sequence to open in Timeline

5. Clip is added to sequence
- Timeline's playhead location determines In point for clip's sequence

Figure 9.1 Here's one way to perform a drag-and-drop style edit.

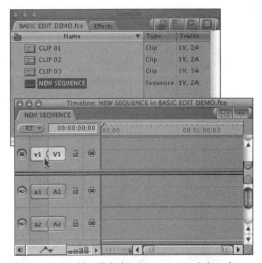

Figure 9.2 Double-click the new sequence's icon in the Browser to open it for editing. Examine the open sequence in the Timeline to check that destination tracks are assigned correctly and that the playhead is positioned at the beginning of the sequence.

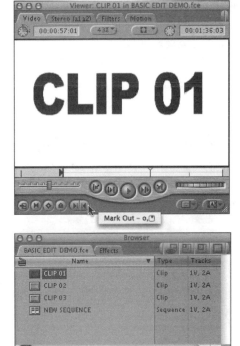

Figure 9.3 Double-click the clip to open it in the Viewer; then mark In and Out points to specify which portion of the source clip you want to use.

Basic Editing Step-by-Step

Here's a step by step breakdown of a simple rough-assembly-style edit in Final Cut Express. After you've reviewed this basic editing procedure, find out how to perform more specific types of edits in the sections that follow.

To add the first clip to your sequence:

1. In the Browser, press Command-N to create a new sequence.

2. Double-click the new sequence to open it in the Canvas and the Timeline (**Figure 9.2**).

   The new, empty sequence opens in the Timeline window. The Timeline's playhead is positioned at the beginning of the sequence.

   Before you insert a clip in a sequence, you need to check the target tracks (the destination tracks for your clip in the sequence).

3. In the Timeline, check the destination track assignment for your first clip. In a new sequence, default destination tracks will already be assigned to V1, A1, and A2. If necessary, you can target different destination tracks by clicking the target track controls.

4. In the Browser, double-click the first clip you want to insert in your new sequence; that clip opens in the Viewer.

5. In the Viewer, select the portion of the clip you want to use in the sequence by setting In and Out points (**Figure 9.3**). (See "Working with In and Out Points" in Chapter 8.)

continues on next page

BASIC EDITING STEP-BY-STEP

6. Click the Viewer's image area and drag the clip to the Canvas window.

   The Canvas edit overlay menu appears.

7. Drop the clip on the Overwrite edit area (**Figure 9.4**). (Overwrite is the default edit type in FCE unless you specify another type.)

   The clip will be inserted at the beginning of your new sequence (**Figure 9.5**).

Figure 9.4 Drag the source clip from the Viewer to the Canvas edit overlay; then drop the clip on the Overwrite edit area.

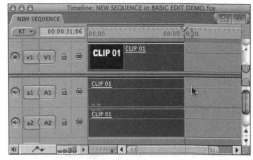

Figure 9.5 The source clip has been added to the sequence. The Timeline playhead's position was used as the sequence In point, so the clip's In point has been placed at the beginning of the sequence.

Many Ways to Make an Edit

Dragging your source clip to the Canvas edit overlay is just one way to execute an edit. Once you have defined your edit points, you can also do the following:

◆ Drag the clip directly from the Viewer to the Timeline (**Figure 9.6**).

◆ Drag one or more clips directly from the Browser to the Timeline (now *that's* a rough edit).

◆ Use a keyboard shortcut to perform the edit. The keyboard shortcut for each edit type is listed in Appendix B.

Figure 9.6 You can edit by dragging a clip directly from the Viewer or Browser and dropping it into a sequence in the Timeline.

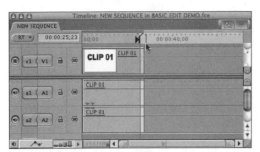

Figure 9.7 Position the Timeline playhead where you want your second clip to start; then press I to set a sequence In point.

Figure 9.8 The second source clip, displayed in the Viewer with In and Out points set.

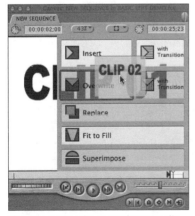

Figure 9.9 Drag the second source clip to the Canvas edit overlay; then drop the clip on the Overwrite edit area.

To insert additional clips:

1. In the Timeline, park the playhead on the frame where you want your new clip to start. You can press I to set a sequence In point on that frame, but it's not required (**Figure 9.7**).

2. In the Viewer, set In and Out points on your second clip (**Figure 9.8**).

3. Drag the clip from the image area of the Viewer to the Canvas window.

   The Canvas edit overlay menu will appear.

4. Drop the clip on the Overwrite edit area (**Figure 9.9**).

   The second clip will be inserted starting where you set the sequence In point (**Figure 9.10**).

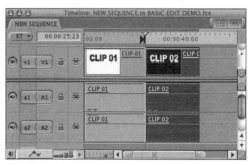

Figure 9.10 The sequence displayed in the Timeline, with the second clip inserted at the sequence In point.

FCE Protocol: Three-Point Editing

In a three-point edit, you can define any three points of an edit, and Final Cut Express will calculate the fourth point for you. Here's an example:

1. Specify In and Out points for your source clip.

2. Park the playhead in the Canvas at the sequence In point (the point where you want your new clip to start).

When you insert the new clip into your sequence, Final Cut Express uses the duration of the new clip insert to calculate the sequence Out point.

At least three edit points must be set in the Viewer and Canvas to complete an edit. But if you specify fewer than three points and begin an edit, FCE will calculate your edit based on the following protocols:

◆ If no In or Out point is set in the Canvas, the Canvas playhead location is used as the sequence In point.

◆ If no In or Out point is set in the source, FCE assumes that you want to use the entire source clip. The playhead's location in the sequence (Timeline and Canvas) is used as the sequence In point. FCE calculates the Out point for the sequence.

◆ If one edit point (In or Out) is set in a source clip, the second point is the beginning or the end of the media (depending on whether the user-defined point is an In or an Out point). The Canvas playhead is used as the sequence In point, and FCE calculates the Out point.

There are three exceptions to the three-point editing rules:

◆ Fit to Fill editing requires four user-specified points, because FCE adjusts the speed of the specified source clip to fill a specified sequence duration.

◆ Replace editing ignores the In and Out points set in the source clip and uses the boundaries of the clip under the Canvas playhead as sequence In and Out points. Replace edits affect the target track media. To replace an audio track, turn off targeting for all video tracks.

◆ If In and Out points are set for both the source clip and the sequence, FCE ignores the source clip's Out point and uses the clip's In point and the sequence In and Out points.

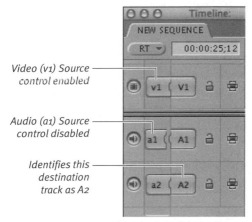

Video (v1) Source control enabled

Audio (a1) Source control disabled

Identifies this destination track as A2

Figure 9.11 The target track controls in the Timeline. A control's left side identifies which source clip track is assigned to this destination track; the right side identifies the destination track by number. Timeline base tracks are enabled by default; you can click either side of the control to *disconnect* (disable) a track.

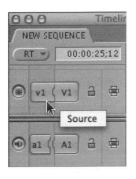

Figure 9.12 Set a target track by connecting a video Source control. The Source control is connected to the destination indicator when the track is targeted.

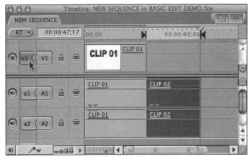

Figure 9.13 Click to disconnect a Video Source control. Audio tracks remain targeted.

Specifying target tracks

Each time you add clips to a sequence, you can specify which tracks the media will occupy. You specify target tracks using the Timeline's target track controls (**Figure 9.11**): the lozenge-shaped icons located on the left in the Timeline. The Destination (right) side of the control identifies the track. Set the Source control (the left side of the control) to specify which source track is assigned to that destination track and whether the track is enabled to receive a source clip. You can target one video target track plus one audio target track for each audio track in your source clip.

For more information on targeting and mapping track assignments, see "Mapping Timeline target track assignments" in Chapter 10.

To select target tracks in the Timeline:

◆ In the Timeline, click the target track control on the left side of the track you want to use.

The Source control is connected to the Destination track indicator when a track is targeted (**Figure 9.12**).

To use audio only from an audio+video clip:

◆ Click the left (Source) side to disconnect the target indicator of the video track before you perform your edit (**Figure 9.13**).

To use one channel of two-channel audio from the source clip:

◆ Click the left (Source) side to disconnect the target indicator of the track you want to exclude (**Figure 9.14**).

✔ Tips

■ Once you've used the target track controls to route your source clips to their proper tracks, you might want to lock the tracks to prevent further changes to edited clips on those tracks. See "FCE Protocol: Lock vs. Target" in Chapter 10 to learn the hows and whys of track locking.

■ When you are ready for big-time multi-track editing, be aware that FCE offers a raft of keyboard shortcuts for target track selection. Check them out in Appendix B, "Keyboard Shortcuts."

Moving the playhead

You can jump the playhead to the edit point of your choice with a single keystroke or mouse click. Most of these shortcuts work in the Viewer as well.

To move the playhead to the In point:

◆ Press Shift-I; or Shift-click the Mark In button.

To move the playhead to the Out point:

◆ Press Shift-O; or Shift-click the Mark Out button.

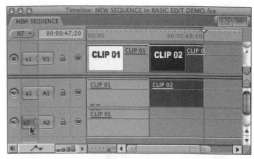

Figure 9.14 With A2 targeting turned off, channel 2 audio is excluded from the sequence.

To jump the playhead to an adjacent edit point:

Do one of the following:

◆ Click the Previous Edit or the Next Edit button in the transport controls.

◆ Press the Up or the Down Arrow key.

◆ Open the Mark menu and choose from the Next or Previous submenu.

◆ Press Option-E (to go to the previous edit point) or Shift-E (to go to the next edit point).

✔ Tip

■ If you need to define the edit points for a clip, you'll find information on marking In and Out points on a source clip in Chapter 8, "Working with Clips in the Viewer."

FCE Protocol: Editing Multiple Tracks in Final Cut Express

Final Cut Express sequences can have multiple video and audio tracks. The first video clip you add to a sequence will be the base layer (V1). Video frames you place on track 2 (V2) are superimposed over any video frames at the same point in time on track 1. In a sequence with multiple layers, the base track becomes the background, and media on each higher-numbered track obscures the media on tracks below it. The result appears in the Canvas (after a little rendering).

Audio tracks A1 and A2 are the designated base tracks for stereo audio. Final Cut Express can mix and play back several audio tracks in a sequence in real time.

How Many Audio Tracks?

The number of audio tracks you can mix in real time depends on your Macintosh's configuration (available RAM, processor speed, hard drive data transfer rate, and so on), the number of audio files requiring real-time sample rate conversion or filtering, and the number of simultaneous audio transitions you have included in your sequence. You can specify how many tracks you want FCE to attempt to handle in real time by setting the Real-Time Audio Mixing preference (see "Specifying User Preferences and System Settings" in Chapter 3). However, increasing your real-time audio track budget is no guarantee that you'll be able to play back the number of tracks you specify, and if you set this preference too high, you could trigger dropped frames during playback or dropouts in audio.

Eight tracks of real-time audio is the FCE default setup, but you can have up to 99 tracks in a sequence.

In calculating the number of audio tracks you need for a sequence, note that each simultaneous audio crossfade or transition increases the track count by one. So if your sequence requires seven audio tracks, adding a pair of crossfades increases the count to nine tracks. It may also require rendering to preview.

You can reduce your audio track overhead by choosing Sequence > Render Only > Mixdown. Mixdown renders all the audio tracks in a sequence along with their transitions, and it filters and consolidates them into one render file. For more information on working with audio in FCE, see Chapter 12, "Audio Tools and Techniques."

Using FCE's Many Edit Types

One powerful editing option unique to Final Cut Express is the Canvas edit overlay. When you drag a clip directly into the Canvas image area, the Canvas edit overlay appears with fields for each type of edit (**Figure 9.15**). Select the type of edit you want to perform by dropping your clip on the corresponding overlay area. The default type is an Overwrite edit.

Final Cut Express offers many types of edits and many ways to perform those edits. Keep reading to find a rundown of the types of edits you can perform in FCE, along with variations they impose on the basic editing procedure.

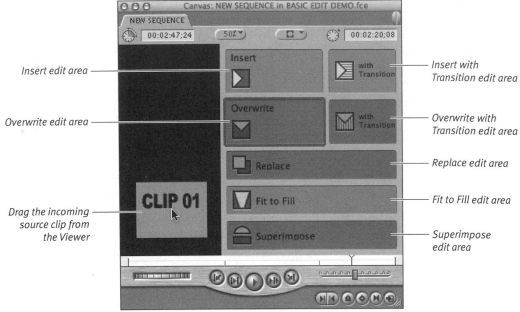

Figure 9.15 The Canvas edit overlay allows drag-and-drop editing for seven types of edits.

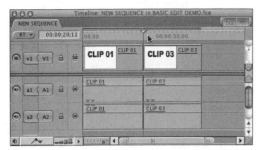

Figure 9.16 Position the Timeline playhead to set your sequence In point.

Figure 9.17 Drag the source clip from the Viewer to the Canvas edit overlay; then drop the clip on the Insert edit area.

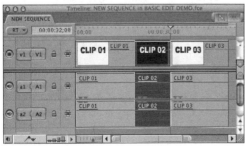

Figure 9.18 The completed Insert edit in the Timeline. Clip 02, inserted between Clip 01 and Clip 03, pushes Clip 03 to the right.

Insert edit

When you perform an Insert edit, the sequence clips at the In point move to the right to make room for the new source clip.

✔ Tips

- Insert edits can also be performed by dragging the source clip directly to the Timeline. See "Performing Edits in the Timeline," later in this chapter.

- Heads up! When you perform an insert edit, any sequence clips that span the In point are automatically split to accommodate the new clip.

To perform an Insert edit:

1. Set the sequence In point by positioning the Timeline (or Canvas) playhead where you want the edit to occur (**Figure 9.16**).

2. Drag the source clip from the Viewer to the Insert edit area in the Canvas overlay (**Figure 9.17**); or press F9.

   The source clip is inserted into the sequence (**Figure 9.18**).

USING FCE'S MANY EDIT TYPES

Overwrite edit

In an Overwrite edit, the source clip overwrites sequence clips past the sequence In point. Overwrite edits use the source In and Out points to calculate the edit duration, replacing sequence material with the incoming source clip, with no time shift in the existing sequence.

✔ Tip

■ You can also perform Overwrite edits by dragging the source clip directly to the Timeline. See "Performing Edits in the Timeline," later in this chapter.

To perform an Overwrite edit:

1. Set the sequence In point by positioning the Timeline (or Canvas) playhead where you want the edit to occur (**Figure 9.19**).

2. Drag the source clip from the Viewer to the Overwrite edit area in the Canvas overlay (**Figure 9.20**); or press F10.

   The source clip is added to the sequence, overwriting any existing sequence material on the targeted tracks that falls between the sequence In and Out points (**Figure 9.21**).

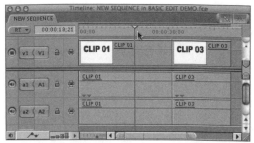

Figure 9.19 Position the Timeline playhead to set your sequence In point.

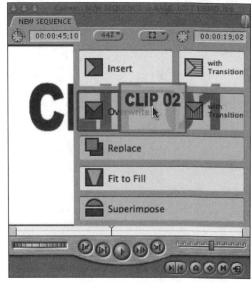

Figure 9.20 Drag the source clip from the Viewer to the Canvas edit overlay; then drop the clip on the Overwrite edit area.

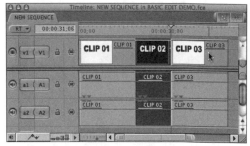

Figure 9.21 The completed Overwrite edit in the Timeline. Clip 02 overwrites the portion of Clip 01 that extends beyond the sequence In point, without moving Clip 03.

Replace edit

A Replace edit replaces the contents of a sequence clip with source clip material.

The Replace edit uses the playhead position in the Viewer, not the source In and Out points, to calculate the Replace edit; your source In and Out points will be ignored. If you don't set sequence In and Out points, FCE uses the boundaries of the clip under the Timeline playhead.

You can use a Replace edit to simply replace a shot in a sequence with footage from another shot with the same duration. Replace editing can also be a powerful tool for matching action: for example, when you're cutting between multiple-camera coverage of different angles on the same action (in your big-budget dreams). Park the Canvas playhead at the point in the action that you want to match in your source clip. Find the source clip frame that matches the action in the sequence frame. Mark In and Out points in the Canvas to select the section of the sequence you want to replace with the new material. The material between the sequence In and Out points is replaced by corresponding material from the source clip on either side of the frame that was matched.

Hate Your Edit? Do Undo

Undo is one of the great technological contributions to civilization. Especially when you're editing.

As you build your edited sequence, keep in mind that the fastest way to repair your sequence after you've done something brilliant but basically bad is to use the Undo feature. You can set your FCE user preferences to allow up to 99 Undos; 10 is the default.

Undo is particularly useful when you've just performed an unsuccessful (or accidental) Overwrite edit and replaced some clips in your sequence. Deleting the clips that wiped out part of your sequence won't restore your original footage, but if you undo (Command-Z) your Overwrite edit, your sequence footage will be restored.

So go forth and be bold. Experiment with your edit. You can always Undo.

To perform a Replace edit:

1. Position the Viewer playhead on the frame you want to match with a frame in the Canvas (**Figure 9.22**).

2. Position the Canvas playhead on the frame you want to match with the one selected in the Viewer. If you want to specify the duration of the replacement clip, set sequence In and Out points (**Figure 9.23**).

Figure 9.22 Position the Viewer playhead on the frame you want to match with a frame in the Canvas.

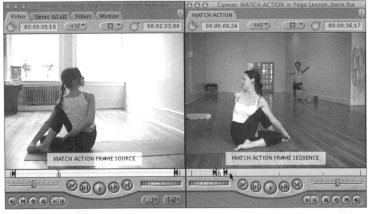

Figure 9.23 Position the Canvas playhead on the frame you want to match with a frame in the Viewer.

USING FCE'S MANY EDIT TYPES

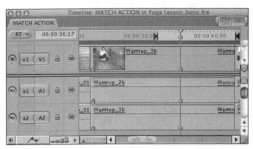

Figure 9.24 The sequence before the Replace edit in the Timeline.

Figure 9.25 The same sequence after performing the Replace edit. The new clip replaces the old, using the match frame you selected as the sync point.

3. Drag the source clip from the Viewer to the Replace edit area in the Canvas overlay; or press F11.

Figure 9.24 shows the Timeline before the Replace edit; **Figure 9.25** shows the Timeline after the Replace edit.

✔ Tip

- Use the Replace edit technique to replace a clip with an offset copy of itself. This is a shortcut to adjust the timing of action in a clip or to sync action to music.

What's a Backtime Edit?

Say you're filling a gap in your edited music video sequence. The In point of the clip you want to use is not critical, but you know exactly where you want this clip to end—and you want the clip to fit your gap exactly. In this case, set up a *backtime* edit by marking the gap as your sequence In and Out points, along with the source Out point you identified in your source clip. FCE will calculate the other In point and back in your clip so it fits the gap perfectly.

Fit to Fill edit

In a Fit to Fill edit, the speed of the source clip adjusts to fill the duration specified by the sequence In and Out points; you must render the clip before you can play it back.

To perform a Fit to Fill edit:

1. In the Timeline, set sequence In and Out points to define the sequence section you want to fill (**Figure 9.26**).

2. In the Viewer, set source In and Out points to define the part of the source clip you want to speed-modify so it fits between your edit points in the sequence (**Figure 9.27**).

3. Drag the source clip in the Viewer to the Fit to Fill edit area in the Canvas overlay; or press Shift-F11.

   The source clip is speed-modified to fit between the sequence In and Out points (**Figure 9.28**).

✔ Tip

■ You've just added a clip to your sequence—but it's too short to fill the gap you're trying to fill. Here's a slick trick: Perform Fit to Fill on a clip that's already edited into your sequence by double-clicking the clip to open it in the Viewer and then dragging it to the Fit to Fill edit area. Voilà! Perfect fit.

Figure 9.26 Setting the sequence In and Out points defines the section you want to fill.

Figure 9.27 Marking a source Out point in the Viewer. Setting source In and Out points defines the section you want to fit into the sequence.

Figure 9.28 The source clip is speed-modified to fit between the sequence In and Out points. Note that the speed change is indicated on the clip.

Figure 9.29 Using the Mark Clip keyboard shortcut (X) is a fast way to mark In and Out points at the clip boundaries of a clip you want to superimpose over.

Figure 9.30 In the Viewer, set a source In or Out point to specify the part of the source clip that you want to superimpose on the sequence.

Figure 9.31 Drag the source clip from the Viewer to the Canvas edit overlay; then drop the clip on the Superimpose edit area.

Superimpose edit

In a Superimpose edit, the source clip is placed on a new track above the target track, starting at the sequence In point. The target track does not change. If the clip has audio, the source audio is added to new tracks below the target audio track.

To perform a Superimpose edit:

1. Position the Canvas playhead or set a sequence In point where you want the source clip to start (**Figure 9.29**).

2. In the Viewer, set a source In or Out point to define the part of the source clip you want to add to the sequence (**Figure 9.30**).

3. Drag the source clip from the Viewer to the Superimpose edit area in the Canvas overlay (**Figure 9.31**); or press F12.

   The source clip is placed on a new track above the target track, starting at the sequence In point (**Figure 9.32**).

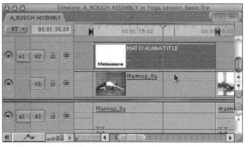

Figure 9.32 The source clip is placed on a new track above the target track, starting at the sequence In point.

USING FCE'S MANY EDIT TYPES

Transition edits

FCE offers two types of edits that incorporate transitions: Insert with Transition and Overwrite with Transition. A transition edit automatically places a cross-dissolve (FCE's default transition) at the head of the edit. When using either of the transition edit types, you'll need at least 15 extra frames in each clip at the edit point where the transition is applied in order to create the transition. (The additional frames necessary are equal to half of the default transition's 30-frame duration; see Chapter 13, "Creating Transitions," for more on using transitions.)

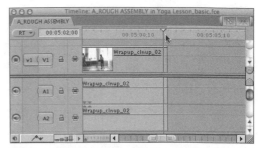

Figure 9.33 Positioning the Timeline playhead to set a sequence In point.

To perform a Transition edit:

1. Set the sequence In point by positioning the Timeline (or Canvas) playhead where you want the edit to occur (**Figure 9.33**).

2. In the Viewer, set source In and Out points to define the part of the source clip you want to add to the sequence (**Figure 9.34**).

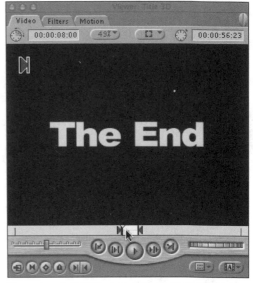

Figure 9.34 In the Viewer, set source In and Out points to specify the part of the source clip that you want to use.

Figure 9.35 Drag the source clip from the Viewer to the Canvas edit overlay; then drop it on either of the Transition edit areas.

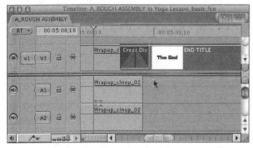

Figure 9.36 The Timeline, showing the source clip inserted into the sequence with the default transition at the head.

3. Drag the source clip from the Viewer to either the Insert with Transition or the Overwrite with Transition edit area in the Canvas overlay (**Figure 9.35**).

The source clip is inserted in the sequence with the default transition applied at the sequence In point (**Figure 9.36**).

✔ Tips

- You'll find a few transitions that will play in real time, but you must render most Transition edits before you can play them back. Real-time transitions appear in the Effects menu with their names in bold type.

- If you've customized a transition in your sequence that you want to reuse, you can select it in the Timeline and drag it to your Favorites folder on the Effects tab in the Browser. You can copy a Favorite transition from the folder and paste it into a sequence wherever you want it. Setting up a customized Favorite transition is easy, so it's worth doing even if you're building a fairly short sequence.

Deleting clips from a sequence

Two types of edits can be used to remove material from a sequence:

◆ **Lift** removes the selected material, leaving a gap.

◆ **Ripple Delete** removes the selected material and closes the gap.

To perform a Lift edit:

Do one of the following:

◆ Select the clip in the Timeline and press Delete.

◆ Select the clip in the Timeline; then choose Sequence > Lift.

◆ Select the clip in the Timeline and press Command-X (Cut).

◆ Control-click the selected clip in the Timeline; then choose Cut from the shortcut menu. (Cut also lets you paste the deleted clip in another location in the sequence.)

Figure 9.37 shows a sequence in the Timeline before a Lift edit; **Figure 9.38** shows the same sequence after a Lift edit.

Figure 9.37 A clip selected in the Timeline. Press Delete to perform a Lift edit by deleting the clip from the sequence; or press Command-X to cut the clip for pasting elsewhere.

Figure 9.38 The sequence after a Lift edit. The rest of the sequence clips hold their positions.

Figure 9.39 Control-click the selected sequence clip to access the shortcut menu.

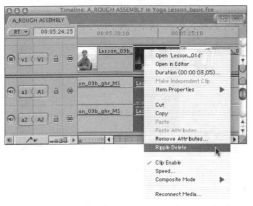

Figure 9.40 From the shortcut menu, choose Ripple Delete.

Figure 9.41 The sequence after a Ripple Delete edit. Material to the right of the deleted clip has been pulled up to close the gap.

To perform a Ripple Delete edit:

Do one of the following:

◆ Select the clip in the Timeline and press Shift-Delete.

◆ Select the clip in the Timeline; then choose Sequence > Ripple Delete.

◆ Control-click the selected clip in the Timeline (**Figure 9.39**); then choose Ripple Delete from the shortcut menu (**Figure 9.40**).

The clip is deleted from the sequence, and the material on all unlocked tracks to the right of the sequence pulls up to close the gap (**Figure 9.41**).

✔ Tip

■ You can delete a precisely defined section of a sequence by setting sequence In and Out points to mark the section you want to remove and then pressing Delete to lift the section or pressing Shift-Delete to ripple delete it.

USING FCE'S MANY EDIT TYPES

Performing Edits in the Timeline

Editing in the Timeline can be a faster way to go, particularly when you're in the early stages of assembly.

You have a number of ways to control the size and time scale of the Timeline window. You need the Timeline's big-picture view when you deploy multiple tracks of visual or sound effects, but you can also zoom way in when performing precise work. See Chapter 10, "Editing in the Timeline and the Canvas," for details.

◆ You can assemble a sequence by dragging clips directly to the Timeline from the Browser or Viewer.

◆ You can use the Browser Sort function to sort your takes by timecode or by shot number and then drag a whole group of clips from the Browser directly to the Timeline. FCE will place the clips in the Timeline based on your Browser sort order.

◆ You can construct a storyboard in the Browser's Large Icon view (**Figure 9.42**) and then drag all the clips into the Timeline (**Figure 9.43**). If the Browser tab from which you drag the clips is in Icon mode, the clips are placed in storyboard order, from left to right and top to bottom (**Figure 9.44**).

◆ You can designate target tracks in an edit just by dragging a source clip directly to the destination track.

◆ Drag a source clip to the space above your existing tracks, and FCE will automatically create a new track.

Figure 9.42 Using Large Icon view in the Browser, arrange clip icons in storyboard order.

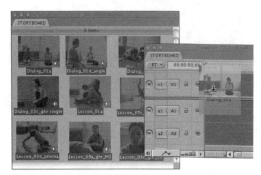

Figure 9.43 Select all clips in the Browser and drag them to the Timeline.

Figure 9.44 The sequence assembles clips in storyboard order.

PERFORMING EDITS IN THE TIMELINE

Figure 9.45 Dragging a clip to the upper third of the Timeline track performs an Insert edit.

Figure 9.46 Dragging a clip to the lower two-thirds of the Timeline track performs an Overwrite edit.

Figure 9.47 When you drop a clip directly onto the Timeline, the Canvas displays details about the two clips adjacent to your edit point.

To perform an Insert edit:

◆ Drag the source clip from the Viewer or Browser to the upper third of the Timeline track (**Figure 9.45**).

  The pointer changes to indicate the type of edit.

To perform an Overwrite edit:

◆ Drag the source clip from the Viewer or Browser to the lower two-thirds of the Timeline track (**Figure 9.46**).

✔ Tips

■ If you drag a clip to the Timeline when it is set to the smallest timeline track size, you'll perform an Overwrite edit. Hold down the Option key to perform an Insert edit.

■ When you drag a clip from the Browser onto a clip or transition in the Timeline, a two-up display appears in the Canvas. This two-up display shows the frame just before your insert on the left, and it shows the frame just after your insert on the right. The names of the sequence clips adjacent to your edit point appear at the top of each display, and the time-code of the displayed frames appears at the bottom (**Figure 9.47**).

Performing split edits

A split edit sets different In and Out points for video and audio in a single clip (**Figure 9.48**). Split edits are commonly used in cutting synchronized dialogue scenes.

To mark a split edit:

1. With the clip open in the Viewer, position the playhead where you want the video to begin.

2. Control-click the Scrubber bar; then choose Mark Split > Video In from the shortcut menu (**Figure 9.49**).

3. Reposition the playhead at your desired Out point and choose Mark Split > Video Out from the shortcut menu.

4. Repeat the process to set your Audio In and Out points (**Figure 9.50**). You could also switch to your clip's Audio tab and mark the audio there.

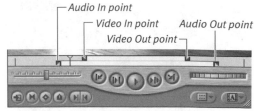

Figure 9.48 Split edit points as they appear in the Viewer's Scrubber bar.

Figure 9.49 Control-click anywhere on the Scrubber bar to call up the shortcut menu; then choose Mark Split > Video In.

Figure 9.50 Using the Scrubber shortcut menu to mark the Audio Out point. (Alternatively, you can switch to the clip's Audio tab to do this.)

Figure 9.51 Moving split In points by dragging them in the Scrubber. The Audio and Video In points will shift in tandem. Video edit points appear in the top half of the Scrubber; audio points appear in the bottom half.

Figure 9.52 Shift-dragging moves all four points at once. The timecode readout in the Viewer displays the current In point location of the point that you drag.

To move split edit points:

◆ Open the clip in the Viewer. In the Scrubber bar, drag either the In points or the Out points to a new position.

The video and audio edit points move in tandem in a split edit (**Figure 9.51**).

To slip all split edit points at once:

◆ In the Scrubber bar, press Shift while dragging any of the edit points.

All the edit points *slip*, or move in unison (**Figure 9.52**).

The respective video and audio durations specified in the split edit don't change, but the frames that are included in the marked clip shift.

✔ Tip

■ As you slip a split edit, the updated In point frame with the timecode for the edit point you selected is displayed on the Viewer image, and the edit's Out point frame with timecode is displayed on the Canvas. Awesome.

Tips for Quicker Split Edits

Split edits are commonly used in cutting synchronized dialogue scenes. You can mark a split edit before you insert a clip into a sequence for the first time (as shown here), but a common split edit approach to a dialogue sequence starts by making straight cuts of both video and audio tracks based on the rhythm of the dialogue and then going back and using the Roll tool to adjust the edit points on the video track only. Hold down the Option key as you click the edit point to select only the video track of your clip. Check out "Tips on Tools" in Chapter 11 for more information.

Another approach is to include only video or only audio in your edit by targeting only the video or audio track in the Timeline.

As you play back your footage, you can use one of these keyboard shortcuts to mark a split edit on the fly:

◆ Mark Video In: Control-I

◆ Mark Video Out: Control-O

◆ Mark Audio In: Command-Option-I

◆ Mark Audio Out: Command-Option-O

To move only one edit point in a split edit:

◆ In the Scrubber bar, press Option while dragging the edit point you want to modify (**Figure 9.53**).

A display pops up as you drag to indicate the duration of the offset between Video In and Audio In, or Video Out and Audio Out. The Scrubber bar in the Viewer updates to reflect the new edit points.

To remove a split edit point:

Do one of the following:

◆ In the Scrubber bar, Control-click; then choose Clear Split and, from the shortcut submenu, select the point you want to clear (**Figure 9.54**).

◆ Drag the edit point above or below the Scrubber bar until it disappears.

◆ Press Option I to remove both Audio and Video In points; press Option-O to remove both Audio and Video Out points.

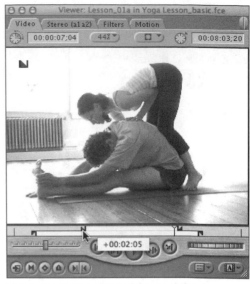

Figure 9.53 Option-click and drag to shift only one edit point in a split edit. The pop-up display shows the offset duration between Video and Audio In points.

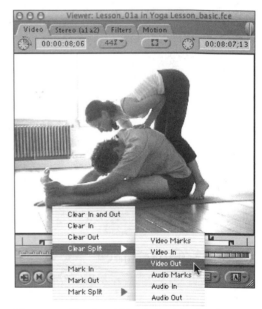

Figure 9.54 Clearing a Video Out point using the Scrubber shortcut menu. Control-click the Scrubber bar to access this menu.

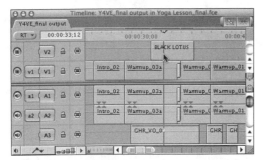

Figure 9.55 In the Timeline, place the playhead over the clip that you want to use to mark the sequence.

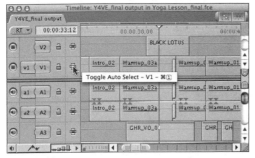

Figure 9.56 Track V1's Auto Select control is disabled, so track V2 is the lowest-numbered auto-selected track.

Figure 9.57 Choose Mark > Mark Clip.

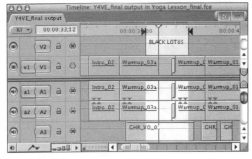

Figure 9.58 The sequence In and Out points are set to match the boundaries of the clip on track V2.

Shortcuts for Marking Sequence Edit Points

Use the same commands and keyboard shortcuts that you use to mark In and Out points in the Viewer to mark your sequence In and Out points in the Timeline and the Canvas.

FCE also offers a couple of handy commands specifically for marking edit points in a sequence:

◆ Use the Mark Clip command to set the sequence In and Out points to match the edit points of a particular clip in the sequence.

◆ Use Mark Selection to set the sequence In and Out points to match a multiple-clip selection or a selection that includes only part of a clip.

To use the Mark Clip command:

1. Place the playhead over a clip in the Timeline (**Figure 9.55**).

2. Check that your selected clip's track is the lowest-numbered auto-selected track (**Figure 9.56**).

3. Choose Mark > Mark Clip (**Figure 9.57**); or press X.

   The sequence In and Out points are set to match the boundaries of the clip (**Figure 9.58**).

✔ Tips

■ Mark Clip is a quick way to mark sequence In and Out points if you want to super-impose something over a particular clip.

■ Turn on the Auto Select controls added to Timeline tracks, and FCE automatically selects sequence material between sequence In and Out points. For more information, see "To use Auto Select to select items between In and Out points" in Chapter 10.

SHORTCUTS FOR MARKING SEQUENCE EDIT POINTS

To use the Mark Selection command:

1. Make a selection in the Timeline. The selection can range from an entire sequence to a part of a single clip (**Figure 9.59**). See Chapter 10, "Editing in the Timeline and the Canvas," for information on using the Tool palette's selection tools.

2. Choose Mark > Mark Selection (**Figure 9.60**).

   The sequence In and Out points are set to the boundaries of the selection (**Figure 9.61**).

Figure 9.59 Selecting a region of the sequence. Use Range Select from the toolbar if you want to include just part of a clip.

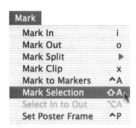

Figure 9.60 Choose Mark > Mark Selection.

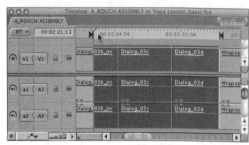

Figure 9.61 Sequence In and Out points are set to match the boundaries of the selected region.

Figure 9.62 Park the Canvas playhead on the frame that you want to match in the source clip.

Figure 9.63 FCE displays the match frame for the frame at the playhead position on the lowest-numbered Auto Select-enabled track.

Locating a match frame

Final Cut Express offers two commands you can use to locate the source clip for any frame in your sequence. Match Frame quickly locates the source for a clip you've used, which is convenient when you'd like to select another part of that clip for use elsewhere in your sequence.

◆ View > Match Frame > Master Clip locates the master clip affiliated with your sequence clip in the Browser and opens it in the Viewer. The playhead is positioned on the frame matching the sequence frame, and the master clip's In and Out points are matched to those in the sequence copy of the clip.

◆ View > Match Frame > Source File locates the original source clip in the Browser and opens it in the Viewer, but does not set matching In and Out points. Use Match Frame > Source File when you're looking for footage that's located in the original source file on disk, but outside the boundaries of your master clip.

To find a source frame of video matching a sequence clip frame:

1. In the Canvas or the Timeline, park the playhead on the frame for which you want to locate the source clip (**Figure 9.62**).

2. Set the track containing the clip to be the lowest-numbered Auto Select-enabled track (**Figure 9.63**).

continues on next page

3. *Do one of the following:*

◆ Choose View > Match Frame > Master Clip (**Figure 9.64**); or press F to locate the master clip affiliated with your sequence clip.

◆ Choose View > Match Frame > Source File; or press Command-Option-F to locate the original source clip for your sequence clip.

The matching clip opens in the Viewer. The current frame in the Viewer matches the current frame on the target track in the Canvas (**Figure 9.65**).

Figure 9.64 Choose View > Match Frame > Master Clip.

Figure 9.65 The master clip that matches the sequence clip opens in the Viewer. The frame displayed in the Viewer matches the current frame displayed in the target track in the Canvas.

EDITING IN THE TIMELINE AND THE CANVAS   10

The previous chapter introduced basic editing procedures in Final Cut Express; this chapter outlines your display, navigation, and editing options in the Timeline and Canvas windows. You'll also learn about the Tool palette, a deceptively tiny floating toolbar that's packed with editing, selection, and display tools. The Tool palette is key to efficient workflow in the Timeline.

The Timeline and the Canvas work together, but they present two different views of your edited sequence. The Timeline displays a chronological diagram of all the clips in your sequence; the Canvas is a monitor where you view playback of an edited sequence. That's why the Canvas and Timeline playheads are locked together. The Canvas always displays the frame at the current position of the Timeline's playhead.

When you open a sequence, it appears simultaneously in the Timeline and the Canvas. Any changes you make to the sequence in the Timeline are reflected in the Canvas playback, and any changes you make in the Canvas are reflected in the Timeline display.

Double-clicking a sequence clip in the Timeline opens it in the Viewer; sequence clips are identified in the Viewer by two lines of dots in the Scrubber bar. Why the identification? Remember that when you insert a clip into a sequence, you are inserting a copy of the clip from the Browser. If you change the sequence version of the clip, your changes will be reflected in the sequence only. Opening the same clip directly from the Browser in a Viewer window opens a different copy of the clip. If you change the Browser copy (for example, by making audio-level adjustments or adding motion effects), these changes will not affect the copy of the clip in the sequence. It's important to understand the difference between working with clips that have been opened from the Browser and clips that have been opened from the Timeline. (For more information, see "FCE Protocol: Clips and Sequences" in Chapter 4.)

Anatomy of the Canvas

The Canvas window (**Figure 10.1**) looks like the Viewer and has many of the same controls. You can use the controls in the Canvas window to play edited sequences, mark sequence In and Out points, add sequence markers, and set keyframes. In addition to the Viewer-like marking controls, the Canvas features a pop-up overlay where you can perform various types of drag-and-drop edits. The Canvas edit overlay appears only when you drag a clip from the Browser or the Viewer to the Canvas.

You can also use the Canvas window to plot out motion effects. Learn about applying filters and effects in Chapter 14, "Compositing and Effects Overview."

✔ Tips

- You can use tooltips to identify most of the control buttons in the window. Place your pointer over a button and then wait a moment, and a name label will appear. (Enable tooltips in the User Preferences window if they're not showing up.)

- Two playback options don't have interface controls: Play Every Frame (Option-P) and Loop Playback (Control-L).

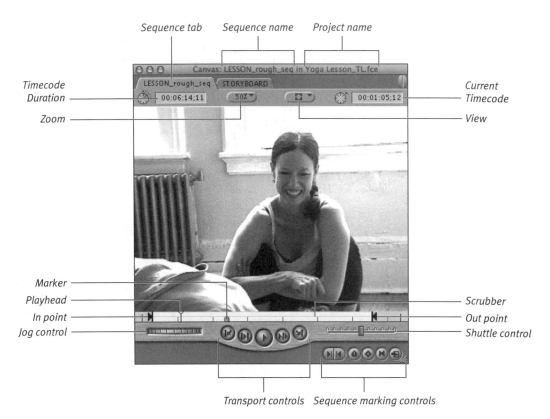

Figure 10.1 An overview of the Canvas window. Use the Canvas to play sequences, perform edits, and set keyframes.

ANATOMY OF THE CANVAS

Previous Edit *Play In to Out* *Play Around Current*
Play *Next Edit*

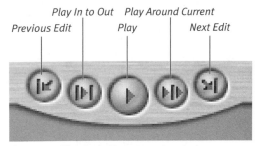

Figure 10.2 The Canvas's transport controls.

Figure 10.3 The Shuttle control.

Figure 10.4 The Jog control.

Figure 10.5 The Scrubber and playhead.

Onscreen controls and displays

The Canvas controls include transport controls, Canvas display options, and editing controls.

Note that all the Canvas controls listed here (except the overlay) appear in the Viewer window as well and operate in the same way.

Transport controls

The Canvas's transport controls are shown in **Figure 10.2**.

◆ **Previous Edit:** Click to jump the playhead back to the previous edit, the In point, or the Out point.

◆ **Play In to Out:** Click to play the clip from the In point to the Out point.

◆ **Play:** Click to play the clip from the current position of the playhead. Click again to stop playback.

◆ **Play Around Current:** Click to play the part of the clip immediately before and after the current position of the playhead. The pre-roll and post-roll settings (in the User Preferences window) determine the duration of the playback.

◆ **Next Edit:** Click to move the playhead to the next edit, the In point, or the Out point.

◆ **Shuttle control:** Drag the control tab away from the center to fast forward or rewind. Speeds vary depending on the tab's distance from the center. A green control tab indicates normal playback speed (**Figure 10.3**).

◆ **Jog control:** Drag the control to the left or right to step through a sequence one frame at a time (**Figure 10.4**).

◆ **Scrubber and playhead:** The Scrubber is the strip immediately below the image window. Move through the sequence by dragging the playhead, or click the Scrubber to jump the playhead to a new location (**Figure 10.5**).

Clip-marking controls

All the onscreen controls you use to mark clips are grouped in the lower-right corner of the Canvas (**Figure 10.6**):

◆ **Mark In (left) and Mark Out (right):** Click to set the In point or the Out point for a sequence at the current playhead position.

◆ **Add Marker:** Click to add a marker to the sequence at the current playhead position.

◆ **Add Keyframe:** Click to add a keyframe to the sequence clip at the current playhead position.

◆ **Mark Clip:** Click to set the sequence In and Out points at the outer boundaries of the clip at the position of the playhead in the target track.

◆ **Match Frame:** Click to display in the Viewer the frame currently showing in the Canvas. This control is useful for synchronizing action.

View selectors

◆ **Zoom:** Adjust the Canvas's image display size (**Figure 10.7**). (This pop-up selector does not affect the actual frame size of the image.)

◆ **View:** Select a viewing format. You can access Title Safe and Wireframe modes from this pop-up menu (**Figure 10.8**).

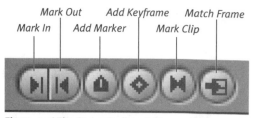

Mark Out   Add Keyframe   Match Frame
Mark In   Add Marker   Mark Clip

Figure 10.6 The Canvas's clip-marking controls.

Figure 10.7 The Zoom pop-up selector.

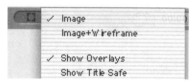

Figure 10.8 The View pop-up selector.

ANATOMY OF THE CANVAS

Figure 10.9 The Timecode Duration display.

Figure 10.10 The Current Timecode display.

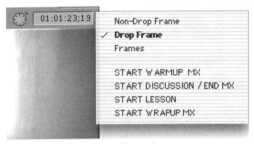

Figure 10.11 The Current Timecode pop-up menu. Select a sequence marker from the list to jump to that marker's location.

Timecode navigation and display

Two timecode displays, located in the upper corners of the Canvas window, are useful for precisely navigating to specific timecode locations.

◆ **Timecode Duration:** This display shows the elapsed time between the In and Out points of a clip. If no edit points are set, the beginning and the end of the sequence serve as the In and the Out points (**Figure 10.9**).

◆ **Current Timecode:** This display shows the timecode at the current position of the playhead. You can enter a timecode in this display to jump the playhead to that point in the sequence (**Figure 10.10**).

✔ Tips

■ Control-click the Current Timecode field to see a pop-up menu of sequence markers in the current sequence (**Figure 10.11**). Select one to jump the playhead to that marker's location. The same list of sequence markers is available from the Timeline ruler's shortcut menu.

■ You can use keyboard shortcuts to step through both sequence and clip markers in the Timeline, but you must open a clip in the Viewer to make changes to that clip's markers. For details, see "Using Markers in the Timeline and the Canvas" later in this chapter.

ANATOMY OF THE CANVAS

251

Anatomy of the Canvas edit overlay

When you drag clips from the Viewer and drop them on the Canvas, the edit overlay appears (**Figure 10.12**). The edit overlay and its related edit procedures are detailed in Chapter 9, "Basic Editing." You can perform the following types of edits:

◆ **Insert edit:** This type of edit inserts a source clip into a sequence by pushing back the part of the sequence that's past the sequence In point, making room for the new source clip.

◆ **Overwrite edit:** The source clip overwrites sequence clips past the sequence In point. Overwrite uses the source In and Out points to calculate the edit duration. The incoming source material replaces the sequence material; there is no time shift in the existing sequence.

◆ **Replace edit:** This edit type replaces the contents of a sequence clip with the source clip material. It allows you to specifically align single frames in the source clip and sequence. The material between the sequence In and Out points is replaced by corresponding material from the source clip on either side of the frame that was matched.

◆ **Fit to Fill edit:** The speed of the source clip will be modified to fill the duration specified by the sequence In and Out points; the clip must be rendered before the edit can be played back.

◆ **Superimpose edit:** The source clip is placed on a new track above the target track, starting at the sequence In point. The target track is not changed. If the clip has audio, the source audio is added to new tracks below the target audio track.

◆ **Transition edits:** The source clip is inserted into the sequence with the default transition at the source clip's head.

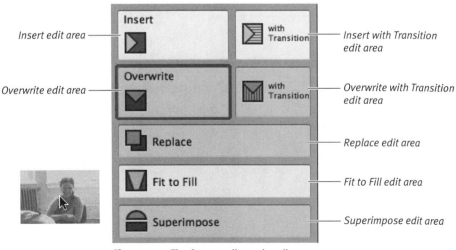

Figure 10.12 The Canvas edit overlay allows drag-and-drop editing for seven types of edits.

Figure 10.13 Selecting Image+Wireframe from the View pop-up selector.

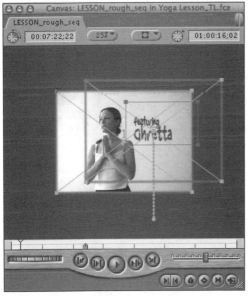

Figure 10.14 Motion paths, filters, and scaling can be directly applied in the Canvas window, but only when Image+Wireframe mode is enabled.

Using the Canvas Window

The Canvas and the Viewer windows operate in much the same way. If you review the sections in Chapter 8, "Working with Clips in the Viewer," that detail operating the Viewer window, you'll know how to use the Canvas window as well.

Editing in the Canvas is detailed in Chapter 9, "Basic Editing."

So what does that leave for this section? Just a few odds and ends.

To open a sequence in the Canvas:

◆ Start in the Browser. Double-click the sequence icon. The sequence opens in the Canvas and the Timeline.

To composite or add effects to a sequence in the Canvas:

1. Start in the Canvas with your sequence cued to the location to which you want to add effects.

2. Choose Image+Wireframe from the View selector in the Canvas (**Figure 10.13**).

   The Canvas acts as your monitor as you compose and review effects or create motion paths (**Figure 10.14**). Learn more about creating effects in Chapter 14, "Compositing and Effects Overview."

Creating and exporting still frames

It's easy to turn a single video frame into a freeze-frame image and use it in a sequence. If you want to convert this image into a graphics file and work with it outside of FCE, you'll need to export it using the Export command on the File menu.

To create a still image from a Canvas frame:

1. In the Canvas, position the playhead on the desired frame.

2. Choose Modify > Make Freeze Frame; or press Shift-N.

   The new freeze-frame image opens in the Viewer window as a clip. It has the default duration for stills, as specified on the Editing tab of the User Preferences window. You can modify the freeze-frame clip's duration by setting In and Out points before you edit it into your sequence.

To export a still image from a Canvas frame:

1. In the Canvas, position the playhead on the desired frame.

2. Choose File > Export > Using QuickTime Conversion (**Figure 10.15**).

3. In the dialog box, type a new name for your exported still image in the Save As field and select a destination folder.

4. Select Still Image from the Format pop-up menu (**Figure 10.16**).

5. To set export format options, click the Options button.

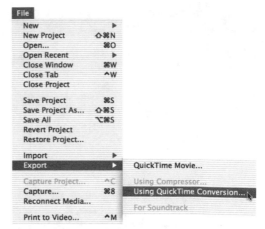

Figure 10.15 Locate the frame; then choose File > Export > Using QuickTime Conversion to export a still image directly from the Canvas or Viewer.

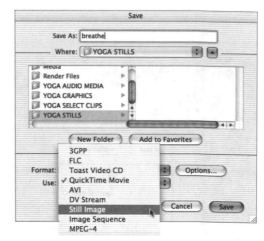

Figure 10.16 Select Still Image from the Format pop-up menu.

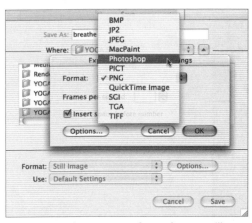

Figure 10.17 Select an export format for your still image from the pop-up menu.

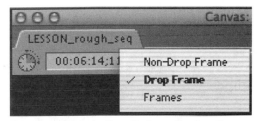

Figure 10.18 Select a time display option from the shortcut menu in the Canvas's Current Timecode display.

6. In the Export Image Sequence Settings dialog box, select an export format from the Format pop-up menu at the top (**Figure 10.17**); click OK. You can ignore the frame rate settings because you are exporting a single frame.

7. Back in the Save dialog box, click Save.

To set the time display view:

◆ In the Canvas, Control-click either of the timecode display fields; then select a time display option from the shortcut menu (**Figure 10.18**).

✔ Tips

■ Check the time display mode to quickly determine which type of timecode is currently specified in your sequence settings. The timecode type specified in your sequence settings appears in bold.

■ Changing the timecode display in the Canvas won't alter your sequence's timecode settings; you're just selecting a different display mode.

Adjusting the Canvas Display

You can set up the Canvas to show clips in a variety of display formats and magnifications. FCE also lets you overlay an array of useful information on your clip image, or you can turn off everything.

Display options operate the same way in the Canvas and the Viewer. Learn more about Canvas display options by reading "Adjusting the Viewer Display" in Chapter 8.

Anatomy of the Tool Palette

The Tool palette contains tools for selecting and manipulating items in the Timeline, Canvas, and Viewer. As you work in the Timeline with an assembly of clips in a rough sequence, you use the tools in the palette to do the following:

◆ Select anything, from a sliver of a single clip to all the tracks in your sequence.

◆ Select and adjust edit points in your sequence.

◆ Adjust the scale of the Timeline so you can see what you are doing.

◆ Crop or distort an image.

◆ Add and edit keyframes in the Timeline.

Figure 10.19 shows the Tool palette as it appears in the program.

Figure 10.20 shows the Tool palette with all its pop-up selectors fully extended. When you actually use the Tool palette to select a tool, you will see only one of these selectors at a time, but they are assembled in this illustration to show the location of every available tool.

Here's a complete rundown of the tools you'll find in the Tool palette.

Figure 10.19 The Tool palette as a compact floating toolbar.

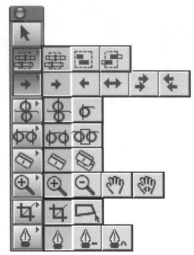

Figure 10.20 The Tool palette with every pop-up selector displayed. You'll see only one of these bars at a time when you select a tool.

Selection tools

 Selection: Selects individual items.

 Edit Selection: Selects just the edit points inside your selection.

 Group Selection: Selects whole clips or groups of whole clips.

 Range Selection: Selects the area inside the selection marquee you draw. Select partial clips with this tool.

 Select Track Forward: Selects all the contents of the track after the selection point.

 Select Track Backward: Selects all the contents of the track before the selection point.

 Track Selection: Selects the entire contents of a single track.

 Select All Tracks Forward: Selects the contents of all tracks after the selection point.

 Select All Tracks Backward: Selects the contents of all tracks before the selection point.

Edit tools

 Roll: Rolls edit points.

 Ripple: Ripples edit points.

 Slip: Slips a clip's In and Out points.

 Slide: Slides a clip in a sequence.

 Razor Blade: Cuts a single clip into two sections.

 Razor Blade All: Cuts clips on all tracks at the selection point into two sections.

Learn more about performing these edits in Chapter 11, "Fine Cut: Trimming Edits."

View tools

 Zoom In: Zooms in on an image or within the Timeline.

 Zoom Out: Zooms out from an image or within the Timeline.

 Hand: Moves the Timeline or image view from side to side.

 Video Scrub Hand: Scrubs the thumbnail image displayed on Timeline clips.

Image modifiers

 Crop: Crops the edges of an image in the Viewer or the Canvas (in Wireframe mode).

 Distort: Distorts a selection by click-dragging corner points.

Keyframe tools

 Pen: Adds a keyframe.

 Pen Delete: Deletes a keyframe.

Pen Smooth: Smoothes a curve by adding Bézier handles to the selected keyframe.

You can use the Pen tools in keyframe graphs on the Viewer effects tabs, in keyframe overlays in the Timeline, and on a motion path in the Canvas or the Viewer.

Using the Tool Palette

When you click and hold the mouse on a tool in the palette, the Tool palette extends to display multiple tools on pop-up selectors. Each pop-up selector displays all the tools available from its palette button. After you've made a selection from the pop-up display, your selected tool will be displayed on the palette.

✔ Tip

■ See Appendix B for a complete list of keyboard shortcuts for tool selection. Shortcuts are also listed in tooltips and on FCE menus.

To select a tool from the palette:

Do one of the following:

◆ Click the tool to select it (**Figure 10.21**).

◆ Click and hold on the tool icon; then make a selection from the pop-up display of related tools (**Figure 10.22**).

◆ Use a keyboard shortcut. To quickly see the proper key, rest the pointer over the tool icon in the palette. A tooltip displaying the name of the tool and its shortcut will appear (**Figure 10.23**).

Figure 10.21 Click a tool to select it from the Tool palette.

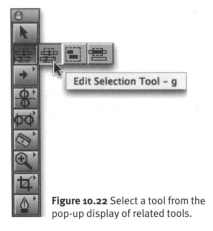

Figure 10.22 Select a tool from the pop-up display of related tools.

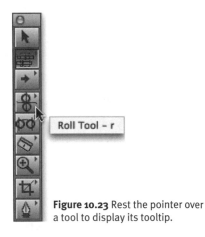

Figure 10.23 Rest the pointer over a tool to display its tooltip.

Anatomy of the Timeline

The Timeline displays multiple video and audio tracks along a time axis (**Figure 10.24**). The base layers of video (V1) and audio (A1 and A2) appear toward the center of the Timeline window. Additional audio tracks extend below the base layer; additional video tracks stack above the base layer.

If you have multiple sequences open, the Timeline and the Canvas display a tab for each sequence.

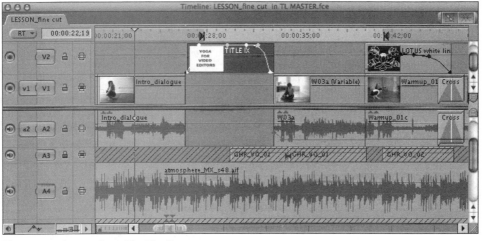

Figure 10.24 An overview of the Timeline.

Onscreen controls and displays

Use the controls in the Timeline window to move the playhead, view the tracks in your edited sequence, and perform edits and keyframe adjustments. Timeline controls and displays include track icons, sequence edit points, and clip and sequence markers (**Figures 10.25**, **10.26**, and **10.27**).

Sequence controls and displays
(**Figure 10.25**)

◆ **Sequence tabs:** Each open sequence in the Timeline has its own sequence tab. To make a sequence active, click its tab.

◆ **Real-Time Effects (RT) pop-up menu:** Select a level of playback quality for real-time effects. Your trade-off is the number of effects you can see in real time versus the visual quality of the playback. For more details, see Chapter 18, "Real Time and Rendering."

◆ **Current Timecode field:** This field displays the timecode at the current position of the playhead. You can enter a time in the display to jump the play-head to that point in the clip. This display/control operates like the Current Timecode fields in the Viewer and the Canvas.

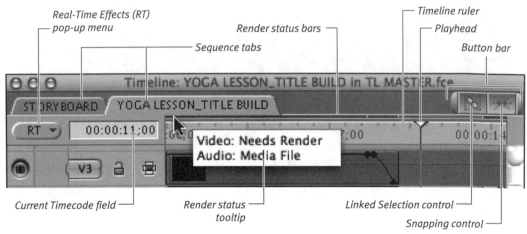

Figure 10.25 Sequence controls and displays in the Timeline.

ANATOMY OF THE TIMELINE

◆ **Render status bars:** Two render status bars indicate which parts of the sequence have been rendered. The upper bar is for video tracks, and the lower bar is for audio tracks. Red bars indicate material that requires rendering before playback. Gray bars indicate material that does not require rendering. A blue-gray bar indicates material that has already been rendered. On real-time-capable systems, a green status bar indicates that the material can be played back in real time, dark green indicates an effect that can be played back and output to video at full quality in real time, orange indicates an effect that probably exceeds the real-time capabilities of the system and could result in dropped frames during playback, and yellow indicates real-time playback with a proxy (lower-quality) version of the material.

◆ **Timeline ruler:** This ruler displays the timecode for the current sequence and sequence In and Out points. Edit point overlays are displayed along the ruler. Adjust the ruler's time scale with the Zoom slider or the Zoom control.

◆ **Playhead:** The playhead reflects the chronological position in the sequence of the frame displayed in the Canvas. The playhead in the Timeline always moves in tandem with the Canvas playhead.

◆ **Button bar:** The Timeline button bar has two buttons that are displayed by default, but you can add other buttons and customize to your taste. See "Customizing Final Cut Express" in Chapter 3.

  ◆ **Linked Selection control:** The Linked Selection indicator controls whether linked selection is active or disabled. Note: This control toggles the Linked Selection feature, not Link/Unlink. One click on this tiny icon does not permanently unlink the linked clips in your sequence. You typically disable linked selection to select just the audio or video track of a linked AV clip—to adjust a split edit in a sync sequence, for example.

  ◆ **Snapping control:** Click to toggle snapping on and off.

ANATOMY OF THE TIMELINE

Timeline track controls (Figure 10.26)

◆ **Track Visibility control:** Click to make a track invisible. When the track is invisible, the contents remain in the Timeline but are not played or rendered with the sequence. Invisible tracks appear dimmed in the Timeline. Caution: Video render files can be lost if the track is made invisible.

◆ **Lock Track control:** Lock a track to prevent any changes to its contents. Locked tracks are crosshatched in the Timeline.

◆ **Auto Select control:** Use sequence In and Out points to define a selected area; then disable any tracks you want to exclude from your selection. You can cut, copy, search, delete, or ripple delete an auto-selected area. You can also apply copies of a filter to all the clips in an auto-selected area in a single operation.

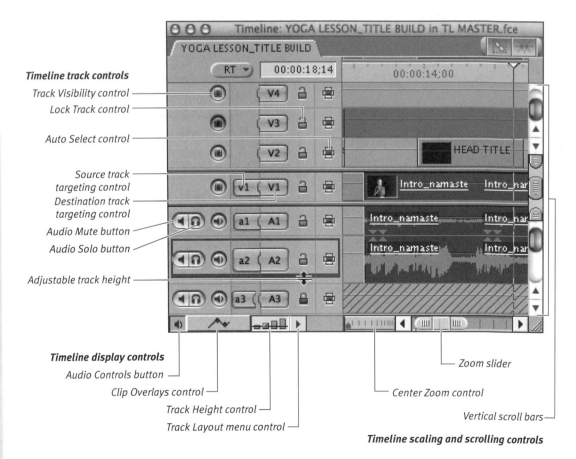

Figure 10.26 Display and Track controls in the Timeline.

ANATOMY OF THE TIMELINE

◆ **Source and Destination controls for targeting tracks:** Set the Source control to specify which source track is assigned to a destination track and whether the track is enabled to receive a source clip. The Destination control identifies the track. You can target one video target track plus one audio target track for each audio track in the source clip.

◆ **Audio Solo button:** Click to mute playback of any other audio tracks, except those tracks where Solo is enabled.

◆ **Audio Mute button:** Click to mute a track's audio playback.

◆ **Adjustable track height:** Drag the lower border of any individual track to adjust its height.

Timeline display controls (Figure 10.26)

◆ **Audio Controls button:** Click to toggle the display of Mute and Solo buttons. Controls are hidden by default.

◆ **Clip Overlays control:** Click to toggle the display of Audio Level line graphs over audio clips and Opacity Level line graphs in video clips.

◆ **Track Height control:** Click to switch among the four track display sizes in the Timeline.

◆ **Track Layout menu control:** Click the triangle to display a pop-up menu containing Timeline display options and to access saved custom track layouts.

Timeline scaling and scrolling controls (Figure 10.26)

◆ **Center Zoom control:** Click to jump between different time scale views.

◆ **Zoom slider:** Use this slider to scroll through your sequence and to adjust the time scale of your view.

◆ **Vertical scroll bars:** This two-part scroll bar allows the video and audio tracks to scroll independently. Adjust the thumb tabs between the scroll controls to create a static area in the center of the Timeline.

Clip controls and displays (Figure 10.27)

- **Link indicators:** Linked clips are displayed in the Timeline with their names underlined. When a linked clip is selected, moved, or trimmed, items linked to it are affected in the same way. Linked selections can be switched on and off as a sequence preference.

- **Out-of-Sync indicators:** This display indicates the number of frames by which a clip's video and audio tracks are out of sync.

- **Clips:** You can display clips as solid bars or as video frames. Clips that have been disabled appear dimmed in the Timeline. Clips on locked tracks are crosshatched in the Timeline. Clips with a speed change applied display the current speed setting.

- **Stereo Pair indicators:** These indicators appear as two triangles. These two audio clips are linked as a stereo pair.

- **Item Level Render Status indicator:** Audio clips that require rendering display this render status indicator. The indicator's color coding is the same as the render indicators above the Timeline ruler. Audio clips rendered at item level can be moved or edited without losing their render files.

- **Through edit indicator:** This indicates an edit point joining two clips with the same reel number and contiguous timecode (such as a clip divided in two with the Razor Blade tool).

- **Transition:** An effect applied at the edit point between two clips. See Chapter 13, "Creating Transitions."

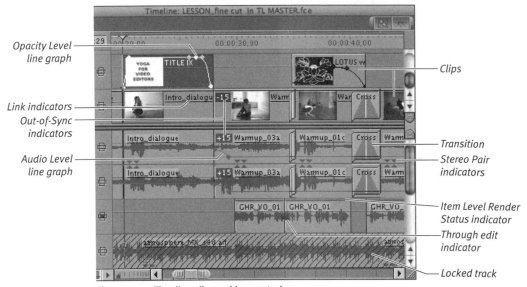

Figure 10.27 Timeline clip marking controls.

Table 10.1

Color Coding in the Timeline

COLOR	ITEM
Purple	Video sequences
Cyan	Video clips
Aquamarine	Video graphics
Green	Audio clips
Light green	Audio sequences
White	Offline video or audio clips

- **Locked track:** A track whose contents cannot be moved or edited.

- **Opacity Level line graph:** Adjust and apply keyframes to this editable overlay to set the opacity level of a video clip.

- **Audio Level line graph:** Adjust and apply keyframes to this editable overlay to set the level of an audio clip.

Color coding in the Timeline

Final Cut Express uses a color-coding system to identify the various clip and sequence types found in the Timeline. **Table 10.1** lists the file types and their colors.

Customizing Timeline Display Options

Every sequence is different, which is why you can customize Timeline display options for each one—perhaps you don't need to see thumbnails in a complicated sequence, or maybe it's easier to edit a short montage using larger tracks. These display settings are modified in the Sequence Settings window. Your custom display settings will apply only to the sequence that's open on the top tab of the Timeline; if you want the same appearance every time you create a new sequence, you can specify your preferred Timeline display setup on the Timeline Options tab of the User Preferences window. This section details your choices for the Timeline display options you're most likely to adjust often; for complete preferences setting details, see "Customizing the Timeline Display" in Chapter 3.

To set clip display mode on video tracks for the current sequence:

1. Make the Timeline active; then choose Sequence > Settings; or press Command-0 (zero).

2. When the Sequence Settings window appears, click the Timeline Options tab.

3. From the Thumbnail Display pop-up menu, select from three thumbnail display options (**Figure 10.28**):

   ◆ Name displays the name of the clip with no thumbnail images.

   ◆ Name Plus Thumbnail displays the first frame of every clip as a thumbnail image and then the name of the clip.

   ◆ Filmstrip displays as many successive thumbnail images as possible for the current zoom level of the Timeline.

4. Click OK.

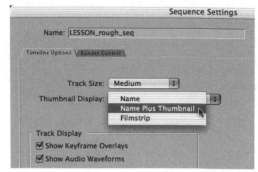

Figure 10.28 Select a name display option from the Thumbnail Display pop-up menu.

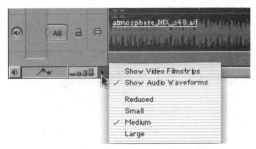

Figure 10.29 The Track Layout menu speeds access to frequently used display options.

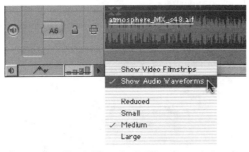

Figure 10.30 Check Show Audio Waveforms to toggle the display of waveforms in the Timeline.

Figure 10.31 Select from the four track display sizes by clicking one of the icons in the Track Height control.

To show or hide audio waveforms for the current sequence:

◆ Click the triangle next to the Track Height display to open the Track Layout pop-up menu (**Figure 10.29**); then select Show Audio Waveforms to toggle the display of waveforms in the Timeline (**Figure 10.30**).

✔ Tip

■ The Timeline's audio waveform display is really useful for tweaking your audio edits, but Timeline display performance suffers when waveforms are visible. If you want to quickly look at the waveforms without taking a trip to the Track Layout pop-up menu, press Command-Option-W.

To set the track display size:

Do one of the following:

◆ Click one of the four icons in the Track Height control (**Figure 10.31**).

◆ Press Shift-T to toggle through the four track display sizes.

◆ Select a track display size from the Track Layout pop-up menu.

To resize track height:

Do any of the following:

◆ In the Timeline control area, drag the upper boundary of a single video track or the lower boundary of an audio track (**Figures 10.32** and **10.33**).

◆ Hold down the Shift key while dragging to resize all video and all audio Timeline tracks.

◆ Hold down the Option key while dragging to resize all the video or all the audio Timeline tracks.

◆ Click a Track Height control to reset all the Timeline tracks to one of the four default display settings.

✔ Tip

■ If you hold down the Option key while clicking a Track Height control, you can resize your variously sized Timeline tracks relative to one of the four default display settings.

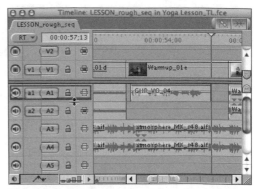

Figure 10.32 Drag the lower boundary of an individual Timeline audio track.

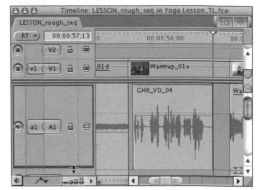

Figure 10.33 The audio track resized. Stretching the height of the waveform display makes it much easier to cut dialogue tracks right in the Timeline.

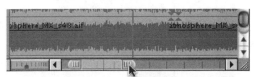

Figure 10.34 Drag a thumb control of the Zoom slider to adjust the scale of your Timeline view.

Figure 10.35 Click the Zoom control to jump to a new time scale. This control keeps the playhead or selected clip centered in view as you change zoom levels.

Timeline scaling and scrolling

Final Cut Express has state-of-the-art zoom features and scroll bars. The time scale in the Timeline is continuously variable; you can transition smoothly from viewing several minutes of your sequence down to a single frame. The horizontal scroll bar—the Zoom slider—is a combination zoom and scroll control. The Zoom control is handy—you can jump to any time scale with a single mouse click.

The vertical scroll bar separating the video and audio tracks allows you to set a static area in the center of the Timeline window, so your base tracks are always in view.

To adjust the time scale of the Timeline display:

Do one of the following:

◆ Click either thumb control and drag it to adjust the time scale, keeping the selected clip (or the playhead, if no clip is selected) centered in the Timeline as it scales (**Figure 10.34**). (The thumb controls are the ribbed-looking ends of the Zoom slider.)

◆ Shift-click and drag a thumb control to lock the position of the thumb control on the other end of the Zoom slider and to make the zoom adjustment only to the side you're dragging.

◆ Click the Zoom control to the left of the Zoom slider to jump to a different time scale (**Figure 10.35**). This Zoom control keeps the playhead or selected clip centered in view as you change zoom levels.

To zoom the view of the Timeline:

1. From the Tool palette, select the Zoom In or the Zoom Out tool (**Figure 10.36**); or press Z.

2. *Do one of the following:*

   ◆ Click in the Timeline or drag a marquee around the section you want to display (**Figure 10.37**).

   ◆ Use a keyboard shortcut. (See Appendix B for a complete list of shortcuts.)

   ◆ Choose View > Zoom In (or Zoom Out).

✔ Tips

■ When the Timeline is zoomed in or out to the maximum, the plus sign (+) or minus sign (–) disappears from the Zoom tool's pointer.

■ Pressing Option while using the Zoom In tool toggles the tool to Zoom Out.

Figure 10.36 Click the Zoom In tool to select it from the Tool palette.

Figure 10.37 Drag a marquee around the section you want to zoom in on.

Best Zoom Shortcuts

Final Cut Express has a jillion ways to zoom and scroll program windows. Which shortcuts are most useful in the Timeline?

◆ **Option-+ (plus) / Option- – (minus):** This keyboard combo zooms the Timeline even if the Canvas is currently selected, and it keeps the selected clip (or the playhead, if no clip is selected) centered in the Timeline as it scales. This shortcut is the best way to zoom in and out of the Timeline.

◆ **Command-+ (plus) / Command- – (minus):** This shortcut works like Option-plus and Option-minus, but it zooms the selected program window.

◆ **Shift-Z:** When the Timeline is selected, this key combination adjusts the time scale to fit the entire sequence in the Timeline window.

◆ **Shift-Page Up / Shift-Page Down:** This shortcut scrolls the Timeline one full length of the Timeline window at the current scale.

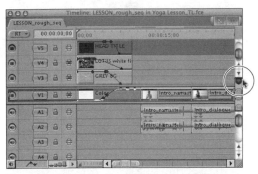

Figure 10.38 Drag the thumb tab up the scroll bar to create a static display area for a video track in the Timeline.

Figure 10.39 Drag the thumb tab down the scroll bar to create a static display area for an audio track in the Timeline.

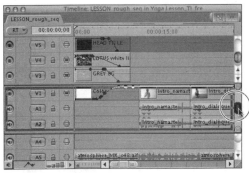

Figure 10.40 Use the center tab in the scroll bar to move the static display area up or down the Timeline display.

To scroll through your sequence:

◆ Drag the Zoom slider across the scroll bar.

To set up the vertical scroll bars:

1. In the Timeline, click and hold the uppermost thumb tab near the center of the vertical scroll bar. Drag the thumb tab up the scroll bar to create a static area for as many video tracks as you want to keep in constant view (**Figure 10.38**).

   You can use the upper scroll bar to scroll through higher video tracks in the upper portion of the Timeline.

2. Click and hold the lowest thumb tab in the vertical scroll bar. Drag the thumb tab down the scroll bar, creating a static area for as many audio tracks as you want to keep in constant view (**Figure 10.39**).

   You can use the lower scroll bar to scroll through additional audio tracks in the lower portion of the Timeline window.

3. Once you have set up your static view area, use the center tab on the scroll bar to move the static area up or down in the window (**Figure 10.40**).

CUSTOMIZING TIMELINE DISPLAY OPTIONS

Navigating in the Timeline

Many of the tasks described here can be accomplished with the help of keyboard shortcuts. Final Cut Express has an army of key commands; many professional editors prefer a keyboard-intensive working style. This section demonstrates some other ways to approach the Timeline interface because, frankly, keystrokes don't make good illustrations. Check out the keyboard shortcuts in Appendix B. Before you flip to the back of the book, though, consider the alternatives in this section. You keyboard diehards might find something here you actually like.

Figure 10.41 Click a point in the Timeline ruler to jump the playhead to that location.

✔ Tip

■ You can use the playhead's locator line to help identify the exact timecode location of an item way down at the bottom of the Timeline window. Set the playhead's locator line on the point you want to identify, and the Current Timecode display will give you its exact timecode location.

Positioning the playhead in a sequence

The playhead in the Timeline can be positioned by the same methods as those used for the Canvas and the Viewer playheads.

The playhead sits on the Timeline ruler and has a vertical locator line that extends down through the Timeline track display.

To scrub through a sequence in the Timeline:

◆ Drag the playhead along the Timeline ruler.

To jump the playhead to a new location:

◆ Click the location on the Timeline ruler to move the playhead to that location (**Figure 10.41**).

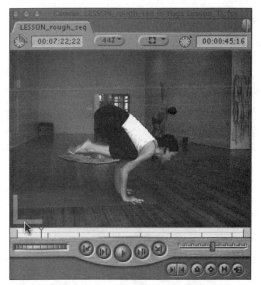

Figure 10.42 An L-shaped icon in the lower left of the Canvas indicates the first frame of a clip after an edit point.

To jump the playhead from edit to edit:

Do one of the following:

◆ Press the Up Arrow key (for the previous edit) or the Down Arrow key (for the next edit).

◆ Press ; (semicolon) for the previous edit or ' (apostrophe) for the next edit. (These are the most convenient alternative if you use J-K-L keys for navigation.)

◆ In the Canvas, click the Previous Edit button or the Next Edit button.

◆ Choose Mark > Previous (or Next) > Edit.

◆ Press Option-E (for the previous edit) or Shift-E (for the next edit).

◆ Press Home to jump to the beginning of the sequence.

◆ Press End to jump to the end of the sequence.

The playhead jumps to the first frame of the clip. If you've enabled Show Overlays on the View menu, an L-shaped icon appears in the lower left or right of the Canvas window, indicating that you are on the first or last frame of the sequence clip (**Figure 10.42**).

NAVIGATING IN THE TIMELINE

Navigating with timecode in the Timeline

Just as in the Viewer, using timecode values to position the playhead in the Timeline and the Canvas will result in frame-accurate positioning. Final Cut Express's timecode input function is very flexible (see "FCE Protocol: Entering Timecode Numbers" in Chapter 8 for protocol and entry shortcuts).

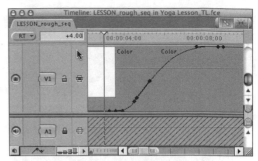

Figure 10.43 Type +4.00 to move the playhead 4 seconds later in the sequence.

To navigate using timecode values:

1. Start in the Timeline. Make sure all clips are deselected, or you'll move the selected clip and not the playhead.

2. Enter a new timecode number, or use the shorthand methods noted in Chapter 8. You don't need to click in the field to begin entering a new timecode; just type the numbers (**Figure 10.43**).

3. Press Enter.

    The playhead moves to the new timecode value, and the new timecode position appears in the Current Timecode field at the upper left of the Timeline (**Figure 10.44**).

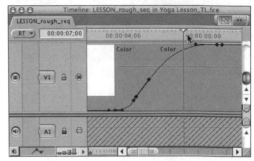

Figure 10.44 The playhead is repositioned 4 seconds later in the sequence.

✔ Tip

- Deselecting everything in the Timeline can be tricky—unless you know the keyboard shortcut. Press Shift-Command-A and you're completely deselected.

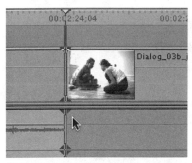

Figure 10.45 The Timeline with snapping turned on. The playhead's locator line displays small triangles to show that it has snapped to an edit.

Figure 10.46 You can activate Timeline snapping by clicking the Snapping control on the right side of the Timeline. The control turns green when snapping is enabled.

Figure 10.47 Snapping a clip to an edit point. You can toggle Timeline snapping even in mid-edit by pressing N at any time.

About snapping in the Timeline

Snapping is an interface state that makes certain points in the Timeline "sticky." With snapping turned on, the edges of clips will snap together, or a clip will snap to an edit point on an adjacent track when dragged close to it. The playhead snaps to edits, clip and sequence markers, and keyframes (if displayed) on all visible tracks. If you drag the playhead across the Timeline ruler, it snaps to items in the Timeline when it encounters them. Small triangles flanking the playhead locator line appear above or below the edit, marker, or keyframe, showing you what the playhead has snapped to (**Figure 10.45**).

To turn snapping on or off:

Do one of the following:

◆ Choose View > Snapping.

◆ Click the Snapping control located in the upper-right corner of the Timeline window (**Figure 10.46**).

To toggle snapping on or off on the fly:

◆ Press N; then drag the playhead, or your selected clip, to the new location (**Figure 10.47**).

Snapping remains in the toggled state until you press the N key again. Snapping can be toggled at any time, even in mid-edit.

✔ Tip

■ Use the "gear-down dragging" option to make precision adjustments to clips, levels, or edits in the Timeline—hold down the Command key while dragging an item.

NAVIGATING IN THE TIMELINE

Using markers in the Timeline and the Canvas

Final Cut Express has two types of markers (**Figure 10.48**):

◆ Sequence markers appear on the Timeline ruler.

◆ Clip markers appear on individual clips in the Timeline.

If you open a Timeline clip in the Viewer, the clip markers appear in the Viewer Scrubber bar.

You can learn more about working with markers in Chapter 8, "Working with Clips in the Viewer."

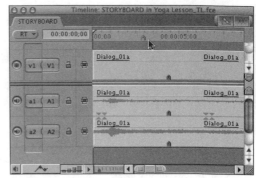

Figure 10.48 Sequence markers appear on the Timeline's ruler; sequence marker data is stored with the sequence. Clip markers appear on individual clips, and clip marker information is stored with the clip.

To set a sequence marker:

1. In the Timeline, position the playhead at the point where you want to set the marker. Make sure no clips are selected at the playhead's location.

2. Press M.

   A sequence marker appears in the Canvas scrubber and on the Timeline ruler. Press M a second time to open the Edit Marker dialog box.

✔ Tips

■ You can set a sequence marker only if no clips are selected at the playhead position in the Timeline. With a selected Timeline clip under the playhead, your marker will be set as a clip marker on that clip.

■ You can delete sequence markers only if no clips are selected in the Timeline.

■ Any two adjacent sequence markers can be used to set sequence In and Out points. Just position your Timeline playhead anywhere between the two markers you want to use; then choose Mark > Mark to Markers, or press Control-A.

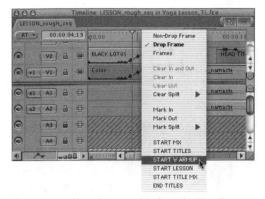

Figure 10.49 Choosing a marker from the Timeline ruler's shortcut menu.

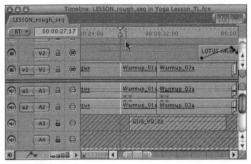

Figure 10.50 Selecting the marker jumps the playhead to that marker's location.

To position the playhead on a specific sequence marker:

◆ Control-click the Timeline ruler; then choose a marker from the list of sequence markers in the shortcut menu (**Figure 10.49**).

The playhead jumps to the selected marker's position (**Figure 10.50**).

To jump the playhead to the next or the previous sequence marker:

Do one of the following:

◆ Choose Mark > Previous (or Next) > Marker.

◆ Press Option-M for the previous marker.

◆ Press Shift-M for the next marker.

These are the same commands you use to locate clip markers in the Viewer; when you use them in the Canvas or the Timeline, FCE looks for sequence markers only, unless you have selected a Timeline clip. With a Timeline clip selected, these commands will locate both clip and sequence markers in the selected clip.

To position the playhead on a specific Timeline clip marker:

◆ In the Timeline, Control-click the clip; then choose a marker from the list of clip markers in the shortcut menu (**Figure 10.51**).

The playhead jumps to the selected marker's position.

✔ Tip

■ Say you have a specific phrase in the middle of a narration track that you'd like to align with an action in your video track. You can place a clip marker in the audio track and a sequence marker in the video clip at a key point and then grab the audio clip by its marker and drag it to align it to your video clip marker (**Figure 10.52**). This procedure works best with snapping enabled.

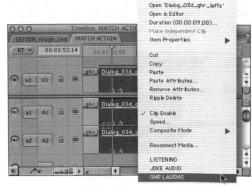

Figure 10.51 Selecting a clip marker from a Timeline clip's shortcut menu jumps the playhead to that marker's location.

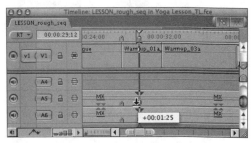

Figure 10.52 You can grab a Timeline clip by its marker and drag it to align it to another marker or to an edit point.

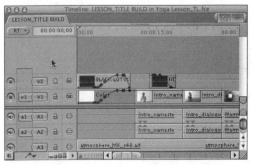

Figure 10.53 A sequence in the Timeline. Note the open space above the last video track.

Figure 10.54 Adding new video tracks to the sequence. The location specified is after the last track.

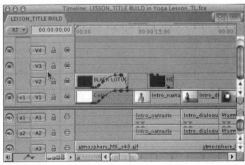

Figure 10.55 Two new video tracks (V3 and V4) have been added at the specified location above V2.

Working with Timeline Tracks

Editing operations in Final Cut Express frequently involve configuring tracks. Timeline tracks can be locked, unlocked, targeted, added, deleted, and made visible or invisible. There is a difference between tracks and the contents of tracks. The procedures described in this section affect whole tracks. To learn about editing procedures that affect individual sequence clips, edit points, and keyframes, see "Working with Items in the Timeline" later in this chapter.

To add tracks to a sequence:

1. Open the sequence in the Timeline (**Figure 10.53**).

2. Choose Sequence > Insert Tracks.

3. In the Insert Tracks dialog box, select the appropriate check box if the Insert field is inactive; then enter the number of new video or audio tracks you want to add. Final Cut Express supports up to 99 tracks for video and 99 tracks for audio.

4. Select from options for inserting tracks:
   ◆ Choose Before Base Track to insert your tracks before the first track in the Timeline.
   ◆ Choose After Last Track to insert your tracks after the last track in the Timeline (**Figure 10.54**).

5. Click OK to insert the tracks.
   The new tracks are added at the specified location (**Figure 10.55**).

To add a track to a sequence quickly:

Do one of the following:

◆ Drag a clip to the area above the top video track or below the bottom audio track (**Figure 10.56**).

A new track will be added to the sequence automatically (**Figure 10.57**).

◆ Control-click anywhere on the track header; then choose Add Track from the shortcut menu.

To delete a single track from a sequence:

◆ Control-click anywhere on the track header; then choose Delete Track from the shortcut menu (**Figure 10.58**).

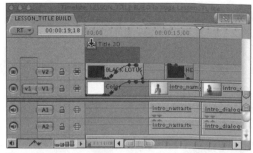

Figure 10.56 Drag and drop a clip in the area above the top video track.

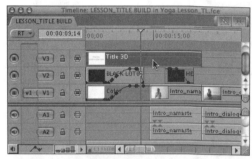

Figure 10.57 A new track is created automatically, and the clip is added to the sequence.

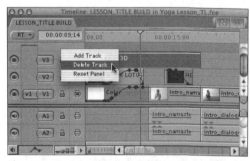

Figure 10.58 In the Timeline, delete a track by Control-clicking the track's header and then choosing Delete Track from the shortcut menu.

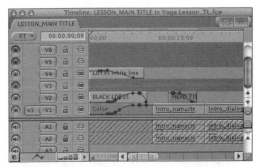

Figure 10.59 Open the sequence in the Timeline; then choose Sequence > Delete Tracks.

Figure 10.60 Click the appropriate check box to specify the track type you're deleting.

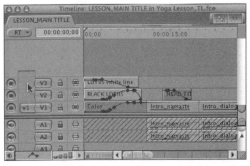

Figure 10.61 All the empty tracks are deleted from the sequence, and the remaining tracks are renumbered.

To delete empty tracks from a sequence:

1. Open the sequence in the Timeline (**Figure 10.59**).

2. Choose Sequence > Delete Tracks.

3. In the Delete Tracks dialog box, select from the options for deleting tracks:

   ◆ Click the Video Tracks and/or Audio Tracks check boxes to select track types.

   ◆ Choose All Empty Tracks to delete every empty track in the Timeline (**Figure 10.60**).

   ◆ Choose All Empty Tracks at End of Sequence to delete all empty tracks above (or below) the highest-numbered track used in the Timeline.

4. Click OK to delete the tracks.

   The selected tracks are deleted from the sequence; remaining tracks are renumbered consecutively (**Figure 10.61**).

To lock a Timeline track:

Do one of the following:

◆ In the Timeline, click the Track Lock control on the left side of the track. Click again to unlock the track (**Figure 10.62**).

◆ To lock a video track, press F4 plus the track number of the track you are locking.

◆ To lock an audio track, press F5 plus the track number of the track you are locking.

To lock all Timeline video tracks:

◆ To lock all video tracks in the sequence, press Shift-F4.

To lock all Timeline audio tracks:

◆ To lock all audio tracks in the sequence, press Shift-F5.

✔ Tip

■ Option-click a Track Lock control to toggle locking on all other audio or video tracks except the selected track.

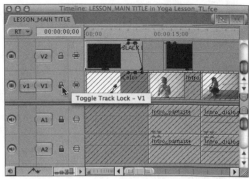

Figure 10.62 Lock a Timeline track by clicking the Track Lock control. Click again to unlock the track.

FCE Protocol: Lock vs. Target

One of the tasks when learning a new program is getting in sync with the logic behind the program design. If you are coming to Final Cut Express from another editing system, you'll probably notice a few things that FCE does differently. Understanding the difference between locking and targeting is important to your editing happiness, so let's get it straight.

Locking a track keeps it out of trouble. So unless you're working on a particular track, you might as well keep it locked so that your editing operations don't have unforeseen consequences, like trimming or moving tracks that are stacked above or below the base tracks, out of your Timeline view (spooky music here). You have to take the responsibility for locking tracks because FCE defaults to unlocked tracks (unlike many other editing systems, which disable tracks by default until you enable them).

Here are the keyboard shortcuts for locking tracks:

◆ Shift-F4 locks all video tracks.

◆ F4 plus the track number locks that video track.

◆ Shift-F5 locks all audio tracks.

◆ F5 plus the track number locks that audio track.

Lock 'em. Just do it. You're welcome.

Even if you've selected a specific edit on one track with the Selection tool, any unlocked track is capable of responding to changes you make to that edit. If you have locked all the tracks that you don't want cut or moved, this capability is a great thing. For example, you can make multitrack cuts, moves, and lifts to dialogue tracks or multicamera sync setups and leave your locked music track right where it is.

Target track controls are a scheme for mapping each source clip to its proper Timeline track. Even though you don't always need to specify a target track to perform an edit, it's a good habit to check your target assignments whenever you perform an edit.

FCE also uses targeting as a way to specify the track when you perform a specific operation. For example, you target a track when you are getting ready to delete it.

Mapping Timeline target track assignments

Final Cut Express's track-targeting scheme has been adapted to accommodate multi-channel audio source clips. Targeting Timeline tracks to receive source clips is a two-step process: First you map which source tracks are going to what destination tracks. Once your source clip's audio and video are mapped to the proper destination tracks, you have the option of disabling track targeting when you want to exclude selected source tracks from a pending edit. For information on simple track targeting, see "Specifying target tracks" in Chapter 9. To learn how to operate the Timeline's track-targeting controls and the protocols that govern target track behavior, read on.

Figure 10.63 Choose a new destination track from the Source control shortcut menu.

Figure 10.64 Drag a Source control to your desired destination track.

To map a source clip's destination tracks in the Timeline:

Do one of the following:

◆ Control-click the Source control; then choose a new destination track from the shortcut menu (**Figure 10.63**).

◆ Drag a Source control to your desired destination track (**Figure 10.64**).

◆ Control-click the Destination control of the track you want to target; then select a source track from the shortcut menu (**Figure 10.65**).

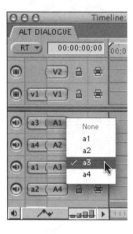

Figure 10.65 Select a source track from the Destination control shortcut menu.

✔ Tips

■ When you load a clip into the Viewer, the number of Source controls available in the Timeline automatically updates to match the number of tracks in that source clip.

■ You can click the Destination control on a track you want to target, and the closest Source control will be assigned. Video targeting is limited to one track, so this is a quick way to target any video track with a single click.

Figure 10.66 Choose Reset Panel from the track control area shortcut menu to reset the Timeline patch panel.

Figure 10.67 To disable a track, click the Source control to disconnect the target indicator of the track before you perform your edit.

To return destination track mapping to default settings:

◆ Control-click in the Timeline track control area; then choose Reset Panel from the shortcut menu (**Figure 10.66**).

✔ Tip

■ When you open that shortcut menu, you'll see a menu item that allows you to assign your audio tracks to audio output channels. Assigning output channels is independent of destination track mapping. Unless your FCE system has additional audio hardware that supports multiple audio output channels, you're limited to two channels of audio output: A1 and A2. For more information on FCE audio, see Chapter 12, "Audio Tools and Techniques."

To disable a targeted track:

◆ Click the Source control to disconnect the target indicator of the track before you perform your edit (**Figure 10.67**).

FCE Protocol: Target Tracks

◆ Once you specify target tracks, your edits will use the same target tracks until you change your target selection.

◆ If the target track is locked, it will not accept any additional audio or video.

WORKING WITH TIMELINE TRACKS

Making a Timeline track invisible

You can temporarily hide a track by making it invisible so that the contents of that track do not appear in the sequence when you play it back. This is useful when you tweak multilayered composited sequences.

You can also single out a track by making all the other tracks in the sequence invisible. This lets you focus on the contents of a single track temporarily. You can single out video and audio tracks independently.

Audio render files are protected from loss, but note that changing the visibility of a video track will cause a loss of any render files associated with the track. A warning dialog box appears when you attempt to change visibility on a track.

If you've invested a lot of rendering in a sequence, you can use a couple of workarounds to avoid re-rendering just because you turned a track off for a moment:

◆ You don't need to turn off the entire track. You can disable an individual clip by Control-clicking the clip in the Timeline and unchecking Clip Enable in the shortcut menu. If you are interested in a short section of your sequence, you can disable just the clips you want to hide, and you'll sacrifice only the render file for that clip, preserving your render files for the rest of the sequence.

◆ Undo and Redo might work. FCE has many layers of undo, and if you haven't been messing around too much in the interim, you can revert to the state before the render file loss.

Dragging Is Different

Final Cut Express has the common sense to allow drag-and-drop edits to override track target assignments. When you insert a clip into a sequence by dragging it to a specific track in the Timeline, the clip will be placed on that track even if you did not target it previously.

If you've disabled a targeted track by disconnecting its Source control, things work a little differently.

If you disable the *video* target and then drag an audio+video clip to an *audio* track, the video will be excluded from the edit. With disabled *audio* target tracks, dragging an audio+video clip to a *video* track will exclude the audio from the edit.

Drag audio into target-disabled audio tracks (or video to disabled video tracks), and the drag-and-drop edit *will* override your disabled target controls.

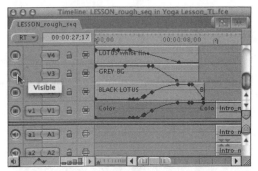

Figure 10.68 Click the Track Visibility control to make a track invisible.

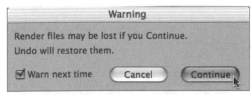

Figure 10.69 If making a track invisible will cause a loss of render files, you'll see this warning. You can turn off the warning on the Editing tab of User Preferences.

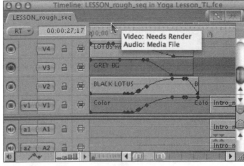

Figure 10.70 The invisible track will be excluded from playback, and the render status bar updates to remind you about your lost render files.

To make a track invisible:

1. In the Timeline, click the Track Visibility control at the far left of the track you want to affect (**Figure 10.68**).

2. If the sequence has been rendered, a dialog box will appear warning you about the impending loss of render files. If you don't need your render files, click Continue (**Figure 10.69**).

3. The track is made invisible. The render status bar updates to show which sections of your sequence have been altered and may require re-rendering (**Figure 10.70**).

✔ Tips

■ You can still edit invisible tracks. Lock invisible tracks if you don't want them to respond to edits.

■ Next time you build a sequence involving multiple takes or a multicamera shoot, try loading your synchronized clips into tracks above and below the base layer (V1 and A1 to A2), keeping the base layer clear to assemble your cut. You can turn on single tracks for viewing and then copy and paste your selections into the base layers.

To single out a track for visibility:

Do one of the following:

◆ Option-click the Track Visibility icon.

◆ Select items in the track; then choose Sequence > Solo Item(s) or press Control-S.

The contents of all the video or audio tracks except the selected one are dimmed in the Timeline and are hidden from view in the Canvas (**Figure 10.71**). All audio tracks except the selected track are muted.

✔ Tip

■ In addition to the Track Visibility control, each Timeline audio track has its own Solo and Mute buttons. These controls are hidden by default, but you can unearth them by clicking the Audio Controls button at the extreme lower left of the Timeline window (**Figure 10.72**).

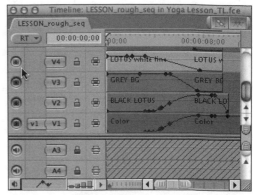

Figure 10.71 Video track V4 will play back alone. All other tracks are made invisible.

Figure 10.72 Click the Audio Controls button in the lower-left corner of the Timeline window to reveal the Solo and Mute buttons.

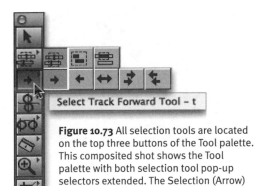

Select Track Forward Tool - t

Figure 10.73 All selection tools are located on the top three buttons of the Tool palette. This composited shot shows the Tool palette with both selection tool pop-up selectors extended. The Selection (Arrow) tool is at the top, marquee selection tools are second from the top, and track selection tools are third from the top.

Working with Items in the Timeline

This section covers Timeline editing procedures that affect individual sequence clips, edit points, and keyframes. Manipulating Timeline items requires extensive use of the tools in the Tool palette (**Figure 10.73**). Final Cut Express boasts some great selection tools but very few keyboard equivalents. If you haven't used the Tool palette yet, review "Anatomy of the Tool Palette" earlier in this chapter.

Selecting items in the Timeline

All the selection tasks described here use tools from the Tool palette.

Items you can select in the Timeline:

◆ **Clips,** including multiple clips or ranges of clips

◆ **Transitions,** which can be trimmed or deleted

◆ **Edits,** which can be modified in several ways

◆ **Gaps,** which can be closed or filled with media

◆ **Keyframes,** which can be moved when they're displayed over the Timeline clip

Items you cannot select in the Timeline:

◆ **Tracks:** You can't select a track, but you can select the contents of a track.

To select the entire contents of the Timeline:

◆ Press Command-A.

To deselect the entire contents of the Timeline:

◆ Press Shift-Command-A.

Selecting items with the track selection tools

The track selection tools offer a variety of ways to select the contents of one or more tracks. Don't forget: If you select an item that you've included in a linked selection, all the items involved in that linked selection will be affected by whatever operation you're about to perform.

✔ Tip

■ Deselect an individual Timeline item from a group selection by Command-clicking the item.

To select all items on a single track:

◆ From the Tool palette, choose the Select Track tool and click anywhere in the track.

To select all items on a single track forward or backward from the selected point:

1. From the Tool palette, choose the Select Track Forward or the Select Track Backward tool (**Figure 10.74**).

2. In the Timeline track, click the first clip to include in the selection.

    That entire clip is selected, plus all the items in front of or behind it (**Figure 10.75**).

Figure 10.74 Choose the Select Track Forward tool from the Tool palette.

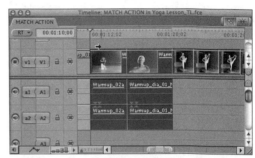

Figure 10.75 Using the Select Forward tool to click the first clip on any track to be included in the selection.

Figure 10.76 Choose the Select All Tracks Forward tool from the Tool palette to select clips on all tracks forward from the selection point.

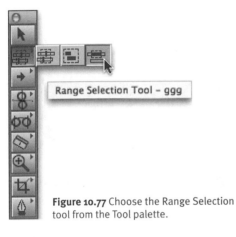

Figure 10.77 Choose the Range Selection tool from the Tool palette.

Figure 10.78 Drag the tool across a Timeline clip to define the range you want to select. You can select partial clips with this tool.

To select all items on all tracks forward or backward from the selected point:

1. From the Tool palette, choose the All Tracks Forward or the All Tracks Backward tool (**Figure 10.76**).

2. In the Timeline, click the first clip on any track that should be included in the selection.

   The contents of all tracks from that point forward or backward are selected.

✔ Tips

- The Track Forward and Track Backward tools select entire clips only; they do not make range selections.

- When one of the Select All Tracks tools is active, you can quickly switch to the corresponding Select Track tool by holding down the Shift key.

To select an entire clip:

1. From the Tool palette, choose the Selection tool; or press A.

2. In the Timeline, use the Selection tool to click the clip you want to select.

   The Canvas indicates the selection by displaying a cyan border around the video of the selected clip.

To select part of a clip or a larger selection including partial clips:

1. From the Tool palette, choose the Range Selection tool (**Figure 10.77**).

2. In the Timeline, click at the point in the clip where you want to start your selection and then drag a marquee around the range to select it (**Figure 10.78**).

   A two-up display in the Canvas shows the first and last frames of your selection.

WORKING WITH ITEMS IN THE TIMELINE

To select multiple whole clips:

1. From the Tool palette, choose the Group Selection tool (**Figure 10.79**).

2. In the Timeline, drag a marquee around all the clips you want to select. You don't need to include the entire clip; any clip you touch will be included in its entirety.

To select multiple noncontiguous clips:

1. From the Tool palette, choose the appropriate selection tool.

2. In the Timeline, Command-click the items you want to select (**Figure 10.80**). Command-click again on a selected item to deselect it.

To select all items between the In and Out points:

1. Set the sequence In and Out points in the Timeline or in the Canvas.

2. In the Timeline Track control area, click to enable the Auto Select controls on tracks you want to include in your selection.

3. Choose Mark > Select In to Out; or press Option-A.

   All items between the In and Out points on tracks with Auto Select enabled are selected.

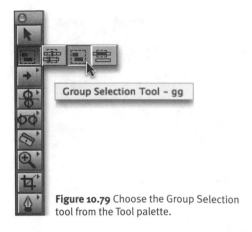

Figure 10.79 Choose the Group Selection tool from the Tool palette.

Figure 10.80 Command-click to select discontinuous clips in the Timeline or to deselect an individual clip from a group selection.

Figure 10.81 Click to enable the Auto Select controls on tracks you want to include in your selection. Enabled controls are dark.

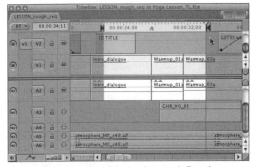

Figure 10.82 Set In and Out points to define the portion of the sequence you want to select.

To use Auto Select to select items between In and Out points:

1. In the Timeline Track control area, click to enable the Auto Select controls on tracks you want to include in your selection (**Figure 10.81**).

2. Set In and Out points to define the part of the sequence you want to select (**Figure 10.82**).

   You can cut, copy, delete, ripple delete, or search the auto-selected area. These operations will include only the selected sequence section (defined by In and Out points) and only tracks with Auto Select enabled.

✔ Tips

- Option-click a video track's Auto Select control to select just that track and deselect all other video tracks. The process works the same for audio tracks.

- Auto-selected areas are automatically highlighted, so it's easy to see what's included in your auto-selection.

- See "To use Auto Select to apply a filter to multiple clips" in Chapter 16 to learn another slick Auto Select move.

FCE Protocol: Auto Select

◆ When you paste cut or copied clips into a sequence, the clips will be pasted into the same tracks you cut them from *unless you make a change to the Auto Select controls after you cut (or copy) but before you paste.* If you do make that change, then the Auto Select controls determine the track destination of pasted tracks. Clips will be pasted starting at the lowest-numbered Auto Select–enabled track.

◆ Audio and video paste destinations are tracked separately. For example, if you enable a video Auto Select control between cutting and pasting but leave the audio Auto Select controls untouched, the video portion will be pasted according to your Auto Select setting, but the audio portion will be pasted into the same tracks you cut them from.

◆ The Tool palette's Selection, Range Selection, and Edit Selection tools can override the Auto Select feature. No need to click those teeny control buttons: select a selection tool and then just—select.

To set In and Out points around a selected part of a sequence:

1. From the Tool palette, choose the Range Selection tool. If your desired selection is composed of whole clips, use the Group Selection tool.

2. In the Timeline, drag a marquee around the range you want to select.

3. Choose Mark > Mark Selection; or press Shift-A.

    The bounds of the selection become the sequence In and Out points (**Figure 10.83**).

To set In and Out points at two markers:

1. Position the Timeline playhead anywhere between the two markers you want to use.

2. Choose Mark > Mark to Markers; or press Control-A.

    Sequence In and Out points are now set at the markers' Timeline locations.

Figure 10.83 The boundaries of your selection become the sequence In and Out points.

Figure 10.84 Select the sequence clips you want to link in the Timeline.

Linking clips

Linking clips is Final Cut Express's scheme for grouping clips. When clips are linked, any action performed on one clip affects the other clips as well. Check out the sidebar "FCE Protocol: Linked Clips" later in this chapter, for the rules governing linked clips and the operation of linked selections.

To link a group of unrelated clips:

1. In the Timeline, select the clips you want to link (**Figure 10.84**).

   You can select one video and up to 24 audio clips from different tracks.

2. Choose Modify > Link; or press Command-L.

   In the Timeline, an underline appears beneath the linked clips' names, indicating their linked status.

To permanently unlink a group of linked clips:

1. Select the linked items.

2. Choose Modify > Link; or press Command-L.

   In the Timeline, the underline beneath the linked clips' names disappears, indicating their unlinked status.

✔ Tip

- You can unlink a group of linked clips in a single operation, but linking operations must be performed one clip at a time.

Merged Clips and Linking

When you're editing sync video with production audio that has been recorded separately, you can sync up your audio and video takes in FCE and use the Modify > Link command to create linked audio+video clips. Select your newly linked Timeline clips and drag them back into the Browser to create merged clips. Merged clips will load into the Viewer as if they were a single clip. Audio and video will reference each other, keeping track of changes in sync, but original audio and video timecode data is preserved; it's stored with the merged clip.

Using linked selection

You can temporarily override the rules that govern a linked clip's selection. Editors frequently disable linked selection to select just the video (or audio) track of a linked clip, in order to create a *split edit* (that's an edit where a clip's audio and video tracks have different lengths).

You can disable linked selection for the entire sequence or for a single selection operation.

To turn linked selection on or off:

Do one of the following:

◆ Click the Linked Selection control on the right side of the Timeline window. (**Figure 10.85**).

◆ Choose Sequence > Linked Selection.

◆ Press Shift-L to toggle linked selection on and off.

To select an item without selecting any items that are linked to it:

◆ Hold down the Option key when you select the item.

Figure 10.85 Activate linked selection by clicking the Linked Selection control. The control is enabled when the shading moves to the top half of the button.

FCE Protocol: Linked Clips

Here's how Final Cut Express handles linked clips:

◆ Video and audio clips that originated from the same media file are linked automatically.

◆ You can set up multiple linked clip groups.

◆ You can switch linked selection on or off.

◆ When linked selection is turned on, FCE treats your linked items as a single entity for most operations.

◆ If you switch linked selection off, all your linked items will be treated as if they were unlinked, with the following exception: audio and video clips that were captured in sync continue to reference each other even when linked selection is disabled and will display out-of-sync indicators if moved out of sync with each other.

◆ Locking a track overrides a linked selection. If a linked item is on a locked track, it won't be modified, even if you modify an item it's linked to.

◆ Moving a linked clip's video to a higher track (for example, from track V1 to track V2) will automatically move the clip's audio to higher-numbered audio tracks (for example, from tracks A1 and A2 to tracks A3 and A4).

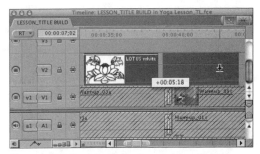

Figure 10.86 Dragging a clip to a new location. The pop-up indicator shows the offset from the clip's original location.

Figure 10.87 Dropping the clip performs an Overwrite edit in the new location.

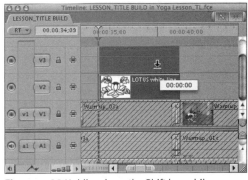

Figure 10.88 Holding down the Shift key while dragging the clip to a higher track.

Moving Timeline clips

As with most things in Final Cut Express, you have a choice of methods for moving clips within and between sequences. There are a variety of drag-and-drop methods, plus the timecode entry method, which offers greater precision but a little less flexibility.

To drag a clip to a new position:

1. In the Timeline, select the clip and drag it to a new position (**Figure 10.86**).

2. In the new position, *do one of the following:*

   ◆ Drop the clip to perform an Overwrite edit (**Figure 10.87**).

   ◆ Drop the clip while holding the Option key to perform an Insert edit.

To shift a clip to another track at the same timecode location:

1. In the Timeline, select the clip you want to move.

2. Hold down the Shift key while dragging the clip vertically to another track (**Figure 10.88**).

   The clip maintains its timecode position at the new track location.

To copy a clip to a new location:

1. In the Timeline, select the clip you want to move.

2. Hold down the Option key while dragging the clip to another location (**Figure 10.89**).

   A copy of the selected clip is edited into the new location.

✔ Tips

- You can make copies of sequence clips by dragging them from the Timeline into the Browser. Select and then drag multiple clips to make a copy of each clip in a single operation. Remember that this clip copy will include any changes you have made to the clip in the sequence.

- A quick way to make a Browser copy of every clip you've used in a sequence is to select the entire sequence in the Timeline (Command-A) and then drag the clips over to a Browser folder. Don't worry about wiping out your sequence—remember, you're making copies.

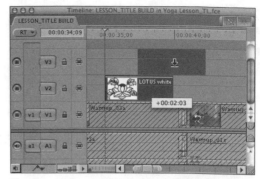

Figure 10.89 Press the Option key as you start to drag to copy the clip. Continue pressing Option as you drop the clip copy to perform an Insert edit; or release the key before you drop to perform an Overwrite edit.

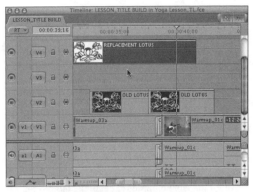

Figure 10.90 Select the clip you want to copy and paste.

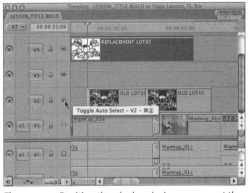

Figure 10.91 Position the playhead where you want the pasted clip to start; then target the track you want to paste into by ensuring that it's the lowest-numbered track with Auto Select enabled.

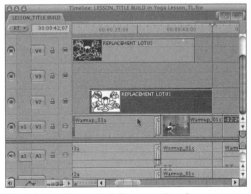

Figure 10.92 The pasted clip overwrites the contents of the destination track.

To copy and paste a clip into the Timeline:

1. Working in the Timeline, select the clip (**Figure 10.90**); or use the Group Selection tool from the Tool palette to select clips from multiple tracks.

2. Cut or copy the selected material to the clipboard, and then *do one of the following*:
   - ◆ To paste the material into the same tracks you cut or copied from, position the playhead where you want to paste the clip.
   - ◆ To assign different destination tracks for your pasted material, set the destination track by enabling its Auto Select control (and ensuring that all Auto Select controls on lower-numbered tracks are disabled), and then position the playhead where you want to paste the clip (**Figure 10.91**).

3. Choose Edit > Paste; or press Command-V.
   The pasted material overwrites the sequence clips, starting at the playhead location in the destination track and extending for the duration of the pasted material (**Figure 10.92**).

✔ Tip

- ■ Press Shift-V to insert-edit the pasted material in the new sequence location.

WORKING WITH ITEMS IN THE TIMELINE

299

To reposition an item in the Timeline by entering a timecode:

1. In the Timeline, select the clip you want to move.

2. Enter a new timecode number; or use the shorthand methods detailed in Chapter 8, "Working with Clips in the Viewer."

   As you type, a text entry window appears below the Timeline ruler (**Figure 10.93**).

3. Press Enter.

   The clip is repositioned, if there is space at the new timecode location.

   If you had selected an edit tool from the Tool palette before making the timecode entry, an edit of that type is performed in the direction indicated by the timecode.

✔ Tip

■ Moving clips around via timecode entry is wonderfully mouseless and precise, but there are limitations: When you're repositioning a clip by entering a timecode, FCE won't allow you move the clip so that it overwrites another clip. Your clip will move as far as possible without overwriting, and you'll see a "clip collision" error message.

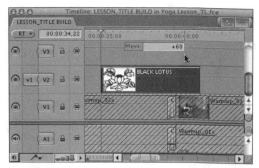

Figure 10.93 Type +60 and then press Enter to position the clip 60 frames (2 seconds) later in the sequence.

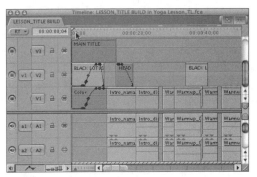

Figure 10.94 Pressing the Home key positions the playhead at the beginning of the sequence.

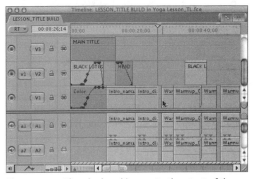

Figure 10.95 The playhead jumps to the start of the first gap found.

Finding and closing gaps

As you assemble a sequence, all that cutting and pasting and slipping and sliding may create gaps in your sequence tracks. Sometimes the gaps are too small to see in the Timeline, but a gap of even a single frame is easily detectable in Canvas playback.

This section contains a repertoire of techniques for detecting and closing gaps and explains FCE protocol for defining gaps.

To find gaps in a sequence:

1. Make the sequence active; then press the Home key to position the playhead at the beginning of the sequence (**Figure 10.94**).

2. Choose Mark > Next > Gap; or press Shift-G.

   The playhead moves to the beginning of the first gap found (**Figure 10.95**).

3. If you want to close the gap, use one of the procedures described in the next section, "To close a gap."

4. Repeat steps 2 and 3 until you reach the end of the sequence.

✔ Tip

■ Press Option-G to jump the playhead back to the previous gap.

FCE Protocol: Gaps and Track Gaps

Final Cut Express defines two classes of gaps: gaps and track gaps.

◆ A gap is any empty spot across all unlocked video or audio tracks.

◆ A track gap is any empty spot on an individual track in a sequence; if you have a gap on one track, but a clip bridges the gap on a higher or lower track, FCE defines that as a track gap.

Some gap-closing techniques, such as Ripple Delete, work only with gaps, not track gaps. To close track gaps, lock all other tracks, leaving the gapped tracks as the only unlocked tracks in your sequence.

To close a gap:

1. Make the sequence active; then position the playhead anywhere in the gap.

2. *Do one of the following:*

   ◆ Select the gap and press Delete.

   ◆ Control-click the gap; then select Close Gap from the shortcut menu (**Figure 10.96**).

   ◆ Choose Sequence > Close Gap.

   Clips to the right of the gap will shift left to close the gap. These clips adjust their timecode location to occur earlier, and the sequence duration may change (**Figure 10.97**).

Figure 10.96 Control-click the gap; then choose Close Gap from the shortcut menu.

Figure 10.97 Clips to the right of the gap shift left to close the gap.

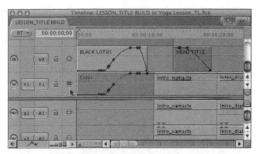

Figure 10.98 To select a track to search for track gaps, target the track and enable the Auto Select control.

Figure 10.99 The playhead jumps to the start of the first track gap found.

Figure 10.100 The Close Gap command is dimmed when a gap can't be closed because clips don't have space to shift back. Resizing one of the adjacent clips to fill the gap looks like a better option here.

To find track gaps in a Timeline track:

1. In the Timeline, target the track you want to search (**Figure 10.98**).

2. Press the Home key to position the playhead at the beginning of the sequence.

3. Choose Mark > Next > Track Gap.

   The playhead moves to the beginning of the first track gap found (**Figure 10.99**).

To close a track gap:

Do one of the following:

◆ Open the shortcut menu over the gap and choose Close Gap.

◆ Select the gap and press the Delete key.

◆ Position the playhead anywhere within the gap; then choose Sequence > Close Gap.

✔ Tip

■ Sometimes a gap can't be closed because clips don't have space to shift back. If the command can't be completed, the Close Gap command will appear dimmed (**Figure 10.100**). Try the track-locking technique discussed next.

To close a track gap without affecting other tracks in a sequence:

1. Press Shift-F4 to lock all video tracks in your sequence.

2. Press Shift-F5 to lock all audio tracks in your sequence.

3. Click the Track Lock control of the gapped track.

   Your selected track is now the only unlocked track in the sequence (**Figure 10.101**).

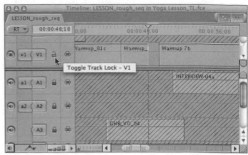

Figure 10.101 Locking every track but the gapped track allows you to close the gap by shifting material on the unlocked track only.

4. *Do one of the following:*
   - ◆ Select the gap and press Delete.
   - ◆ Control-click the gap; then select Close Gap from the shortcut menu (**Figure 10.102**).
   - ◆ Choose Sequence > Close Gap.

   Clips to the right of the gap will shift left to close the gap. These clips adjust their timecode locations to occur earlier, and the sequence duration may change (**Figure 10.103**).

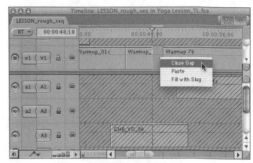

Figure 10.102 Control-click the gap; then choose Close Gap from the shortcut menu.

5. If you want to unlock your sequence tracks after closing the gap, press Shift-F4 and Shift-F5 again to toggle track locking off.

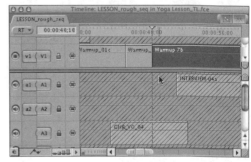

Figure 10.103 Clips to the right of the gap shift left to close the track gap. Clips on the locked tracks have not moved.

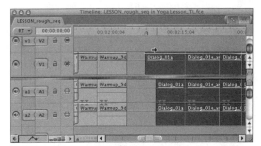

Figure 10.104 Use the Select Track Forward tool to click the first clip to the right of the track gap.

Figure 10.105 Drag the selected clips to the left until they snap to close the gap; then drop them as an Overwrite edit.

FCE Protocol: Deleting Items in the Timeline

You can delete items in the Timeline simply by selecting them and then pressing Delete. But if the Timeline window is active and you press Delete with no items selected in the Timeline, FCE protocol dictates that all material between the Timeline and Canvas In and Out points is deleted on all unlocked tracks.

Learn more about performing Delete edits in Chapter 9, "Basic Editing."

To close a track gap with the Select Forward tool:

1. Snapping must be on; if necessary, choose View > Snapping to turn it on.

2. From the Tool palette, choose the Select Track Forward tool; then click the first clip to the right of the track gap (**Figure 10.104**).

   The clips to the right of the sequence are selected, and the pointer changes to a four-headed arrow.

3. Drag the selected clips to the left until they snap to close the gap; then drop them as an Overwrite edit (**Figure 10.105**).

To close a gap by extending an adjacent clip (an Extend edit):

◆ In some cases, you may prefer to close a gap in a sequence by extending the duration of a clip that's adjacent to the gap. One advantage of an Extend edit is that all the clips in your sequence can stay put, and you won't develop sync problems. To learn how to perform an Extend edit, see Chapter 11, "Fine Cut: Trimming Edits."

✔ Tips

■ When you fine-tune gaps in sequences, take advantage of the Zoom tools to scale your view so you can see what you're doing. You may also find that turning on snapping simplifies selection and manipulation of gaps and track gaps.

■ Here's a quick way to read a gap's duration: Select the gap in the Timeline and then press Shift-A. The Mark Selection command sets sequence In and Out points, and your gap's duration appears in the Timecode Duration field in the Canvas. Wow—it actually takes longer to describe it than to do it.

Copying and pasting clip attributes

A clip's *attributes* comprise the settings applied to a particular media file in Final Cut Express. You can paste all the attributes of one clip onto another clip, or you can select and paste some of a clip's settings onto another clip without affecting other attributes. For example, you can apply just the filter settings from clip A to clip B without changing the video frames of clip B. Conversely, you can replace the video frames of clip B without disturbing the filters that have been applied to it by pasting only the video frames from another clip. If you just paste into a sequence without selecting a clip in the Timeline or the Canvas, the clip's media contents and selected attributes are included.

The Remove Attributes command offers an easy way to strip selected settings from a clip or to remove selected settings from multiple clips in a single operation.

To paste the attributes of a copied clip into another clip:

1. In the Timeline or the Browser, select a clip whose attributes you want to copy (**Figure 10.106**); then press Command-C to copy the clip to the clipboard.

2. Select the clip that will inherit the attributes; then choose Edit > Paste Attributes or press Option-V.

3. In the Paste Attributes dialog box, select the attributes that you want to transfer to the selected clip (**Figure 10.107**).

   ◆ **Scale Attribute Times:** Check this box to adjust the timing of the incoming keyframes to fit the duration of the clip inheriting the attributes. If this option is not selected, leftover keyframes will be cropped off the end.

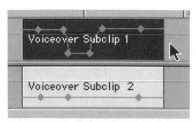

Figure 10.106 Select the clip whose attributes you want to copy; then press Command-C.

Figure 10.107 Selecting audio levels in the Paste Attributes dialog box.

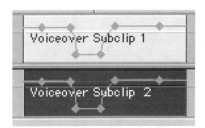

Figure 10.108 The audio levels from Voiceover Subclip 1 have been copied and pasted into Voiceover Subclip 2.

✔ Tip

- Pasting audio levels can be a quick way to add an audio element—say, another sound effects track—to a scene you have already mixed. You can "borrow" the mix levels from a track that has already been adjusted to match action and paste those levels onto your new effects track. You can apply the same idea to video compositing: paste the motion path from one video layer to another that you want to track the same path, or paste and then offset the timing of the motion path.

Video Attributes:

- ◆ **Content:** Paste the video frames only. If the receiving clip is a different length, incoming video frames are cropped or lengthened to match the duration of the receiving clip. The clip speed is not affected.

- ◆ **Basic Motion, Crop, Distort, Opacity, Drop Shadow, Motion Blur, and Filters:** You can pick and choose among these options to apply the parameter values and keyframes you have set for each attribute.

- ◆ **Speed:** Apply the same speed settings.

- ◆ **Clip Settings (Capture):** Paste all capture settings that are logged with a clip. (You can review these settings on the Clip Settings tab of the Capture window.)

Audio Attributes:

- ◆ **Content:** Paste the audio waveform only. If the receiving clip is a different length, the incoming audio file is cropped or lengthened to match the duration of the receiving clip. The clip speed is not affected.

- ◆ **Levels, Pan, and Filters:** Apply the parameter values and keyframes you have set for each attribute.

4. Click OK.

   The selected attributes are pasted into the receiving clip (**Figure 10.108**).

To remove attributes from a clip:

1. In the Timeline, select the clip or clips whose attributes you want to remove.

2. Choose Edit > Remove Attributes.

3. In the Remove Attributes dialog box, check the attributes you want to remove (**Figure 10.109**); then click OK.

Making multiclip adjustments

Use the Modify > Levels command to adjust multiclip selections:

◆ Use Modify > Levels to adjust levels for a group of audio clips.

◆ Use Modify > Opacity to adjust opacity levels for a group of video clips.

To adjust audio levels for a group of clips:

1. In the Timeline, select a group of audio clips whose levels you want to adjust (**Figure 10.110**).

2. Choose Modify > Levels.

3. In the Gain Adjust dialog box, *do one of the following:*

    ◆ Choose Relative from the pop-up menu; then use the slider to adjust each clip's volume relative to its current level by the dB value indicated next to the slider (**Figure 10.111**).

    ◆ Choose Absolute from the pop-up menu; then use the slider to set each clip's volume to the dB value indicated next to the slider.

4. Click OK.

✔ Tip

■ Use FCE's audio level meters to check your audio level adjustments. Choose Window > Audio Meters to display the meters.

Figure 10.109 Select the attributes you want to remove; then click OK.

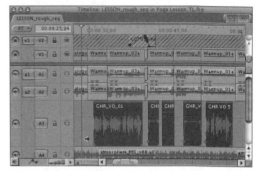

Figure 10.110 Selecting multiple audio clips with the Select Track Forward tool.

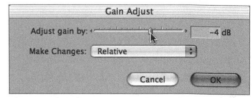

Figure 10.111 Adjusting the audio levels relative to their current levels.

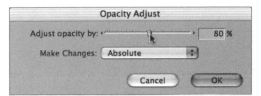

Figure 10.112 Setting opacity levels to 80 percent for all selected clips.

To adjust opacity levels on a group of clips:

1. In the Timeline, select just the video portion of a group of clips whose levels you want to adjust.

2. Choose Modify > Levels.

3. In the Opacity Adjust dialog box, *do one of the following:*

    ◆ Choose Relative from the pop-up menu; then use the slider to adjust each clip's opacity relative to its current level by the percentage value indicated next to the slider.

    ◆ Choose Absolute from the pop-up menu; then use the slider to set each clip's opacity to the percentage value indicated next to the slider (**Figure 10.112**).

4. Click OK.

Changing the playback speed of a clip

Changing the playback speed of a clip adjusts its duration by duplicating or skipping clip frames and creates either a slow-motion or a fast-motion effect. For example, if you start with a 1-minute clip and set the playback speed to 50 percent, Final Cut Express will duplicate each frame, doubling the clip length to 2 minutes. Your adjusted 2-minute clip will appear to play back at half speed. If you start with the same 1-minute clip and increase the playback speed to 200 percent, the adjusted clip will skip every other frame and appear to play back at double speed in 30 seconds. You can specify frame blending when modifying a clip's speed to smooth out the slow-motion or fast-motion effect.

✔ Tip

■ When a clip is simply too short to fit that gap in your montage, the Fit to Fill edit is a one-step solution that automatically speed-modifies the clip so it fills that gap perfectly. See "Fit to Fill edit" in Chapter 9.

To change the playback speed of a clip:

1. Select the clip in the Timeline (**Figure 10.113**).

2. Choose Modify > Speed; or press Command-J.

3. Choose from the options in the Speed dialog box (**Figure 10.114**):

   ◆ You can modify the clip speed by a percentage or specify a duration for the adjusted clip. Changing the clip speed or duration automatically adjusts the other value.

   ◆ The Reverse check box renders the clip's frames in reverse order; the adjusted clip plays in reverse.

   ◆ The Frame Blending option smoothes motion at slow or fast speeds.

4. Click OK.

   The adjusted duration of the modified clip will be calculated based on the clip's original In and Out points (**Figure 10.115**).

✔ Tip

■ Speed effects can be applied only to whole clips, but if you want to speed-modify only a portion of a clip, you can use the Time Remap feature, or use the Razor Blade tool to break out the portion of the clip that you want to process.

Figure 10.113 Select the clip in the Timeline.

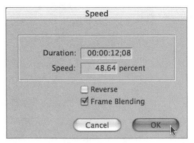

Figure 10.114 Modify your entire clip's speed by a percentage or specify a duration; then click OK.

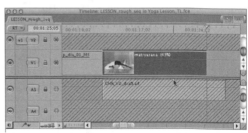

Figure 10.115 The size of the Timeline clip increases to reflect the duration change caused by modifying the playback speed, and the adjusted speed appears next to the clip's name.

Using offline clips

An offline clip is defined as a placeholder for an actual media file. An offline clip could be:

◆ Logged but not yet captured

◆ A stand-in for the actual media file, which has been moved or deleted

◆ A stand-in for media that is not yet available

You can treat offline clips just like regular clips: You can set In and Out points, add transitions and filters, rename the clips, and so on. Later, you can replace an offline clip by recapturing it or reconnecting to the original source media.

Final Cut Express is so advanced, you can edit media that doesn't even exist yet!

To create an offline clip:

◆ Choose File > New > Offline Clip.

An offline clip is inserted into the Browser.

See "Reconnecting Offline Files" in Chapter 4 for more information on offline clips.

WORKING WITH ITEMS IN THE TIMELINE

Working with keyframes in the Timeline

Final Cut Express has two types of keyframes:

◆ **Keyframe overlays** indicate clip opacity for video clips and volume level for audio clips. Keyframe overlays are displayed as line graphs right on top of the track display in the Timeline (**Figure 10.116**).

◆ **Motion effect keyframes** appear in the Canvas (or Viewer). You can view, add, or modify motion keyframes only when the window is in Image+Wireframe mode (**Figure 10.117**). Working with keyframes to create motion effects is covered in Chapter 15, "Motion."

For more information about using these keyframing tools, see "Working with Keyframes in the Timeline" in Chapter 14.

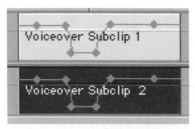

Figure 10.116 Keyframe overlays allow you to sculpt audio levels right in the Timeline.

Figure 10.117 Motion keyframes also appear on the Timeline clip's overlay.

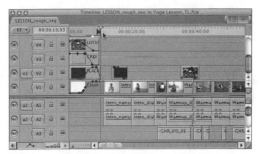

Figure 10.118 Position the playhead at the beginning of the section you want to search.

Searching for Items in the Timeline

The Final Cut Express search engine is built to search for other items beyond clips and sequences. Use FCE's Find command to search the Timeline for clip names, marker text, and clip timecodes. You can search for items forward or backward. You can also search for and close gaps in all tracks in a sequence or in individual tracks.

✔ Tip

■ This might be a good time to mention that when you place a clip in a sequence, the new sequence clip is a separate version from the one that stays in the Browser, even though the two clips may have the same name. So if you are searching for the sequence version of a clip, you need to search in that sequence.

To search for items in the sequence:

1. Open the sequence in the Timeline.

2. *Do one of the following:*

   ◆ To search the entire sequence, position the playhead at the start of the sequence.

   ◆ To search a selected portion of the sequence, set the sequence In and Out points to specify the search area; or position the playhead at the beginning of the section you want to search (**Figure 10.118**).

3. Choose Edit > Find; or press Command-F.

continues on next page

4. From the Search pop-up menu, choose the type of item to search for (**Figure 10.119**):

- ◆ **Names/Markers:** Search for the text in clip names, marker names, and marker comments.
- ◆ **Timecode Options:** Search for any source or auxiliary timecode in a clip.

5. From the Where pop-up menu, choose which tracks to search:

- ◆ **All Tracks:** Search all tracks in the sequence.
- ◆ **Auto Select Tracks:** Search only tracks with Auto Select controls enabled.
- ◆ **From In to Out:** Search between the sequence In and Out points on all tracks (**Figure 10.120**).

6. To perform the search, *do one of the following:*

- ◆ Click Find to find the item.
- ◆ Click Find All to find all occurrences of clips that match the search criteria (**Figure 10.121**).

Clips matching the search criteria are selected in the Timeline (**Figure 10.122**). If the search returns a marker, the playhead is positioned on the marker.

To cycle through items in the Timeline that match the criteria:

- ◆ Follow the search procedure outlined in the preceding steps; then press F3.

To search for an item backward from the position of the playhead:

- ◆ Follow the search procedure outlined in the preceding steps; then press Shift-F3.

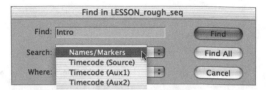

Figure 10.119 Specifying a search for clips or markers with "Intro" in their names.

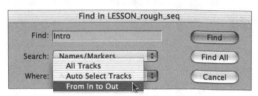

Figure 10.120 Specifying a search of the sequence from the sequence In to the sequence Out point.

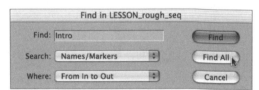

Figure 10.121 Clicking Find All causes FCE to highlight all clips in the sequence that match the search criteria.

Figure 10.122 Two clips whose names contain the phrase "Intro" are highlighted in the Timeline. Only the section between the sequence In and Out points has been searched.

FINE CUT: TRIMMING EDITS

11

What's the difference between performing an edit and trimming an edit? An edit adds new material to a sequence; a trim adjusts previously assembled sequence material. The development of nonlinear editing has expanded the repertoire of trim edit types. Some trim edit types (like Ripple and Roll) date back to the tape-to-tape days of video editing; others (like the Slide edit) could not have existed before the advent of nonlinear systems.

In this chapter, you'll learn about the types of trim edits available in Final Cut Express. Each can be performed in a variety of ways (with tools, with timecode entry, and with keystrokes) and in a few different locations (the Timeline, the Trim Edit window, and the Viewer), so you'll learn how and where you can perform each type. This chapter also introduces the Trim Edit window, a specialized work environment for making fine adjustments to your edits.

Note that when editors talk about performing certain types of edits, the edit type is used as a verb, as in "Roll that cut forward 30 frames." That's easier to say than "Perform a Roll edit on that edit point, which will move the edit point forward 30 frames." In the editing suite, time is money.

Types of Trimming Operations

Each trim edit type can solve a particular editing problem, so it's a good idea to become familiar with the whole palette—maybe even try them all in advance. (If you would like to review FCE's basic editing types, return to Chapter 9, "Basic Editing.")

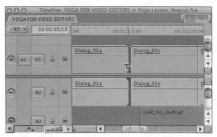

Figure 11.1 A Ripple Left edit, as performed in the Timeline.

- ◆ **Ripple:** A Ripple edit adjusts the length of one clip in a sequence by changing either the In or the Out point of that clip. A Ripple edit accommodates the change by rippling (or shifting) the timecode location of the clips that come after the adjusted edit, without affecting the clips' duration. Use a Ripple edit if you want to adjust the length of a clip in a sequence without losing sync or creating a gap. Locked tracks will not be rippled. For example, the Close Gap command in the Timeline performs a Ripple Delete edit.

  Figure 11.1 shows a Ripple Left edit, in contrast to **Figure 11.2**, which shows a Ripple Right edit. Note the differences in the pointer and in the selected edit points.

Figure 11.2 A Ripple Right edit, as performed in the Timeline.

- ◆ **Roll:** A Roll edit (**Figure 11.3**) adjusts the location of an edit point shared by two clips. A rolling edit makes the change by subtracting frames from clip A on one side of the edit to compensate for the frames added to clip B on the other side of the edit. The overall duration of the sequence remains unchanged, but the location of the edit in the sequence is changed.

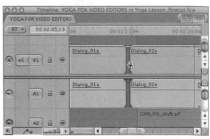

Figure 11.3 A Roll edit, as performed in the Timeline.

- ◆ **Slip:** A Slip edit (**Figure 11.4**) is an adjustment made within a single clip. When you slip a clip, you select a different part of that clip to include in the sequence, while maintaining the same clip duration and timecode location in the sequence. Surrounding clips are not affected, and the sequence duration does not change.

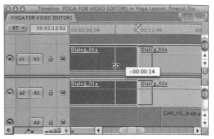

Figure 11.4 A Slip edit, as performed in the Timeline. The selected portion of the clip has shifted −14 frames.

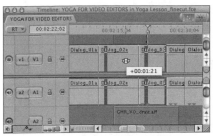

Figure 11.5 A Slide edit, as performed in the Timeline. The selected clip has slid 1 second, 21 frames later in the sequence.

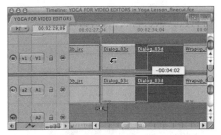

Figure 11.6 A Swap edit, as performed in the Timeline. The two clips will swap positions.

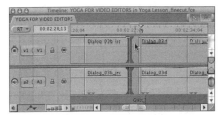

Figure 11.7 An Extend edit. Select the edit point of the clip you want to extend to the playhead position.

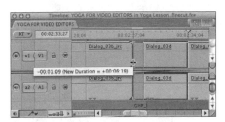

Figure 11.8 Resizing a clip in the Timeline. Drag an edit point with the Selection tool to adjust the clip's duration.

◆ **Slide:** A Slide edit (**Figure 11.5**) moves a single clip in relation to those before and after it, so that the durations of the clips on either side change, but the In and Out points of the clip you're sliding remain the same. The clips immediately adjacent to the sliding clip accommodate the change; the overall sequence duration does not change.

◆ **Swap:** A Swap edit (**Figure 11.6**) doesn't alter any sequence clips, but it does change the order in which the clips appear in the sequence. Perform a Swap edit in the Timeline by selecting a clip, dragging it to a new location, and placing it into the sequence using an Insert edit.

◆ **Extend:** An Extend edit (**Figure 11.7**) moves a selected edit point to the playhead position by extending the clip's duration, rolling over any gaps or clips that are encountered. You can extend an edit only to the maximum length of that clip's media. An Extend edit is a useful way to fill sequence gaps without affecting the sequence duration.

◆ **Resize:** The Selection (or Arrow) tool can be used to resize a clip in the Timeline by dragging an edit point (**Figure 11.8**). You can drag the edit point to create a gap (by making the duration of the clip smaller) or to cover an existing gap.

✔ Tip

■ Press the Command key to gear down the onscreen tools while performing fine adjustments to a trim. With the Command key engaged, your manipulation of the onscreen trim tools will result in much smaller adjustments to your edit points.

Selecting an Edit for Trimming

The first step in trimming an edit in the Trim Edit window or the Timeline is selecting the edit. If you use a trimming tool from the Tool palette to select the edit, you can select and define the type of trim to perform at the same time. You can select only one edit per track.

If an edit point you select for trimming has been linked to others, the edit points of the linked items are also selected. Any adjustments you make will be applied to all clips in the linked selection, so if you find that you can't trim an edit point, the conflict may be with one of the linked items. You can toggle linked selection off by holding down the Option key as you select the edit.

With snapping turned on, edit points will stick to markers, keyframes, the playhead, and edit points on other tracks. Snapping can simplify alignment of edits in the Timeline. To toggle snapping on the fly, press the N key while dragging edit points.

✔ Tips

■ Many trim operations will ripple all of your unlocked tracks as part of the trim process. If you don't want your tracks taking unplanned trips when you are trimming, lock all tracks except the ones you want to adjust.

■ If FCE refuses to execute a trim edit that would ripple your unlocked tracks backward, check to see if other tracks in your sequence contain clips that can't move back in time without bumping into other clips.

Tips on Tools

FCE's edit tools get a heavy workout when you transform your rough assembly into a fine cut. You can review the contents of the Tool palette's selection and edit tools in "Anatomy of the Tool Palette" in Chapter 10, but here are some other ideas for making efficient use of these tools:

◆ Use the keyboard shortcuts to call up an edit tool. See **Table 11.1** for a list of basic selection shortcuts. Check out Appendix B for more shortcuts.

◆ Once you've selected an edit tool, press U to cycle through the three principal trim types: Roll, Ripple Left, and Ripple Right.

◆ You can use the Ripple and Roll tools to directly select the edit you're adjusting. With one click, you've selected the edit and specified the edit type.

◆ After you've selected your first Timeline edit point, use the Up and Down Arrow keys to jump to your next or previous edit. FCE automatically selects each edit point as you jump to it.

◆ Pressing the Option key to override linked selection works on all edit tools, not just the Selection arrow.

◆ Pressing the Command key while dragging an edit tool on a selected edit in the Timeline will gear down the tool and allow you to make fine adjustments.

◆ Turn off snapping to make fine adjustments that don't align with an existing edit point, marker, or clip boundary.

◆ Turn on snapping to align an edit to another existing edit point or marker.

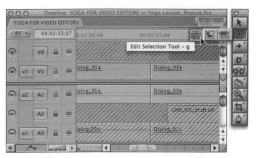

Figure 11.9 Choose the Edit Selection tool from the Tool palette. This tool is designed to detect and select edits only.

Table 11.1

Tool Selection Shortcuts

TOOL	SHORTCUT
Roll	R
Ripple	R+R
Slip	S
Slide	S+S
Razor Blade	B
Razor Blade All	B+B
Selection	A
Edit Selection	G

Quick Navigation Keys

Option and Shift modifier keys are used throughout FCE's keyboard shortcuts for navigation. Here's a set of keyboard short-cuts to help you motor through your sequence while you fine-tune your edit.

KEY	FUNCTION	SHIFT + KEY	OPTION + KEY
I	Set In	Go to In	Clear In
O	Set Out	Go to Out	Clear Out
M	Set Marker	Next Marker	Previous Marker
E	Extend Edit	Next Edit	Previous Edit
G		Next Gap	Previous Gap
K		Next Keyframe	Previous Keyframe

To select an edit in the Timeline:

Do one of the following:

◆ From the Tool palette, choose the Edit Selection tool (**Figure 11.9**); or press G. Then click an edit point in the Timeline. The Trim Edit window opens.

◆ From the Tool palette, choose the Selection tool; then click the edge of the clip in the Timeline. Double-click the edit if you want the Trim Edit window to open as well.

◆ From the Tool palette, choose the Ripple tool or the Roll tool; then click the edge of the clip in the Timeline.

◆ Press V to select the edit point nearest the playhead's location.

✔ Tips

■ If you are having trouble selecting Timeline edit points, use the Zoom slider to magnify your view, or try again with the Ripple tool or the Roll tool; they're designed to select edit points only, so you can't accidentally select a clip.

■ Using the Option key to override linked selection works with any edit tool, just as it does with the Selection tool.

■ These keyboard combos can help you snag edit points on audio clips composed of multiple linked stereo clips: Command-click the edit point of a stereo pair to add both audio channels to your selection. Command-Option click to restrict your selection to a single audio edit point.

To select multiple edits in the Timeline:

Do one of the following:

◆ From the Tool palette, choose the Edit Selection tool; then draw a marquee around the edit points of one or more Timeline tracks (**Figure 11.10**). You can select one edit per track; the selected edits don't have to be aligned in time.

The Trim Edit window opens as you release the mouse button.

◆ From the Tool palette, choose the Selection tool; then Command-click the edge of the clips in the Timeline. Double-click any selected edit if you want the Trim Edit window to open as well.

◆ From the Tool palette, choose the Ripple tool or the Roll tool; then Command-click the edge of the clips in the Timeline.

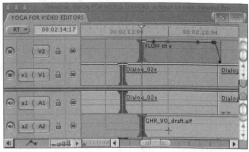

Figure 11.10 Draw a marquee around the edit points you want to select.

All Keys: Mouseless Trimming in FCE

You can work your way through your edit without touching the mouse. Here's one possible scenario:

1. Press Shift-E to jump the playhead to the next edit in the Timeline.

2. Press V to select the nearest edit.

3. Press \ (backslash) to play the sequence before and after the selected edit point.

4. Press R to select the Roll tool.

5. Press + (plus) or – (minus) and then enter a number of frames to roll the edit.

So many keyboard shortcuts in FCE—and so many ways to speed your work while you give your mouse hand a rest. To learn more, check out the keyboard shortcuts in Appendix B.

Anatomy of the Trim Edit Window

The Trim Edit window is a work environment optimized for making fine adjustments to a single edit point. You can trim the selected edit by one frame or several frames, quickly switch between Ripple and Roll edits, and play back the edit to review your trim adjustments. The Play Around Edit button is designed to loop playback of your edit while you fine-tune it. The looping is not seamless, though; a slight interruption occurs in the playback when you nudge the edit point.

Figure 11.11 shows an overview of the Trim Edit window.

- **Outgoing clip name:** Displays the name of the outgoing clip.

- **Outgoing clip duration:** Displays the elapsed time between the In and Out points of the outgoing clip. This value updates to reflect trim adjustments.

- **Outgoing clip current timecode:** Displays the clip's source timecode at the current position of the playhead.

continues on next page

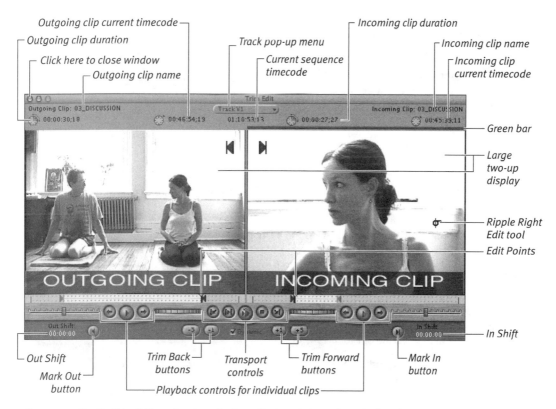

Figure 11.11 Use the Trim Edit window to make fine adjustments to a selected edit point.

◆ **Track pop-up menu:** Displays a list if multiple edits have been selected. Select the track you want to edit in the Trim Edit window.

◆ **Current sequence timecode:** Displays the sequence timecode location of the edit point. Enter + or − and a duration to roll the edit point. You don't need to click in the field; just start typing.

◆ **Incoming clip current timecode:** Displays the clip's source timecode at the current position of the playhead.

◆ **Incoming clip duration:** Displays the elapsed time between the In and Out points of the incoming clip. This value updates to reflect trim adjustments.

◆ **Incoming clip name:** Displays the name of the incoming clip.

◆ **Large two-up display:** The left screen displays the last frame before the edit. The right screen displays the first frame after the edit.

◆ **Green bar:** Indicates which side of the edit you are trimming.

◆ **Edit points:** Indicate the current Out and In points for the two clips in the Trim edit window. You can trim by dragging the outgoing clip's Out point or the incoming clip's In point with an edit tool.

◆ **Playback controls for individual clips:** The outgoing and incoming clips have separate playback controls. Use these controls to play only that clip without changing the current edit point location.

◆ **Out Shift:** Indicates the number of frames that the Out point has been adjusted.

◆ **Mark Out button:** Click to set a new Out point for the outgoing clip at the current playhead position.

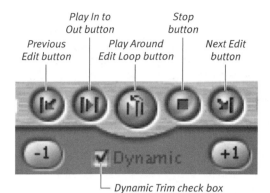

Previous
Edit button

Play In to
Out button

Play Around
Edit Loop button

Stop
button

Next Edit
button

Dynamic Trim check box

Figure 11.12 Trim Edit window transport controls detail. The Dynamic Trim check box is located beneath the transport controls.

◆ **Trim Back buttons:** Nudge the selected edit point to the left. Trim by single-frame increments or by another frame increment you specify on the Editing tab of FCE's User Preferences window.

◆ **Trim Forward buttons:** Nudge the selected edit point to the right.

◆ **Mark In button:** Click to set a new In point for the incoming clip at the current playhead position.

◆ **In Shift:** Indicates the number of frames that the In point has been adjusted.

Figure 11.12 shows the Trim Edit window's transport controls.

◆ **Previous Edit button:** Click to move the previous edit into the active area of the Trim Edit window.

◆ **Play In to Out button:** Click to play from the start of the first clip to the end of the second clip.

◆ **Play Around Edit Loop button:** Click to loop playback of the edit point plus the specified pre-roll and post-roll. Playback loops until you click Stop. You can continue trimming the edit while playback is looping.

◆ **Stop button:** Click to stop playback and position the playhead on the edit point.

◆ **Next Edit button:** Click to move the next edit into the active area of the Trim Edit window.

◆ **Dynamic Trim check box:** Check to enable dynamic trimming mode. See "To use dynamic trim mode to adjust an edit point" later in this chapter.

ANATOMY OF THE TRIM EDIT WINDOW

Using the Trim Edit Window

The Trim Edit window offers plenty of flexibility to accommodate your editing style; you can mix and match trimming methods in a single trim operation. This window features two good-sized screens displaying the clips on either side of the edit you are adjusting, as well as Duration and Current Timecode displays for each side.

✔ Tip

■ If you're using Timecode entry in the Trim Edit window, you can cancel an edit by pressing the Esc key while the Timecode field is still active. You can also undo an edit at any time by pressing Command-Z.

FCE Protocol: Trimming Error Messages

When you attempt a trim operation that can't be executed, Final Cut Express will warn you by displaying one of the following error messages:

◆ **You cannot set the In later than a disabled Out:** When you're adjusting an In or Out point in the Trim Edit window, you can't position your clip's In point later than its Out point. Likewise, Out points cannot be placed before In points. The word *disabled* in the message refers to Trim Edit window protocol. Only the outgoing clip's Out point and the incoming clip's In point are active while you're in the Trim Edit window.

◆ **Clip collision:** A trimming operation would cause clips to collide or one clip to overwrite another. Specifies the track number where the error occurred.

◆ **Transition conflict:** A transition duration adjustment would be required to accommodate the trimming change. Specifies the track number where the error occurred.

◆ **Media limit:** The source clip does not include sufficient media to complete the edit as specified. Specifies the track number where the error occurred.

◆ **Insufficient content:** The same as the "Media limit" error; the source clip does not contain sufficient media to complete the edit.

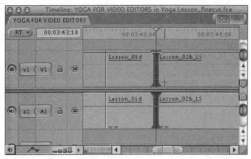

Figure 11.13 Click an edit point in the Timeline with the Edit Selection tool.

Figure 11.14 The Trim Edit window opens automatically.

Figure 11.15 Close the Trim Edit window by clicking the close button in the upper-left corner.

To open the Trim Edit window:

Do one of the following:

◆ Press Command-7.

The playhead jumps to the closest edit on the target track, and the Trim Edit window opens with a Roll edit selected.

◆ In the Timeline, click an edit with the Edit Selection tool (**Figure 11.13**).

The edit is selected, and the Trim Edit window opens automatically (**Figure 11.14**).

◆ Click an edit with the Ripple or Roll tool, and the Trim Edit window opens with that edit type already selected.

◆ Choose Sequence > Trim Edit.

◆ In the Timeline, double-click an edit.

To close the Trim Edit window:

Do one of the following:

◆ Move the Timeline or the Canvas playhead away from the edit.

◆ Click anywhere in the Timeline away from an edit to deselect all edits in the Timeline.

◆ Click the close button in the upper-left corner of the Trim Edit window (**Figure 11.15**).

✔ Tip

■ All the plus and minus adjustments you make in the Trim Edit window refer to the location of the edit point, not the duration of either clip. That's especially important to remember when you're making adjustments on the right side of the edit point.

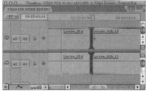

USING THE TRIM EDIT WINDOW

To trim an edit in the Trim Edit window:

1. Select one or more edit points to trim, using any of the methods described earlier in this section. Then, if the Trim Edit window has not opened automatically, press Command-7 to open the Trim Edit window.

2. In the Trim Edit window, select the type of trim operation by clicking in the appropriate image area (the pointer changes to indicate whether you've selected Ripple Left, Roll, or Ripple Right):

    ◆ Click the left image to trim the outgoing clip with a Ripple Left edit.

    ◆ Click the right image to trim the incoming clip with a Ripple Right edit (**Figure 11.16**).

    ◆ Click the area between the images to select a Roll edit.

    ◆ A green bar appears above the clip image, indicating the side of the edit that is selected for trimming.

3. Trim the edit using *one of the following methods:*

    ◆ Use the Trim Forward and Trim Back buttons to move the edit point to the left or right by frame increments (**Figure 11.17**).

    ◆ Trim the edit point by typing + or – and a duration to add or subtract. You don't need to click the field—just start typing and then press Enter. The type of trim performed depends on the edit selection you made in step 2.

    ◆ Drag an edit point in the Scrubber bar.

    ◆ Use the individual playback controls under either clip to play the clip; then mark a new Out point for the outgoing clip or a new In point for the incoming clip.

Figure 11.16 Click the image on the right in the Trim Edit window to select a Ripple Right edit.

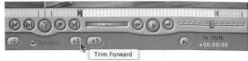

Figure 11.17 Clicking this Trim Forward button moves the edit point to the right by single-frame increments.

Figure 11.18 Review your trim by clicking the Play In to Out button to play from the beginning of the incoming clip to the end of the outgoing clip.

Figure 11.19 Use the Track pop-up menu to choose another selected edit point for trimming. Even when you're trimming an audio clip, you'll still see video playback in preview mode, and you'll be able to hear all the audio tracks at that edit point in your sequence.

The In Shift and Out Shift fields update to show the total cumulative shift in the edit point. These fields will track the shift, even if you perform the trim as several small adjustments. The Timeline display updates to reflect your trim.

4. Use the transport controls to review your edit.

   ◆ Click the Play In to Out button to play from the start of the first clip to the end of the second clip (**Figure 11.18**).

   ◆ Click the Play Around Edit Loop button to loop playback of the edit point plus the specified pre-roll and post-roll.

   ◆ Click the Stop button to stop playback and position the playhead on the edit point.

5. When you finish trimming, close the Trim Edit window.

✔ Tips

■ The right amount of pre- and post-roll can establish a perfect rhythm and pace that helps you nail a tricky edit. You can adjust the default pre-roll and post-roll settings on the Editing tab of the User Preferences window.

■ You can use the Previous Edit and Next Edit buttons in the Trim Edit window to move to the next edit on the current track without leaving the Trim Edit window.

■ If you have selected multiple edits to trim, use the Track pop-up menu to select the track to view in the Trim Edit window (**Figure 11.19**).

USING THE TRIM EDIT WINDOW

New in FCE HD: Audio Monitoring Options in the Trim Edit Window

The FCE pit crew has been swarming over the Trim Edit window, and the latest edition has new audio monitoring flexibility that editors have been asking for. The implementation of this feature is a little tricky, so prick up your ears:

Two new audio monitoring preferences appear on the Editing tab of the User Preferences window. You can enable and disable either monitoring option without leaving the Trim Edit window by using a keyboard shortcut.

Trim with Sequence Audio (Command-Option-A) allows you to monitor all audio tracks at the playhead position when trimming an edit in the Trim Edit window. Disable this preference to limit Trim Edit audio monitoring to the selected clip's audio.

Trim with Edit Selection Audio (Mute Others) (Command-Option-Z) limits audio monitoring in the Trim Edit window to just the audio tracks included in the edit you selected for trimming in the Trim Edit window. With this preference enabled, you'll hear all selected audio, whether or not it is linked to the selected edit point. Disable this preference to limit Trim Edit audio monitoring to audio that's linked to the edit point you selected for trimming.

Here comes the tricky part: These audio monitoring configurations are in effect *only* when you use the JKL keys to play back incoming or outgoing clips. If you use the spacebar to play through your edit point, you'll hear all the sequence audio tracks regardless of your audio monitoring preference settings. Also remember—the Trim Edit window's Dynamic Trim mode uses JKL keys to perform trim edits; if you just want to review your audio without adjusting the edit point when you hit the K key, be sure to disable Dynamic Trim mode first.

Figure 11.20 Click the Play Around Edit Loop button to loop the playback of your edit point plus the specified pre-roll and post-roll.

To adjust an edit point on the fly:

1. In the Trim Edit window, select the type of trim operation by one of the methods described in the previous task.

   A green bar appears above the clip image, indicating the side of the edit that is selected for trimming.

2. Click the Play Around Edit Loop button (or press the spacebar) to loop playback of the edit point (**Figure 11.20**).

3. As the preview loop plays, tap the I key to set a new In point on the incoming clip, or tap the O to set a new Out point on the outgoing clip (**Figure 11.21**).

   The corresponding In or Out edit point is adjusted accordingly. The looped playback hesitates briefly and then resumes.

Figure 11.21 As the playback loops in preview mode, you can use the I and O keys or the Mark buttons to adjust the edit point on the fly.

To use dynamic trim mode to adjust an edit point:

1. In the Trim Edit window, enable dynamic trim mode by checking its box.

2. Position the mouse pointer in the image area of the clip you want to trim.

   The pointer changes to the Ripple Left, Ripple Right, or Roll tool depending on the pointer's location; the Play control on the affected clip is highlighted (**Figure 11.22**).

3. Use the JKL keyboard transport commands to play the clip you're adjusting.

4. Click the K key to stop the playhead at the point you want to set as your new edit point.

   The edit point adjusts to the playhead position automatically.

✔ Tip

- For more information on using the JKL keys for transport control, see "JKL Keys: The Way to Move" in Chapter 8.

To slip an edit in the Trim Edit window:

1. In the Trim Edit window, Shift-drag the active edit point on either Scrubber bar to slip that clip (**Figure 11.23**); or drag the edit point with the Slip tool.

   The Current Time display switches to show the adjusted timecode location for the edit point you are slipping.

2. Release the mouse button to complete the Slip edit.

   The Current Time display reverts to displaying the timecode location at the clip's current playhead position.

Figure 11.22 Dynamic Trim mode uses the mouse pointer's location to determine which side of the edit you're trimming and lets you use the JKL keys to control playback and mark edit points.

Figure 11.23 Shift-dragging an active edit point in the Trim Edit window slips the selected clip. During the slip, the display changes to show the new In and Out points.

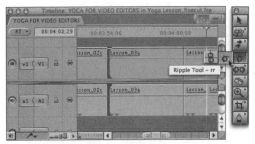

Figure 11.24 Choose the Ripple tool from the Tool palette.

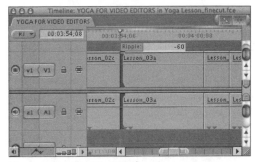

Figure 11.25 After selecting the edit you want to ripple, type + or – followed by the number of frames to add to or subtract from the edit point.

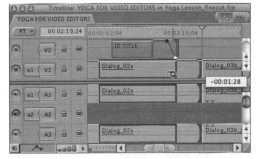

Figure 11.26 Performing a Ripple edit on multiple tracks in the Timeline.

✔ Tip

■ Holding down the Shift key while you perform a trim toggles the pointer between the Ripple and Roll tools.

Trimming Edits in the Timeline

The Timeline can be a good place to trim your sequence if you need to keep tabs on multiple tracks in relation to one another. You can perform all types of trim edits in the Timeline: Ripple, Roll, Slip, Slide, Extend, Swap, and Resize.

✔ Tip

■ Set up your Timeline display to optimize the efficiency of your trim operation. Things to check include the time scale, track size, snapping, and vertical scroll bar setup. You'll find details on Timeline display options in Chapter 10, "Editing in the Timeline and the Canvas."

To perform a Ripple edit in the Timeline:

1. From the Tool palette, choose the Ripple tool (**Figure 11.24**).

2. In the Timeline, select the edit by clicking near the edge of the clip.
   The selected side of the edit will be highlighted.

3. Ripple the edit using *one of the following methods:*
   ◆ Drag the edit to adjust the duration of the clip in the sequence.
   ◆ Type + or – followed by the number of frames to add to or subtract from the current edit point (**Figure 11.25**); then press Enter.

To perform a Ripple edit on multiple tracks simultaneously:

◆ Command-click to select multiple edit points; then use the Ripple tool to perform the Ripple edit across all the tracks (**Figure 11.26**).

To perform an asymmetric Ripple trim in the Timeline:

1. Make a Ripple Left edit selection on the video track clip by clicking the left side of the edit point with the Ripple tool. If the clip is linked, you must Option-click to override linked selection.

2. On the audio track clip, use the Ripple tool again to make a Ripple Right edit selection on the other side of the audio track's edit point. If you're working on a linked clip, Command-click to select just the right side of the edit point with the Ripple tool (**Figure 11.27**).

3. Type + or – followed by the number of frames to add to or subtract from the current edit points (**Figure 11.28**); then press Enter.

   The video track edit point shifts back, while the audio track edit point shifts ahead by the same amount (**Figure 11.29**).

✔ Tip

■ Use asymmetric trimming to create a split edit without changing the sync relationship of your sequence clips.

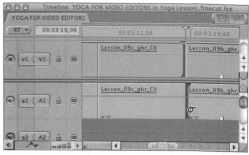

Figure 11.27 Command-clicking the right side of this edit with the Ripple tool selects just the audio edit point of this linked clip to ripple right.

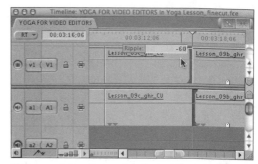

Figure 11.28 Use timecode entry to adjust the edit point. In this example, typing –60 trims 60 frames off the end of the V1 track of the left clip and 60 frames off the head of the A1 track of the right clip.

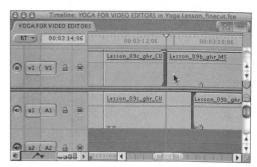

Figure 11.29 The completed asymmetric Ripple edit produces a split edit. Both clips were rippled by the same number of frames without affecting the sync of the downstream clips—note that the position of the clip markers is unchanged.

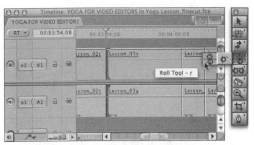

Figure 11.30 Choose the Roll tool from the Tool palette.

Figure 11.31 During a Roll edit, the Canvas window converts to dual-screen mode, displaying the outgoing Out point on the left and the incoming In point on the right.

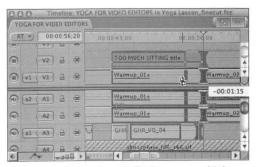

Figure 11.32 Performing a Roll edit across multiple tracks in the Timeline.

To perform a Roll edit in the Timeline:

1. From the Tool palette, choose the Roll tool (**Figure 11.30**).

2. In the Timeline, select the edit point.

3. Roll the edit *using one of the following methods:*
   - ◆ Drag in either direction. As you drag, the Canvas display changes to two smaller screens that show the Out point of the outgoing clip on the left and the In point of the incoming clip on the right (**Figure 11.31**).
   - ◆ Type + or – followed by the number of frames to add to or subtract from the current edit point; then press Enter.

To roll multiple tracks simultaneously:

- ◆ Command-click to select multiple edit points; then use the Roll tool to perform the Roll edit across all the tracks (**Figure 11.32**).

✔ Tip

- ■ If you're still dragging but your Roll edit stops rolling, your clip has reached the end of the media.

To slip a clip in the Timeline:

1. In the Tool palette, choose the Slip tool (**Figure 11.33**).

2. In the Timeline, select the clip and drag it left or right. As you drag:
   - An outline of the complete clip appears, indicating the amount of media available.
   - The Canvas display changes to two smaller screens that show the In point frame on the left and the Out point frame on the right (**Figure 11.34**).

3. Release the mouse button when you have positioned the clip at its new location.

✔ Tip

- Try turning off snapping in the Timeline before you slip your clip. Your clip will slip more smoothly.

To slip a clip in the Timeline using numerical timecode entry:

1. Select the clip in the Timeline.

2. In the Tool palette, choose the Slip tool.

3. Type + or – and the number of frames to slip; then press Enter.

Figure 11.33 Choose the Slip tool from the Tool palette.

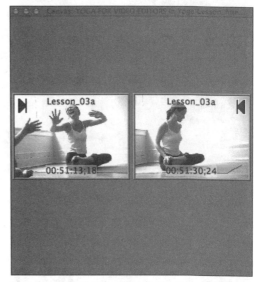

Figure 11.34 During the Slip edit, the Canvas window converts to dual-screen mode, displaying the In point frame on the left and the Out point frame on the right.

Figure 11.35 Select the clip with the Slide tool.

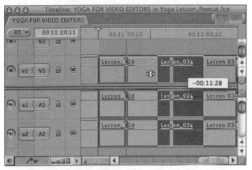

Figure 11.36 During the Slide edit, an outline of the complete clip appears in the Timeline, indicating the amount of media available outside the clip's edit points.

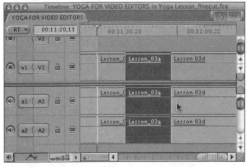

Figure 11.37 The clip in its new sequence location.

To slide a clip in the Timeline:

1. In the Tool palette, choose the Slide tool.

2. In the Timeline, select the entire clip (**Figure 11.35**) and drag it left or right. As you drag:

   ◆ An outline of the complete clip appears, indicating the amount of media available (**Figure 11.36**).

   ◆ The Canvas display changes to two smaller screens, which show the Out point frame of the clip to the left of the sliding clip and the In point frame of the clip to the right of the sliding clip.

3. Release the mouse button when you have positioned the clip at its new location (**Figure 11.37**).

To slide a clip in the Timeline using numerical timecode entry:

1. Select the clip in the Timeline.

2. In the Tool palette, choose the Slide tool.

3. Type + or – and the number of frames to slide; then press Enter.

TRIMMING EDITS IN THE TIMELINE

To perform a Swap edit in the Timeline:

1. In the Timeline, select the clip you want to move.

2. Drag the clip from its current sequence location to the new location (**Figure 11.38**).

3. Align the head of the selected clip with the head of the clip in the Timeline at the insert location (**Figure 11.39**); then press Option without releasing the mouse button.

   The pointer becomes a curved arrow.

4. Drop the selected clip at the insertion point you selected (**Figure 11.40**).

   The inserted clip and the sequence clip swap positions; no sequence clip durations are altered (**Figure 11.41**), but the order in which they appear has changed.

✔ Tips

- The Swap edit is one way to go if you want to preserve render files you've already created. The swapped clips don't change duration, and they maintain the linkage to their previously rendered files.

- You can perform Swap edits only with single clips.

Figure 11.38 Drag the Timeline clip from its current sequence location to the edit point at the new location.

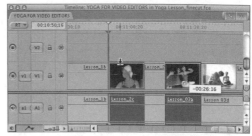

Figure 11.39 Use snapping to help you line up the head of the clip you are moving with the edit point where you want to insert the clip.

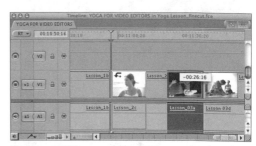

Figure 11.40 When you press Option as you drop the clip into the Timeline, the pointer changes to a curved arrow. Drop the clip at the insertion point.

Figure 11.41 The inserted clip pushes the rest of the sequence clips down without altering any sequence durations.

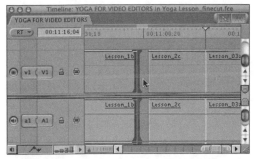

Figure 11.42 Use the Selection (or the Edit Selection) tool to select the edit point of the clip you want to extend.

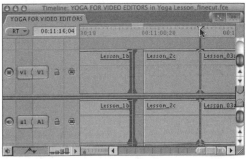

Figure 11.43 Position the playhead to mark the new edit point for the edit; then press E.

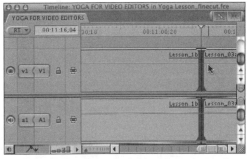

Figure 11.44 The clip on the left lengthens, extending to the playhead position, overwriting any gaps or clips.

To perform an Extend edit in the Timeline:

1. Check the Snapping control to make sure snapping is on. (An Extend edit is a little easier to perform with snapping turned on.)

2. From the Tool palette, choose the Selection tool or the Edit Selection tool.

3. In the Timeline, click the edit point of the clip you want to extend (**Figure 11.42**).

4. Move the playhead to the position that the edit will extend to (**Figure 11.43**); then press the E key.

   The clip with the selected edit extends to the playhead position. An Extend edit will overwrite any gaps or clips it encounters, up to the position of the playhead (**Figure 11.44**).

   If there is not enough media to reach your selected playhead position, an "insufficient content for edit" error message appears, and the edit is canceled.

✔ Tips

- Use an Extend edit to create a split edit on the fly. In the Timeline, select the edit you want to adjust by Option-clicking it; then play back your sequence and press the E key when you see your new edit location. The edit point will move to the playhead's position at the moment you press E—if you have enough media in your clip to extend it to that point.

- Extend edits are also a neat way to clean up the tail ends of a stack of clips with different durations. Select the edit points of the shorter clips, position the playhead at the end of the longest clip, and press E (**Figure 11.45**). If you have enough media available, all the clips will align their durations to match that of your longest clip (**Figure 11.46**).

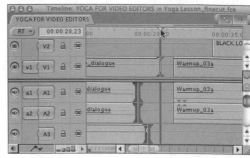

Figure 11.45 Select the edit points of the shorter clips; position the playhead at the end of the longest clip and then press E.

Figure 11.46 The edit extends the duration of all the selected clips to match that of the longest clip.

Figure 11.47 Choose the Selection tool from the Tool palette. The Selection arrow changes to a Resize pointer when you position it near an edit point.

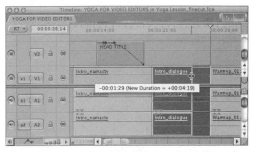

Figure 11.48 Dragging the edit point of the selected clip in the Timeline resizes the clip.

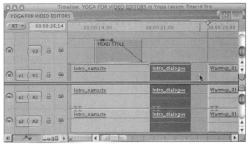

Figure 11.49 The clip, resized to a shorter duration, leaves a gap in its Timeline track.

To resize the duration of a clip in the Timeline:

1. In the Tool palette, choose the Selection tool (**Figure 11.47**).

2. In the Timeline, select an edit point and drag it (**Figure 11.48**).

   You can drag the edit point to create a gap (by making the duration of the clip shorter; **Figure 11.49**) or cover an existing gap (by making the duration of the clip longer).

To divide (razor-blade) a clip in the Timeline:

1. Set your target track to the one that contains the clip you want to divide (**Figure 11.50**).

2. In the Timeline, position the playhead at the point where you want to divide the clip (**Figure 11.51**); then press Control-V to add an edit point.

   The added edit point will create an additional clip that starts at the playhead position (**Figure 11.52**).

   Or do this:

   Press B to select the Razor Blade tool; then click at the point where you want to divide the clip.

✔ Tips

- Both halves of a divided clip will have the same name as the original, so if you plan on keeping both of them around, you may want to give them new names that reflect their history as two halves of a bladed clip—for instance, intro_01.1 and intro_01.2. Remember, though, that renaming an affiliate clip causes all other affiliates and the master clip they reference to be renamed as well. If you've bladed an affiliate clip, you'll need to change the status of each additional piece to Independent or Master in order to give it a unique name. Learn more about FCE's clip-handling grammar in Chapter 4, "Projects, Sequences, and Clips."

- Use the Razor Blade All tool to divide clips on all Timeline tracks at the same point.

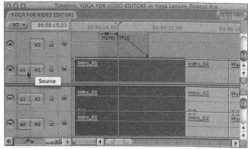

Figure 11.50 Target the track that contains the clip before you select its division point.

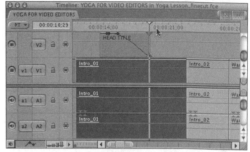

Figure 11.51 Position the playhead at the point where you want to divide the clip.

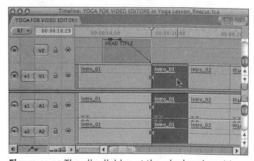

Figure 11.52 The clip divides at the playhead position. The added edit point creates an additional clip that starts at the playhead position.

TRIMMING EDITS IN THE TIMELINE

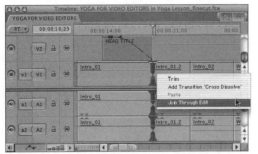

Figure 11.53 Control-click the through edit indicator; then choose Join Through Edit from the shortcut menu.

About through edits

FCE defines a through edit as an edit point joining two clips with the same reel number and contiguous timecode (such as a clip you've divided in two with the Razor Blade tool). You have the option of removing the through edit and merging the two adjacent clips into one continuous clip.

To remove a through edit:

Do one of the following:

◆ In the Timeline, select the through edit indicator and press Delete.

◆ Control-click the through edit indicator in the Timeline; then choose Join Through Edit from the shortcut menu (**Figure 11.53**).

The edit point disappears, and the divided clip is rejoined. The newly merged clip adopts the properties (filters, opacity, audio levels, and so on) of the first (left) clip.

TRIMMING EDITS IN THE TIMELINE

Trimming Edits in the Viewer

You can perform four types of trim operations in the Viewer: Ripple, Roll, Slip, and Resize. Remember that you can perform trim operations only on sequence clips, so all these trim operations require you to open the sequence clip in the Viewer by double-clicking it in the Timeline.

To perform a Ripple edit in the Viewer:

1. From the Tool palette, choose the Ripple tool.

2. In the Timeline, double-click the clip to open it in the Viewer.

3. In the Viewer's Scrubber bar, drag either the In or the Out point to ripple the clip (**Figure 11.54**).

To perform a Roll edit in the Viewer:

1. From the Tool palette, choose the Roll tool.

2. In the Timeline, double-click the clip to open it in the Viewer.

3. In the Viewer's Scrubber bar, drag either the In or the Out point to roll the edit.

   If you run out of media to accommodate the shift in your edit point, an overlay appears on the image in the Viewer warning you of a "Media limit" error on the track that's run out of frames.

Figure 11.54 Dragging the Out point with the Ripple tool. The edit point will be rippled to the left.

TRIMMING EDITS IN THE VIEWER

Figure 11.55 As you slip the edit, the Viewer displays the first frame of the clip, and the Canvas displays the last frame.

Figure 11.56 Dragging the edit point in the Viewer's Scrubber bar resizes the selected clip.

To slip a clip in the Viewer:

1. From the Tool palette, choose the Slip tool.

2. In the Timeline, double-click the clip to open it in the Viewer.

3. In the Viewer's Scrubber bar, drag either the In or the Out point to slip the clip.

   As you slip, the Viewer displays the first frame of the clip; the Canvas displays the last frame of the clip (**Figure 11.55**).

✔ Tip

■ You can also slip a clip in the Viewer by Shift-dragging either the In or the Out point with the Selection tool.

To resize a clip in the Viewer:

1. In the Tool palette, choose the Selection tool.

2. In the Timeline, double-click the clip to open it in the Viewer.

3. In the Viewer's Scrubber bar, drag either the In or the Out point to resize the clip (**Figure 11.56**).

   You can drag the edit point to create a gap (by decreasing the duration of the clip) or cover an existing gap (by increasing the duration of the clip).

Correcting Out-of-Sync Clips

When you insert a sync clip into a sequence, the audio and video are automatically linked. That means you'll have to go out of your way to knock them out of sync, because linked items are selected and moved together. However, if you have turned linked selection off, it's possible to knock a sync clip out of sync.

Boxes appear on the clips that are out of sync. These indicators display the number of frames that the audio and video portions of the clip are out of sync in relation to each other.

Final Cut Express offers two options for correcting a sync problem:

◆ You can move a clip into sync, which repositions the selected portion of the clip so that the sync is corrected.

◆ You can slip a clip into sync, which corrects the sync problem by performing a Slip edit on the selected portion of the clip (keeping the clip in the same position and shifting the contents of the clip).

Occasionally, you'll want to move a clip out of sync intentionally—for example, when you combine the video from one take with substitute audio from another take.

In that case, you might want to mark the video and the substitute audio as being in sync if you don't want to be warned of a sync problem.

To move a clip into sync:

◆ In the Timeline, Control-click the out-of-sync indicator (the red box on the clip; **Figure 11.57**); then choose Move into Sync from the shortcut menu (**Figure 11.58**).

The portion of the clip you selected is repositioned to correct the sync (**Figure 11.59**).

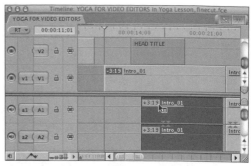

Figure 11.57 Control-click the out-of-sync indicator on the part of the clip you wish to reposition.

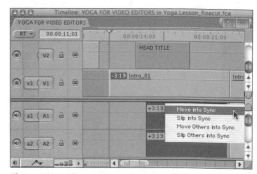

Figure 11.58 Choose Move into Sync from the shortcut menu.

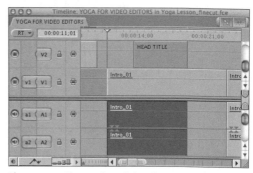

Figure 11.59 The portion of the clip you selected is repositioned in the Timeline so the sync is corrected. Note that you can move a clip into sync only if there is a gap in the track to accommodate the move.

CORRECTING OUT-OF-SYNC CLIPS

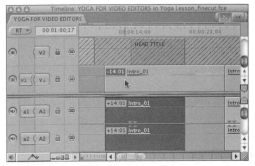

Figure 11.60 Select the audio and video clips you want to mark as in sync.

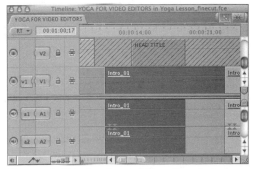

Figure 11.61 The clips do not shift position, but are marked as in sync.

To slip a clip into sync:

◆ In the Timeline, Control-click the out-of-sync indicator (the red box) on the clip portion you want to slip into sync; then choose Slip into Sync from the shortcut menu.

To mark clips as in sync:

◆ In the Timeline, select the audio and video clips you want to mark as in sync (**Figure 11.60**); then choose Modify > Mark in Sync.

The two selected clips are marked as in sync, without shifting their positions in the Timeline (**Figure 11.61**).

Audio Tools and Techniques

The basic editing and finishing features in Final Cut Express operate in the same way for video and audio clips. This chapter covers the few tools and techniques unique to audio editing, audio effects, and mixing.

You can learn about other aspects of audio elsewhere in this book. Capturing audio is covered in Chapter 5, "Capturing Video." Steps for importing digital audio from CDs or other digital sources appear in Chapter 6, "Importing Digital Media," and exporting audio back to tape or to another digital format is covered in Chapter 19, "Creating Final Output." Also, audio transitions are covered in Chapter 13, "Creating Transitions," and rendering audio is explained in Chapter 18, "Real Time and Rendering."

Locating Audio Tools in the FCE Interface

The FCE interface has five areas where you edit and finish audio.

◆ **The Audio tab in the Viewer:** The Audio tab displays audio-only clips, as well as the audio portion of audio+video clips. This is where you can audition and mark edit points in audio clips and use keyframes to set audio level and pan settings. The Audio tab is the only place in FCE where you can get a large view of your audio clip's waveforms and make subframe adjustments to edit points.

◆ **The Audio tracks in the Timeline:** The Timeline is the only place where you can view all audio tracks at once. Turn on the Timeline's audio waveform display (it's off by default), and you can edit audio quite nicely; you can do everything from basic assembly to fine trimming. Track height is completely adjustable, so when you need to concentrate on fine-tuning an edit, you can expand the track until the waveform display is a healthy size.

You can use keyframes to set and sculpt audio levels using the Timeline's clip overlays. Playback on the Audio tab and in the Trim Edit window is independent of Timeline/Canvas playback, so the Timeline is the only place you can trim audio on the fly as you watch your sequence play back.

◆ **The Voice Over tool:** FCE's audio recording tool can record multiple tracks of sync audio as FCE plays back a selected portion of your sequence. Sounds complicated, but it's easy to use and very useful.

◆ **The Filters tab in the Viewer:** Apply and adjust audio filters and effects on the Filters tab of the Viewer.

◆ **The Trim Edit window:** The latest edition of the Trim Edit window is the best yet (dynamic trimming, improved performance), and if the Trim Edit window displayed large-size waveforms as you fine-tuned your audio edits, it would be a great place to do fine cutting of dialogue or music. Unfortunately, you can't see waveforms in this window, so it's not a top choice for tight audio editing.

Audio Tracks vs. Timeline Tracks

One small clarification: *audio track* is an old expression describing an audio recording, such as a soundtrack or an album track.

In Final Cut Express, *track* refers to an empty layer in the Timeline where you assemble video and audio clips, but not to the clips themselves.

In an attempt to avoid confusion, this book uses the term *CD track* to refer to an audio recording on a CD, *audio tracks* to refer to Timeline tracks that hold audio clips, *audio clips* to refer to the individual items you manipulate in FCE, and *audio files* to refer to the source media files those audio clips reference.

So—are we avoiding confusion yet?

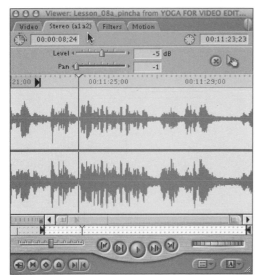

Figure 12.1 The two audio channels that make up a stereo pair appear on a single Audio tab. Any adjustments made to one channel are automatically applied to both channels.

Figure 12.2 Ch 1 + Ch 2 audio format appears in the Viewer with two Audio tabs. Each channel is distinct and can be adjusted independently.

FCE's Audio Formats

In the audio world, *format* has entirely too many meanings.

There are media formats, such as DV, CD, and DAT, which describe the media used to record the original audio. There are also digital audio file formats, such as AIF, MP3, and WAV.

And then there are the audio formats discussed here, which describe the structure of multiple-channel audio recordings such as stereo or mono. These audio formats apply to audio captured with video, as well as to imported clips or audio-only clips captured with the Voice Over tool.

◆ **Stereo:** Both channels have been captured as a stereo pair. Stereo pairs are always linked, so anything applied to one track applies to both. Waveforms for the two channels that make up the stereo pair appear on a single Audio tab (**Figure 12.1**).

◆ **Ch 1 + Ch 2:** Both channels have been captured but are distinct and can be adjusted independently of one another. Two Mono Audio tabs appear in the Viewer (**Figure 12.2**).

◆ **Mono:** The audio consists of a single mono channel, or both channels from the tape mixed into a single track. A single Audio tab appears in the Viewer. The source track designation (a1, a2, and so on) refers to the audio format of these tracks' source media at the time of capture.

Modifying audio channel formats

Two linked audio clips behave differently than two linked audio clips defined as a stereo pair.

◆ Two linked audio clips will be selected together, but their levels and filters must be controlled separately. Two linked audio clips can appear in two separate Audio tabs in the Viewer.

◆ Two audio clips defined as a stereo pair share everything except their audio content and their Timeline tracks. The two stereo channels appear on a single Audio tab in the Viewer, and they are always selected together. Any filter, panning, or level modification applied to one stereo channel is automatically applied to the other.

You can modify the audio format of captured audio using the Modify > Stereo Pair and Modify > Link commands. For example, toggling Stereo Pair off will convert a pair of clips captured as a stereo pair to two linked clips in A1 + A2 (Ch 1 + Ch 2) format.

✔ Tip

■ Converting two single audio clips to form a stereo pair is a quick way to apply identical level changes to a couple of clips. You can always toggle stereo off after you have made your level adjustments.

About 16-bit, 24-bit, and 32-bit Resolution

DV cameras usually offer a choice between 12-bit, 32 kHz and 16-bit, 48 kHz audio recording resolution; 16 bits is the highest bit depth available. Meanwhile, the latest pro digital audio hardware records and outputs 24-bit audio. Final Cut Express HD cannot capture 24-bit audio, but you can import 24-bit audio files captured in another program. Final Cut Express will preserve their 24-bit quality because in FCE, audio mixing is calculated at a 32-bit floating-point resolution. Mixing audio in the digital domain is a mathematical process; the added accuracy of floating-point calculation plus the extra dynamic range resolution provided by 32 bits ensures that your 24-bit audio preserves its original quality. You can then output 24-bit audio AIFF files from FCE.

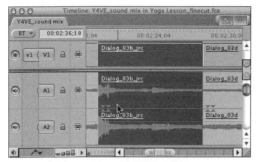

Figure 12.3 Select the stereo audio clip in the Timeline; then choose Modify > Stereo Pair (or press Option-L) to toggle stereo off.

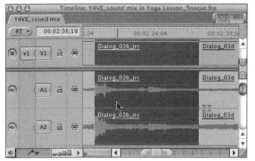

Figure 12.4 The stereo audio clip converted to Ch 1 + Ch 2 format. Note that the small triangles indicating a stereo pair are gone, but the clip names remain underlined because the two audio channels remained linked.

To convert a stereo pair to A1 + A2 format:

◆ Select the stereo audio clip in the Timeline (**Figure 12.3**); then choose Modify > Stereo Pair to toggle stereo off.

The stereo audio clip is converted to dual mono (Ch 1 + Ch 2) format, but the two audio channels remain linked (**Figure 12.4**). If you want to convert these to two completely independent audio clips, select the linked audio clips in the Timeline; then choose Modify > Link to toggle linking off.

✔ Tips

■ Toggling stereo off will automatically unlink audio-only clips.

■ FCE's Capture window captures only video+audio clips, and it always formats audio channels as a stereo pair. If you want your clip's audio to be formatted as A1 + A2 format, you'll need to select the two channels of your audio clip in the Timeline and then choose Modify > Stereo Pair to toggle stereo off.

To convert two audio clips to stereo pair format:

◆ Select the two audio clips in the Timeline; then choose Modify > Stereo Pair to toggle stereo on.

FCE'S AUDIO FORMATS

The Browser's audio format columns

You'll find four Browser columns devoted to information about the formatting of your audio clips (**Figure 12.5**); this summary will help you decode what each column tells you about your audio files.

◆ **Tracks:** The number of audio and video tracks used in a clip or sequence. Note the higher total number of tracks in the sequences.

◆ **Audio:** The audio clip's format as defined inside FCE. "A1 + A2" indicates the dual mono format.

◆ **Aud Format:** The audio format of the audio's source media file. The number (8, 12, 16, or 24) indicates the audio's bit depth. Note the 32-bit floating-point bit depth listed for sequences.

◆ **Aud Rate:** The sample rate of the audio's source media file.

✔ Tip

■ Final Cut Express allows you to mix audio tracks with different sample rates within the same sequence. The program can convert the sample rate of nonconforming audio on the fly as you play back a sequence. Real-time sample-rate conversion does take processor power, however, and can occasionally produce nasty audible artifacts, so for best results, you should convert the sample rates of all your audio tracks to match the sequence settings. For more information, see "To export audio only from a clip or sequence" in Chapter 19.

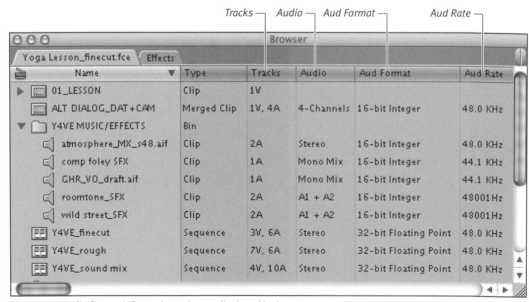

Tracks ── Audio ── Aud Format ── Aud Rate ──

Name	Type	Tracks	Audio	Aud Format	Aud Rate
01_LESSON	Clip	1V			
ALT DIALOG_DAT+CAM	Merged Clip	1V, 4A	4-Channels	16-bit Integer	48.0 KHz
Y4VE MUSIC/EFFECTS	Bin				
atmosphere_MX_s48.aif	Clip	2A	Stereo	16-bit Integer	48.0 KHz
comp foley SFX	Clip	1A	Mono Mix	16-bit Integer	44.1 KHz
CHR_VO_draft.aif	Clip	1A	Mono Mix	16-bit Integer	44.1 KHz
roomtone_SFX	Clip	2A	A1 + A2	16-bit Integer	48001Hz
wild street_SFX	Clip	2A	A1 + A2	16-bit Integer	48001Hz
Y4VE_finecut	Sequence	3V, 6A	Stereo	32-bit Floating Point	48.0 KHz
Y4VE_rough	Sequence	7V, 6A	Stereo	32-bit Floating Point	48.0 KHz
Y4VE_sound mix	Sequence	4V, 10A	Stereo	32-bit Floating Point	48.0 KHz

Figure 12.5 Audio format information columns displayed in the Browser.

What's Bit Depth and Sampling Rate Got to Do with My Audio Quality?

Digital audio is recorded at a bit depth and a sampling rate.

The bit depth indicates the fidelity of the recording's dynamics (volume levels), and the sample rate determines the fidelity of the recording's frequency response.

The bit depth defines the resolution of the dynamic range—the number of possible steps between the softest and loudest sound—of the recording.

An 8-bit digital audio recording uses 256 levels to represent the possible dynamic range. A 16-bit digital recording has a range of 65,536 levels.

The recording's sampling rate tells you how many times per second audio samples are saved to memory or disk. A 22-kHz sample rate means that 22,000 audio samples will be recorded each second, in contrast, a 48-kHz sample rate recording will take 48,000 audio samples each second.

Remember: Your audio recording's fidelity is set at the time you record the original. You can't improve a recording by choosing a higher sample rate later; you can, however, convert an audio file to a lower bit depth and sample rate.

If you're looking for audio fidelity, more is better, so go for the highest possible bit depth and sampling rate when you record original audio.

For more information on measuring dynamic range, see "FCE Protocol: Measuring Digital Audio in Decibels (dB)" later in this chapter.

Anatomy of the Viewer's Audio Tab

The Audio tab in the Viewer window is where you review, mark, and edit single audio clips opened from the Browser or the Timeline. You can see the audio waveforms of audio clips, and in addition to the editing functions, you can use onscreen controls to adjust the level and stereo pan settings (**Figure 12.6**).

Before you start marking up audio clips, make sure you understand how and where FCE saves your changes. See the sidebar "FCE Protocol: Clips and Sequences" in Chapter 4.

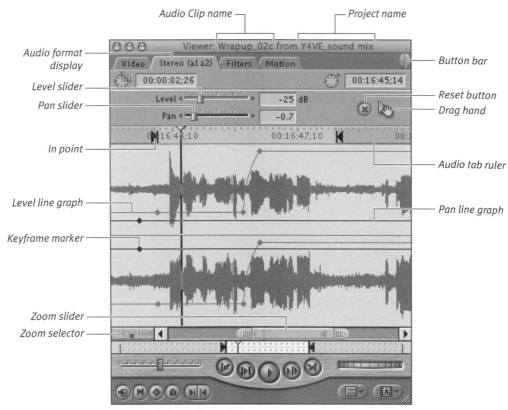

Figure 12.6 The Audio tab in the Viewer window.

Onscreen controls and displays

Editing digital audio requires different interface tools than editing digital video. When you open an audio clip in the Viewer, a graph of the audio waveform appears on the Audio tab, and the playhead travels across a stationary waveform image.

The Audio tab retains the transport controls from the Video tab interface in the lower part of the tab, but it has its own set of onscreen controls in the upper part.

Here's a brief rundown of the onscreen controls unique to the Audio tab (**Figures 12.7** and **12.8**):

◆ **Level slider:** Use to adjust the amplitude or volume of the audio clip.

◆ **Pan slider:** Use to adjust stereo panning or swapping of the left and right channels. Single channel (mono) clips use the Pan slider for left/right positioning of mono audio.

◆ **Reset (X) button:** Use to delete all marked points in the audio timeline and reset the level and pan values to their original settings.

◆ **Drag hand:** This is your handle for drag-and-drop editing. Drag to move the audio clip with edits to another window, such as the Browser or the Timeline.

◆ **Audio tab ruler:** This shows the time-code for the audio displayed. Edit point overlays appear along the ruler. You can adjust the time scale with any Zoom tool, selector, or slider.

◆ **In and Out points:** These appear in both the Scrubber bar and the ruler.

◆ **Level line graph:** Both a tool and an indicator, it graphs level changes by indicating the amplitude of the audio. You can also drag the Level line graph to adjust the overall level of your audio clip, or you can drag keyframes to create dynamic volume effects.

continues on next page

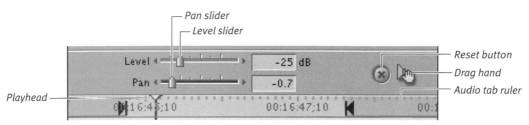

Figure 12.7 Controls displayed in the upper half of the Audio tab.

ANATOMY OF THE VIEWER'S AUDIO TAB

◆ **Pan line graph:** This has the same basic operation as the Level line graph. Drag to adjust the stereo spread (for stereo clips) or pan (for mono clips).

◆ **Keyframe marker:** Use the Pen tool to add keyframes to level lines, creating dynamic changes to volume and pan settings.

◆ **Zoom selector:** Click to jump between different time scale views. The Zoom selector keeps your playhead centered as you change time scales.

◆ **Zoom slider:** Use to scroll through an audio file and to adjust the time scale of your view.

✔ Tip

■ You can link two single audio clips to form a stereo pair. This is a quick way to apply identical level changes to a couple of clips. You can always unlink them after you have made your level adjustments. For more information, see "Modifying audio channel formats" earlier in this chapter.

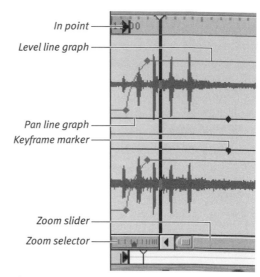

Figure 12.8 Controls displayed in the lower half of the Audio tab.

Figure 12.9 When you review a long, unedited audio recording, the wide Viewer window is a great place to set markers in preparation for breaking the clip into subclips.

Figure 12.10 Click the Audio tab to access the audio portion of an audio+video clip.

Using the Audio Tab

The capture settings for a clip determine how its audio appears in the Viewer. Stereo clips are panned full left and full right by default, and clips with one or two channels of discrete audio are panned center.

To open an audio clip:

Do one of the following:

◆ Double-click the clip icon in the Browser or the Timeline.

◆ Select a clip icon and choose View > Clip; or press Return.

◆ Select the clip in the Browser or the Timeline and choose View > Clip in New Window.

✔ Tip

■ Don't forget: You can stretch the Viewer window across your monitor to make a wide view—great when you're working with audio. You can see more of the clip, which makes marking and level adjustments easier (**Figure 12.9**). Resize it manually or click the green zoom button in the upper-left corner of the window.

To access the audio channel for an audio+video clip:

◆ Open the clip in the Viewer and click the Audio tab (**Figure 12.10**).

Scaling and scrolling an audio file

The Zoom slider is located along the bottom of the Audio tab. You use it to scroll through an audio file and to adjust the time scale of your view. You can view several minutes of audio in the window or focus on a fraction of a frame. The Zoom slider also appears on the Filters tab, the Motion tab, and the Timeline.

To scroll through your file:

◆ Drag the Zoom slider across the scroll bar (**Figure 12.11**).

To adjust the time scale:

Do one of the following:

◆ Press Command-+ (plus) to zoom in, expanding the time scale, and Command- – (minus) to zoom out, shrinking the time scale. These zoom keyboard shortcuts are useful on the Audio tab, because your view stays centered on the current playhead position.

◆ The thumb controls are the ribbed-looking ends of the Zoom slider (**Figure 12.12**). Click a thumb control and drag it to shrink the time scale and expose more of your audio file (**Figure 12.13**).

◆ Click the Zoom selector to the left of the Zoom slider to jump to a different time scale (**Figure 12.14**); the current playhead position stays centered in the view area.

Figure 12.11 Drag the Zoom slider across the scroll bar to navigate through an audio file. This control doesn't move the playhead, just the view.

Figure 12.12 Use the thumb controls to vary time scaling. A smaller Zoom slider indicates an expanded time scale.

Figure 12.13 Drag the thumb control. A longer Zoom slider indicates a more compressed time scale.

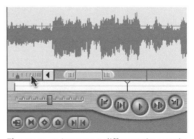

Figure 12.14 Jump to a different time scale with one click using the Zoom selector.

Setting edit points on the Audio tab

You set In and Out points and markers on the Audio tab in the same way you do on the Viewer's Video tab. The overlays for these markers appear on the Audio tab ruler at the top of the waveform display.

Because video is captured and stored as frames, the smallest adjustment you can make to a video edit point is a single frame. Digital audio, however, is captured in subframes as samples forming a continuous waveform. In FCE, audio edit points can be set to an accuracy of 1/100 frame. The Audio tab is the only place you can make subframe adjustments to an audio clip's In and Out points. Most likely, you'll need this kind of fine-tuning when you are finessing a music edit.

You can also place keyframes with the same precision—a lifesaver when you are working your way through a really good dialogue take with a couple of bad clicks or pops. The subframe precision allows you to use audio level keyframes to silence that audio just for the few milliseconds it takes to mute the click.

Lost in the Waveforms? Audio Tab Editing Tips

When you're trying to fine-tune an audio edit point on the Audio tab, it's easy to lose track of your location as you zoom and scroll through your audio clip's waveforms. Here's a navigation method to try while editing on the Audio tab:

◆ Start by playing back the clip.

◆ When you hear the spot where you think your edit point should be, tap the spacebar to pause the playhead at that spot.

◆ Use the marquee selection feature of the Zoom tool to draw a narrow selection box around the playhead. You won't lose track of the playhead this way.

◆ While you're zoomed in, take advantage of the detailed waveform display to get a precision edit. Press I or O to mark your edit point at the current playhead position.

◆ When you finish tweaking, press Shift-Z to zoom out and fit the clip to the window with a single keystroke.

To make subframe adjustments to an audio clip's edit points:

1. Open the audio clip on the Audio tab; then jump the playhead to the edit point you want to adjust.

2. Use the marquee selection feature of the Zoom tool (**Figure 12.15**) to zoom in until the playhead looks like a bar.

3. Hold down the Shift key; then click the Audio tab playhead and drag it to the subframe location of the new In or Out point (**Figure 12.16**).

4. Press I (or O) to stamp a new In (or Out) point (**Figure 12.17**).

✔ Tip

■ To add an audio keyframe in a location that's not on a frame line, you don't need to adjust the playhead; just zoom way in and use the Pen tool to add the keyframe.

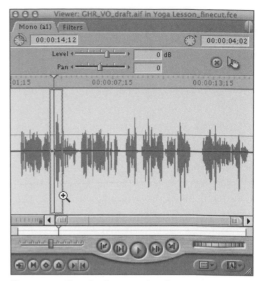

Figure 12.15 Use the Zoom tool to drag a marquee around the playhead. When the view zooms in, the playhead will still be in view.

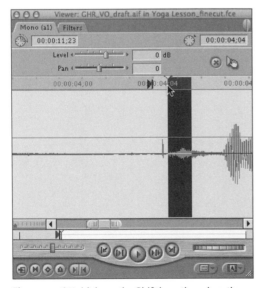

Figure 12.16 Hold down the Shift key; then drag the Audio tab playhead to the exact location of the new In or Out point.

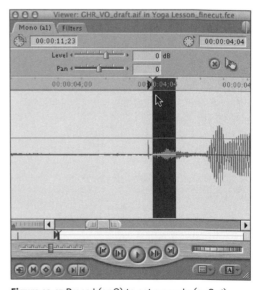

Figure 12.17 Press I (or O) to set a new In (or Out) point. This In point has been adjusted to trim out a small pop at the beginning of a word.

Figure 12.18 Click and hold to grab the drag hand.

Figure 12.19 Drag and drop to insert a clip into a sequence in the Canvas window.

To drag an audio clip into the Timeline or the Canvas window:

1. Start with an open clip and the Viewer window selected.

2. Position the pointer over the drag hand. When the pointer changes to a hand shape, you're in the right spot (**Figure 12.18**).

3. Drag from that spot to the Canvas or the Timeline.

   This inserts your audio clip into the open sequence (**Figure 12.19**).

Sounds Good: Scrubbing Audio with JKL Keys

Use JKL keys to get a better low- and high speed playback; dragging the playhead across the Scrubber produces ghastly chopped up-sounding playback that's not useful for much. (Toggle audio scrubbing off and on by pressing Shift-S; you'll still be able to use the JKL key method.) Here's how to use JKL to zero in on a precise point:

- Press L and K together for slow forward playback; press J and K together for slow reverse playback.

- Release the L (or J) as you keep the K key depressed for precision playhead parking on any frame.

Editing Audio in the Timeline

Editing in the Viewer is fine, but here are a few compelling reasons to do your audio editing right in the Timeline:

◆ Timeline tracks are the only place where you can view all your audio tracks at once.

◆ You can set audio level or filter keyframes and sculpt audio levels right in the Timeline.

◆ Canvas and Timeline playback are locked together, so the Timeline is a good place to trim audio on the fly as you watch your sequence play back.

Most of the tools and techniques collected here are discussed in Chapter 10, "Editing in the Timeline and the Canvas." These techniques can give you more control when you need to fine-tune a particular bit of dialogue or a sound effect in a busy soundtrack (**Figure 12.20**).

◆ **Track height:** Use the largest track size for fine-tuning and close work; use the smallest size for a multitrack overview. Press Shift-T to cycle through the track sizes. If you're using the waveform display to fine-tune an edit, you can stretch just the track you're focusing on.

◆ **Turn on audio waveforms:** Displaying audio waveforms in the Timeline can be a big help when you edit audio, but displaying waveforms slows the Timeline's performance. Toggle audio waveforms off and on by pressing Command-Option-W.

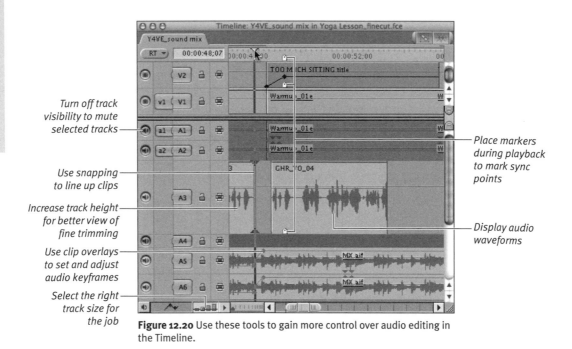

Turn off track visibility to mute selected tracks

Use snapping to line up clips

Increase track height for better view of fine trimming

Use clip overlays to set and adjust audio keyframes

Select the right track size for the job

Place markers during playback to mark sync points

Display audio waveforms

Figure 12.20 Use these tools to gain more control over audio editing in the Timeline.

◆ **Markers:** When you're trying to hit the perfect spot for a sound effect or music cue, you can set a Timeline marker right at the sweet spot by tapping the M key as you watch your sequence play back. You can also hold down the M key while you watch and then set a marker by releasing the key at the perfect moment.

◆ **Soloing and muting tracks:** As you build up your audio tracks, *track soloing*—silencing all but one audio track so you can concentrate on one sound—makes it much easier to trim precisely or isolate problem sounds in a busy track. Click the Solo button on the track you want to hear. The Mute button offers another route to selective monitoring: just mute the tracks you want to silence.

◆ **Snapping:** Snapping makes certain points in the Timeline "sticky." With snapping on, the edges of clips snap together, or a clip will snap to an edit point on an adjacent track when dragged close to it. When you're making fine adjustments to your audio, snapping can be a help (like when you're trying to line up a stack of audio clips to a marker or the playhead position) or a hindrance (when you're trying to drag a sound effect to the perfect location, and snapping jerks your clip to the nearest edit point). Remember: You can toggle snapping on or off *at any time*—even midmove—by pressing the N key.

Editing Clips with Multiple Audio Channels

Final Cut Express 2 introduced official support for *merged clips*—a type of clip created in FCE by permanently linking up to 24 audio clips with a single video clip. Earlier versions of the program used workarounds to support clips composed of audio and video linked inside Final Cut Express, but "official" merged clips make it possible to reliably sync video with production audio recorded separately, while preserving separate audio timecode. Open the Item Properties window on any audio+video clip, and you'll see that each audio channel has its own data column (**Figure 12.21**).

Merged clips appear in the Viewer with multiple Audio tabs sufficient to accommodate the number of audio channels in the clip (**Figure 12.22**). When you open a merged clip in the Viewer, additional source track-targeting controls automatically appear in the Timeline—one for each audio channel in the merged clip (**Figure 12.23**).

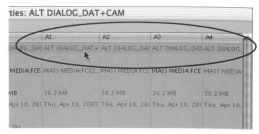

Figure 12.21 The Item Properties window displays separate tracking data for each audio channel.

Figure 12.22 This merged clip contains four channels of stereo audio, so two Audio tabs appear in the clip's Viewer—one tab for each of the two stereo audio pairs.

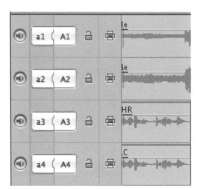

Figure 12.23 When a clip with multiple audio channels is opened in the Viewer, additional source track-targeting controls automatically appear in the Timeline.

You can set separate source In and Out points for video and audio (**Figure 12.24**), but you can mark only a single set of audio edit points. Those audio edit points will be used on all audio channels when you perform the edit (**Figure 12.25**).

You can trim edit points on individual tracks in the Timeline by overriding linked selection (**Figure 12.26**). You can also exclude selected audio channels from an edit by disconnecting source track-targeting controls on the tracks you wish to exclude before you perform the edit (**Figure 12.27**).

Figure 12.24 You can mark split video and audio edit points in a merged clip, but you can mark only a single set of audio edit points.

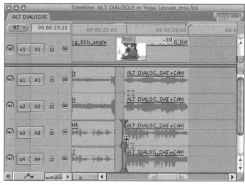

Figure 12.26 Once the merged clip has been edited into the Timeline, you're free to trim the individual audio channels.

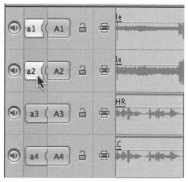

Figure 12.27 Disconnect the source targeting controls on tracks you want to exclude from a multichannel audio edit.

Figure 12.25 When you perform the edit, the same audio edit points will be used on all audio channels.

Recording Audio with the Voice Over Tool

The Voice Over tool is a nifty gadget designed to record synchronous audio as FCE plays back a selected portion of your sequence. Here's a brief rundown of its features:

◆ You can monitor your existing tracks through headphones as you record.

◆ Each completed audio take is automatically placed on a new Timeline track in the portion of the sequence you specified.

◆ When you record multiple takes, FCE automatically creates a new Timeline track for each take's clip.

◆ The Voice Over tool automatically records before and after your Mark In and Mark Out points, so your recorded track won't be cut off if your voiceover runs over.

◆ Once you complete your recording, you are free to reposition, trim, and polish your new voiceover tracks just as you would any other FCE clip.

Anatomy of the Voice Over tool

The Voice Over tool is a self-contained audio recording interface within FCE. When you set up for your recording session, use the Input controls to configure your audio input hardware settings and set audio recording levels, and use the Headphones controls to set monitoring levels. When you're ready to record, use the transport controls for preview and capture. The status display helps you keep in step with FCE's playback without having to watch the picture.

To open the Voice Over tool:

◆ Choose Tools > Voice Over.

The Tool Bench appears with the Voice Over tool displayed (**Figure 12.28**).

Transport controls

◆ **Record/Stop button:** Click to start audio recording and Timeline playback. Once recording starts, this button changes to the Stop button. Click again (or press the Escape key) to stop recording. If you stop recording before your specified Out point, the audio you recorded is saved to disk, and the partial clip is placed in the Timeline.

◆ **Review button:** Click to play back the Timeline section you've specified, without recording. Use Review while you rehearse your voiceover.

◆ **Discard button:** Click to delete the clip and media file from the previous take. The Discard button is dimmed until you've recorded your first voiceover clip. *Using the Discard button to delete a take is not undoable.*

Status display

◆ **Status area:** A progress bar indicates what proportion of your specified Timeline section has been recorded, along with a message indicating the Voice Over tool's current state.

Status messages include:

◆ **Ready to Record:** Indicates that the Voice Over tool is standing by to record.

◆ **Starting:** Appears during the 5-second countdown before Timeline playback reaches your specified In point. FCE records audio during this pre-roll period, to ensure that your performance is preserved even if you jump the gun and start speaking too soon.

continues on next page

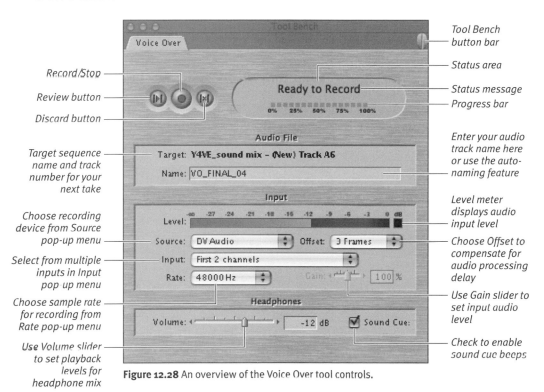

Figure 12.28 An overview of the Voice Over tool controls.

◆ **Recording:** Appears when Timeline playback reaches your specified In point. The Recording status message displays a countdown (accompanied by audio cue beeps in your headphones) during the last 5 seconds before your specified Out point.

◆ **Finishing:** Appears when FCE reaches your specified Out point. FCE continues to record 2 seconds past your specified Out point to ensure that your last word won't be cut off, preserving your take if you run a little over.

◆ **Saving:** Appears while FCE saves your voiceover recording from RAM to a file on your specified scratch disk.

Audio File area

◆ **Target:** This field shows the sequence name and track number where your next voiceover take will be placed. The target track updates automatically, moving down to the next available track for each subsequent take.

◆ **Name:** Enter a name for your voiceover recording here. The filename will automatically increment as you record subsequent takes. This name is used for both the clip and the source media file on disk. If the name is already in use by another clip in the same capture folder, FCE automatically appends a number to the duplicate name.

Input controls

Use the Input controls to select the source, configure the format, and adjust the incoming audio signal that you're recording with the Voice Over tool. These settings are for the Voice Over tool only; they won't affect your capture preset settings.

◆ **Level:** This audio meter displays the input recording levels you set with the Gain slider, located at the bottom right of the Input controls section.

◆ **Source:** Choose your audio input device from this pop-up menu. The specific external recording equipment you have connected will determine your choices.

◆ **Input:** If your audio input device has multiple inputs, select which input you want FCE to record from this pop-up menu.

◆ **Rate:** Choose an audio sample rate for your recording from this pop-up menu. Only sample rates that your selected audio device supports should appear. If you can, select the rate that matches the audio sample rate of your sequence settings. If your audio device doesn't support your sequence's sample rate, choose the highest sample rate available.

◆ **Offset:** Choose an offset to compensate for any processing delay in your incoming audio signal.

◆ **Gain:** Use this slider to adjust the input levels from your microphone or other recording device.

✔ Tip

■ DV camcorders typically introduce a delay of 3 frames; an average USB capture device introduces a delay of 1 frame. If you use the Voice Over tool to record replacement dialogue, even a couple frames of delay can be a bother when you are trying to judge quickly whether the lip sync in a take is good enough.

Headphones controls

◆ **Volume:** Use this slider, or enter a value in decibels, to adjust the playback volume in your headphones.

◆ **Sound Cues:** Check this box to hear cue beeps in your headphones during recording. The beeps won't be recorded in your voiceover recording.

✔ Tip

■ If you don't plan to monitor your program's existing soundtrack during your voiceover recording, be sure to mute any speakers that are within range of your microphone, or mute the playback here in the Headphones control panel. Set the Volume slider to −60 dB and disable the Sound Cues check box.

Voice Over tool setup checklist

The Voice Over tool may streamline your recording process, but remember: You're still setting up for a recording session. If you intend to use these tracks in a final product, you should plan on running a full test to check your audio quality before starting your recording session. Here's a list of setup tasks:

◆ **Set up your external recording device.** You can hook up any audio recording device that's compatible with the Apple Sound Manager; options include the built-in DV microphone on your DV camera, a PCI audio card, or a USB audio capture device. If your Mac has one (and you're not too picky), you can use the built-in microphone port on the back of the computer.

◆ **Set up headphones.** Plug headphones into your computer's built-in headphone jack. You may want to configure your setup to allow headphone monitoring for both the recordist and the voiceover talent.

◆ **Calculate the offset of your audio recording device.** Digital recording devices typically introduce a short delay while the device processes the analog audio signal from your microphone. This delay can offset your voiceover clips from your performer's original timing. You could go back and adjust all your clips by hand, but the Voice Over tool allows you to set a compensating offset that will put your tracks right back in sync. See Chapter 22 of Apple's *Final Cut Express Help* PDF for details on the offset calibration process.

◆ **Test your setup.** Listen to playback of your audio away from the whir and whine of your editing workstation. Better yet, set up an external video monitor away from your computer and drives and isolate your voiceover talent from the sound of your CPU and drives when recording voiceover.

✔ Tip

■ If you select your DV camera's microphone as your audio recording device, you won't be able to record until you turn off your external video feed by choosing View > External Video > Off.

To record synchronous audio with the Voice Over tool:

1. Follow the Voice Over tool setup procedure outlined earlier.

2. In the Timeline, mark In and Out points to specify the duration of your recording by defining the section of your sequence you want to record over (**Figure 12.29**). If you do not set In and Out points, recording will start at the playhead position and stop at the end of the last clip in the Timeline.

3. Specify the target location of your new voiceover audio clip by choosing the Timeline audio track immediately *above* your desired voiceover track position, and set that track as the channel 2 target track (**Figure 12.30**).

4. Choose Tools > Voice Over.

   The Tool Bench appears with the Voice Over tab displayed.

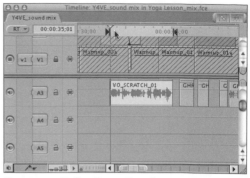

Figure 12.29 Define the section of your sequence you want to record by marking In and Out points in the Timeline.

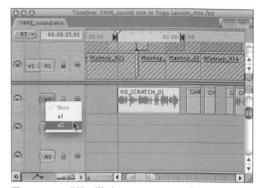

Figure 12.30 FCE will place your new audio on a new track immediately below the track you set as the a2 target track.

Cue Beep Choreography

The Voice Over tool offers the option of hearing cue beeps along with the audio track playback in your headphones. These beeps are invaluable if you can't watch the screen because your eyes are glued to the script you're about to read. Unfortunately, you can't easily adjust the beep level independently of the rest of the headphone playback mix, and a little beep goes a long way.

Here's the sequence and timing of the cue beeps:

1. Three beeps mark off the first 3 seconds at the start of the 5-second pre-roll. The last 2 seconds before playback reaches your In point are beepless.

2. Exactly 15 seconds before playback reaches your Out point, you'll be cued with a single warning beep.

3. During the last 5 seconds of recording, you'll hear five beeps—the last beep is longer and has a lower pitch. Try not to panic. Remember—you still have those 2 seconds of post-roll recording as protection.

Figure 12.31 Click the Record button or press Shift-C to start recording and playback.

Figure 12.32 When playback reaches your specified In point, the Voice Over tool status display turns red, and the message switches to "Recording."

5. On the Voice Over tab, click the Record button (**Figure 12.31**).

The Timeline playhead jumps back 5 seconds before your specified In point. FCE starts playback and recording and displays the "Starting" status message during this 5-second pre-roll countdown. When FCE reaches your specified In point, the status message area displays "Recording" (**Figure 12.32**).

6. Start speaking, or cue your voiceover talent.

FCE continues recording for 2 seconds after the playback reaches your specified Out point, and the Status message area displays "Finishing." FCE saves your new audio clip in the capture folder specified in your Scratch Disk preferences. Your new audio clip appears in the Timeline (**Figure 12.33**), and the Voice Over tool is reset so that it displays the "Ready to Record" status message.

7. If you want to record additional takes, mute the previous take by turning off its Timeline track before you record (**Figure 12.34**).

continues on next page

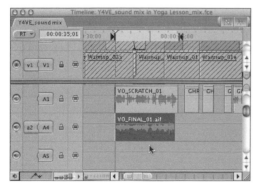

Figure 12.33 Your new audio clip appears in the Timeline.

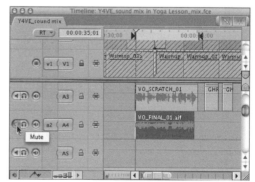

Figure 12.34 Click the Audio Mute button to silence the Timeline track of the previous take before you record a second take.

RECORDING AUDIO WITH THE VOICE OVER TOOL

371

8. Repeat steps 5 and 6 to record additional takes in the same Timeline location.

Your additional takes appear as audio clips on new Timeline tracks that appear below your first take (**Figure 12.35**). The a2 track target automatically moves down one track, and you're ready to record another take on the newly created track.

✔ Tips

■ Did your voiceover take get cut off at the head or tail of the clip? Never fear. FCE was recording during the entire pre- and post-roll. You can adjust the In and Out points of your truncated take's audio clip (**Figure 12.36**) and retrieve your first consonant or your last gasp.

■ Does this sound familiar? You got tongue-tied when you recorded "VO Take 1," so you deleted that take from your Timeline and you're ready to record a new take 1. Maybe you're wondering why the Voice Over tool stubbornly refuses to let you reuse the name "VO Take 1." Here's why—you deleted the clip reference to "VO Take 1" from the Timeline, but the audio file created when you recorded the first "VO Take 1" remains in your capture folder. FCE wisely forbids having two files with the same name in the same folder. If you want to reuse the name "VO Take 1," delete the audio file with that name from your capture folder.

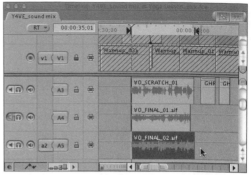

Figure 12.35 Additional takes appear as audio clips on new Timeline tracks inserted below your first take.

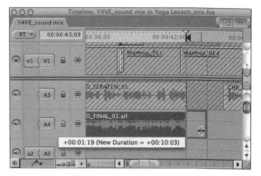

Figure 12.36 Adjusting the Out point of an audio clip to restore the end of the take that extended past the specified Out point during recording.

Mixing and Finishing Audio

This section covers all the ways you can adjust your audio clips' volume (levels), stereo pan position, and sound quality. You'll get a few tips on mixing and learn how to apply and tweak FCE's audio filters.

Setting audio levels

A sequence clip's levels and pan position are adjustable from several locations (**Figure 12.37**):

◆ On the Viewer's Audio tab, set levels and pan by visually editing the line graph that appears as an overlay on your audio waveform or by adjusting the Level and Pan sliders. See "Adjusting levels and pan on the Audio tab" later in this chapter.

continues on next page

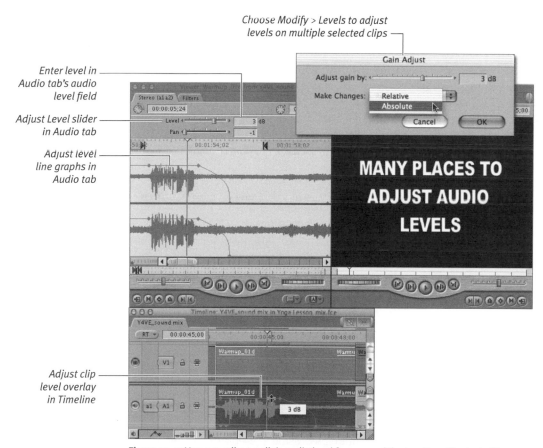

Choose Modify > Levels to adjust
levels on multiple selected clips

Enter level in
Audio tab's audio
level field

Adjust Level slider
in Audio tab

Adjust level
line graphs in
Audio tab

Adjust clip
level overlay
in Timeline

Figure 12.37 You can adjust a clip's audio level from any of the locations illustrated here.

◆ In the Timeline, adjust a clip's audio levels with the Audio Level line clip overlay. For more information about using these keyframing tools, see "Working with Keyframes in the Timeline" in Chapter 14.

◆ You can use the Modify > Levels command to set levels for multiple audio clips in a single operation. See "Making multiclip adjustments" in Chapter 10.

Remember: Adjusting a sequence clip's levels or pan position in *any* of these locations will be reflected in the other locations.

FCE Protocol: Measuring Digital Audio in Decibels (dB)

Decibels (dB) is a unit of measurement for audio levels. Several decibel scales are used in the audio/video world (and some excellent technical articles on the Web explain them in detail). All of these scales describe amplitude as perceived by the human ear, but they measure different amplitude-tracking indicators. The scales all express amplitude in relationship to a fixed reference point, but different scales use different reference points. Professional analog audio uses a reference point of 0 dBVU and expresses dynamic range by adding *headroom* (range above 0 dBVU) plus *signal to noise* (the range from 0 dBVU down to the device's *noise floor*). For instance, an analog audio device with a "signal-to-noise ratio" of 76 dB and 22 dB of headroom has a total dynamic range of 98 dB.

Digital audio behaves differently and therefore requires a different structure for expressing dynamic range. There's no such thing as headroom in audio that's stored as binary numbers. Digital audio signal quality improves as levels approach 0 dBfs, but exceed the maximum level allowed by even a hair, and the audio levels are clipped.

That's why the *dBfs scale*, the standard decibel scale used for digital audio, uses a reference point that corresponds to the *highest* value that can be expressed in a particular bit depth and calls that value 0 dBfs. The amplitude measurement of dBfs scales down from 0 dBfs to the lowest level that can be expressed at that bit depth. For example, 16-bit digital audio has a dynamic range of 0 dBfs (the maximum) to –96 dBfs (the smallest value). Greater bit depth increases digital signal processing resolution; FCE uses 32-bit floating-point resolution to compute audio mixes. Even with this increased accuracy, the dBfs scale still maintains the same maximum allowable level; the extra dynamic resolution accommodates the intermediate bit values generated by blending and processing multiple digital audio streams during the mixing process. The extended dynamic range (–177 dBfs) of 32-bit resolution seems enormous, but it's necessary for accurate processing of 24-bit digital audio.

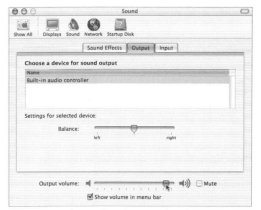

Figure 12.38 The Macintosh's Sound preferences pane.

Monitor levels and mixing

It's important to keep your speaker levels constant when you adjust audio levels for a sequence. There's more than one place to adjust your monitoring level. Take a moment before you start working to set up everything, and note your settings so that you can recalibrate if necessary.

If you'll be recording out to an external video deck or camera, check the audio output levels on the recording device's meters. Play the loudest section of your program. If your recording device has no meters, record a test of the loudest section and review the audio quality.

Check your Macintosh's Sound preferences pane to make sure your computer's sound output level is set high enough (**Figure 12.38**). Next, set a comfortable listening level on the amplifier that drives your external speakers. Now you are in a position to make consistent volume adjustments to the audio in your sequence.

✔ Tip

- There's no way to adjust computer audio levels within Final Cut Express. Instead, adjust your levels from your Mac's Sound preferences pane (see Figure 12.38).

Adjusting levels and pan on the Audio tab

The Audio tab is a good place to make fine level and pan adjustments, but you must open and adjust each clip separately. To make multiclip level and pan adjustments, use the Timeline level line overlays.

To set audio clip levels on the Audio tab:

1. Start with an open clip and the Viewer window selected.

2. *Do one of the following:*

◆ Drag the Level slider to the right to increase clip volume, or to the left to decrease clip volume (**Figure 12.39**).

◆ Drag the pink Level line graph displayed over the audio waveform: dragging higher increases volume; dragging lower decreases volume (**Figure 12.40**).

◆ Press Control-+ (plus) or Control- – (minus) to adjust audio levels by single-decibel increments.

◆ Choose Modify > Audio and make a gain selection from the submenu (**Figure 12.41**). Note that the submenu lists keyboard shortcuts for nudging audio levels.

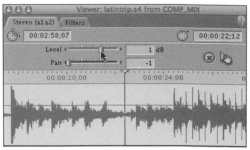

Figure 12.39 Dragging the Level slider to the right increases the clip volume.

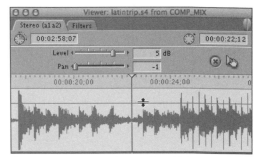

Figure 12.40 Dragging the Level line higher increases the volume.

Figure 12.41 Choose Modify > Audio and make a gain selection from the submenu. Note the keyboard shortcuts listed to the right of the submenu choices.

MIXING AND FINISHING AUDIO

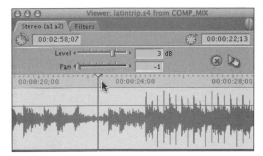

Figure 12.42 Move the playhead to the location where you want the level change to start.

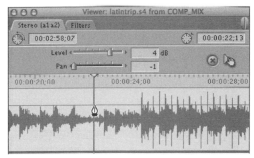

Figure 12.43 Adjust the level with the Level slider and click the level line with the Pen tool to set a keyframe.

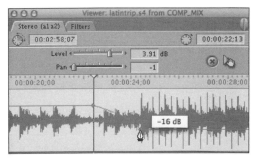

Figure 12.44 At the next location where you want a level change, use the Pen tool to drag the level line to the new level setting.

To create dynamic level changes within a clip:

1. Start with an open clip and the Viewer window selected.

2. Park the playhead where you want to start the level change (**Figure 12.42**).

3. Adjust the level using the Level slider.

4. Select the Pen tool from the Tool palette; then set a keyframe by clicking the level line with the Pen tool (**Figure 12.43**).

5. Move the playhead to the next location where you want a change in the level.

6. With the Pen tool, drag the level line to the new audio level (**Figure 12.44**).

   Another keyframe is set automatically as you drag the level line with the Pen tool.

✔ Tips

- You can use the Audio Tab's Level and Pan sliders to record audio level and pan changes in real time. For more information, see "Real-time audio level and pan adjustment" later in this chapter.

- If you just want to make quick level adjustments to an entire group of clips, it's faster to select the clips in the Timeline and then use the Modify > Levels command to adjust all levels in the selected clips in a single operation. For more information, see "Making multiclip adjustments" in Chapter 10.

- Click the Set Keyframe button in the lower part of the window to set a keyframe on both the Level and Pan line graphs at the current playhead position.

MIXING AND FINISHING AUDIO

Adjusting the pan position

The pan position is the left/right placement of sound for single audio channels. Clips with one or two channels of discrete audio will initially open with pan set to the center.

To set a pan position:

1. Start with an open clip and the Viewer window selected.

2. *Do one of the following:*

   ◆ Drag the Pan slider to the right to pan toward the right; drag the slider to the left to pan toward the left (**Figure 12.45**).

   ◆ Drag the purple Pan line graph displayed over the audio waveform. Drag higher to pan right; drag lower to pan left (**Figure 12.46**).

   ◆ Choose Modify > Audio and make a pan selection from the submenu.

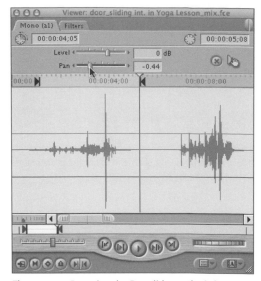

Figure 12.45 Dragging the Pan slider to the left pans your track toward the left channel.

Figure 12.46 Dragging the Pan line graph lower pans your track toward the left channel.

MIXING AND FINISHING AUDIO

Figure 12.47 The Pan slider at its base setting of –1. This setting replicates the original mix of a stereo source track.

Adjusting stereo spread

On stereo audio clips, the Pan control adjusts the *spread* (the degree of stereo separation), and it adjusts left and right channels simultaneously and equally.

You can use the Pan slider or line graph to adjust the stereo spread. The setting options on the Pan slider are as follows:

◆ The base setting of –1 outputs the left audio channel to the left and the right audio channel to the right. This setting accurately reproduces the stereo mix of a track from a music CD.

◆ A setting of 0 outputs the left and right audio channels equally to both sides.

◆ A setting of +1 swaps the channels, outputting the left audio channel to the right and the right audio channel to the left.

To adjust the pan on a stereo audio clip:

1. Start with an open clip and the Viewer window selected.

2. *Do one of the following:*
   ◆ Drag the Pan slider to adjust the stereo pan positioning (**Figure 12.47**).
   ◆ Drag the purple Pan level line graph displayed over the audio waveform at the center line between the two stereo channels. Drag away from the center line for a +1 setting; drag toward the center for a –1 setting.

MIXING AND FINISHING AUDIO

Real-time audio level and pan adjustment

Final Cut Express can record audio level and pan adjustments in real time.

You perform keyframe recording on the Audio tab. Each individual clip must be opened on the Audio tab first, so real-time level and pan adjustment must be performed one clip at a time.

You can freely mix and match real-time level adjustment on the Audio tab with manual tweaking of level and pan keyframes in the Timeline or on the Audio tab; they're just two means of achieving the same end: fine-tuning the dynamic level and pan information stored with each individual clip.

To record audio level or pan keyframes in real time:

1. Open the audio clip on the Viewer's Audio tab.

2. Locate the point where you want to start recording audio keyframes and position the playhead a few seconds before your first planned move (**Figure 12.48**). You might want to loop playback of the section you're working on.

3. Start playback.

4. Position the pointer over the Level or Pan slider control and then press the mouse button to start recording keyframes (**Figure 12.49**). Drag the slider to the desired level, keeping the mouse button held down until you've completed your move; then release the mouse to stop recording keyframes.

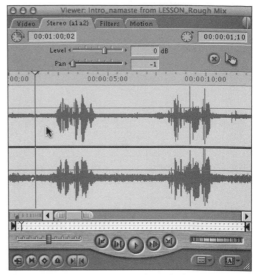

Figure 12.48 Position the Timeline playhead a few seconds before your first planned fader move.

Figure 12.49 Drag the slider to the desired level, holding down the mouse button until you complete your move. If you want to maintain a steady audio level at the end of a move, release the mouse at the end of the move and then press, hold, and drag the mouse again when you want to perform your next move.

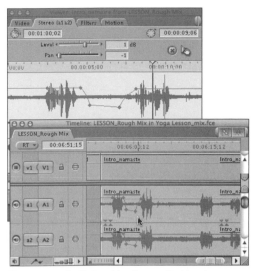

Figure 12.50 Audio level keyframes that track your mixer moves appear on the clip's audio level overlays in the Timeline.

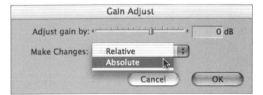

Figure 12.51 Use the Modify > Levels command to reset all selected clip levels to a specific decibel level in a single operation.

Final Cut Express sets audio level keyframes that track your moves. These keyframed audio levels appear in the clip's audio level overlays in the Timeline and on the Audio tab of the Viewer (**Figure 12.50**).

✔ **Tip**

■ If you have already applied keyframes to sculpt a clip's audio levels, the new keyframes you just recorded will overwrite any previously applied keyframes.

To delete all audio keyframes from a clip:

1. In the Timeline, select the clip.

2. Choose Edit > Remove Attributes; or press Command-Option-V.

3. In the Remove Attributes dialog box, check Levels and/or Pan; then click OK.

Or do this:

1. In the Timeline, select the clip.

2. Choose Modify > Levels; or press Command-Option-L.

3. In the Gain Adjust dialog box, choose Absolute from the pop-up menu; then use the slider to set a clip volume, or enter a dB value indicated next to the slider (**Figure 12.51**).

   The clip's level is set to the dB value you entered, and all level keyframes are removed from the clip.

✔ **Tip**

■ Both of these methods for resetting audio clip levels can be used on multiclip selections. Quick level resetting will surely save your sanity as you're trying to master the art of real-time audio mixing.

MIXING AND FINISHING AUDIO

Adjusting Audio Filters

Final Cut Express's suite of audio filters is geared toward repairing problems in production audio. That's good, because production audio frequently has problems—problems that don't come to light until you review your footage in the editing room. FCE's equalization, compression, and noise reduction filters are tools you can use to reduce rumble in an exterior street recording or improve crispness in a dialogue track. (Before you ask, there is no filter that will strip background music out of dialogue.)

You apply FCE's audio filters in the same way that you apply video filters.

FCE has improved the real-time previewing of audio filters considerably, but some audio filters have to be rendered before you can hear the results of your settings adjustment. Lack of real-time feedback can make adjusting audio filters in FCE more challenging. Try the method described here to reduce the lag time between when you adjust an audio filter's setting and when you hear the results. If the filter you're adjusting plays back without rendering, so much the better—you get to skip the rendering step.

To adjust an audio filter's settings:

1. Make a short test subclip from a representative section of your audio track (**Figure 12.52**). If you're trying to fix a problem, pick out a worst-case section and then maybe an average-case section to try your worst-case settings on. Make the test subclip long enough so you can evaluate your work—say 5 to 10 seconds.

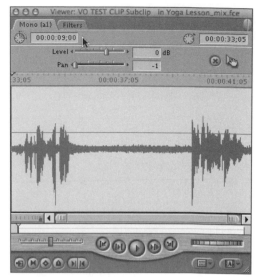

Figure 12.52 Create a test subclip using a representative section of your audio track.

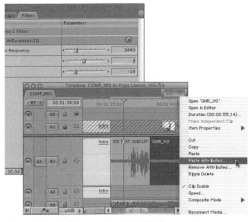

Figure 12.53 When you've tuned in filter settings, copy them and then use the Paste Attributes command to paste the filter and its settings from the test clip to your full-length audio track in the sequence.

Figure 12.54 In the Paste Attributes dialog box, paste just the filters from your test audio clip onto the longer audio clip you're filtering.

2. Open your test clip in the Viewer, apply the filter, and start tweaking the filter settings. If you like, you can pull the Filters tab completely out of the Viewer window so you can view your subclip playing back on the Audio tab as you adjust filter settings.

3. You'll hear a series of beeps (FCE's rendering indicator for audio) if your test clip requires rendering. In that case, you'll need to render the audio before you can hear the effect of the audio filter you've applied. Your short test clip should render quickly.

4. Enable looped playback and then try to get into a rhythm of adjusting and listening. When you think you've zeroed in on your filter settings, copy and paste the filter (and its settings) from the test clip to your full-length audio track in the sequence. Use the Paste Attributes command (**Figure 12.53**) to paste just the filters (**Figure 12.54**).

✔ Tips

- Audio filters applied to audio that is formatted as a stereo pair are applied to both channels equally, and only one set of controls appears on the Viewer's Filters tab.

- You can copy an audio filter with all its current settings and paste it onto other clips or onto an entire nested sequence. If you perfect the EQ setting that cancels out the sound of your camera, you can easily apply the same filter setting wherever it's needed. See "Copying and pasting clip attributes" in Chapter 10.

Smart Filter Tweaking Tips

The best way to pinpoint the frequency of a problem sound in your production audio is to apply an EQ filter that's set to a narrow bandwidth and then boost the filter gain. Sweep that narrow bandwidth slowly across the frequency spectrum until the problem sound is the *most* noticeable. Now that you've identified the problem frequency, attenuate the filter gain and widen the filter's bandwidth until the problem sound is minimized.

Overprocessing your audio to eliminate acoustic deficiencies or noise can actually hurt your overall sound quality. Consider your soundtrack as a whole—is the noise really noticeable, or is it buried in the mix? Audiences are accustomed to ambient noise; we're surrounded by it and are already trained to listen selectively. Sometimes adding a little more ambient noise to a mix creates a constant field that's less noticeable.

This last tip is the most important: If the program you're editing is going to be handed over to a post-production sound crew for finishing, *don't* try to fix your production audio with filters and processing beforehand. Audio specialists can do their best work when you give them unprocessed tracks to work with.

ADJUSTING AUDIO FILTERS

CREATING
TRANSITIONS

Transitions are a small, but essential, part of film grammar. Over the years, transitions have developed an important role in film story language. Filmmakers rely on the audience's knowledge of the transition "code." This grammar of transitions and what they signify in movie language has grown up with the movies. These days, viewers are hardly aware of the translations that they make while watching film: fade-out/fade-in means the passage of time, a ripple dissolve means "it was all a dream," and a heart-shaped iris wipe means you're watching reruns of *The Dating Game*.

Final Cut Express offers a library of more than 50 transition effects, which range from simple dissolves to complex 3D transitions. This chapter introduces the procedures for working with transitions in an editing context. For information on modifying effects settings to sculpt transitions, see Chapter 14, "Compositing and Effects Overview."

Adding Transition Effects

You can add transitions along with clips as you assemble your sequence by performing one of the two transition edit types available in the Canvas edit overlay, or you can apply transitions to edit points after you have assembled your sequence. Once you've applied transitions, you can go back and modify them as you refine your cut.

Final Cut Express displays transitions as overlays within a single Timeline track—an efficient use of screen real estate (**Figure 13.1**). You can adjust a transition directly in the Timeline window, or you can make more complex adjustments in the Transition Editor. The following procedures for adding a transition to a sequence are performed in the Timeline.

Figure 13.1 Transitions appear as overlays within a single Timeline track. The dark gray diagonal shading on the transition's Timeline icon indicates the transition's direction, alignment, and speed.

FCE Protocol: Transitions

◆ Because transitions are created by overlapping material from two adjacent clips, each source clip must have enough additional frames to span half of the transition's duration. If a source clip is too short to create the transition at your specified duration, Final Cut Express will calculate and apply the transition with a shorter duration, or not apply it at all if you have no additional frames.

◆ You can add transition effects as you edit a clip into a sequence, or you can add transitions to a previously edited sequence.

◆ You can place a transition so that it is centered on the cut, starts at the cut, or ends at the cut.

◆ When you use the Transition edit in the Canvas overlay to add a clip to your sequence, FCE always centers the transition on the cut between the two clips. If you want to add a transition that either starts or ends at the cut, add the transition after the clips are placed in the sequence.

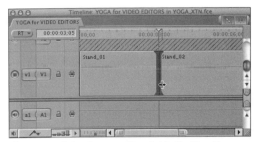

Figure 13.2 Selecting an edit point in the Timeline.

Figure 13.3 Choosing Cross Dissolve from the Effects menu.

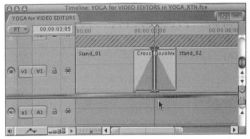

Figure 13.4 The Cross Dissolve transition is applied to the selected edit point in the Timeline.

To add a transition effect that's centered on a cut:

1. In the Timeline, select the edit point between two clips on the same Timeline track (**Figure 13.2**).

2. To add the transition effect, *do one of the following:*

   ◆ Choose Effects > Video Transitions; then select from the submenu's list of effects (**Figure 13.3**).

   ◆ Drag a transition effect from the Effects tab in the Browser onto the cut, centering it over the cut.

   ◆ To add the default transition, Control-click the edit point; then choose Add Transition from the shortcut menu.

   The transition is applied to the selected edit point (**Figure 13.4**).

✔ Tip

■ You can change the alignment of an existing transition by Control-clicking the selected transition in the Timeline and then choosing a different alignment from the shortcut menu.

ADDING TRANSITION EFFECTS

To add a transition effect that starts or ends at a cut:

◆ Drag a transition effect from the Effects tab in the Browser onto the edit point in the Timeline, aligning it so that it starts or ends at the cut (**Figure 13.5**).

✔ Tips

■ Create a fade-to-black transition by dragging the Cross Dissolve transition from the Effects tab of the Browser to the final clip in your sequence, aligning it so that it ends at the cut.

■ To fade up from black, drag the Cross Dissolve transition onto the beginning of the first clip in your sequence, aligning it to start at the first frame of the sequence.

Figure 13.5 Dragging the transition from the Effects tab of the Browser to the edit point in the Timeline. This Dip to Color Dissolve transition is aligned to end at the cut, creating a fade-out.

FCE Protocol: Saving Changes to Modified Transitions

When saving changes to a transition, remember that transitions follow the same protocols as clips and sequences. (For more information, review "FCE Protocol: Clips and Sequences" in Chapter 4.) Here's a summary of the main points:

◆ When you add a transition to a sequence by dragging it from the Browser to the Timeline, a copy of the transition is inserted into the sequence.

◆ You can open a transition from the Browser (outside a sequence) or from the Timeline (within a sequence).

◆ If you modify a transition from the Browser before you insert the transition into a sequence, the transition that is placed in the sequence includes the changes made in the Browser.

◆ Any changes you make to a transition from within a sequence are not made to the transition in the Browser. If you want to reuse a transition you've designed within a sequence, drag a copy of your revised transition from the Timeline back to the Browser.

ADDING TRANSITION EFFECTS

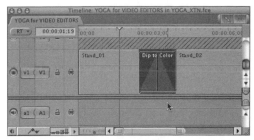

Figure 13.6 Select the transition you want to replace.

Figure 13.7 Choose a replacement transition from the Effects menu.

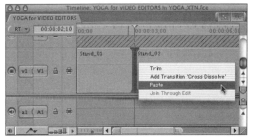

Figure 13.8 Control-click the edit point; then choose Paste from the shortcut menu.

To delete a transition from a sequence:

◆ In the Timeline, select the transition; then press the Delete key.

To replace one transition with another:

1. In the Timeline, select the transition you are replacing (**Figure 13.6**).

2. Choose Effects > Video (or Audio) Transitions; then select a replacement transition from a submenu (**Figure 13.7**).

To copy a transition and paste it in another location:

1. In the Timeline, select the transition you want to copy; then press Command-C.

2. Control-click the edit point where you want to paste the transition; then choose Paste from the shortcut menu (**Figure 13.8**).

✔ Tip

■ You can copy and apply a transition to another edit point in one stylish move. Select your desired transition and then hold down Option while dragging the transition to another edit point in the Timeline. This technique works with clips, too.

ADDING TRANSITION EFFECTS

Working with Default and Favorite Transitions

Final Cut Express offers one default video transition—a 1-second cross-dissolve (**Figure 13.9**)—and one default audio transition—a 1-second cross-fade (**Figure 13.10**). The default transitions are available from the Effects menu, the edit point's shortcut menu, and as keyboard commands. A transition edit, available in the Canvas edit overlay, automatically includes the default transition at the time you perform the edit. You can also designate a transition (or any other type of effect) as a Favorite by dragging the effect from the Browser, Viewer, or Timeline and placing it in the Favorites folder on the Effects tab in the Browser. Using Favorites is an easy way to save a transition's settings so you can reproduce the effect later. You can build up a small group of favorite transitions for a particular project.

To apply the default video transition:

Do one of the following:

◆ Select the edit point where you want to place the transition; then choose Effects > Default - Cross Dissolve.

◆ Control-click the edit point; then choose Add Transition 'Cross Dissolve' from the shortcut menu (**Figure 13.11**).

◆ Select the edit point; then press Command-T.

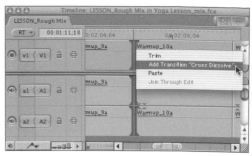

Figure 13.9 FCE's default video transition is a 1-second cross-dissolve.

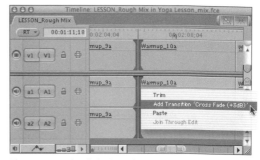

Figure 13.10 The default audio transition is a 1-second +3dB cross-fade.

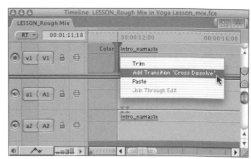

Figure 13.11 Control-click the edit point; then choose Add Transition 'Cross Dissolve' from the shortcut menu.

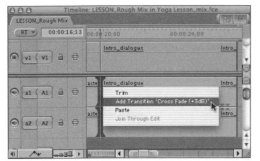

Figure 13.12 Control-click the edit point; then choose Add Transition 'Cross Fade (+3dB)' from the shortcut menu.

Figure 13.13 Dragging a modified transition from the Timeline to the Favorites folder, located on the Effects tab of the Browser.

To apply the default audio transition:

Do one of the following:

◆ Select the audio edit point where you want to place the transition; then choose Effects > Default - Cross Fade (+3dB).

◆ Control-click the edit point; then choose Add Transition 'Cross Fade (+3dB)' from the shortcut menu (**Figure 13.12**).

To create a favorite transition by saving its settings:

◆ In the Transition Editor or the Timeline, drag the transition icon to the Favorites folder on the Effects tab in the Browser (**Figure 13.13**).

WORKING WITH DEFAULT AND FAVORITE TRANSITIONS

391

To create a favorite transition before using it in a sequence:

1. On the Effects tab in the Browser, double-click the transition (**Figure 13.14**).

The transition opens in the Transition Editor.

2. Adjust the transition's settings in the Transition Editor; then use the drag handle to drag the modified transition into the Favorites folder (**Figure 13.15**).

3. In the Favorites folder, rename the new transition (**Figure 13.16**).

To delete a favorite transition from the Favorites folder:

◆ In the Favorites folder, select the transition you want to delete; then press Delete.

Figure 13.14 Double-click the transition you want to customize to open it in the Transition Editor.

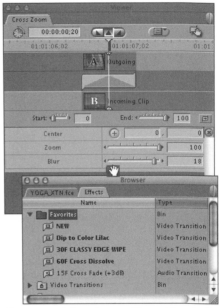

Figure 13.15 Adjust the transition settings in the Transition Editor and then drag the customized transition into the Favorites folder.

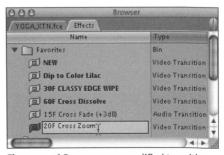

Figure 13.16 Rename your modified transition in the Favorites folder.

WORKING WITH DEFAULT AND FAVORITE TRANSITIONS

Figure 13.17 The Timeline playhead, positioned at the selected edit point; the playhead position will be used as the sequence In point.

Figure 13.18 Set source In and Out points in the Viewer. Be sure to leave at least 15 extra frames at the beginning of your clip to accommodate the transition.

Figure 13.19 Drag the source clip from the Viewer to the Canvas edit overlay; then drop the clip on the Overwrite with Transition edit area.

About transition edits

There are two types of transition edits: Insert with Transition and Overwrite with Transition. A transition edit automatically places your default transition at the head of the edit. When using either of the transition edit types, you'll need enough footage in your source clip to create the transition. Each source clip will need additional frames equal to half of the transition's duration.

To perform a transition edit:

1. Set the sequence In point by positioning the Timeline playhead where you want the edit to occur (**Figure 13.17**).

2. In the Viewer, set source In and Out points to define the part of the source clip you want to add to the sequence (**Figure 13.18**).

3. Drag the clip from the Viewer to either the Insert with Transition or the Overwrite with Transition edit overlay in the Canvas (**Figure 13.19**).

✔ Tip

■ Scenario: You need to apply the same 1-second dissolve to 101 sequence clips before your client arrives for a screening, and she just pulled into the parking lot. Don't panic. Here's a slick trick: Use the Group Select tool to select all 101 sequence clips; then drag the whole group of clips from the Timeline to the Canvas edit overlay and drop them on the Overwrite with Transition area. Final Cut Express will apply the default cross-dissolve transition to all 101 clips in a glorious display of computer automation—that is, if you remembered to allow handles on your clips. Try it sometime.

Editing Video Transitions

You can make dramatic changes to a video transition even after you have added it to your sequence. You can adjust its duration and placement and customize its appearance. Opening your transition in the Transition Editor will give you maximum access to the transition's settings, but you can perform many adjustments directly in the Timeline.

Figure 13.20 shows an overview of the Transition Editor interface.

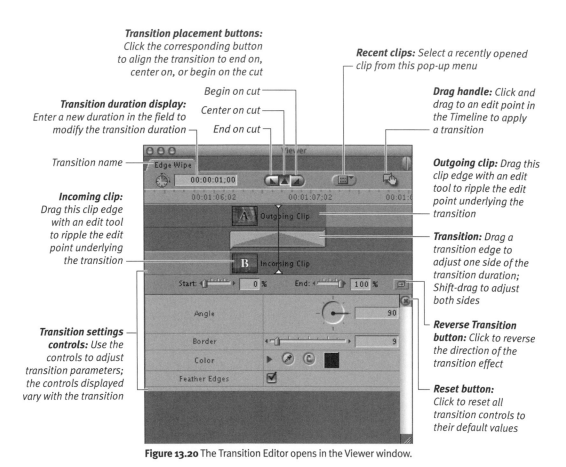

Transition placement buttons: Click the corresponding button to align the transition to end on, center on, or begin on the cut

Recent clips: Select a recently opened clip from this pop-up menu

Transition duration display: Enter a new duration in the field to modify the transition duration

Begin on cut

Center on cut

End on cut

Drag handle: Click and drag to an edit point in the Timeline to apply a transition

Transition name

Incoming clip: Drag this clip edge with an edit tool to ripple the edit point underlying the transition

Outgoing clip: Drag this clip edge with an edit tool to ripple the edit point underlying the transition

Transition: Drag a transition edge to adjust one side of the transition duration; Shift-drag to adjust both sides

Transition settings controls: Use the controls to adjust transition parameters; the controls displayed vary with the transition

Reverse Transition button: Click to reverse the direction of the transition effect

Reset button: Click to reset all transition controls to their default values

Figure 13.20 The Transition Editor opens in the Viewer window.

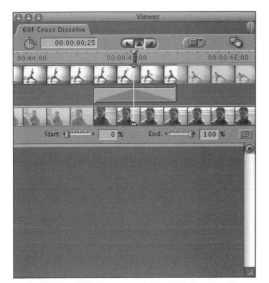

Figure 13.21 The Transition Editor with Thumbnail Display set to Filmstrip.

Using the Transition Editor

The Transition Editor (sometimes called the Transition Viewer) is a special version of the Viewer window that you use to make detailed adjustments to transition settings. Use the Transition Editor to do the following:

◆ Adjust the duration of the transition.

◆ Reverse the direction of the transition.

◆ Trim the edit point underlying the transition.

◆ Adjust the placement of the transition relative to the edit point. You can set a transition to end on the cut, center on the cut, begin on the cut, or occur anywhere in between.

◆ Adjust the starting and ending effect percentages. The default settings of a simple cross-dissolve would range from 0 to 100 percent. However, in a transition effect that incorporates a motion path, effect percentages specify the portion of the full path that will be included in the transition.

The Timeline's Thumbnail Display option controls the way clips appear in the Transition Editor (**Figure 13.21**). You can adjust the thumbnail display on the Timeline Options tab of the Sequence Settings window.

EDITING VIDEO TRANSITIONS

To open a transition in the Transition Editor:

Do one of the following:

◆ Control-click the transition; then choose Open *'name of the transition'* from the shortcut menu (**Figure 13.22**).

◆ In the Timeline, double-click the transition to open it in the Transition Editor.

◆ Select the transition's icon in the Timeline; then choose View > Transition in Editor.

To change the duration of a transition in the Transition Editor:

Do one of the following:

◆ Type a new duration in the Duration field; then press Enter (**Figure 13.23**).

◆ Drag either end of the transition (**Figure 13.24**).

The change in duration applies equally to both sides of the transition.

✔ Tip

■ FCE transitions apply equally to both sides of an edit point, so if you need an asymmetrical effect—where the transition effect is not applied to an equal number of frames on either side of the edit point—you must build it yourself. Here's how to build an asymmetrical dissolve. Place the incoming and outgoing clips on separate Timeline tracks and allow the areas you want to include in the dissolve to overlap. Then ramp the opacity levels to cross-dissolve from one clip to the other.

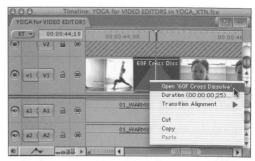

Figure 13.22 Control-click the transition; then choose Open *'name of the transition'* from the shortcut menu.

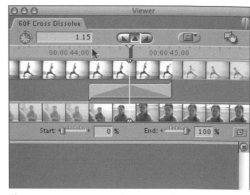

Figure 13.23 Type a new duration in the Duration field of the Transition Editor.

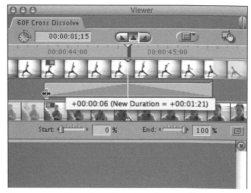

Figure 13.24 Dragging the edge of a transition to adjust its duration.

EDITING VIDEO TRANSITIONS

Figure 13.25 Positioning the pointer on the incoming clip's In point in the Transition Editor.

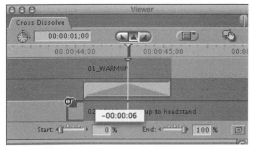

Figure 13.26 Performing a Ripple edit on the incoming clip's In point. Drag the edge of the clip to ripple the edit point underlying the transition.

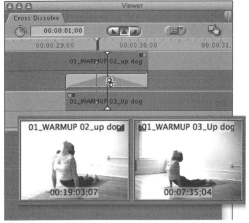

Figure 13.27 As you drag the Roll Edit tool on the transition, a two-up display in the Canvas shows the frames adjacent to the new edit point.

To perform a Ripple edit on a transition in the Transition Editor:

1. Position the pointer on the edit point you want to trim (**Figure 13.25**).

   In the Transition Editor, the edit points appear on the clip icons displayed in the tracks above and below the transition icon.

   The pointer changes to the Ripple Edit tool.

2. Drag the edit point (**Figure 13.26**).

   A Ripple edit is performed on the edit point underlying the transition as the Canvas display changes to show your new In point.

To perform a Roll edit on a transition in the Transition Editor:

◆ Place the pointer anywhere on the transition. When the pointer changes to the Roll Edit tool, drag it on the transition to perform a Roll edit on the edit point underlying the transition.

   As the Roll edit is performed, a two-up display in the Canvas changes to show the two frames adjacent to your new edit point (**Figure 13.27**).

To change the settings for a transition:

Do one or more of the following:

◆ To change the starting and ending effect percentages, drag the Start and End sliders (**Figure 13.28**) or type percentage values in the text boxes.

◆ To change the direction of the effect, click the Reverse button.

◆ To have the transition center on, start on, or end on the edit, click the corresponding placement button at the top center of the Transition Editor. Once you've changed the center point of a transition, these controls won't remember the original edit point.

◆ Make other settings as desired for the transition. For more information on modifying effects settings, see Chapter 14, "Compositing and Effects Overview."

To preview a transition in the Canvas:

1. Open the transition in the Transition Editor.

2. Position the Transition Editor's playhead at any point in the transition (**Figure 13.29**).

Figure 13.28 Using the slider to adjust end position settings for a wipe transition.

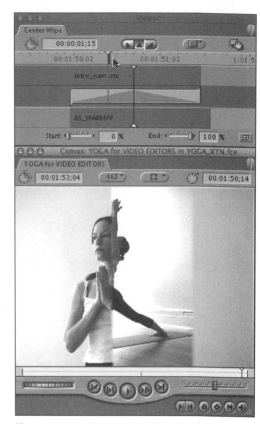

Figure 13.29 Position the Transition Editor's playhead at any point in the transition. The Canvas displays a preview of the transition at the selected playhead location.

3. Adjust the transition settings.

The Canvas display updates to reflect any adjustments made to the transition settings (**Figure 13.30**).

4. To preview a frame at another point in the transition, reposition the Transition Editor playhead (**Figure 13.31**).

✔ Tip

■ Hold down the Option key as you scrub the Canvas's Scrubber bar to preview your transition. You can also step through a transition one frame at a time by pressing the Right Arrow key to advance the transition by single frames. Press the Left Arrow key to step backward. A slow-motion view of the transition appears in the Canvas.

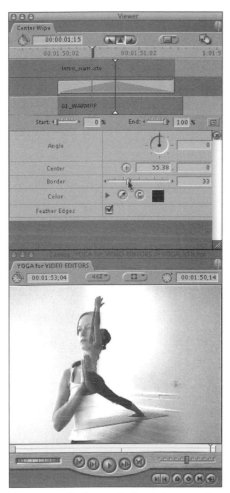

Figure 13.30 The Canvas display updates to reflect an adjustment to the transition's border width settings. A Center Wipe with wide, transparent border settings and soft edges can make a subtle replacement for yet another cross-dissolve.

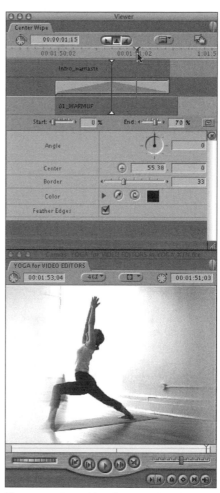

Figure 13.31 Reposition the Transition Editor's playhead, and the Canvas displays a preview of a frame later in the transition.

Editing transitions in the Timeline

You can streamline transition editing in the Timeline by using the shortcut menus. Control-clicking the transition itself opens one of the shortcut menus. A different shortcut menu is available for the edit point underlying the transition. Edit points that have transitions applied to them can still be trimmed in the same way as other edits; you can use the Trim Edit or Viewer windows or drag directly in the Timeline. For more information about trimming operations, see Chapter 11, "Fine Cut: Trimming Edits."

To adjust the duration of a transition in the Timeline:

◆ With the Selection tool, drag one edge of the transition to adjust its length.

Or do this:

1. Control-click the transition; then choose Duration from the shortcut menu (**Figure 13.32**).

2. In the Duration dialog box, enter a new duration (**Figure 13.33**); then click OK.

✔ Tip

■ Control-D is the keyboard shortcut to open the Duration dialog box for a selected clip or transition.

To trim an edit point underlying a transition:

Do one of the following:

◆ From the Tool palette, select the appropriate edit tool; then drag the edit point underlying the transition (**Figure 13.34**).

◆ Double-click an edit point with any edit tool to open the Trim Edit window.

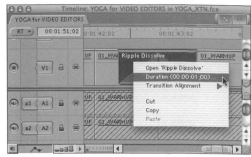

Figure 13.32 Control-click the transition; then choose Duration from the shortcut menu.

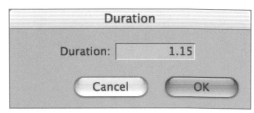

Figure 13.33 Enter a new duration for your transition.

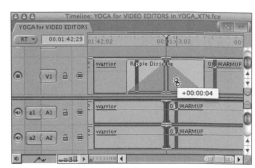

Figure 13.34 Trim an edit point underlying a transition by dragging the edit point with an edit tool. This Roll edit will shift the edit point downstream by 4 frames.

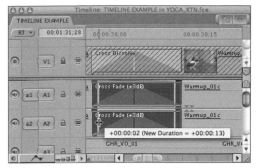

Figure 13.35 Adjusting the duration of an audio transition in the Timeline. Dragging a transition's edge affects the length of the transition but does not alter any underlying edit points.

Modifying Audio Transitions

Final Cut Express offers only two audio transitions; both are cross-fades. One is a 0 dB (decibel) cross-fade. The standard default is a +3 dB cross-fade. The +3 dB amplitude increase of the default cross-fade is designed to compensate for any perceived volume drop during the transition, but the only way to decide which cross-fade works best to finesse your audio edit is to try them both and trust your ears. You can adjust only the duration of audio transitions.

To modify the duration of an audio transition:

◆ With the Selection tool, drag one edge of the transition to adjust its length (**Figure 13.35**).

Or do this:

1. Control-click the transition; then choose Duration from the shortcut menu.

2. In the Duration dialog box, enter a new duration.

3. Click OK.

✔ Tip

■ Duration is the only adjustable parameter for the audio cross-fade transitions in Final Cut Express, but you can build your own cross-fades. Set up the audio clips you want to transition between on adjacent tracks. You can adjust the clips' overlap and then set Level keyframes to sculpt your special-purpose cross-fade.

Rendering Transitions

If you are using a real-time FCE system, you can preview many transitions without rendering, but you'll also find many transitions you must render before you can play them back. With the advent of FCE scalable Real Time architecture, your rendering options have become a bit more complex: before you can render, you must specify which of the six video and two audio Timeline playback states you want to include in the render operation (**Figure 13.36**). Thank goodness for real-time preview, eh? For more information, see Chapter 18, "Real Time and Rendering."

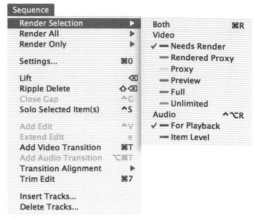

Figure 13.36 In FCE's render menus, you'll encounter six video and two audio render categories. You can specify which render categories you want to include in your render operations.

Real-Time Transitions

If your Final Cut Express system supports real-time effects, you can play certain transitions without rendering them first. The real-time transitions available on your particular system appear in bold type in the Effects menu (**Figure 13.37**) and on the Browser's Effects tab. For more information on real-time systems and rendering, see Chapter 18, "Real Time and Rendering."

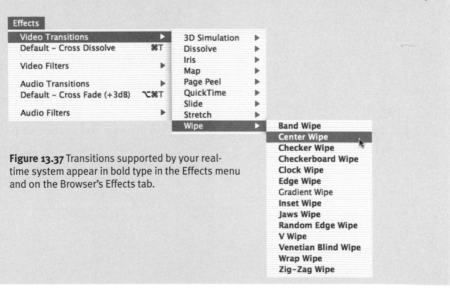

Figure 13.37 Transitions supported by your real-time system appear in bold type in the Effects menu and on the Browser's Effects tab.

COMPOSITING AND EFFECTS OVERVIEW

Creating digital motion effects could be the most fun you'll ever have without getting arrested. Modern mass media relies heavily on the same techniques you'll be introduced to in this chapter. Once you understand the role of each basic building block of effects creation, you'll never look at movies and TV in the same way again, because you'll be able to see how complex visuals are constructed.

The effects creation tools found in Final Cut Express are designed to be easy to use, but effects tools are the most challenging part of the FCE interface to master.

This chapter offers an overview of the basic elements you combine and sculpt to create effects, provides details on how to apply effects to your sequence, and shows where you can modify those effects.

As you start to apply effects, it's important to keep this in mind: Adding a clip from the Browser to a sequence in the Timeline places a copy of the clip in the sequence. By placing a clip in a sequence, you create a new instance of the clip. Before you modify a clip with effects, be sure you have selected the correct copy of the clip you want to change. This rule is central to understanding editing in Final Cut Express. For more information, see "FCE Protocol: Clips and Sequences" in Chapter 4.

Basic Building Blocks of Effects Creation

The basic building blocks you use to create video effects are fairly simple. You can generate complex effects by combining and then animating images using the processes described here.

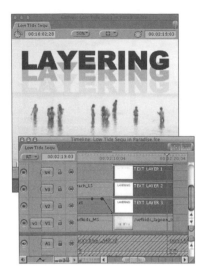

◆ **Layering** is an arrangement of multiple clips at one point in time, each clip in its own track. Superimposing a title over a video clip is a simple example of layering, with the video clip forming the background layer and the title forming the foreground layer. Other layering arrangements require making the upper layers semitransparent, so you can see the image in the background layer.

◆ **Compositing** can be any process that combines two or more image layers to create an effect. Compositing techniques can include the adjustment of one or more image layers' transparency and the selection of a Composite mode, which is the algorithm that controls the way the image layers are combined.

◆ **Motion properties** are image modification tools that control a clip's size and shape, its position in the frame, and its designated center point, among other characteristics. The tools that are grouped together on the Motion tab don't always have an obvious connection to image movement; for example, the Opacity controls are located there. However, making incremental adjustments to a clip's size, position, and angle of rotation are basic steps in animating a static element—that's when things start to move.

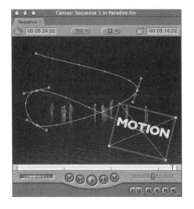

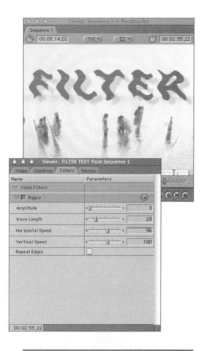

♦ **Filters** are image modifiers that process the image data in a clip. Over time, filters have developed into a diverse effects category that includes everything from basic tools, such as brightness, contrast, and color controls, to complex 3D simulators.

♦ **Opacity** refers to a clip's level of transparency. A clip with an opacity level of 100 percent is completely opaque; one with an opacity level of 0 percent is completely transparent. Adjusting opacity is a basic procedure in compositing layers of images. Alpha channels and mattes are a means of adjusting opacity in selected portions of an image. You can adjust a clip's opacity on the Viewer's Motion tab or by using the opacity clip overlay in the Timeline.

♦ **Generators** are effects that create (or generate) new video information rather than modify existing video. Generators are useful for producing utility items such as black frames (known as slug), a plain-colored background, or text titles.

Locating and Applying Effects

You can access Final Cut Express's effects features in a variety of places:

◆ The Browser's Effects tab (**Figure 14.1**) displays folders containing all the types of effects available in Final Cut Express except motion properties.

◆ The same effects found on the Browser's Effects tab are also available from the Effects menu (**Figure 14.2**).

◆ Motion properties are applied to every clip automatically. Open a clip in the Viewer and click the Motion tab to access a clip's motion controls.

You can apply effects to clips and sequences in the following ways:

◆ Select a clip in the Timeline and then choose an effect from the Effects menu.

◆ Select an effect from a folder on the Effects tab of the Browser and drag it onto the clip.

◆ Select a customized effect or motion from the Favorites folder on the Effects tab of the Browser and drag it to the clip to apply it.

◆ Choose a generator from the Generator pop-up menu in the lower-right corner of the Viewer.

◆ Open a Timeline or a Browser clip in the Viewer; then use the controls on the clip's Motion tab to apply motion effects.

◆ Open a Timeline clip in the Canvas; then use the Canvas's Image+Wireframe mode overlay to animate a motion path.

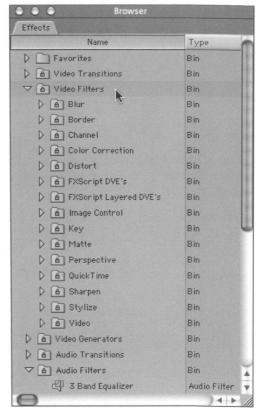

Figure 14.1 The Browser's Effects tab organizes available effects in folders.

Figure 14.2 The same library of effects is available from the Effects menu.

Effects Production Shortcuts

Creating effects can be time consuming and repetitive. Here are a few production shortcuts.

Copying and pasting clip attributes: Clip attributes are settings applied to a particular media file in Final Cut Express. You can copy and paste selected settings from one clip to another clip in the Timeline or in the Canvas, or you can use the Remove Attributes command to restore a clip's default settings. For more information, see Chapter 10, "Editing in the Timeline and the Canvas."

Nesting sequences: When you place a Final Cut Express sequence within another sequence, it's called *nesting* a sequence. Nested sequences can streamline and enhance your effects work in a variety of ways. You can use nested sequences to protect render files, to force effects to render in a different order, or to group clips so you can apply a single filter or motion path to all of them in one operation. Nested sequences are discussed in Chapter 4, "Projects, Sequences, and Clips."

"Effecting" multiple clips: FCE allows you to adjust opacity levels for a group of clips. You can also adjust audio levels for multiple clips in a single operation. See "Setting a clip's opacity in the Timeline" in Chapter 15.

Favorites: Favorites are customized effects presets. For example, if you need to apply the same color correction to a large group of clips, you can tweak the settings once, save that filter configuration as a Favorite, and then apply it to the whole group without having to make individual adjustments. Favorites are discussed in the next section.

LOCATING AND APPLYING EFFECTS

Onscreen effects controls

You can make adjustments to effects you've already applied in the following ways:

- Double-click the clip in the Timeline; then select the Audio, Filters, or Motion tab in the Viewer and use the controls to make your adjustments. **Figure 14.3** illustrates the operation of the controls found on the Filters, Motion, and Controls tabs.

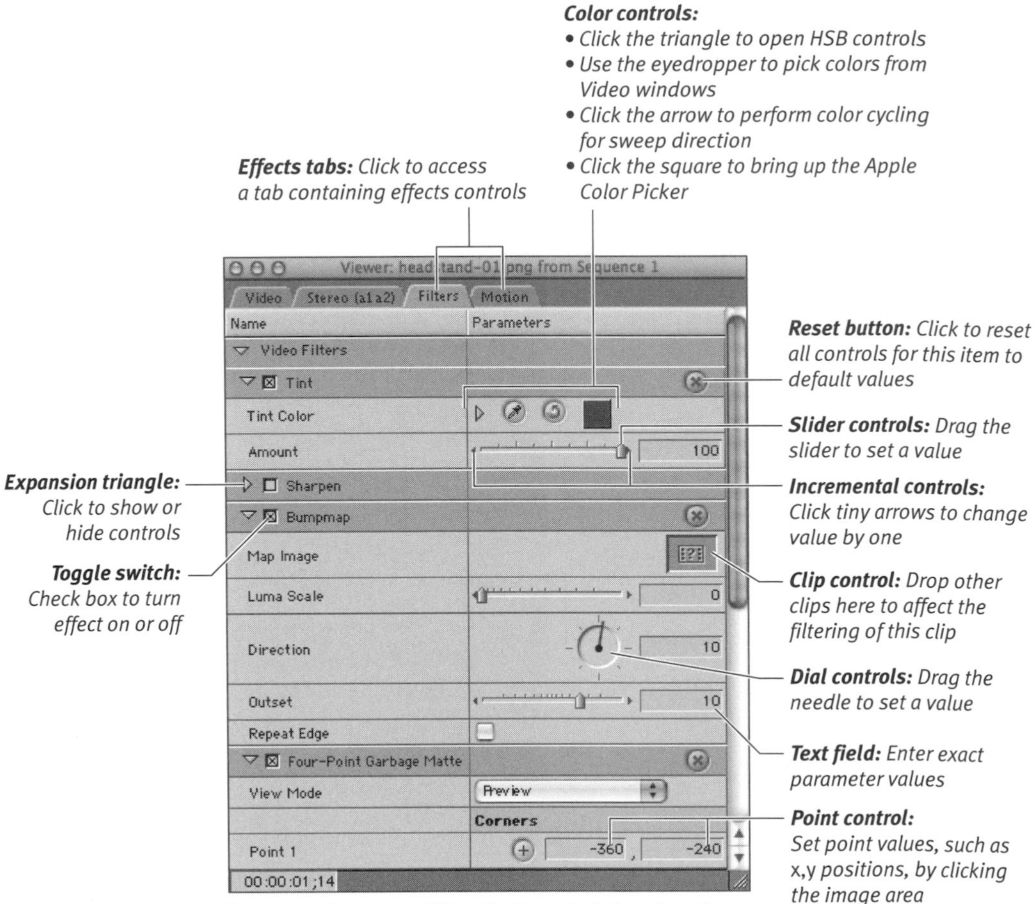

Color controls:
• Click the triangle to open HSB controls
• Use the eyedropper to pick colors from Video windows
• Click the arrow to perform color cycling for sweep direction
• Click the square to bring up the Apple Color Picker
Effects tabs: Click to access a tab containing effects controls
Reset button: Click to reset all controls for this item to default values
Slider controls: Drag the slider to set a value
Incremental controls: Click tiny arrows to change value by one
Clip control: Drop other clips here to affect the filtering of this clip
Dial controls: Drag the needle to set a value
Text field: Enter exact parameter values
Point control: Set point values, such as x,y positions, by clicking the image area
Expansion triangle: Click to show or hide controls
Toggle switch: Check box to turn effect on or off
Video
Filters
Motion
Name
Parameters
Video Filters
Tint
Tint Color
Amount
100
Sharpen
Bumpmap
Map Image
Luma Scale
0
Direction
10
Outset
10
Repeat Edge
Four-Point Garbage Matte
View Mode
Preview
Corners
Point 1
-360
-240
00:00:01;14

Figure 14.3 Overview of the effects controls found on the Filters, Motion, and Controls tabs in the Viewer window.

◆ In the Timeline, adjust opacity or audio level keyframe locations in the clip's clip overlay level line. **Figure 14.4** shows an overview of the effects tools and procedures available in the Timeline window.

◆ In the Canvas, turn on Image+Wireframe mode and adjust a clip's motion properties (motion properties also include a static clip's size, position, and opacity) or use motion keyframes to animate a motion path. For more information, see Chapter 15, "Motion."

Clip & Sequence markers:
Linked to markers in Viewer; used to align keyframes over multiple tracks

Opacity keyframe:
Curve type

Clip overlays: *Display opacity level for video and audio level for audio clips*

Opacity keyframe:
Corner type

Video clip:
Double-click to access an effects tab in the Viewer

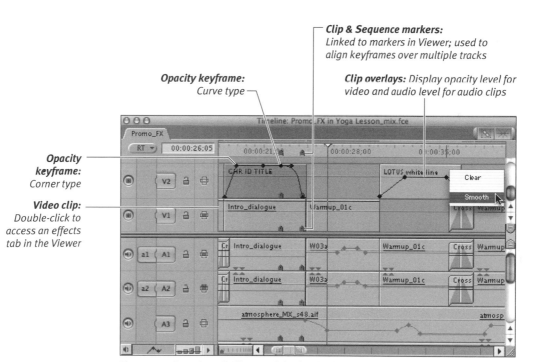

Figure 14.4 Overview of effects tools in the Timeline.

Tuning in Effects: Using Dial, Slider, and Point Controls

Here are some keyboard/mouse combos you can use to enhance your control over any effect parameter with a dial interface:

◆ Hold down the Shift key to constrain the dial to 45-degree increments.

◆ Hold down the Command key to gear down the dial's movement and make precise adjustments.

◆ Drag way, way out of the dial to reset the effect to the previous value.

◆ Scroll-wheel mouse users can make precise dial adjustments by positioning the pointer over the dial and nudging the scroll wheel.

Here are a few tips for effect parameters with slider interfaces:

◆ Expand the horizontal throw of any slider by widening the Parameters column in the column title bar. A longer slider makes it easier to adjust values.

◆ Hold down the Command key to gear down the slider's movement and make precise adjustments.

◆ Scroll-wheel mouse users can nudge the scroll wheel to make single-digit adjustments to slider values.

◆ Hold down the Shift key to add two decimal places of accuracy to a slider's value. (This command could be more useful if it incorporated gearing down as well.) You need to expand the horizontal throw of the slider by widening the Parameters column on the Filters or Controls tab before the double-digit accuracy becomes useful.

◆ The Point control is that little crosshairs button you use to select location coordinates for a clip's center point. You can select the Point control and then click the Canvas to specify a center point. That's very handy, but here's a way to use the Point control that's even better: Once you've clicked, keep the mouse button pressed, and you can drag the center point location around the canvas until you find a position you like. The Canvas will update even while you hold down the mouse button.

Using Keyframes

Whenever you create motion paths, change filters over time, sculpt audio levels, or just fade to black, you need to use keyframes. Think of a keyframe as a kind of edit point—you set a keyframe at the point at which you want to change the value of an effect's parameter. Keyframes work the same way wherever they are applied.

You don't need keyframes to set a single level or value that applies to an entire clip; keyframes are required only if you want to change the value at some point within the clip. After you have added the first keyframe to a clip, Final Cut Express adds a new keyframe automatically whenever you change an effect setting for that clip at a different point in time.

When you use a keyframe to change a parameter, you have the option of making that keyframe a *curve type*. Curve-type keyframes have two added controls: *Bézier handles*, which you can use to fine-tune the shape of the motion path's curve, and *ease handles*, which you can use to fine-tune a clip's speed immediately before and after the keyframe location. You can also use curve-type keyframes to fine-tune the rate of change in an effect parameter's level. Converting a keyframe from a *corner type* to a curve type is sometimes called smoothing a keyframe. For more information on keyframe types, see "Adjusting motion path curves and corners" in Chapter 15.

continues on next page

USING KEYFRAMES

Final Cut Express has two types of keyframe graphs: clip overlays and motion paths.

- **Clip overlays** (or *keyframe overlays*) are displayed as line graphs right on top of the track display in the Timeline (**Figure 14.5**) and over the waveform display on the Viewer's Audio tab. Keyframe overlays indicate clip opacity (for video clips) and volume level and stereo pan position (for audio clips).

  For more information, see "Working with keyframes in the Timeline" later in this chapter.

- **Motion keyframes** are set and sculpted in the Image+Wireframe display in the Canvas (**Figure 14.6**) or in the Viewer. Enable Image+Wireframe mode, and a wireframe overlay appears on your clip image. This wireframe overlay features controls you can use to graphically manipulate the size, shape, and position of your clip's image. Image+Wireframe mode is the best mode to use to manipulate a clip's motion properties and to create motion paths.

  For information on working with motion keyframes, see Chapter 15, "Motion."

Keyframe navigation shortcuts

Table 14.1 shows keyboard shortcuts for jumping forward and backward through a series of keyframes and for adding a motion keyframe. These keyboard shortcuts work for the Timeline's clip overlays and the Canvas's wireframe overlay. These shortcuts will boost your speed and accuracy and are highly recommended.

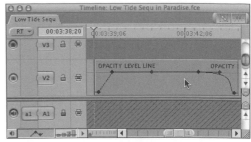

Figure 14.5 Clip overlays are displayed as line graphs right on top of the track display in the Timeline. The overlay in this figure controls opacity. Corner-style keyframes appear at the beginning of the clip; a curve-type keyframe with Bézier handles appears at the clip's end. Hide and show level line overlays by clicking the Clip Overlays button in the lower-left corner of the Timeline.

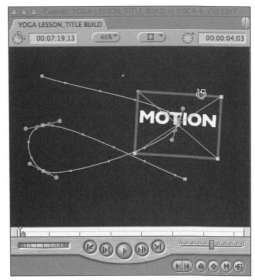

Figure 14.6 Motion keyframes appear on the wireframe overlay in the Canvas (or the Viewer) when Image+Wireframe mode is enabled.

Table 14.1

Keyboard Shortcuts for Keyframes	
Go to Next Keyframe	Shift-K
Go to Previous Keyframe	Option-K
Add Motion Keyframe	Control-K

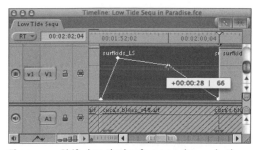

Figure 14.7 Shift-drag the keyframe to change both the value and the keyframe's point in time simultaneously.

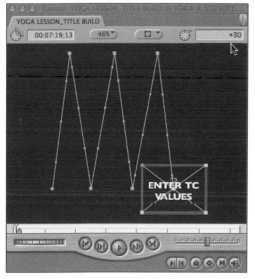

Figure 14.8 Enter timecode values to set keyframes at frame-accurate intervals.

Precision control of a keyframe's positioning

Even in a compact screen layout, FCE offers a variety of techniques to help you get a grip on your keyframe's positioning:

◆ On the effect's Viewer tab, use the incremental controls (the tiny arrows at either end of the effect parameter control sliders) to nudge values by +1 or by –1, or enter an exact numeric value in the parameter's text field.

◆ In the Timeline or the Viewer, hold down the Command key while you drag a keyframe. This enables gear-down dragging, which allows you to move the keyframe in precise increments.

◆ Shift-drag to change both the value and the keyframe's point in time simultaneously (**Figure 14.7**).

◆ To set keyframes at precise intervals, use timecode entry to jump the Timeline or Canvas playhead by a precise number of frames (**Figure 14.8**); then add your keyframe.

Working with keyframes in the Timeline

You can edit and adjust keyframes in the Timeline's keyframe overlay. These graphs are overlaid on top of the track display in the Timeline. Video clips display the clip opacity level; audio clips display the volume level and stereo pan position.

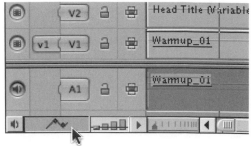

Figure 14.9 Click the Clip Overlays control in the Timeline window to toggle the display of keyframe overlays.

To display keyframe overlays in the Timeline:

◆ In the Timeline, click the Clip Overlays control in the lower-left corner (**Figure 14.9**).

To add an overlay keyframe to a track:

1. From the Tool palette, select the Pen tool.

2. On the selected clip's keyframe overlay graph, click where you want to place the keyframe (**Figure 14.10**).

   A new keyframe is added to the overlay.

Figure 14.10 Use the Pen tool to add a keyframe to a clip's keyframe overlay graph.

✔ Tips

■ Any time you're working with the Selection tool, the fastest way to a Pen tool is to press Option. The Selection tool switches to Pen tool mode as long as you're holding down the Option key.

■ Did you just add one keyframe too many? Press Option, and your Pen tool toggles to Pen Delete mode. Click that extra keyframe to delete it; then release the Option key.

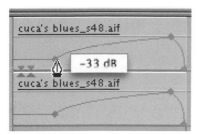

Figure 14.11 A tooltip displaying the current level updates as you adjust the keyframe.

To adjust the values of individual overlay keyframes:

Do one of the following:

◆ Using the Pen tool or the Selection tool, drag overlay keyframes vertically to adjust their values. As you drag, a tooltip appears, displaying the parameter's value (**Figure 14.11**).

◆ Using the Selection tool, drag the level line between two overlay keyframes to adjust its position.

◆ Using the Pen tool, Shift-drag the level line between two overlay keyframes to adjust its position.

To delete overlay keyframes:

Do one of the following:

◆ Drag keyframes off the track completely to delete them.

◆ With the Pen tool selected, press the Option key to toggle to the Pen's Delete mode. Click the keyframe you want to delete.

The keyframes (except for the last one) are removed, and the keyframe path adjusts to reflect the change.

USING KEYFRAMES

415

Saving Effects Settings as Favorites

You can designate an effect, transition, or generator as a Favorite. Favorite effects are placed in the Favorites folder on the Browser's Effects tab. Favorites provide an easy way to save an effect that you want to reproduce later. For more information on creating and using favorites, see "Working with Default and Favorite Transitions" in Chapter 13.

To create a Favorite effect by saving its settings:

1. In the Timeline, double-click the clip with the effect you want to make a Favorite.

   The clip opens in the Viewer.

2. Select the Filters or the Controls tab to access the selected effect's controls.

3. Select the effect in the Name column (**Figure 14.12**); then drag the effect's name from its control bar to the Favorites folder on the Browser's Effects tab.

✔ Tip

- If you've created a set of Favorite effects for use in a particular project, you can archive those effects by dragging the Favorites folder (or selected Favorite effects) from the Browser's Effects tab onto your project tab. Your project's Favorite effects are saved with the project file.

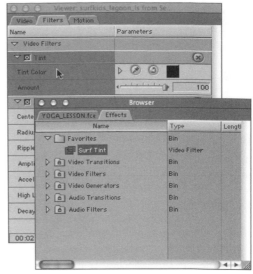

Figure 14.12 Save customized effects settings by selecting an effect in the Name column and dragging it to the Favorites folder.

Figure 14.13 On the Browser's Effects tab, select an effect and drag it to the Favorites folder.

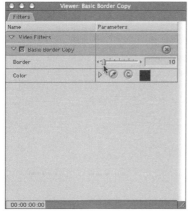

Figure 14.14 Configure the effect's settings.

Figure 14.15 In the Favorites folder, rename the customized effect.

To create a Favorite effect before changing its settings:

1. On the Effects tab in the Browser, select an effect and drag it to the Favorites folder (**Figure 14.13**).

2. Open the Favorites folder; then double-click the effect.

   The effect opens in the Viewer.

3. Adjust the effect's settings (**Figure 14.14**); then close the Viewer.

4. In the Favorites folder, rename the new effect (**Figure 14.15**).

✔ Tip

- You can also select an effect in the Browser and then choose Edit > Duplicate. A copy of the effect appears in the Favorites submenu of the Effects menu.

SAVING EFFECTS SETTINGS AS FAVORITES

417

15

MOTION

Unlike filters or generators, motion properties are already present on every clip. You can access them by loading a clip or sequence into the Viewer and then selecting the Motion tab.

A few of the controls you find on the Motion tab, such as Opacity, Crop, Distort, and Drop Shadow, don't have any obvious connection to movement.

The first part of this chapter introduces motion properties as static image modification tools that can be used in either static or animated compositions. The second part of the chapter, "Animating Clip Motion with Keyframes," discusses motion paths: the time-based uses of motion properties.

Setting Motion Properties

The motion properties listed here are present automatically on every clip, and their controls can be adjusted on the clip's Motion tab in the Viewer (**Figure 15.1**) or on the clip's Image+Wireframe mode overlay in the Canvas (**Figure 15.2**).

◆ **Scale:** Adjusts the size of the clip to make it smaller or larger than the sequence frame size.

◆ **Rotation:** Rotates the clip around its anchor point without changing its shape.

◆ **Center:** The *x,y* coordinates specify the center point of the clip.

◆ **Anchor Point:** The *x,y* coordinates specify another point relative to the clip's center point to use as a pivot point for rotating, scaling, or animating the motion path of the clip.

◆ **Crop:** Crops (removes) a portion of the clip from the side you specify.

◆ **Distort:** Changes the shape of the clip by adjusting its corners. The Aspect Ratio parameter sets the clip's height:width proportions.

◆ **Opacity:** Makes a clip opaque or translucent; 100 percent is completely opaque, and 0 percent is completely transparent.

◆ **Drop Shadow:** Places a drop shadow behind the selected clip, with a color, softness, and opacity you specify.

◆ **Motion Blur:** Blurs moving images by a specified percentage, by combining the images of adjacent frames to create the effect.

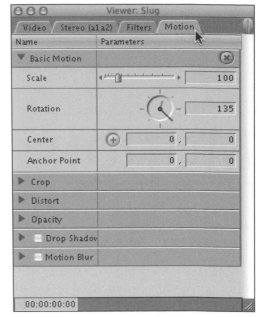

Figure 15.1 Use the controls on the Viewer's Motion tab to adjust motion properties.

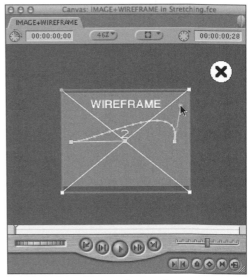

Figure 15.2 You can also adjust motion properties graphically, using the Canvas wireframe overlay.

Locating *x,y* coordinates

Final Cut Express uses *x,y* coordinates to specify a clip's position in the frame. For example, in the DV-NTSC frame size (720 by 480 pixels), you can specify locations outside the visible frame by using coordinate values greater than plus or minus 360 on the *x* axis, or plus or minus 240 on the *y* axis. You'll often see *x,y* coordinates specified like this: (50,25). The first number (50) is the *x* coordinate; the second number (25) is the *y* coordinate. **Figure 15.3** illustrates *x,y* coordinate locations in a DV-NTSC frame (720 by 480 pixels).

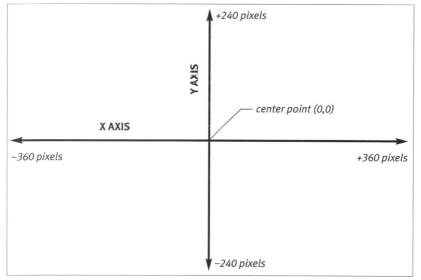

Figure 15.3 The *x,y* coordinate locations for a DV-NTSC frame size (720 by 480 pixels).

Motion Properties Modify an Image or Make It Move

Motion properties perform basic image modifications when used as static composition tools, but they can also create motion effects when you adjust their values over time. For example, you might use the Rotation control as a static composition tool to display a title at a 90-degree angle (**Figure 15.4**) or animate rotation by setting incrementally increasing values over time (**Figure 15.5**).

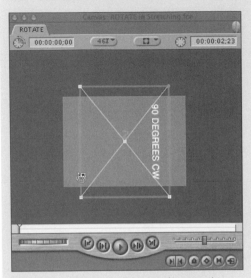

Figure 15.4 Use the Rotation control as a static composition tool to set a title clip at a 90-degree angle.

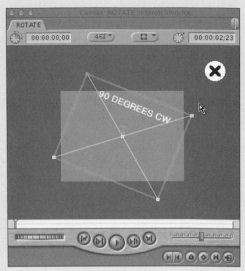

Figure 15.5 Use the Rotation control to animate the title clip's rotation by setting incrementally increasing values over time.

Using Wireframes

Enabling Image+Wireframe mode in the Canvas or the Viewer activates a wireframe overlay that appears on your clip image. You must be in Image+Wireframe mode to graphically manipulate a clip's motion properties in the Canvas or the Viewer.

The elements of the wireframe aren't just indicators; they're also controls you can use to manipulate the size, shape, and position of your clip's image. Select the appropriate tool from the Tool palette; then drag a handle on the clip's wireframe. **Figure 15.6** offers a key to wireframe handles and tools.

✔ Tip

■ While you work in Image+Wireframe mode, note that the selected track's number appears just above the clip's center point. The track number helps you remember which layer you've selected. If you're working on an effects sequence with many layered elements, that's a big help.

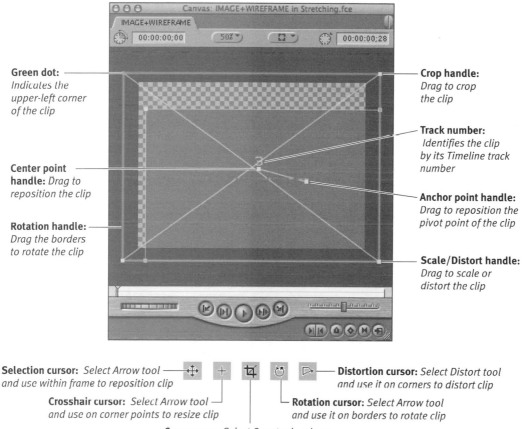

Green dot: Indicates the upper-left corner of the clip

Center point handle: Drag to reposition the clip

Rotation handle: Drag the borders to rotate the clip

Crop handle: Drag to crop the clip

Track number: Identifies the clip by its Timeline track number

Anchor point handle: Drag to reposition the pivot point of the clip

Scale/Distort handle: Drag to scale or distort the clip

Selection cursor: Select Arrow tool and use within frame to reposition clip

Crosshair cursor: Select Arrow tool and use on corner points to resize clip

Crop cursor: Select Crop tool and use it on borders or corners to crop clip

Distortion cursor: Select Distort tool and use it on corners to distort clip

Rotation cursor: Select Arrow tool and use it on borders to rotate clip

Figure 15.6 To manipulate motion properties in Image+Wireframe mode, select a tool; then drag the appropriate handle on the clip's wireframe.

Wireframe keyframe indicators

Wireframe mode uses green highlighting to indicate whether a keyframe is present on a frame and what type of keyframe it is (**Figure 15.7**).

To enable Wireframe mode:

Do one of the following:

◆ Press W once to place the Viewer or the Canvas in Image+Wireframe mode. (Press W again to return to Image mode.)

◆ Choose Image+Wireframe from the View pop-up menu at the top of the Viewer or the Canvas (**Figure 15.8**).

◆ Choose View > Image+Wireframe.

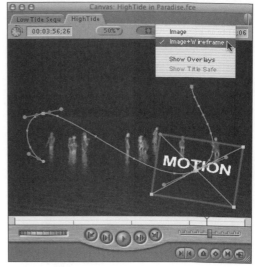

Figure 15.8 Choose Image+Wireframe from the View pop-up menu at the top of the Viewer or Canvas.

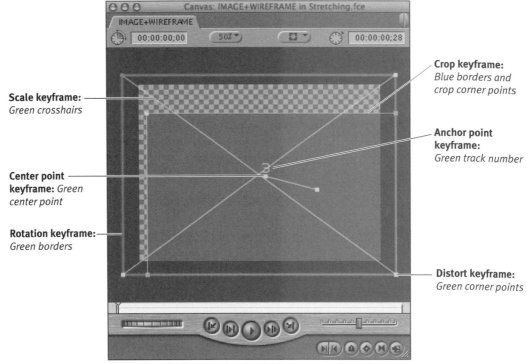

Scale keyframe: *Green crosshairs*

Center point keyframe: *Green center point*

Rotation keyframe: *Green borders*

Crop keyframe: *Blue borders and crop corner points*

Anchor point keyframe: *Green track number*

Distort keyframe: *Green corner points*

Figure 15.7 Wireframe mode uses highlighting to indicate the presence of keyframes.

USING WIREFRAMES

Using Motion Properties to Change a Clip's Appearance

In Final Cut Express, when you want to make a clip's image larger or smaller, tilted or skewed, opaque or transparent, you adjust the clip's motion properties—even if the clip's not moving. Not very intuitive, is it?

As long as you're not animating the clip (changing the size and shape of the clip's image over time), you don't need to add any motion keyframes. Simply open the clip and adjust the clip's default motion properties settings. FCE offers two ways to modify a clip's motion properties: by adjusting the controls and entering numerical values on the clip's Motion tab in the Viewer, or by using the Tool palette's image modification tools to manipulate the clip's image directly in the Canvas wireframe overlay. When you're going for precision and consistency, you'll probably end up working both numerically and graphically.

All operations described in this section can be performed in both places. Start each operation by following the general setup procedure for each respective mode; the setup tasks are described in the sections that follow.

Pressin', Clickin', and Draggin': Using Keyboard Shortcuts with Wireframes

Many of the scaling and positioning tools have keyboard modifiers—keys you press as you drag the tool on the wireframe handles in the Canvas or in the Viewer—that you can use to create complex alterations to a clip.

◆ **Option:** Use this key to force automatic rendering while you drag the clip.

◆ **Shift:** Use this key to enable nonproportional scaling (modification of a clip's aspect ratio while scaling). You can use the Shift and Option keys together.

◆ **Command:** Use this key to rotate and scale the clip simultaneously. You can use the Command and Option keys together.

To set up for motion properties adjustment in the Canvas Wireframe mode:

1. In the Timeline, select the clip you want to reposition (**Figure 15.9**). If you are working with a layered composition, be sure to choose the layer you want to affect.

2. From the Tool palette, choose the appropriate image modification tool for the motion property you want to adjust. Refer to the key to wireframe handles and tools in Figure 15.6.

3. If the Canvas's Image+Wireframe mode is not already activated, press W to turn it on.

   The outline of the wireframe overlay appears on the selected clip's image (**Figure 15.10**).

To set up for motion properties adjustment on the Viewer's Motion tab:

1. Double-click the clip in the Timeline or the Browser to open it in the Viewer.

2. In the Viewer, click the Motion tab.

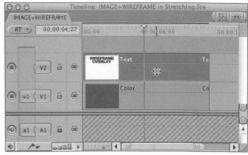

Figure 15.9 In the Timeline, select the clip you want to reposition.

Figure 15.10 Press W to activate Image+Wireframe mode, and the wireframe overlay appears on the selected clip's image.

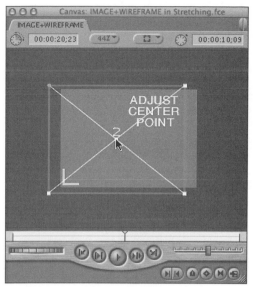

Figure 15.11 Click anywhere in the clip's wireframe and then drag the wireframe to a new position.

Figure 15.12 Click the Point Select button, which is located to the left of the Center value field.

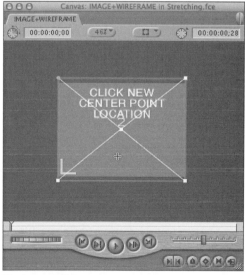

Figure 15.13 Click a new center location in the Canvas to specify new center coordinates.

Positioning clips

Clips start out positioned at the center of the Canvas or the Viewer. You can reposition a clip's center point by dragging it to a new position in the Canvas or in the Viewer, or you can specify new center point coordinates on the clip's Motion tab. You can position a clip partially or completely outside the sequence frame.

To adjust a clip's center point using Wireframe mode:

◆ Follow the setup steps for Wireframe mode presented earlier; then click anywhere inside the clip's image and drag it to a new position (**Figure 15.11**).

To adjust a clip's center point on the Viewer's Motion tab:

Follow the setup steps for the Motion tab mode described earlier; then *do one of the following:*

◆ Enter new x,y coordinates for the clip's center location. Enter the x coordinate in the left value field and the y coordinate in the right value field.

◆ Click the Point Select (+) button (**Figure 15.12**) (located to the left of the Center value field) and then specify new center coordinates by clicking the new center location in the Canvas (**Figure 15.13**) or on the Video tab of the Viewer.

Scaling clips

A clip placed in a Final Cut Express sequence plays at the same frame size at which it was captured, regardless of the sequence frame size. A clip whose native size is smaller than the sequence frame size appears in the center of the sequence frame; a clip whose native size is larger than the sequence frame size shows only the portion of the clip that fits inside the sequence frame dimensions.

You can adjust the scale of a clip to change its frame size (for the current sequence only). If you want to create a media file of your clip at a different size that does not need to be rendered before it can be played back, you should export a copy of the clip at the frame size you need.

To scale a clip in Wireframe mode:

1. Follow the setup steps for Wireframe mode presented earlier.

2. Drag a corner handle to scale a clip while maintaining its proportions (**Figure 15.14**).

✔ Tips

- Smooth your keyframes with Bézier curves when you animate scale. Curve type keyframes produce a change in the rate of scale at the beginning and the end of the scaling animation, making the movement less mechanical. To learn how to convert a keyframe to a Bézier curve type, see "To refine a motion keyframe" later in this chapter.

- When you're scaling a clip, it's easy to drift away from the clip's original aspect ratio, but not easy to find the control that resets your clip to its native proportions. Go to the clip's Motion tab and scroll down to the Distort controls. That's where you'll find the Aspect Ratio parameter. Reset the value to 0, and you'll restore height:width sanity to your scaled clip.

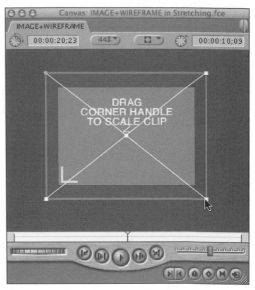

Figure 15.14 Dragging a corner handle scales a clip while maintaining its proportions.

FCE Protocol: Center Point vs. Anchor Point vs. Origin Point

All three types of points—the center point, anchor point, and origin point—are used to define position, but each serves a different purpose:

Center point: Establishes the clip's position inside the Canvas area. The center point's default position (0,0) is the same as the anchor point's.

Anchor point: Establishes the pivot point for a clip's movement inside the Canvas area. Rotation and Scale properties and motion paths are all based on the anchor point. The anchor point's default position (0,0) is the same as the center point's.

Origin point: Appears on the Motion tab for text generators and establishes the positioning of text elements placed inside the clip.

Figure 15.15 Adjust the Scale slider on the Motion tab to scale the clip.

Figure 15.16 To rotate a clip in Wireframe mode, drag in an arc around the clip's center point.

To scale a clip on the Viewer's Motion tab:

Follow the setup steps for Motion tab mode presented earlier, then *do one of the following:*

◆ Adjust the Scale slider (**Figure 15.15**).

◆ Enter a percentage in the text field located to the right of the slider; 100 percent is equal to the clip's native size.

Rotating clips

Rotation is an important part of modern video effects (as you know if you've watched a TV commercial break recently).

A clip rotates around its anchor point. The default anchor point location matches the clip's center point, but you can rotate a clip around a different pivot point by changing the location of the anchor point. You can position a clip at the edge of your sequence frame and rotate your clip partially or completely outside the Canvas, so it appears on the screen for only a portion of its rotation. You can also rotate a clip up to 24 revolutions in either direction or use the Rotation control to angle a clip as part of a static composition.

To adjust a clip's rotation angle in Wireframe mode:

Follow the setup steps for Image+Wireframe mode presented earlier; then *do one of the following:*

◆ Click an edge of the border and drag in an arc around the clip's center point (**Figure 15.16**).

◆ Click a border edge and then drag farther away from the clip's center point to get more precise control over the rotation.

◆ Hold down the Shift key while dragging to constrain the rotation positions to 45-degree increments.

◆ Drag around the clip multiple times without releasing the mouse to specify a number of rotations.

To adjust a clip's rotation angle on the Viewer's Motion tab:

Follow the setup steps for the Motion tab mode described earlier; then *do one of the following*:

◆ Drag the black rotation needle around the dial to set a rotation position (**Figure 15.17**); the red needle indicates the number of complete revolutions.

◆ Enter a new value in the text box.

   The clip realigns at the new rotation angle for the selected frame.

✔ Tip

■ To create an animated rotation effect on the Motion tab, you must set individual keyframes for each rotation angle value (see "Animating Clip Motion with Keyframes" later in this chapter).

Cropping clips

You can crop a clip either by dragging with the Crop tool or by specifying the number of pixels to crop from the borders. Use the Edge Feather option to create a soft border at the crop line.

When you use the Crop tool to remove part of a clip's image, the selected parts are hidden, not deleted. You can restore the cropped sections to view by clicking the Reset button next to the Crop controls on the Viewer's Motion tab.

Figure 15.17 Drag the rotation control dial needle to set a rotation position. The black hand indicates the current angle of the clip, and the small red hand indicates the total number of rotations forward or backward that have been specified.

MOTION PROPERTIES TO CHANGE APPEARANCE

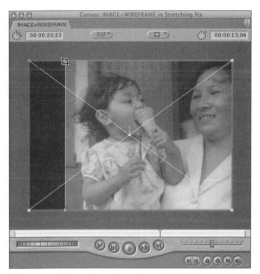

Figure 15.18 Drag from the edges of the clip to crop out elements in the image.

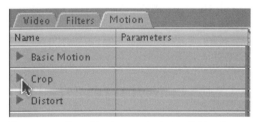

Figure 15.19 Open the Crop controls by clicking the Crop expansion triangle.

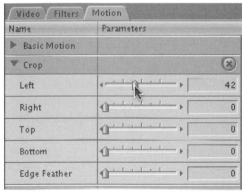

Figure 15.20 Crop a clip by dragging the slider for the side you want to crop and setting it to a new value.

To crop a clip in Wireframe mode:

1. Follow the setup steps for the Image+ Wireframe mode presented earlier; then select the Crop tool from the Tool palette.

2. *Do one of the following:*
   - ◆ Drag from the edges of the clip to hide elements in the image (**Figure 15.18**).
   - ◆ Shift-drag to constrain the clip's aspect ratio as you crop.
   - ◆ Command-drag to trim both horizontal edges or both vertical edges simultaneously.
   - ◆ Use Option in combination with Shift and Command to force rendering while you perform a crop operation.

To crop a clip on the Motion tab:

1. Follow the setup steps for the Motion tab mode described earlier; then open the Crop control bar by clicking the expansion triangle on the left (**Figure 15.19**).

2. To crop the clip from a specific side, *do one of the following:*
   - ◆ Drag the slider for that edge to a new value (**Figure 15.20**).
   - ◆ Enter a new value in the corresponding text field.

3. To soften the cropped edges of the clip, *do one of the following:*
   - ◆ Adjust the Edge Feather slider to specify the width of the feathered edge.
   - ◆ Specify a value in the Edge Feather text field.

Distorting a clip's shape

Use the Distort tool to make independent adjustments to each corner point of a clip's wireframe, or use the Viewer's Motion tab to numerically specify *x,y* coordinates for the location of each corner point.

To distort the shape of a clip in Wireframe mode:

1. Follow the setup steps for the Wireframe mode presented earlier; then select the Distort tool from the Tool palette (**Figure 15.21**).

2. To distort the clip's image, *do one of the following:*
   - ◆ Drag a corner handle of the clip's wireframe (**Figure 15.22**).
   - ◆ Shift-drag to change the perspective of the image.

To distort a clip on the Viewer's Motion tab:

1. Follow the setup steps for the Motion tab mode presented earlier; then open the Distort control bar by clicking the expansion triangle.

2. To specify new locations for the corner points, *do one of the following:*
   - ◆ Enter new values for the corner points you want to move.
   - ◆ Adjust the Aspect Ratio parameter to change the clip's height:width ratio, relocating all four corner points. A clip's original aspect ratio has a value of zero.

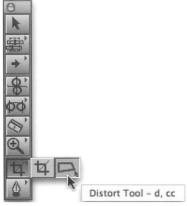

Figure 15.21 Select the Distort tool from the Tool palette.

Figure 15.22 Drag a corner handle of the clip's wireframe to distort it.

Figure 15.23 The title is 100 percent opaque and completely obscures the background.

Figure 15.24 The superimposed title with opacity set to less than 100 percent appears semitransparent.

Figure 15.25 Type a value between 0 and 100 in the Opacity text field.

Adjusting opacity

Final Cut Express clips start out 100 percent opaque (**Figure 15.23**). If you superimpose a clip over another clip in the base track of your sequence, the background image will be completely hidden until you adjust the opacity of the superimposed clip to less than 100 percent, making it semitransparent (**Figure 15.24**).

Layering multiple, semitransparent images is a basic compositing technique, and one you may be familiar with if you have ever worked with Adobe Photoshop.

You can adjust a clip's opacity on the Viewer's Motion tab or with the opacity clip overlay in the Timeline.

To set a clip's opacity on the Viewer's Motion tab:

1. Follow the setup steps for the Motion tab mode described earlier; then open the Opacity control bar by clicking the triangle.

2. To set the opacity level, *do one of the following:*
   ◆ Use the slider control.
   ◆ Enter a value between 0 and 100 in the Opacity text field (**Figure 15.25**).

Setting a clip's opacity in the Timeline

A clip's opacity can be adjusted directly in the Timeline using the clip overlay for opacity, a level line graph that appears over the clip icon in the Timeline. To display clip overlays, click the Clip Overlays control in the lower-left corner of the Timeline.

For information on adjusting clip overlays in the Timeline, see "Working with Keyframes in the Timeline" in Chapter 14.

Use the Modify > Levels command to adjust opacity levels for a group of Timeline clips in a single operation.

To adjust opacity levels on a group of clips:

1. In the Timeline, select a group of clips whose levels you want to adjust (**Figure 15.26**).

2. Choose Modify > Levels.

3. In the Opacity Adjust dialog box, *do one of the following:*
   - ◆ Choose Relative from the pop-up menu. Adjust each clip's opacity relative to its current level by specifying a percentage value (**Figure 15.27**).
   - ◆ Choose Absolute from the pop-up menu; then set an absolute value for all clips' opacity by specifying a percentage value.

4. Click OK.

✔ Tip

- ■ Choose Relative to adjust the opacity percentage but maintain the curves of any sculpted opacity levels. Choose Absolute to remove all keyframes and flatten all the opacity levels to the specified percentage value.

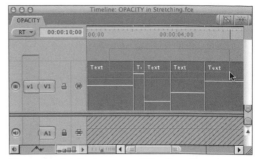

Figure 15.26 Select a group of Timeline clips whose opacity levels you want to adjust.

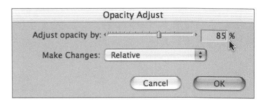

Figure 15.27 Choose Relative in the Opacity Adjust dialog box to adjust the opacity of all the selected clips by the percentage you specify.

Figure 15.28 Drop shadows add depth to a superimposed title.

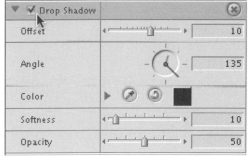

Figure 15.29 Check the box to enable the Drop Shadow option.

Adding a drop shadow to a clip

Drop shadows add the illusion of dimensional depth to the 2D television screen (**Figure 15.28**). Titles pop out from the backgrounds, or clips softly float over other clips; complex silhouettes can add a special depth to your sequences. You can add a drop shadow to any clip whose display size is smaller than the sequence frame size.

You can apply drop shadows to clips that were captured at a smaller frame size and to clips that have been scaled, cropped, moved, or distorted. You can also add a drop shadow to a full-size clip with an alpha channel.

To add a drop shadow to a clip:

1. Double-click the clip in the Timeline or the Browser to open it in the Viewer.

2. In the Viewer, click the Motion tab; then check the Drop Shadow check box (**Figure 15.29**).

3. To adjust your drop shadow settings, *do any of the following:*

- Enter Offset settings to specify the shadow's distance from the clip.

- Enter Angle settings to specify the position of the shadow relative to the clip edge.

- Enter Softness settings to specify the degree of blending in the shadow's edge.

- Enter Opacity settings to specify the shadow's degree of transparency.

continues on next page

MOTION PROPERTIES TO CHANGE APPEARANCE

435

4. In the Color control bar, click the expansion triangle; then pick a color by *doing one of the following:*

◆ Drag the hue, saturation, and brightness sliders to new values.

◆ Enter numeric color values in the text fields.

◆ Click the eyedropper and click in the Canvas to sample a color.

◆ Click the color swatch and use one of the color pickers to choose the desired color (**Figure 15.30**).

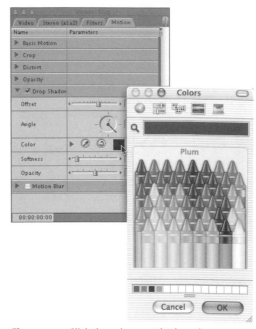

Figure 15.30 Click the color swatch; then choose a color from one of the color pickers.

Figure 15.31 Motion blur produces soft-focus effects based on movement within your video image.

Figure 15.32 You can apply motion blur to a static graphic as well, but you must animate the graphic with a motion path first.

Adding a motion blur effect

The motion blur effect enhances the illusion of movement by compositing the images of adjacent frames (**Figure 15.31**). This is definitely one control to experiment with, particularly for creating interesting, animated, soft-focus background textures. If you're using graphics or stills, you must combine motion blur with other motion effects—scaling, rotation, or motion paths, for example—to see the motion blur effect, but you can use it to create a lot of action in your composition, even with static elements (**Figure 15.32**).

✔ Tip

■ Nest a clip containing an element you want to blur. By increasing the frame size when you nest, you can create a roomier bounding box that will accommodate the larger size of your blurred element.

To add motion blur to a clip:

1. Double-click the clip in the Timeline or the Browser to open it in the Viewer.

2. In the Viewer, click the Motion tab; then check the Motion Blur check box near the bottom of the tab (**Figure 15.33**).

3. Click the Motion Blur expansion triangle to reveal the controls for blurring motion.

4. Use the % Blur slider or enter a value in the text field. Values range from 1000%, which blurs a frame's image across 10 frames, to 100%, which blurs the image on a single frame.

5. To change the quality of the motion blur, adjust the sample rate by choosing a value from the Samples pop-up menu (**Figure 15.34**).

    The sample rate is the number of in-between images FCE calculates when it compares two adjacent frames to calculate motion blur. A low sample rate produces more visible intermediate steps; a high sample rate produces a smoother look but takes longer to render.

Figure 15.33 Check the Motion Blur check box to enable motion blurring.

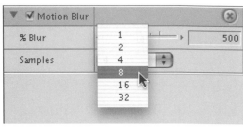

Figure 15.34 Specify a number of samples by selecting a value from the Samples pop-up menu. The sample rate changes the quality of the motion blur. Fewer samples creates more visible intermediate steps.

MOTION PROPERTIES TO CHANGE APPEARANCE

Figure 15.35 Click the Add Motion Keyframe button on the Canvas to set a keyframe.

Animating Clip Motion with Keyframes

The previous section explained how to use motion properties to alter a clip's shape, size, and transparency in a static composition. In this section, you'll finally learn how to use motion properties to actually move clips around.

Working with basic motion keyframe commands

The best place to use motion keyframes to animate a motion path is either the Canvas or the Viewer when it is in Image+Wireframe mode—all the operations described in this section are performed in Wireframe mode.

You can work with motion keyframes in both the Canvas and the Viewer, but because keyframing more commonly happens in the Canvas, the directions in this section mention only the Canvas.

To set a motion keyframe:

1. In the Canvas, position the playhead at the frame where you want to set the keyframe.

2. Click the Add Motion Keyframe button (**Figure 15.35**); or press Control-K.

continues on next page

The Best Way to Fine-Tune a Motion Sequence: Jump Around

Using the Shift-K and Option-K keyboard shortcuts to step through a series of keyframes, you can review your clip's settings at each keyframe. For best results, keep an eye on both the Canvas and the Motion tab—the Canvas wireframe overlay updates to show the way your composition looks, and the clip's Motion tab updates to show the precise value of each keyframe's settings.

3. To set an additional keyframe, move the playhead to the next location where you want to set a keyframe; then *do one of the following:*

◆ Add another keyframe; then adjust the Motion tab parameter control or make a graphical adjustment to the clip's wireframe.

◆ Make an adjustment to a Motion tab parameter control or make a graphical adjustment to the clip's wireframe.

Final Cut Express adjusts the values and then automatically adds the keyframe (**Figure 15.36**).

✔ Tip

■ Clicking the Add Motion Keyframe button in the Canvas sets a motion keyframe across all motion parameters for the current frame.

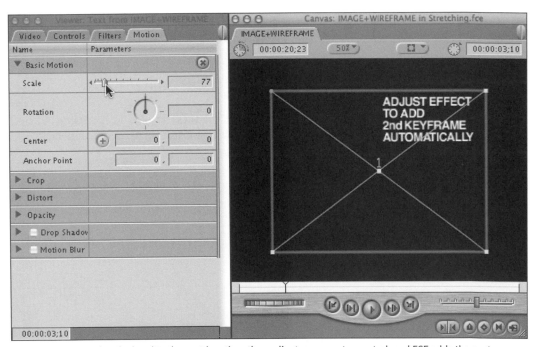

Figure 15.36 Move the playhead to the next location; then adjust a parameter control, and FCE adds the next keyframe automatically.

ANIMATING CLIP MOTION WITH KEYFRAMES

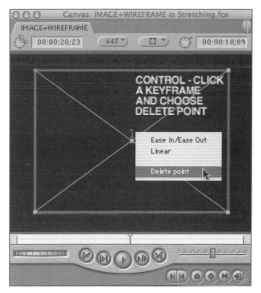

Figure 15.37 To delete the keyframe, Control-click it and choose Delete Point from the shortcut menu.

Figure 15.38 Another way to delete a motion keyframe is to Option-click it with the Selection tool or the Pen tool.

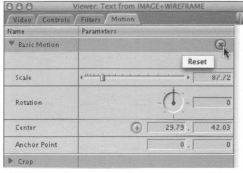

Figure 15.39 Click the Reset button next to a motion property on the clip's Motion tab to delete all keyframes for that motion property.

To navigate between motion keyframes:

◆ Press Shift-K to move to the next motion keyframe.

◆ Press Option-K to move to the previous keyframe.

The playhead moves to the next keyframe in the appropriate direction, and the Canvas updates to show the new position of the clip.

✔ Tip

■ Toggle the Auto Select control off for any track you want to exclude from your keyframe review. FCE will ignore the keyframes on that track.

To delete a motion keyframe:

In the Canvas wireframe overlay, *do one of the following:*

◆ Control-click the keyframe and choose Delete Point from the shortcut menu (**Figure 15.37**).

◆ Option-click the keyframe with the Selection tool or the Pen tool (**Figure 15.38**).

To delete all keyframes:

◆ On the clip's Motion tab, click the Reset button to delete all keyframes for that parameter and return the parameter to its original setting (**Figure 15.39**).

To refine a motion keyframe:

1. Control-click the keyframe and choose Ease In/Ease Out from the shortcut menu (**Figure 15.40**).

   The keyframe changes into a curve type, and Bézier handles appear.

2. Drag the small blue circle at the end of the Bézier handle to adjust the motion path leading up to (or away from) the keyframe (**Figure 15.41**).

✔ Tip

■ Refine opacity and audio level overlay keyframes in the Timeline by Control-clicking the overlay keyframe and selecting Smooth from the shortcut menu.

To move a motion keyframe:

◆ In the Canvas wireframe overlay, click the motion keyframe with the appropriate selection tool and drag it to a new location.

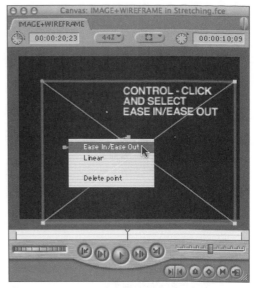

Figure 15.40 To smooth a corner type keyframe to a Bézier curve type, Control-click the keyframe and choose Ease In/Ease Out from the shortcut menu.

Figure 15.41 Drag the small blue circle at the end of the Bézier handle to adjust the motion path leading away from the keyframe.

Figure 15.42 To add the first keyframe, click the Add Keyframe button on the Canvas.

Figure 15.43 Click the Current Timecode field at the bottom left of the Motion tab; then type +30 to add 30 frames to the playhead location.

Setting motion keyframes with timecode entry

Evenly spaced keyframes are essential for smooth, even changes in your effects and for precision synchronization to music or other effects. This is especially true for motion effects. When you animate a program element, using timecode ensures that your keyframes will be set at precise intervals. This task shows you how to rotate a clip using timecode entry to set keyframes.

To set keyframes using timecode entry:

1. In the Timeline, double-click the clip you want to rotate to open it in the Viewer.

2. In the Viewer, click the Motion tab; then press the Home key to jump the playhead to the first frame of your clip.

3. In the Canvas, click the Add Keyframe button (**Figure 15.42**); or press Control-K.

    The clip's first Rotation keyframe is set on the first frame.

4. Verify that the Rotation control is set to zero.

    This establishes the clip's orientation at the beginning of the rotation.

5. Click the Current Timecode field at the bottom left of the Motion tab; then type +30 to move the playhead 30 frames forward (**Figure 15.43**).

    The playhead advances 30 frames.

continues on next page

ANIMATING CLIP MOTION WITH KEYFRAMES

6. Click the Add Keyframe button again; then *do one of the following:*

- ◆ In the Rotation control dial, drag the needle clockwise to set the keyframe value to 180 (**Figure 15.44**).

- ◆ Enter 180 in the Rotation text field.

7. Repeat steps 5 and 6, increasing the Rotation value to 360.

You have set three keyframes, exactly 30 frames apart, causing your clip to complete one full 360-degree rotation in 2 seconds (**Figure 15.45**).

8. Press Option-K to step backward through your three keyframes, noting that the clip flips and the Rotation value updates at each keyframe. Press Shift-K to step forward through the keyframes.

9. You must render your rotating clip before you can play it back. Select the clip; then choose Sequence > Render Selection.

10. Play back your rotation effect.

✔ Tip

- ■ Strictly speaking, it's not necessary to click the Add Keyframe button to set the second and third keyframes; you need only change the keyframe's value on the Motion tab. However, rotation keyframes don't show up in the wireframe overlay even when they are present. Pressing the Add Keyframe button sets a keyframe across all motion parameters, so the green highlighting is visible.

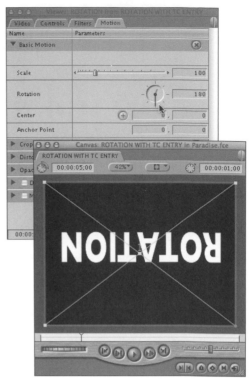

Figure 15.44 Set the keyframe value to 180 by dragging the Rotation dial needle to the right.

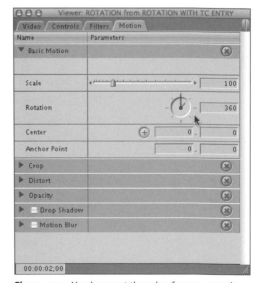

Figure 15.45 You have set three keyframes, exactly 30 frames apart, that program your clip to complete one full 360-degree rotation in 2 seconds.

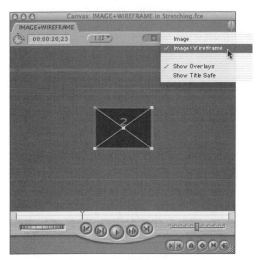

Figure 15.46 Choose Image+Wireframe from the View pop-up menu.

Creating Motion Paths

If you are new to motion paths, try one— if your FCE system is powerful enough to support real-time previewing, you can play back a moving clip without rendering, and you will get a feel for how the Canvas function changes when you are working in Image+ Wireframe mode. You can work in Image+ Wireframe mode in the Viewer as well.

When you animate the center point, you move the whole clip. The following section explains the basic steps for animating a simple motion path.

✔ Tip

- Motion paths are limited to single sequence clips; you must nest sequence clips if you want to create a motion path that includes two or more clips that have been edited together. For more information on nesting items, see Chapter 4, "Projects, Sequences, and Clips."

To create a motion path in the Canvas:

1. In the Timeline, select a sequence clip; then position the playhead on the first frame in your clip.

2. Make the Canvas active; then choose 12% from the Zoom pop-up menu and Image+Wireframe from the View pop-up menu (**Figure 15.46**).

3. To add the first keyframe, click the Add Motion Keyframe button in the Canvas. Final Cut Express sets the first keyframe across all motion parameters for that sequence frame.

continues on next page

4. In the Canvas, drag the wireframe's center handle to the left until the right side of the wireframe aligns with the left edge of the black background. Hold down the Shift key while you drag to constrain the motion path. This makes it easier to drag in a straight line.

Your clip is now positioned just off the screen, at the left (**Figure 15.47**).

5. In the Timeline, position the playhead on the last frame in your sequence clip.

6. In the Canvas, click inside the wireframe and Shift-drag the wireframe to the right. Drag the wireframe across the black background until its left side aligns with the right edge of the black background.

As you drag, the motion path appears across the center of the screen. The white line indicates the motion path of your clip's center point (**Figure 15.48**).

7. To preview your motion path, hold down the Option key while you scrub the Canvas Scrubber bar from side to side.

8. If your computer supports real-time previewing, you can play your moving clip immediately. If not, you must render before playback. Select the clip; then choose Sequence > Render Selection > Video.

✔ Tip

- When your clips and motion paths are so spread out that you need to make the Canvas or the Viewer view smaller than the smallest level listed on the Zoom control (12%), choose Fit All, which will zoom the view out enough to fit all elements of your multilayered composited sequence within the window.

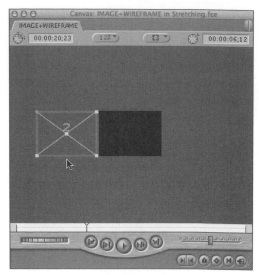

Figure 15.47 Your clip is positioned just off the screen, at the left.

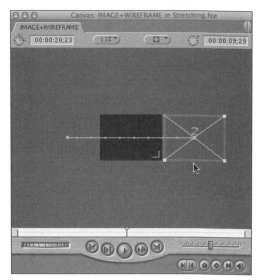

Figure 15.48 The white line indicates the motion path of your clip's center point.

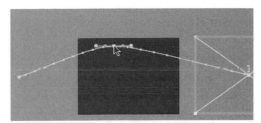

Figure 15.49 As you drag the motion path into a curve, additional keyframes appear with Bézier handles; drag the handles to sculpt the motion path's curves.

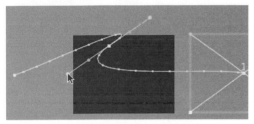

Figure 15.50 Rotate the handle to change the direction of the curve relative to that keyframe.

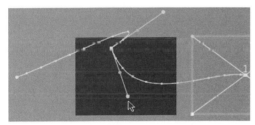

Figure 15.51 Command-drag to restrict rotation to one side of the curve.

To add curves to a motion path:

1. If you don't already have a sequence clip with a motion path applied, follow steps 1 through 6 in the previous task, "To create a motion path in the Canvas."

2. To create a curve in your straight motion path, click the motion path and drag in the direction you want the path to curve.

   As you drag the motion path into a curve, additional keyframes appear on the motion path automatically; the keyframes have little handles, called Bézier handles, which you use to sculpt the motion path's curves (**Figure 15.49**).

3. Click the Canvas Play button to play back the first draft of your edited motion path.

4. To adjust the curve, click a keyframe's Bézier handle; then *do any of the following*:

   ◆ Drag the handle away from the keyframe to deepen the curve.

   ◆ Drag the handle toward the keyframe to reduce the curve.

   ◆ Rotate the handle to change the direction of the curve relative to that keyframe (**Figure 15.50**).

   ◆ Command-drag to restrict rotation to one side of the curve (**Figure 15.51**). Release the Command key to set the new relationship between the two curves.

To reposition an entire motion path:

1. Choose the Selection tool from the Tool palette.

2. In the Canvas, hold down the Command and Shift keys; then place the pointer near the motion path that you want to reposition.

   The Selection tool turns into a Hand pointer when you position it correctly (**Figure 15.52**).

3. Drag the motion path to a new position.

   The entire motion path repositions but does not change its shape or timing (**Figure 15.53**).

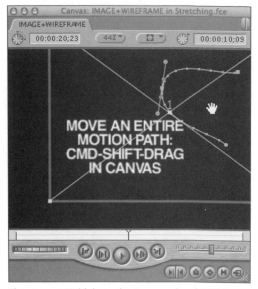

Figure 15.52 Hold down the Command and Shift keys; then place the Selection pointer near the motion path that you want to reposition. The pointer turns into a Hand pointer when you're in the right spot.

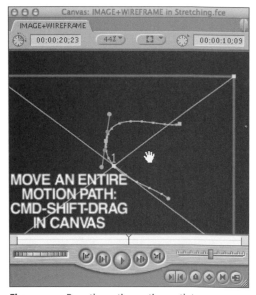

Figure 15.53 Drag the entire motion path to a new position without changing its shape or timing.

CREATING MOTION PATHS

Editing a Motion Path

Once you have created it, you can adjust a motion path directly in the Canvas (or Viewer) by moving or deleting motion path keyframes. When you're working with a motion path in the Canvas, the playhead doesn't need to be over a keyframe for you to move or delete it, nor does the playhead location prohibit you from adding a motion path keyframe.

Remember that a keyframe is like an edit point: It signals a change in an effect. In a motion path, keyframes are placed automatically only when a motion path changes direction. A straight motion path requires only two keyframes: a start keyframe and an end keyframe.

The two motion path variables you are adjusting are your clip's speed of travel (determined by the ratio of duration to distance between keyframes) and the path's route (indicated by the shape of the white line that connects the start and end keyframes). The little dots that appear between the keyframes indicate the duration between path points.

Adjusting motion path curves and corners

Final Cut Express features two types of motion path keyframes: corners and curves. The default motion path keyframe is a corner, which creates an instant change in direction. If you want a smoother motion effect, the curve keyframes have Bézier handles, which you can use to fine-tune the shape of the path's curve, as well as ease handles, which you can use to fine-tune your clip's speed immediately before and after the keyframe location.

You switch a corner type motion path keyframe to a curve type as the first step in smoothing your motion path and finessing its timing.

✔ Tip

- You can use the Shift and Command keys while dragging a Bézier or ease handle to influence the connections between the angles of the curve.

To toggle a keyframe between corner and curve types in Wireframe mode:

With your clip displayed in Wireframe mode in the Canvas, Control-click a keyframe and *choose one of the following options:*

- ◆ Make Corner Point toggles the keyframe from a curve type to a corner type (**Figure 15.54**).

- ◆ Ease In/Ease Out accesses the ease handles, which are discussed later in this section.

- ◆ Linear applies a constant rate of speed to the path immediately before and after the keyframe location.

- ◆ Delete Point deletes the keyframe.

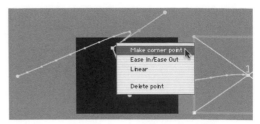

Figure 15.54 Control-click a keyframe on the Canvas; then choose Make Corner Point to toggle the keyframe from a curve type to a corner type.

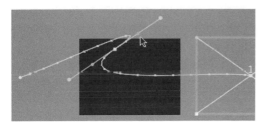

Figure 15.55 Ease handles are located about midway between the Bézier handles and the keyframe's position point.

Setting a Single Motion Path for Multiple Clips

How can you easily apply a single motion path to multiple clips? A couple of different techniques are available; your choice depends on whether you are dealing with a series of clips on a single track or with multiple clips stacked in layers on Timeline tracks.

One approach is to copy and paste just the series of clips into a separate sequence, which you edit back into your main sequence just as if it were a single clip. You can then apply a single motion path to the entire series, because it's contained in a single sub-sequence. You can use the same technique to convert multiple layers into a sub-sequence in order to apply a single motion path.

You also have the option of copying a clip and pasting only its motion path using the Paste Attributes function.

For more information on working with multiple sequences, see Chapter 4, "Projects, Sequences, and Clips."

For more information on the Paste Attributes feature, see Chapter 10, "Editing in the Timeline and the Canvas."

Adjusting speed along a motion path

You can increase the speed of a clip's movement by shortening the timecode duration between two keyframes without changing their spatial coordinates. The clip's speed increases, since it takes less time to travel between the two locations on your motion path. Or keep the time interval the same and move the keyframes farther apart on the motion path, so the clip travels farther in the same amount of time. Other timing factors in your sequence composition will dictate your choice.

Ease handles, located in the Canvas between the Bézier handles and the keyframe's position point (**Figure 15.55**), fine-tune the rate of speed at which a clip approaches and leaves a curve keyframe. The default Ease In and Out setting slows the speed on the motion path by 33 percent before and after the keyframe, but you can customize that setting. Drag both handles to set the clip's ease in and ease out to the same rate, or drag the handles separately to set different ease-in and ease-out rates.

To make a clip ease in and out of a keyframe:

1. With the Canvas in Image+Wireframe mode, start with a curve motion path keyframe.

2. Choose the Selection tool.

3. Click the curve keyframe; then *do one of the following:*

   ◆ Drag the ease handle away from the keyframe to increase the clip's speed as it passes through the keyframe's location on the motion path (**Figure 15.56**).

   ◆ Drag the handle toward the keyframe to slow the clip's speed as it passes through the keyframe's location on the motion path (**Figure 15.57**).

   ◆ Drag either ease handle to adjust the path's timing on both sides of the keyframe equally.

   ◆ Shift-drag one ease handle to adjust the path's timing only on the selected side.

4. Play back in Image+Wireframe mode to see your results.

✔ Tip

■ You can copy and paste motion paths between clips or sequences by using the Paste Attributes command on the Edit menu. Check the Scale Attributes box when you paste attributes onto your destination clip, and you can reuse a motion path on a different clip that's shorter or longer than the original.

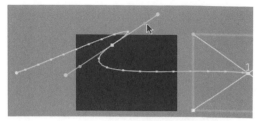

Figure 15.56 Drag the ease handle away from the keyframe to increase a clip's speed as it passes through the keyframe's location on the motion path.

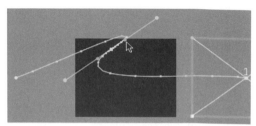

Figure 15.57 Drag the ease handle toward the keyframe to decrease a clip's speed as it passes through the keyframe's location on the motion path.

EDITING A MOTION PATH

FILTERS AND COMPOSITING

Just as the term *motion properties* is used to describe a collection of tools that do a lot more than move things, so the term *filters* applies to a lot more than just tools for tinting or texturing an image. Final Cut Express comes with more than 50 video filters with a wide variety of uses. In addition to a suite of image-control filters for color correction and tinting, Final Cut Express provides filters you can use to blur, twirl, emboss, ripple, flip, mask, and key. For a list of filters, refer to Chapter 29 in Apple's *Final Cut Express Help* PDF.

But wait—there's more. Final Cut Express can also make use of the QuickTime effects that are installed with QuickTime and some FXBuilder-based filters written for Final Cut Pro.

You'll find filters on the Browser's Effects tab or the Effects menu. After installation, QuickTime effects and third-party filters are stored in separate folders within the main Video Filters folders.

For information on working with audio filters, see Chapter 12, "Audio Tools and Techniques."

To apply a filter to a clip:

1. *Do one of the following:*
   - ◆ Drag the filter from the Browser's Effects tab and drop it on the clip in the Timeline (**Figure 16.1**).
   - ◆ Select the clip in the Timeline, choose Effects > Video (or Audio) Filters, and make your filter selection from the submenu.

2. Position the playhead over a frame in the selected clip to see a preview of the effect in the Canvas (**Figure 16.2**).

✔ Tips

- ■ Many filters' default settings have no visible effect on a clip. You must adjust settings before you can detect a difference.

- ■ Final Cut Express renders a clip's filters in the order they appear on the Filters tab. You can drag a filter up or down in the list to rearrange the filter order. Rendering order affects your final results.

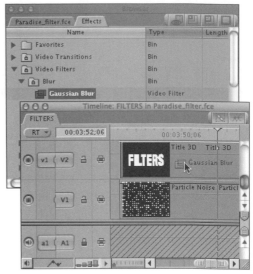

Figure 16.1 Drag the filter from the Effects tab and drop it on the clip in the Timeline.

Figure 16.2 Position the playhead over a frame in the filtered clip to see a preview of the effect in the Canvas.

Figure 16.3 Choose the Range Selection tool from the Tool palette.

Figure 16.4 Choose Effects > Video Filters; then select a filter from the submenus.

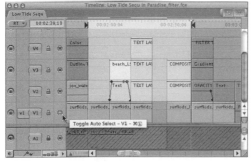

Figure 16.5 Auto-selected clips appear highlighted in the Timeline; In and Out points mark the boundaries of the selection. Disabling the Auto Select control on V1 will exclude V1 clips from the batch filter application. Make sure the Auto Select control is enabled on all tracks where you want the filter to be applied.

To apply a filter to a range of clips or part of a clip:

1. From the Tool palette, choose the Range Selection tool (**Figure 16.3**).

2. In the Timeline, drag to select whole or partial clips.

3. Choose Effects > Video (or Audio) Filters and select a filter from the submenus (**Figure 16.4**).

   If you selected multiple clips, Final Cut Express adds a separate copy of the filter to each clip.

4. Position the playhead over a frame in the selected clip range to see a preview of the effect in the Canvas.

To use Auto Select to apply a filter to multiple clips:

1. In the Timeline, set In and Out points at the boundaries of the section where you want to apply the filter.

2. Make sure the Auto Select control is enabled on all tracks where you want the filter to be applied; disable any tracks containing clips that you want to exclude from filtering (**Figure 16.5**).

3. Choose Effects > Video (or Audio) Filters and select a filter from the submenu.

   If you selected multiple clips, Final Cut Express adds a separate copy of the filter to each clip between the In and Out points on tracks where Auto Select is enabled.

4. Position the playhead over a frame in the selected clip range to see a preview of the effect in the Canvas.

FILTERS AND COMPOSITING

455

To adjust a filter:

1. In the Timeline, double-click a clip to which you've added a filter to open it in the Viewer.

2. In the Viewer, click the Filters tab to access the filter's controls.

3. Configure the filter's settings (**Figure 16.6**). The items you can change vary according to the type of filter.

4. To see your changes, use the arrow keys to move through the clip frame by frame, or try a low-quality real-time preview. For the highest-quality playback, render the clip; then you can play it with a video filter applied.

To disable a filter:

1. In the Timeline, double-click a clip to which you've added a filter; then select the clip's Filters tab.

2. Uncheck the box next to the filter's name on the Viewer's Filters tab.

   The filter is disabled but still applied to the clip. To toggle it on, recheck the box.

✔ Tip

■ If you need more space to adjust sliders (or to read the full name of a filter control), expand the columns containing the effect controls on the Filters, Controls, and Motion tabs. Drag the column header separators to adjust column width (**Figure 16.7**) or drag the lower-right corner of the Viewer to expand it horizontally.

To remove a filter from a clip:

Do *one of the following*:

◆ Select the filter on the Filters tab and press Delete.

◆ Control-click the filter and choose Cut from the shortcut menu.

◆ Select the filter and choose Edit > Clear.

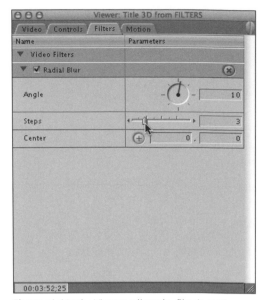

Figure 16.6 In the Viewer, adjust the filter's settings on the clip's Filters tab.

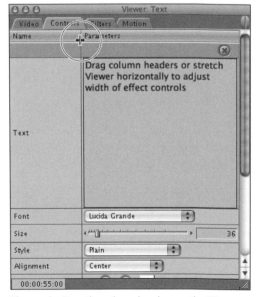

Figure 16.7 Drag the column headers on the Filters, Controls, and Motion tabs to adjust the width of the effect controls.

Useful Filters

There's a boatload of filters in Final Cut Express. Some of them do really useful and cool things that you might not normally associate with the idea of a filter.

Here's a rundown of a few interesting ones that you might have missed:

◆ **Flop:** This Perspective filter flip-flops the image horizontally, vertically, or both directions at the same time. John Huston used this effect in his World War II documentary *The Battle of San Pietro* to keep the Allied forces heading right to left, and the Axis forces heading left to right, regardless of which direction they were actually moving during filming.

◆ **De-interlace:** This Video filter can improve the stability of still images by duplicating either of the two fields that make up a video frame. De-interlace is also useful for correcting jittery high-speed movement, if you can accept a slightly softened image quality. Try the Flicker options for the best control over the effect.

◆ **View Finder:** This Video filter simulates footage from security cameras, home cameras, or pre-production screen tests. Other filters in the Video group—**Blink, Strobe,** and **Image Stabilizer**—are also interesting and can be applied creatively. Check 'em out.

◆ **Sepia:** This Image Control filter tints the clip to an old-time, faded-film color. Why use this filter when the Tint filter does that as well? Well, with Sepia, you can change the color in the same way that you can using the Tint filter, but you have the advantage of being able to tweak the contrast as well, which you can't do using the Tint filter. If you need to adjust color *and* contrast, why not have just one filter doing the math instead of two?

◆ **Echo and Reverb:** These two Audio filters help make that pickup dialogue you recorded in your bedroom sound believable when you cut it into the scene you shot in the gymnasium.

◆ **Film Noise:** This QuickTime filter adds hair, scratches, dust, and the look of old film to your video. Lots of people skip the dust and scratches completely and use Film Noise just for a faded-color-film look that renders quickly. This is not, however, a filter that can be found on the Effects tab in the Browser. To use Film Noise, you have to export your clip as a QuickTime movie and access the filter as described in "To export a clip or sequence in another QuickTime format" in Chapter 19. Be sure to adjust your movie settings to match your audio and video sequence settings. Re-import your processed clip into your project and enjoy your film noise.

◆ **Joe's Filters:** Joe Maller's custom filters, originally written for Final Cut Pro, work just fine in Final Cut Express. Demo versions of these filters are available online. Be sure to check out Joe's documentation for each filter, including the beautiful color illustrations of each filter at work; you can learn a lot about how filters work just by reading his descriptions (www.joesfilters.com). Highly recommended.

Using Color Correction Filters

Like editing, color correction is an invisible art. It's an essential part of post-production that can have a significant impact on a show, but it's not a high-profile part of the process. Final Cut Express introduces an improved set of image-quality measurement and color correction tools that make it feasible to complete a broadcast-quality finished product without leaving the Desktop.

At the most basic level, you can use these tools to ensure that the video levels in your finished program don't exceed broadcast-legal limits. If the video in your program already looks good, careful color correction can make it look even better—if you have exposure problems or intercut shots that don't match, color correction can salvage your show. You can also use color correction tools to completely transform the look of your footage or to create an illusion—one example is "day for night," an old movie trick where scenes shot during the day are printed very dark to simulate night lighting.

This section provides a brief overview of the tools and the basics of working with the Color Correction filter interface, but it does not delve into the complexities of color correction (there are entire books written on the subject). You should supplement your reading with Chapter 31 of Apple's *Final Cut Express Help* PDF, a 20-page introduction to the principles of color correction and the protocols governing the operation of Final Cut Express's color correction tools. Be sure to use the full-color PDF version of the manual; any demonstration of color correction technique is severely handicapped when it's presented in grayscale. The PDF version of the manual is available from FCE's Help menu.

Always Be Color Safe!

It's a fact of life: It's easy to produce video with colors and luminance levels that look great on your Macintosh, but look scary, overblown, and distorted on a home television set. With DV footage, you shouldn't need to worry about color levels, but images created on the computer need to be created correctly. Many colors, including black, white, and quite a few reds, are considered to be outside the color-safe guidelines. While this may not matter so much if you are creating content for the Web, it will matter if you are intending your masterpiece to be premiered on broadcast or cable TV.

It's easy to exceed NTSC broadcast limits for luminance and color intensity; Photoshop and other programs allow you to create images with colors and levels well outside the legal broadcast limits. You can use FCE's color correction tools to tone down your graphics after you import. See "Using the Broadcast Safe filter" later in this chapter.

Be sure to check your work on an external TV monitor as you proceed. The best way to get out of trouble is not to get in.

If your project is headed for national broadcast, you might want to re-create your edit at a professional post-production house for a proper online session, where all the technical demands of broadcast TV can be honored in style.

For more information on FCE's role in handling the conversion of digital video levels to analog video levels, see Apple's Knowledge Base article "Final Cut Express: About Luminance" (article 60864) at the Apple web site: www.info.apple.com/ kbnum/n60864.

Figure 16.8 These five filters make up FCE's color correction suite. Some, like the Color Corrector, are general-purpose color correction tools; others, like the Desaturate Highlights filter, have special uses.

The Color Correction filter suite

You'll find five filters in FCE's Color Correction filter folder (**Figure 16.8**). Some of the filters are general-purpose color correction tools; others have special applications. It's common to use more than one filter type on a single color-corrected clip.

◆ **Broadcast Safe:** This filter is designed to *clamp* (filter out) any illegal luma and chroma levels in your clip. See "Using the Broadcast Safe filter" later in this chapter.

◆ **Color Corrector:** This filter is for general-purpose color correction and offers both numerical controls and graphical onscreen controls. For more information, see "Anatomy of the Color Corrector tab" later in this chapter.

◆ **Desaturate Highlights/Desaturate Lows:** These two filters (actually the same filter with two different default settings) are designed to solve a common color correction problem: altering or increasing the intensity of a color in your image without tinting the highlights or black areas of the image. These filters desaturate (reduce the chroma levels) in those areas of the image, keeping your whites and blacks pure.

◆ **RGB Balance:** This simple RGB color balance filter has separate highlight, midtone, and blacks controls for reds, greens, and blues.

Using the Broadcast Safe filter

The Broadcast Safe filter is a quick fix you can apply to any NTSC or PAL video in your program. The filter offers a menu of presets (**Figure 16.9**) designed to clamp any illegal luma or chroma levels in your clip to within legal limits. The default setting should work well for most clips, but if you want to tweak the settings yourself, you can choose the Custom setting, which enables the individual luma and chroma level controls. The filter displays NTSC or PAL broadcast-safe presets based on your sequence settings.

✔ Tips

- You can apply a single Broadcast Safe filter to your entire sequence by nesting the sequence inside a parent sequence before you apply the filter. To learn more about the care and feeding of nested sequences, see "Working with Multiple Sequences" in Chapter 4.

- Once you've applied the Broadcast Safe filter, your image may appear a little too dark and desaturated on your computer monitor; remember to reserve final judgment until you've scrutinized the picture on an external broadcast monitor.

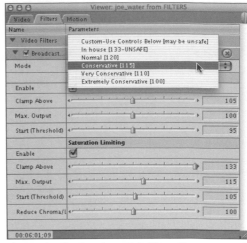

Figure 16.9 The Broadcast Safe filter offers a menu of presets designed to clamp illegal luma or chroma levels in your clip to broadcast-legal limits. The filter's default settings work fine in most cases.

Monitors and Color Correction

A properly calibrated broadcast video monitor is an essential tool for accurate color correction (and most other post-production tasks). Use the best broadcast video monitor you can afford. Follow the procedures outlined in Apple Knowledge Base article 36550, "Final Cut Pro 3: How to Calibrate Your Broadcast Monitor" (available online at the Apple web site), before you color-correct your first clip. You should not color-correct based on the color you see in the image areas of the Viewer or the Canvas.

Anatomy of the Color Corrector tab

The Color Corrector filter—one of the five filters available in FCE's Color Correction filter folder—features graphical onscreen controls in addition to the standard numeric controls found on the Filters tab of the Viewer. The visual controls appear on their own Viewer tab after you apply the Color Corrector filter (**Figure 16.10**).

✔ Tip

■ Position the pointer over a filter control in the interface to display a tooltip with the name of the control and its keyboard shortcut equivalent.

continues on next page

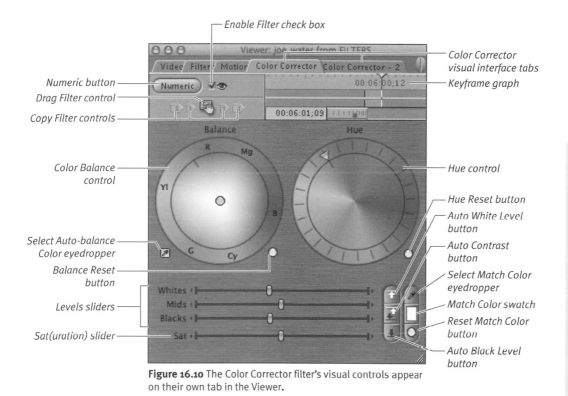

Enable Filter check box

Numeric button

Drag Filter control

Copy Filter controls

Color Balance control

Select Auto-balance Color eyedropper

Balance Reset button

Levels sliders

Sat(uration) slider

Color Corrector visual interface tabs

Keyframe graph

Hue control

Hue Reset button

Auto White Level button

Auto Contrast button

Select Match Color eyedropper

Match Color swatch

Reset Match Color button

Auto Black Level button

Figure 16.10 The Color Corrector filter's visual controls appear on their own tab in the Viewer.

USING COLOR CORRECTION FILTERS

The top section of the tab contains clip controls for keyframing the color correction filter and for copying the filter's settings to other clips in your sequence.

Figure 16.11 Use the Copy Filter controls to copy your filter settings to other clips in your sequence with a single mouse click.

- **Color Corrector Viewer tabs:** The filter's visual controls appear on their own Viewer tab. If you have multiple copies of the Color Corrector filter applied to the clip, a separate numbered tab appears for each copy.

- **Numeric button:** Click this button to switch to the filter's numeric controls on the Filters tab.

- **Enable Filter check box:** Check to enable this filter. Uncheck to disable the filter.

- **Copy Filter controls:** The Copy Filter feature (**Figure 16.11**) is one of the secret weapons of the Color Corrector filter. Once you have color corrected a representative shot in your sequence to your satisfaction, you can use the Copy Filter controls to copy your filter's settings to other clips in your sequence with a single mouse click.

  - **Copy from 2nd Clip Back:** Copies settings from the Color Corrector filter that is applied two clips upstream from the currently selected clip and pastes the settings into this copy of the Color Corrector filter, replacing any previously applied settings. If the source clip has no color correction filter, this control is dimmed.

  - **Copy from 1st Clip Back:** Copies settings from the Color Corrector filter that is applied to the first clip upstream from the currently selected clip and pastes the settings into this copy of the Color Corrector filter, replacing any previously applied settings. If the source clip has no color correction filter, this control is dimmed.

◆ **Copy to 1st Clip Forward:** Copies the settings of this Color Corrector filter into the next clip downstream in your sequence. If no Color Corrector filter is present on the destination clip, FCE applies one automatically.

◆ **Copy to 2nd Clip Forward:** Copies the settings of this Color Corrector filter into the clip located two clips downstream in your sequence. If no Color Corrector filter is present on the destination clip, FCE applies one automatically.

◆ **Drag Filter control:** Drag this button to another Timeline clip to copy the current Color Corrector filter and its settings into that clip.

The tab's center section contains the filter's Color Balance controls and Level and Saturation controls, your everyday color balance tools.

◆ **Color Balance control:** Use the Balance control like a virtual trackball control. Click the dot at the center of the control and drag it across the circular face of the control to adjust the color balance of your clip. The center of the circle represents pure white; drag farther from the center to increase the saturation of your color shift.

Hold down the Shift key while dragging to constrain the angle of the adjustment—a useful technique for adjusting the intensity of a color without shifting its hue.

Hold down the Command key while dragging to gear up the control, increasing the magnitude of the color balance adjustments in response to your mouse movements. (This is the opposite of the Command-drag gear-down modifier implemented elsewhere in FCE, which enables precision adjustments.)

◆ **Select Auto-balance Color eyedropper:** Click the eyedropper icon; then click a color in your image that you want to match to the color you selected with the Hue Match controls. For more information, see "Hue Match controls" later in this section.

◆ **Balance Reset button:** Click to reset the Balance control to its default settings. Shift-click the button to reset the Levels and Sat(uration) sliders to their default values as well.

◆ **Hue control:** Click the outer edge of the Hue control's circular face and rotate the dial to make an overall adjustment to the clip's hue.

◆ **Hue Reset button:** Click to reset the Hue control to its default settings. Shift-click the button to reset the Levels and Sat(uration) sliders to their default values as well.

◆ **Levels sliders:** Use these sliders to make overall adjustments to the luminance levels in your clip. Click the tiny arrow at either end of a slider to nudge the value by a single increment.

  ◆ **Whites slider:** Use the slider to adjust the clip's maximum white level.

  ◆ **Mids slider:** Use the slider to adjust just the midtones in the clip, leaving any black or white areas untouched.

  ◆ **Blacks slider:** Use the slider to adjust the clip's minimum black level.

continues on next page

◆ **Sat(uration) slider:** Move this slider to make overall adjustments to the color saturation levels in your clip. Click the tiny arrow at either end of the slider to nudge the value by single increments. Moving the slider all the way to the left removes all color from the clip, leaving a grayscale image. Moving the slider all the way to the right will almost certainly push your color values into distortion, so use caution and check your work on your broadcast video monitor.

◆ **Auto White Level button:** Click to find the maximum white level in the current frame and automatically adjust the Whites slider to set the maximum white level.

◆ **Auto Contrast button:** Click to set Auto black and Auto white levels in a single operation.

◆ **Auto Black Level button:** Click to find the maximum black level in the current frame and automatically adjust the Blacks slider to set the maximum black level.

◆ **Hue Match controls:** Hue Match controls extend the function of FCE's auto-white balance controls, allowing you to adjust any color in your image to match the color you've selected as the match color. For more information, see "Hue Matching Controls" in Chapter 31 of Apple's *Final Cut Express Help* PDF.

  ◆ **Select Match Color:** Use the eyedropper to select the color hue you want to match.

  ◆ **Match Color:** This swatch displays the color you've selected as the auto-balance target color.

  ◆ **Reset Match Color:** Click to set the match color to white, the default setting.

✔ **Tip**

■ To use Hue Match as an auto-white balance tool, click the Reset Match Color button to set the tool to white, its default setting. Next, use the Select Auto-balance Color eyedropper icon to click a highlight in your image that you want to match to white. The Hue Match control analyzes the hue value of the selected pixel and then automatically adjusts the overall color balance of the image; for example, selecting a light-green highlight will result in an overall color shift toward magenta to correct the green highlight to neutral white.

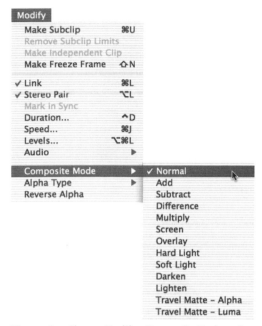

Figure 16.12 Choose Modify > Composite Mode and then select a Composite mode from the submenu. You can also access Composite modes from a Timeline clip's shortcut menu.

Compositing

Compositing can be any process that combines two or more image layers to create an effect. A compositing process can also include filters and motion that have been applied to modify individual layers or to modify the composited image.

Setting Composite mode

A Composite mode is an algorithm, a mathematical formula that controls the way the colors in a clip combine with the clip colors in underlying video layers.

All compositing happens from the top down; the highest-numbered track's image sits on the front plane and obscures the image on a track beneath it, unless the foreground image is made transparent. Each clip's opacity setting influences the final effect of the Composite mode.

For a complete list of Final Cut Express's Composite modes, refer to Chapter 27 of Apple's *Final Cut Express Help* PDF.

To set the Composite mode for a clip:

Select the clip in the Timeline; then *do one of the following:*

◆ Choose Modify > Composite Mode; then select a Composite mode from the submenu (**Figure 16.12**).

◆ Control-click the clip in the Timeline and then select a Composite mode from the submenu.

COMPOSITING

Using alpha channels

An RGB image is composed of three 8-bit grayscale images—the red, green, and blue color channels—that express color information as a gray scale: 256 brightness values (ranging from 0 for black to 255 for white), plus an alpha channel. An alpha channel is a fourth 8-bit channel that can be assigned to an RGB image to track which areas of the image are transparent.

Figures 16.13, 16.14, and **16.15** illustrate how an alpha channel can be manipulated to mask selected areas in an image.

Figure 16.13 A still graphic image.

Figure 16.14 The image's alpha channel. With the alpha channel set to Straight, the white area will be interpreted as transparent.

Figure 16.15 The graphics frame superimposed over video. With the frame's alpha channel set to Straight, the white areas in the alpha channel shown in Figure 16.14 are made transparent here, allowing the video background to show through.

Alpha channels are useful critters with a variety of applications in digital imaging. Final Cut Express video clips automatically have alpha channels assigned to them; it's the alpha channel that's being manipulated when you adjust the opacity of a clip or apply a key or matte filter.

◆ When you import an image that has an alpha channel, Final Cut Express interprets the clip's alpha channel and sets it to Straight, Black, or White (corresponding to the background setting for the clip at the time the clip was created).

◆ When you place a clip in a sequence, Final Cut Express automatically makes the alpha channel area transparent. You can override the automatic setting by modifying the alpha channel type.

◆ You can reverse an alpha channel if you want to invert the transparency of an image, or you can choose to ignore the clip's alpha channel altogether.

To view or modify a clip's alpha channel type:

1. Select the clip.

2. Choose Modify > Alpha Type and select a different alpha channel type from the submenu (**Figure 16.16**).

✔ Tip

■ DV clips do not retain their alpha channel information if you export them in a DV format. If you want to save a clip's alpha channel when you export, use the Animation codec, set to Millions of Colors+. If you're exporting FCE elements for processing in a digital effects creation program such as Adobe After Effects, this is the way to go. Use the Animation codec again when you export from After Effects.

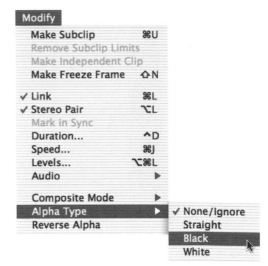

Figure 16.16 Choose Modify > Alpha Type; then select a different alpha channel type from the submenu.

Figure 16.17 Final Cut Express offers a toolbox full of special-purpose matte and key filters. When you create multilayer compositions, use these filters to mask out portions of the frame.

Working with Mattes

Mattes are filters that you shape to define which areas of opaque video clips are to be made transparent during compositing. For example, you could use a circular matte to isolate a clock face from its background, or you could create a matte in the shape of a keyhole to simulate peeking through a key-hole in a door.

Final Cut Express offers many types of matte filters (**Figure 16.17**). "Garbage mattes" are used to quickly rough out large areas of the frame. A *key* is a type of matte that uses a clip's color or luminance information to determine which opaque areas will be made transparent (bluescreen effects are created with color key mattes set to make blue areas transparent). You can combine layers of different types of mattes to create very complex composite shapes.

To apply a matte:

1. *Do one of the following:*
   - Drag the Key or Matte filter from the Browser's Effects tab and drop it on the clip in the Timeline.
   - Select the clip in the Timeline and choose Effects > Video Filters; then select a filter from the Key or Matte submenu.

2. Position the playhead over a frame in the selected clip to see a preview of the effect in the Canvas.

Travel mattes

A travel matte allows one video clip to play through another. The alpha information in a third clip is used as a matte that defines the transparent and opaque areas of the composited image.

When you create a travel matte effect, there are usually three video tracks involved; this is sometimes called a "matte sandwich." The background clip is placed on V1, or the lowest video track available. The matte clip, preferably a high-contrast, grayscale motion clip or still image, goes on the video track just above the background clip, on V2; and the foreground clip sits on V3, or the video track above the matte clip. A Composite mode specifically for creating travel mattes, called Travel Matte - Luma, is applied to the foreground clip. If the matte clip is placed on video track V1 without a background clip, then the background is automatically black.

To create a travel matte:

1. In the Timeline, drag your background clip (**Figure 16.18**) to V1.

2. Drag the clip selected to be the matte clip (**Figure 16.19**) to V2.

Figure 16.18 Drag your background clip to track V1.

Figure 16.19 Drag your matte clip to track V2. The white areas in this clip will define the opaque areas of the foreground clip.

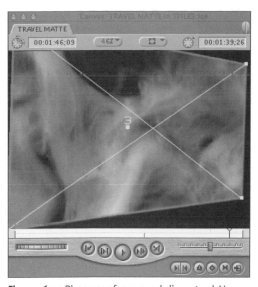

Figure 16.20 Place your foreground clip on track V3.

3. Drag your foreground clip (**Figure 16.20**) to V3.

4. To establish the travel matte, select the foreground clip on V3 (**Figure 16.21**) and choose Modify > Composite Mode > Travel Matte – Luma.

The completed travel matte effect (**Figure 16.22**) uses the matte clip's luminance (or grayscale) levels as the mask. The matte clip's black area creates the shape of the foreground clip's transparent areas, revealing the background clip video. The matte clip's white area creates the shape of the foreground clip's opaque areas— that's where you see the foreground clip's video.

continues on next page

Figure 16.21 To composite the travel matte, select the foreground clip on V3 and choose Modify > Composite Mode > Travel Matte–Luma. The foreground clip on V3 is now composited with the matte clip on V2.

Figure 16.22 The completed travel matte effect.

WORKING WITH MATTES

471

✔ Tips

■ After you composite your travel matte, you can refine the effect by adjusting the matte clip's brightness and contrast.

■ You can apply animated filters and effects, as well any other standard clip motion, to the travel matte on V2 for some very interesting looks.

■ Play with Edge Feather and Edge Thin to soften the halo effect you might find around your matted objects when working with color keys.

■ DV video is not the best video format for creating effects that require critical color key mattes, such as bluescreen or greenscreen effects. DV compression throws out too much color information to give you the best control over edges.

TITLES AND GENERATORS

Generators are a class of effects that create (or *generate*) new video information rather than modify existing video. After you have generated it by rendering, a generated clip can be used just like any other clip. Text is a high-profile member of the generator class of effects; using the text generator to produce titles is covered later in this chapter.

Final Cut Express's generators include the following:

◆ Bars and Tone, which generates NTSC or PAL color bars and includes a 1-kHz audio tone with an adjustable level.

◆ More Bars & Signals, a suite of specialized color bar patterns and gradients.

◆ Matte, which generates solid, single-color clips.

◆ Render, which generates color gradients and different types of "noise."

◆ Shape, which generates an opaque geometric shape on a black background. You can scale or color the shape.

◆ Slug, which generates solid black frames and silent audio. (There are no controls for this effect.)

◆ Text, which generates simple titles using TrueType fonts loaded in your system.

◆ Title 3D and Title Crawl, two text generators from third-party developer Boris. These offer much more precise control over title text, such as individual letter control over kerning. See "Creating titles with Boris Calligraphy" later in this chapter.

To add a generator to a sequence:

1. In the Viewer, choose an item from the Generator pop-up menu in the lower-right corner (**Figure 17.1**).

   The generator effect is loaded into the Viewer as an unrendered clip.

2. Click the Controls tab to access the generator controls (**Figure 17.2**).

3. Adjust the generator's controls; then click the Video tab to view the generator clip in the Viewer.

4. Edit the generator into your sequence just as you would a clip.

5. Render your generated clip. You must render it before you can play it back. Select the clip; then choose Sequence > Render Selection.

✔ Tip

■ When you are configuring settings for a generator clip, it's much easier to see what you're doing if you drag the generator clip's Controls tab out of the Viewer window first. Now you can view the generator image on the Viewer's Video tab as you configure the settings on the Controls tab.

To edit a generator in a sequence:

1. Double-click the generator clip in the Timeline to open it in the Viewer.

2. Click the Controls tab; then make your adjustments.

Figure 17.1 Choose a generator from the Generator pop-up menu in the lower-right corner of the Viewer window.

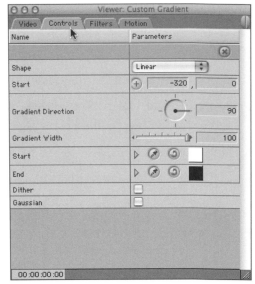

Figure 17.2 Adjust the settings for your generated clip on the clip's Controls tab.

TITLES AND GENERATORS

Always Be Title Safe!

Every TV set is different: different colors, different screen geometries, different projection skews—never the same color, never the same combinations. Since even the middle area of the screen is not reliably centered (especially on home sets!), it's important to keep your text and graphic elements within a screen area that television engineers call *title safe*.

With the Title Safe overlay on, two boxes are superimposed on your clip—the inside border outlines the Title Safe boundary. Keep your graphic elements inside this box, and the edges won't get cropped off, even on consumer TVs. The slightly larger box surrounding the Title Safe boundary is known as the Action Safe boundary. Any visual elements critical to your project should occur within the Action Safe region. You should check Title Safe boundaries on all graphic elements before you invest too much time on a layout. For more information, see "Viewing Title Safe and Action Safe boundaries" in Chapter 8.

Title Safe and Action Safe areas apply only to program material displayed on a TV (both NTSC and PAL). If you plan to show your FCE project on the Web or via some other computer-based format, remember that web-based video displays the entire frame, so check the edges for unexpected surprises—microphones, shadows, dolly grips, and so on. The same caveats apply if you're compositing a Picture in Picture (PiP) effect—every pixel in your frame is included.

Particle Noise = Generator Fun

When you're stuck for a way to add a little flash and color to a title sequence, load up Particle Noise. This generator is a ready source of animated textured backgrounds that range from serene (**Figure 17.3**) to trippy (**Figure 17.4**). Remember: you can stack multiple copies in layers, apply filters, and animate generators with motion keyframes. Now your only problem is how to stop fooling with Particle Noise and finish your title sequence.

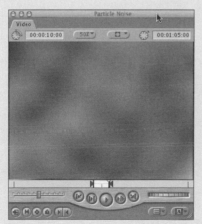

Figure 17.3 The Particle Noise generator in a misty mood.

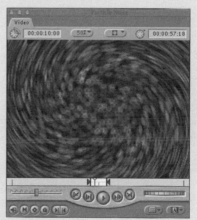

Figure 17.4 Make trippy animated backgrounds in seconds with the Particle Noise generator and the Whirlpool distortion filter.

Generating Text

Use text generators to create text elements and title screens in Final Cut Express. A text generator can create titles using any TrueType font currently loaded in your System Folder. You can specify text size, style, color, tracking, and kerning.

Final Cut Express offers six built-in text generators, which appear in the Text submenu of the Viewer's Generator pop-up menu (**Figure 17.5**):

◆ **Text:** Generates static text in a single size and style. This option allows carriage returns.

◆ **Lower 3rd:** Generates two lines of static text. Each line has separate controls for font, style, and size. The Lower 3rd generator is designed to create the standard titles used to identify interview subjects in news and documentary programs.

◆ **Outline Text:** Generates static text with an adjustable outline stroke and background matte. You can also matte graphics into the text, outline, or background elements.

◆ **Scrolling Text:** Generates animated text that scrolls up or down the screen vertically. A longer clip duration results in a slower scrolling speed. Scrolling text allows carriage returns.

◆ **Crawl:** Generates a single line of animated text that scrolls across the screen horizontally. Crawl speed is determined by the duration of the clip: a longer clip duration results in a slower crawl speed.

◆ **Typewriter:** Generates animated text that appears on the screen one letter at a time, as if typed.

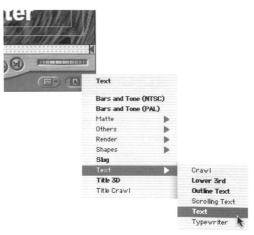

Figure 17.5 Six text generator options are available from the Generator pop-up menu's Text submenu in the Viewer window.

Complex Text: Other Options

If you need to build more complex text elements, your best bet, outside of LiveType, is to use Title 3D and Title Crawl, the (free) Boris Calligraphy text generator plugins that are included on your Final Cut Express CD. These third-party text generators offer a number of additional titling features you can use within FCE. For more information, see "Creating titles with Boris Calligraphy" later in this chapter.

Here's another option: Create your text outside of FCE in a professional graphics program, such as Adobe Photoshop, Illustrator, or After Effects, or Macromedia FreeHand, and then import the text elements as clips.

These built-in generators are the simplest means of adding text to your sequences, but there are some limitations: although text generators offer extensive control over the font, size, style, and positioning of text, except when you use the Lower 3rd generator, you're limited to a single font per text generator.

Final Cut Express also comes with two optional, third-party plugin text generators: Boris Title 3D and Title Crawl. These generators allow you to use as many fonts as you want (and probably more than you should); fancy text fanciers should read "Creating titles with Boris Calligraphy" later in this chapter for more details.

You can edit a text generator clip into a sequence in the Timeline and apply effects, just as with other clips. You can also animate static text by using keyframes to make dynamic adjustments to a text generator clip's motion properties.

Your animation applies to all text in the generator—you cannot control individual letters, words, or sentences.

✔ Tips

- A simple way to fade titles in and out is to keyframe opacity at the head and tail of the text generator clip. If you're building a title sequence, you can copy and paste just the opacity attribute to ensure a consistent look.

- An even simpler way to fade regular text titles in and out is to use the shortcut menu to place a single-ended Cross Dissolve on each end of the generator clip and then drag the transition ends inward to change the fade length.

Assembly-Line Text Generation

If you have a big stack of title or text screens to produce, this assembly-line production technique may help:

1. To produce a title template, create a standard text generator that specifies all basic formatting: font, size, color, position, and so on. Drag it into the Browser.

2. Choose Duplicate as New Master Clip to make an independent copy of your text generator template, rename the copy, and then open it in the Viewer.

3. Choose File > Open to open the text document that contains your title copy. The text document appears in a new window in FCE.

4. Copy and paste the copy for this title from the text window to the Text field in the text generator clip; then add it to your sequence.

5. Repeat steps 2 through 4 until you've banged out all those titles.

Text generator options checklist

On the Controls tab, you can specify the following text control settings (**Figure 17.6**):

♦ **Text:** Enter your text in this field or cut and paste from a word processing program.

♦ **Font:** Choose a font from this pop-up menu.

♦ **Size:** Use the slider or enter a point size for your type.

♦ **Style:** Choose a font style (Plain, Bold, Italic, and so on) from this pop-up menu.

♦ **Alignment:** Choose Center, Left, or Right alignment from this pop-up menu.

♦ **Font Color:** Click the expansion triangle to reveal the full set of color controls; then *do one of the following:*

  ♦ Drag the hue, saturation, and brightness sliders to new values.

  ♦ Enter color values numerically in the text fields.

  ♦ Select the eyedropper and click the Canvas to sample a color.

  ♦ Click the color swatch and use one of the color pickers to select a color.

♦ **Origin:** Click the Point Select (+) button (located to the left of the Origin value fields) and then specify new coordinates for your text's origin point relative to the frame by clicking the new origin location in the Canvas or on the Video tab of the Viewer. Animating the origin point (rather than the center point) of your text allows you to position your text at a starting point outside your frame.

♦ **Tracking:** Use the slider or enter a value to specify the spacing between letters.

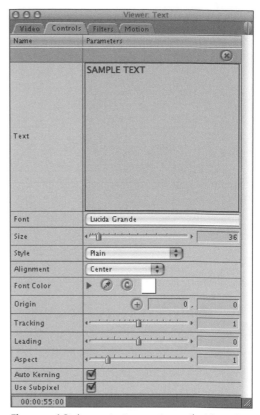

Figure 17.6 Style your text generator on the Viewer's Controls tab.

FCE 1 Projects in FCE HD: Your Text May Vary

If you're working on a project that originated in Final Cut Express 1, you may find that your text tracking has changed, and your titles appear narrower or wider than they did in FCE 1. Check your work before you output.

GENERATING TEXT

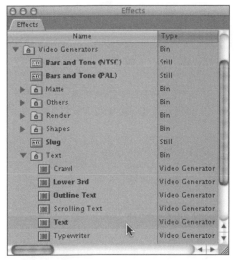

Figure 17.7 Choose the Text generator from the Video Generator folder on the Effects tab of the Browser window.

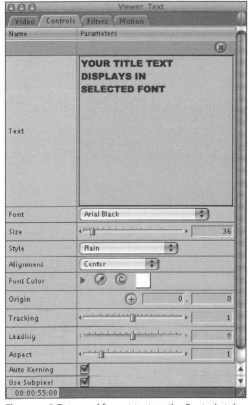

Figure 17.8 Enter and format text on the Controls tab.

◆ **Leading:** Use the slider or enter a value to specify the spacing between lines of text.

◆ **Aspect:** Use the slider or enter a value to specify the height:width proportion of your selected font.

◆ **Auto Kerning:** Check the box to enable automatic adjustment of the spacing between individual letters.

◆ **Use Subpixel:** Check the box to enable subpixel accuracy in your rendered text generator. Subpixel rendering takes longer.

To generate a basic title screen:

1. To generate a title screen, *do one of the following:*

   ◆ From the Generator pop-up menu in the lower right of the Viewer window, choose Text > Text.

   ◆ On the Browser's Effects tab, choose Text from the Video Generator folder (**Figure 17.7**).

   The Text generator appears in the Viewer.

2. In the Viewer, click the Controls tab to access the generator's controls; then specify your text control settings as outlined in the previous section, "Text generator options checklist" (**Figure 17.8**).

   You can specify only one font per text generator.

   continues on next page

GENERATING TEXT

3. Click back to the Viewer's Video tab and edit the text clip into your sequence in the Timeline. If you want to superimpose your text over video, choose the Superimpose edit type when you perform your edit (**Figure 17.9**).

You can edit, filter, and animate text clips as you would any other video element.

Figure 17.9 Drop the text clip on the Superimpose area of the edit overlay. A Superimpose edit automatically places your text clip on a new Timeline track above the target track, starting at the sequence In point.

Tips for Better-Looking Titles

◆ Always check your type on an actual television monitor. (If you are outputting for home viewing on video tape, preferably test it on the absolute worst television set and VCR you can find in the nearest back alley or junkyard.)

◆ Text should be larger than 24 points if you want it to be legible on TV.

◆ Black-and-white titles will never look their best if you use pure white and pure black; these extreme values exceed DV video's capacity to handle contrast. Try using a 10% gray over 90% black. (Compare the results on your video monitor with a title composed using pure white over pure black.) The same principle applies to color titles; using pure red, green, or blue will produce that bad, late-night infomercial look you are probably trying to avoid.

◆ When you superimpose a solid-color title over production video, try setting the title's opacity to 90%.

◆ Don't forget the simple drop-shadow effect found on the Motion tab of any clip. With some tweaks, you can create a professional-quality drop shadow that really pops your title out from any background.

Figure 17.10 The Outline Text generator is composed of three customizable elements: text, an outline stroke, and a rectangular background matte.

Figure 17.11 You can matte graphics into any of the generator's three elements. This composition has a clip matted into the text element.

The Wonders of Outline Text

The Outline Text generator offers three customizable elements in one text generator: text, an outline stroke, and a rectangular background matte (**Figure 17.10**)—perfect for punching titles over hard-to-read backgrounds or creating subtitles that maintain their legibility. You can insert a clip into any of the three elements by dropping the clip on the element's clip well on the Controls tab; the clip's image will be matted into the outline text element you specify (**Figure 17.11**).

To create outline text:

1. To generate an outline text title, *do one of the following:*
   ◆ From the Generator pop-up menu in the lower right of the Viewer window, choose Outline Text (**Figure 17.12**).
   ◆ On the Browser's Effects tab, choose Outline Text from the Video Generator folder.
   The new Outline Text generator appears in the Viewer.

2. In the Viewer, click the Controls tab to access the generator's controls; then specify your text control settings as outlined earlier in this chapter, in the section "Text generator options checklist" (**Figure 17.13**).

3. You can also specify any of the following outline text parameters:
   ◆ **Line Width:** Specify the width of the text's outline.
   ◆ **Line Softness:** Specify the amount of edge feathering applied to the text's outline.

continues on next page

- ◆ **Text Opacity:** Specify the text's transparency level.
- ◆ **Center:** Specify *x,y* coordinates for the text's center point.
- ◆ **Text Color:** Select a color for the text.
- ◆ **Text Graphic:** Drag and drop a graphics clip to be matted into the text element.
- ◆ **Line Color:** Select a color for the text's outline.
- ◆ **Line Graphic:** Drag and drop a graphics clip to be matted into the outline element.

Figure 17.12 Choose Outline Text from the Viewer's Generator pop-up menu.

4. Use the sliders in the Background Settings section to specify the size, edge feathering, opacity, color, and graphics for an optional rectangular matte that sits behind the text and outline. The default Size values are set to zero, so you must increase the size settings to see the background matte.

5. Click back to the Viewer's Video tab and edit the text clip into your sequence in the Timeline. If you want to superimpose your text over video, choose the Superimpose edit type when you perform your edit.

✔ Tip

- ■ If you use a clip as your Back Graphic for your rectangular matte, note that the Back Graphic image will be scaled to fit your background Size values—unless you check the Crop check box. Cropping trims off the sides of the image to fit the matte size you specify, but doesn't scale the image.

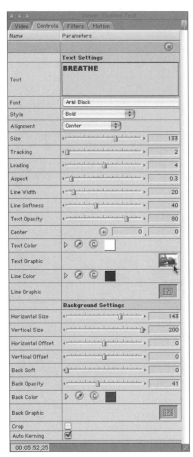

Figure 17.13 Specify your text control settings as outlined in the section "Text generator options checklist."

THE WONDERS OF OUTLINE TEXT

Using Animated Text Generators

Final Cut Express offers three animated text generators: Scrolling Text, Crawl, and Typewriter. These generators offer the font styling and positioning controls of the static text generators, plus simple animation routines built into the generator. You set up the animation on the text generator's Controls tab.

Because these animated titles typically start offscreen, you will not see any text onscreen if your playhead is parked at the beginning or end of the clip. You have to scrub the playhead through the clip to see how your animated title is shaping up.

Creating scrolls

Scrolls are most often found as credit sequences at the end of a show (or at the beginning of *Star Wars* parodies). Scrolling text displays a lot of information in a little time, but take care not to roll your text too quickly. If you set your scroll speed too high, the titles will stutter (they won't appear to scroll smoothly), and no one will be able to read them.

There are several ways to create the scrolling graphic elements. The easiest is to use the Scrolling Text generator found in the Video Generator list, but if you plan to use multiple fonts or specialized tracking, sizing, and kerning, then your best bet is to use the free Boris Calligraphy Title Crawl text generator plugin found on your Final Cut Express CD. See "Creating titles with Boris Calligraphy" later in this chapter.

To generate a scrolling text title:

1. *Do one of the following:*

    ◆ From the Generators pop-up menu in the lower right of the Viewer window, choose Scrolling Text (**Figure 17.14**).

    ◆ On the Browser's Effects tab, choose Scrolling Text from the Video Generator folder.

      The Scrolling Text generator appears in the Viewer.

2. In the Viewer, click the Controls tab to access the generator's controls; then specify your text control settings as outlined earlier in this chapter, in the section "Text generator options checklist" (**Figure 17.15**).

3. You can also specify any of the following scrolling text parameters:

    ◆ **Spacing:** Use the slider or enter a value to specify the spacing between letters (as with Tracking).

    ◆ **Leading:** Use the slider or enter a value to specify the spacing between lines of text.

    ◆ **Indent:** Use the slider or enter a value to set the *x*-axis (left-right) positioning of the scroll's aligned edge, expressed as a percentage of the screen. Indent is enabled only for left- or right-aligned scrolls. The title-safe area begins inside 10% of the screen.

    ◆ **Gap Width:** Use the slider or enter a value to specify the width of the gap between any two text entries separated by an asterisk (*).

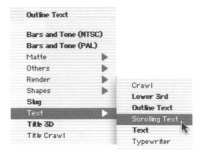

Figure 17.14 Choose Scrolling Text from the Viewer's Generator pop-up menu.

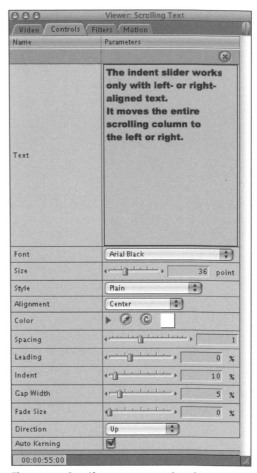

Figure 17.15 Specify your text control settings as outlined in the section "Text generator options checklist."

◆ **Fade Size:** Use the slider or enter a value to set the vertical display area of your scrolling text, expressed as a percentage of the screen. The scrolling text will fade in as it enters (and fade out as it exits) the vertical display area you specify.

◆ **Direction:** Choose Up or Down from this pop-up menu to specify the direction in which the generated text will scroll.

4. Click back to the Viewer's Video tab and edit the text clip into your sequence in the Timeline. If you want to superimpose your text over video, choose the Superimpose edit type when you perform your edit.

✔ Tip

■ Use the Gap Width setting to create a double-column credit scroll with a center gutter. Here's how: Set the Gap Width parameter to specify the width of the gap between any two text entries separated by an asterisk (*). When you assemble the text for your credit scroll, type *Production Credit*Name*—for example, `Visual Effects*Xochi Studios`—and the gutter in your credit scroll will be set to the Gap Width value. How*about*that?

Creating crawl titles

Like the stock market ticker tape creeping along the bottom of your TV screen, a text crawl is an animated title that scrolls horizontally. Text crawls can be useful for displaying short phrases—but keep them short, unless you are trying to annoy your audience.

Stuttering is more pronounced during a text crawl than during any other type of text effect. Take care to test your crawl on an NTSC monitor, and watch for optical jumpiness. Possible remedies include using a wider-stroked font, a larger font size, a slower crawl speed, or a motion blur.

To generate a crawl text title:

1. *Do one of the following:*
   ◆ From the Generator pop-up menu in the lower right of the Viewer window, choose Crawl (**Figure 17.16**).
   ◆ On the Browser's Effects tab, choose Crawl from the Video Generator folder.

   The Crawl text generator appears in the Viewer.

2. In the Viewer, click the Controls tab to access the generator's controls; then specify your text control settings as outlined earlier in this chapter, in the section "Text generator options checklist" (**Figure 17.17**).

continues on next page

Figure 17.16 Choose Crawl from the Viewer's Generator pop-up menu.

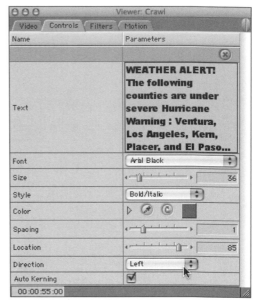

Figure 17.17 On the generator's Controls tab, specify your text control settings as outlined in the section "Text generator options checklist."

USING ANIMATED TEXT GENERATORS

Figure 17.18 Choose Typewriter from the Viewer's Generator pop-up menu.

3. You can also specify any of the following crawl text parameters:

♦ **Spacing:** Use the slider or enter a value to specify the spacing between letters (as with Tracking).

♦ **Location:** Use the slider or enter a value to specify the *y*-axis (top-bottom) positioning of your crawl.

♦ **Direction:** Choose Left or Right from this pop-up menu to specify the direction in which the generated text will scroll.

4. Click back to the Viewer's Video tab and edit the text clip into your sequence in the Timeline. If you want to superimpose your text over video, choose the Superimpose edit type when you perform your edit.

Creating animated typewriter text

The cute little Typewriter text generator automates the animation of single letters popping onto the screen; that's why it's called Typewriter. It's a real time-saver, as anybody who has manually animated simulated typing will tell you.

To generate a typewriter text title:

1. *Do one of the following:*

♦ From the Generator pop-up menu in the lower right of the Viewer window, choose Typewriter (**Figure 17.18**).

♦ On the Browser's Effects tab, choose Typewriter from the Video Generator folder.

The Typewriter text generator appears in the Viewer.

continues on next page

2. In the Viewer, click the Controls tab to access the generator's controls; then specify your text control settings as outlined earlier in this chapter, in the section "Text generator options checklist" (**Figure 17.19**).

3. You can also specify any of the following typewriter text parameters:

◆ **Spacing:** Use the slider or enter a value to specify the spacing between letters (as with Tracking).

◆ **Location:** Use the slider or enter a value to specify the *y*-axis (top-bottom) positioning of your text element.

◆ **Indent:** Use the slider or enter a value to specify the *x*-axis (left-right) positioning of your text element, expressed as a percentage of the screen.

◆ **Pause:** Use the slider or enter a value to specify the timing of your typewriter animation. A larger Pause value results in a longer hold at the end of the clip. The speed of the type-on effect is calculated based on the overall duration of the generator clip minus the pause value you set here.

4. Click back to the Viewer's Video tab and edit the text clip into your sequence in the Timeline. If you want to superimpose your text over video, choose the Superimpose edit type when you perform your edit.

✔ Tips

■ If you're looking for an old-fashioned typewriter font, try Courier.

■ Use a techno-style font like Andale Mono or VT 100 for simulating computer input (and don't forget to add the Blink filter!).

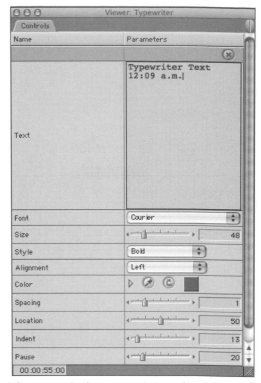

Figure 17.19 On the generator's Controls tab, specify your text control settings as outlined in the section "Text generator options checklist."

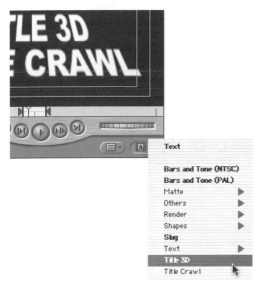

Figure 17.20 If you choose to install them, the Boris Text generators appear in the Generator pop-up menu along with the standard FCE generators.

Figure 17.21 Boris text generators feature a large text input window and myriad text styling options.

Creating titles with Boris Calligraphy

Two Boris Calligraphy text generators, Title 3D and Title Crawl, are available as an installation option in the Final Cut Express installer. Once you install them, these third-party generators show up in the Viewer's Generator pop-up menu along with the standard FCE generators (**Figure 17.20**).

◆ Title 3D features vector-based text you can manipulate in 3D space with pivot control, animated tracking, and a host of text transformations.

◆ Title Crawl is an automated roll and crawl title generator.

In both generators, you can:

◆ Enter text in a larger text-entry field (**Figure 17.21**).

◆ Create static titles.

◆ Set font, size, style, and color properties for individual characters.

◆ Apply drop shadows and borders.

◆ Choose from other 2D title animation options.

◆ Copy and paste text from a word processor.

Note that you can set individual parameters such as font, size, color, and tracking for every character, but you cannot animate individual character properties over time. For more information about Boris Calligraphy, see the Boris Calligraphy user manual, a 44-page, illustrated PDF file, located in the Extras folder on the Final Cut Express application disk.

About LiveType

Who says you can't get a free lunch? LiveType (**Figure 17.22**) is an amazing animated title generator that's bundled into the FCE suite of applications. You can create customized animated fonts, objects, and textures for importing into your FCE project. LiveType offers a library of animated LiveFonts, along with hundreds of pre-set combinations of fonts and backgrounds. It would take another Visual QuickStart Guide to explore all of LiveType's possibilities, so instead, head for the file called *LiveType Help.pdf* found in the Documentation folder on your Final Cut Express application DVD.

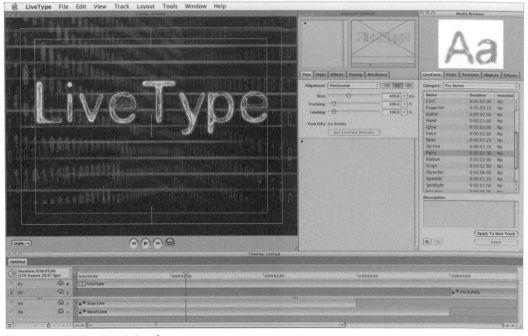

Figure 17.22 LiveType's main interface.

REAL TIME
AND RENDERING

Final Cut Express offers many, many ways to manipulate your raw media—a wild world of complex effects. Someday soon (we all hope), computer processing will speed up enough to dispense with the need to render in Final Cut Express. We enjoy more real time and less rendering in each successive version of Final Cut Express, but the program is not completely renderless yet. Until it is, you'll need to render some clips with effects before you can play back your final result.

This chapter outlines the workings of RT Extreme, FCE's software-only effects previewing feature. Real-time systems use the power of your Mac's CPU to process added effects on the fly, allowing you to play them back without rendering them first. For editors (and their clients) who work extensively with effects, these systems can dramatically improve efficiency and creativity.

Rendering is the process of combining your raw clip media with filters, transitions, and other adjustments to produce a new file. This new file, called the *render file*, can be played back in real time.

This is a chapter with more protocol than most. Understanding rendering protocols can be a big factor in making your post-production work efficient while producing high-quality results. This chapter lays out the rules governing video and audio render files along with some strategies for minimizing render time.

Using Real-Time Effects

Real-time effects take advantage of the G4/5's graphics handling power to compute and display previews of many effects in real time. RT Extreme (RTE), Final Cut Express's software-based effects previewing feature, doesn't require any additional hardware.

RTE effects are computed on the fly and play back in the FCE program windows.

RT Extreme: Scalable software-based real time

RTE's real-time effects previewing may not require extra hardware, but a qualifying G4 and 512 MB of RAM are the minimum system requirements for any RTE functionality. Check the Technical Specifications page of Apple's Final Cut Express web site at www.apple.com/finalcutpro/specs.html for a list detailing which real-time effects are supported on which G4/5 systems.

If your Mac supports real-time effects, FCE will identify your G4/5 model and display the RTE effects it supports in boldface type, both on the Browser's Effects tab (**Figure 18.1**) and on the Effects menu (**Figure 18.2**).

The Timeline's render status bars are color coded to let you know which sections of your sequence will play back in real time, and which sections still require rendering before you can play them. (See "Rendering indicators" later in this chapter.)

Like most cutting-edge technologies, RTE effects come with a list of caveats and trade-offs attached, so let's get those out of the way up front.

◆ RTE's real-time magic works only on DV and HDV format footage.

Figure 18.1 Real-time effects appear in boldface type on the Browser's Effects tab.

Figure 18.2 Real-time effects also appear in boldface in the Effects menu. (Select Unlimited RT from the Timeline's RT pop-up menu, and you'll enable additional real-time effects.)

Figure 18.3 Choose View > Video Out > Canvas Playback to enable real-time effects preview in the Canvas and the Viewer.

Figure 18.4 Choosing Digital Cinema Desktop Preview – Main from the Video Out menu enables full-screen video monitoring on your computer screen, plus real-time effects previewing. Enabling real-time previewing automatically disables your external video feed.

◆ RTE effects are computed on the fly and play back only in the Canvas and the Viewer and in full-screen Digital Cinema mode. You have to disable your DV FireWire to enable RTE's real-time previewing, so you won't be able to see anything on your external TV monitor while you're enjoying your real-time previews. However, you can purchase and install an extra Radeon video display card in your G4 tower and then route the RTE previews to an external TV monitor via S-video. If you're using a qualifying PowerBook G4, you can use the PowerBook's S-video output to feed your external monitor.

◆ Remember that RTE previews are optimized for real-time processing, not resolution. They work great for judging timing and composition, but for critical judgment of color and detail, be sure to render at least a few test frames and view them on your external NTSC or PAL monitor at final output resolution.

For the official word on FCE's real-time capabilities, see Chapter 33 of Apple's *Final Cut Express Help* PDF.

To enable real-time effects:

Do one of the following:

◆ Choose View > Video Out > Canvas Playback (**Figure 18.3**).

◆ Choose View > Video Out > Digital Cinema Desktop Preview - Main (**Figure 18.4**).

Your external video output is disabled and real-time previewing is enabled.

Controlling Playback and Rendering Quality

Final Cut Express's real-time architecture offers flexibility far beyond the simple enabling or disabling of individual effects. Finding the right balance between image quality and system performance for each specific working situation involves some tweaking, but you have a couple of important tools to assist you.

Setting up image quality of real-time playback

You use the settings on the RT pop-up menu to adjust the balance between image quality and playback performance.

Real-time playback quality settings can be adjusted in either of two locations: the Timeline's RT pop-up menu (**Figure 18.5**) and the Playback Control tab of the System Settings window. The RT pop-up menu is the more convenient route.

For details on Playback Control tab settings, see Chapter 3, "Presets and Preferences."

Setting up image quality of rendered material

Use the settings on the Render Control tab of the Sequence Settings window to balance the image quality and rendering speed of rendered material in your current sequence. For more information, see "Changing the Settings of an Existing Sequence" in Chapter 4. For details on Render Control tab settings in your Sequence preset, see Chapter 3, "Presets and Preferences."

✔ Tip

■ Real-time playback quality settings also control the image quality of FCE's Digital Cinema Desktop Preview mode.

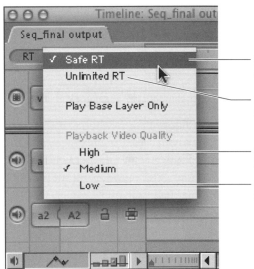

Choose Safe RT to ensure playback without dropped frames

Choose Unlimited RT for more real-time effects and possible dropped frames during playback

Choose High video playback quality with Safe RT to see the highest-quality playback

Choose Low video playback quality with Unlimited RT to see maximum real-time effects

Figure 18.5 Mix and match settings in the Timeline's RT pop-up menu to adjust the balance between playback quality and real-time performance.

Rendering

FCE has made dramatic improvements in real-time effects performance, but when you finally run out of processing power, you must render.

This section outlines FCE's playback and rendering quality settings and rendering protocols and explains how to navigate the Sequence menu's vast forest of Render commands.

For more information, see Chapter 34 of Apple's *Final Cut Express Help* PDF.

Rendering protocols

Here are some general guidelines to help you understand Final Cut Express's rendering protocols.

What needs to be rendered

In general, you must render any transitions, effects, and composited layers that exceed the real-time capacity of your FCE system.

Also, before your sequence can be exported or printed to video, you have to render any source media with frame rate, frame size, or video or audio compression settings that differ from those settings in your sequence.

Audio tracks with transitions or filters, as well as multiple audio tracks over your real-time playback limit, have to be rendered before playback.

Clips whose speed has been changed must also be rendered before playback.

What doesn't need to be rendered

Final Cut Express sequences that include real-time-supported transitions, effects, and composited layers can be played back in real time without rendering, as long as the sequence size and frame rate match those of the original source material.

Multiple audio tracks can be played back in real time without rendering. (See Table 18.1, "Final Cut Express Audio Track Costs," later in this chapter for more information.)

Rendering order

Video frames in sequences are rendered in the following order:

◆ Effects applied within individual tracks are processed first. Speed changes, filters, motion, motion blur, opacity, and transitions are processed next, in that order.

◆ After processing of all the individual tracks is complete, the processed tracks are composited, starting with the top layer of video (the highest-numbered track), which is composited onto the track below it.

It is possible to change the order of rendering by using nested sequences. For more information, see "Working with Multiple Sequences" in Chapter 4.

RENDERING

Rendering indicators

As you build your sequence, you'll encounter the following indicators:

◆ When you try to play video material that requires rendering in the Viewer or the Canvas, a blue background with the word "Unrendered" appears (**Figure 18.6**), indicating that the video can't play in real time.

◆ When you try to play audio material that requires rendering in the Viewer or the Canvas, you'll hear a steady beeping sound, indicating that the audio can't play in real time.

◆ In the Timeline, the rendering indicator above the ruler (**Figure 18.7**) consists of two thin bars. These bars indicate which sections of the sequence currently require rendering to play back smoothly. The upper bar indicates the render status of video tracks; the lower bar shows the audio track status.

◆ A sequence audio clip requiring sample-rate conversion displays a render status indicator overlay right on the clip in the Timeline (**Figure 18.8**).

Non-real-time FCE systems use the following status codes in the rendering indicators:

◆ **Red (Needs Render):** The material needs to be rendered.

◆ **Gray:** No rendering is required.

◆ **Blue-gray:** The material has already been rendered.

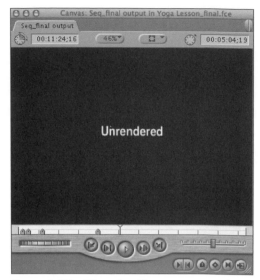

Figure 18.6 The "Unrendered" screen appears when you try to play back video that cannot be played back in real time without rendering.

Figure 18.7 The rendering status bars are located above the Timeline ruler. The upper bar indicates the render status of video tracks. The lower bar shows the audio track status. Pause the pointer over the rendering indicator bars, and a tooltip displays render status details.

Figure 18.8 An audio clip requiring sample-rate conversion displays an item-level render status indicator overlay right on the clip in the Timeline.

Real-time effects previewing adds six (!) more color codes to the render status indicator:

◆ **Dark green (Full):** The material can be played back and output at full quality in real time. No rendering is required.

◆ **Green (Preview):** No rendering is required for real-time playback in the Canvas or the Viewer. For playback on an external device, green indicates a lower-quality output of scaling and motion effects.

◆ **Yellow (Proxy):** Real-time playback is an approximation of the final effect. To get the true final effect, you still need to render the material. You'll see the final effect when playback is stopped or during scrubbing.

◆ **Dark yellow:** The material has been rendered at a quality lower than that currently specified on your sequence's Render Control tab. FCE preserves these render files even if you modify the sequence's render quality settings later.

◆ **Orange (Unlimited):** Indicates effects enabled by selecting Unlimited RT in the Timeline's RT pop-up menu. These effects exceed your computer's "official" real-time playback capabilities and may drop frames during playback, but you can get a rough idea of how a complex effect is shaping up.

FCE Protocol: Audio Rendering Options

Here's the rundown on the audio rendering options available in the Render submenus:

◆ **For Playback:** Only the portions of your sequence audio tracks that require rendering to play back in real-time are processed.

◆ **Item Level:** This option renders individual audio clips that require sample-rate conversion to match the sequence sample rate, and clips with applied audio filters. Item-level processing generates item-level render cache files. Audio levels and multitrack playback are still processed in real time.

◆ **Mixdown Audio:** Your audio tracks, along with all applied filters, levels, and transitions, are processed into a set of render files, a single file for each audio output. This command is available only in the Render Only submenu.

RENDERING

Using Render Commands

Final Cut Express's rendering commands are all about choices. At the top level of the Sequence menu, you'll find three Render commands:

◆ Render Selection processes only the material you select in the Timeline.

◆ Render All creates render files for the entire sequence.

◆ Use Render Only to process a single type of unrendered material. Render Only can process either the portion of the sequence you select or the entire sequence if you don't mark a selection.

Each Render command has a submenu that offers a second tier of choices.

◆ In all three submenus, you can choose to render just video, just audio, or both.

◆ Both the Render Selection and Render All submenus allow you to pick and choose which types of render-eligible sections you want to process in this rendering operation. Check any or all of the render types before you kick off a render (**Figure 18.9**). The render options stay checked until you change them, so once you've set up a render specification, you can render with a simple keyboard command.

✔ Tip

■ HDV users take note: Powering off any FireWire devices that are connected to your computer while an HDV render is underway could trash your render in progress and cause FCE HD to freeze up or quit unexpectedly. Don't touch that off switch until your render is safely completed.

Figure 18.9 Choose Sequence > Render Selection (or Sequence > Render All) and then specify which render types you want to include in this rendering operation by selecting those items from the submenu. Making a selection toggles the checked status on or off; you'll have to select multiple times if you want to include or exclude multiple render types.

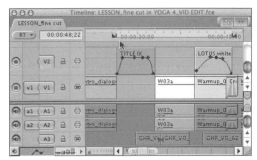

Figure 18.10 Set the Sequence In and Out points to select the area you want to render. (This figure shows split edit points, marking Video In and Video Out.)

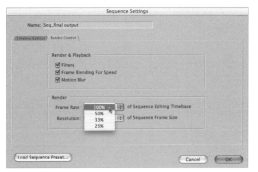

Figure 18.11 Review or adjust the image quality of your rendered material on the Render Control tab of the Sequence Settings window.

Figure 18.12 To start rendering, choose Sequence > Render Selection. Your submenu selection determines whether you render video only (pictured here), audio only, or both audio and video.

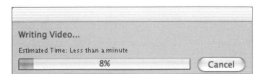

Figure 18.13 A progress bar tracks the speed of the rendering process. More complex effects will take more time to render than simple effects or audio processing.

To render a section of a sequence:

1. *Do one of the following:*
   - ◆ In the Timeline, select a portion of a clip or one or more clips or transitions.
   - ◆ In the Timeline or the Canvas, set the sequence In and Out points to mark the area that you want to render (**Figure 18.10**).

2. Choose Sequence > Render Selection and then select which types of render-eligible material you want to include in this rendering operation by selecting those items from the submenu. Selected types are checked; making a selection toggles the checked status on or off.

3. Press Command-0 (zero) to open the sequence's Sequence Settings window. Verify (or adjust) the settings on the Render Control tab to specify the image quality of this render operation (**Figure 18.11**); then click OK.

4. *Do one of the following:*
   - ◆ Choose Sequence > Render Selection; or press Command-R to render both video and audio in the selected area.
   - ◆ Choose Sequence > Render Selection > Video (**Figure 18.12**) to render just video in the selected area.
   - ◆ Choose Sequence > Render Selection > Audio; or press Control-Option-R to render just the audio in the selected area.

   A progress bar displays the percentage of completed processing while the selected area is being rendered (**Figure 18.13**).

5. Click Cancel if you want to stop rendering. Final Cut Express saves all the rendered frames it has processed, even if you cancel rendering.

USING RENDER COMMANDS

499

To render an entire sequence or multiple sequences:

1. *Do one of the following:*

   ◆ Open the sequence you want to render in the Timeline.

   ◆ In the Browser, select the icon of the sequence you want to render (**Figure 18.14**). You can select multiple sequences in multiple projects.

2. Choose Sequence > Render All and then select which types of render-eligible material you want to include in this rendering operation by selecting those items from the submenu. Selected types are checked; making a selection toggles the checked status on or off.

3. Choose Sequence > Render All.

   A progress bar displays the percentage of completed processing while the sequence is being rendered. Click Cancel if you want to stop rendering. Final Cut Express saves all the rendered frames it has processed, even if you cancel rendering.

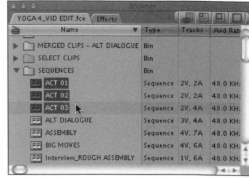

Figure 18.14 You can use the Render All command to render an entire sequence, but you can also use it to batch render multiple sequences. Select the sequences that you want to batch render in the Browser.

Quick Preview Tips

The "instant preview" techniques listed here can show you a quick, temporary preview of an effect or transition before you commit to rendering it. Place the Timeline playhead at the section you want to preview and then use one of these methods:

◆ Press Option-P (the Play Every Frame command) to force a frame-by-frame preview of your unrendered material. FCE displays the frames as fast as they can be processed.

◆ Use the Left and Right Arrow keys to step through your footage a frame at a time.

◆ Scrub the playhead across the Scrubber bar in the Canvas or the Timeline's ruler.

To render a single type of render-eligible material:

1. Select a portion of the sequence, or to render the entire sequence, leave the entire sequence unselected.

2. Choose Sequence > Render Only and select a type of render-eligible material to render from the submenu. Video render options are listed at the top of the submenu; the three options at the bottom are audio only.

To disable rendering:

◆ Press the Caps Lock key to temporarily disable rendering. Press Caps Lock again to cancel.

USING RENDER COMMANDS

FCE Protocol: Estimating Render Processing Time

Render processing times can range from a couple of seconds to many hours. How do you know whether you have just enough time for a quick break or enough for a two-hour lunch? Read on.

◆ Final Cut Express expresses the progress of your rendering operation as an estimate of the time remaining. Even so, the time displayed on the progress bar is based on how long the current frame takes multiplied by the number of remaining frames; so if your effects differ drastically in complexity, predicting the time required to render is difficult—even for Final Cut Express. Watch the progress bar for a few minutes and make a guess, based on the speed of the progress bar and your knowledge of the sequence.

◆ After rendering, or whenever you move a large number of clips, Final Cut Express rebuilds the QuickTime movie used for computer playback of your sequence so that it will be ready to play—wherever you put your playhead. While it's rebuilding, you may see a dialog box that says "Preparing video for display."

Rendering audio

Although real-time video playback in Final Cut Express is usually limited to a single, cuts-only track, FCE can mix and play back up to eight tracks of audio in real time, so audio rendering is not always necessary.

The number of tracks you specify in the Real-Time Audio Mixing preference (located on the General tab of the User Preferences window) determines how many tracks Final Cut Express attempts to play back before it asks for audio rendering.

There's an additional factor that determines whether you have maxed out your real-time audio playback capabilities: All audio tracks are not created equal. When you apply filters or transitions to an audio track, Final Cut Express must allocate processing power to calculate those effects on the fly in order to play back the result in real time—which brings us to track costs. (See the sidebar "FCE Protocol: Track Costs" and **Table 18.1**.)

✔ Tip

■ The Mixdown Audio command produces a render file with a computed mix. Even though the command is called *Mixdown*, you still have individual control over all your audio tracks. Think of Mixdown Audio as a "temp mix" you can use while you're working.

Table 18.1

Final Cut Express Audio Track Costs

ITEM	TYPE	TRACK COST
Each mono track	Track	1
Each mono track with transitions applied	Transition	2
Pair of stereo tracks	Track	2
Sub-sequence containing track	Track	4 (one stereo)
Each track referencing a sub-sequence	Track	Number of audio tracks in sub-sequence
Compressor/limiter	Filter	6
Expander/gate	Filter	6
Vocal de-esser	Filter	6
Vocal de-popper	Filter	6
Reverb/echo	Filter	6
All other filters	Filter	3

FCE Protocol: Track Costs

Final Cut Express uses the concept of track equivalent costs, or *track costs*, to calculate the total processing power needed to play back multiple audio channels. Under certain conditions, you may be able to play back audio tracks with filters or transitions applied. Choose Low Audio Quality playback from the General tab of the User Preferences window, and you'll pick up an extra track or two.

You can estimate the real-time audio capabilities available in your sequence by adding up the audio track costs. Track costs can accumulate quickly when even a couple of unmixed tracks are combined, if you have used filters and transitions. If you exceed your real-time playback capability, you'll hear beeps instead of your audio when you attempt playback. Before you can play back, you'll need to render by selecting Mixdown Audio from the Sequence menu.

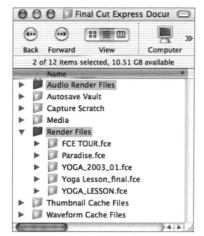

Figure 18.15 Render files are stored in the Final Cut Express Documents folder, along with your Capture Scratch folder.

Managing Render Files

Render files are valuable media elements, stored as actual media files on your hard disk like your original captured media files. Final Cut Express names render files according to its own internal naming protocols. You won't be able to identify individual render files by their filenames, so planning your render file management strategy is a critical part of your post-production work. This will become clear the next time you invest considerable time in a single complex rendering process.

Specifying storage locations for render files

You can specify up to 12 disks for storing captured video, captured audio, or render files. As you create render files, Final Cut Express stores them on the disk with the most available space. If you don't specify disk locations, Final Cut Express saves video and audio render files in separate folders (called Render Files and Audio Render Files), which are located, along with your Capture Scratch folder, in the Final Cut Express Documents folder (**Figure 18.15**). Render files are media files and should be stored on the same media drives as your captured media.

Specify storage locations for your render files on the Scratch Disks tab in the System Settings window. For more information, see Chapter 3, "Presets and Preferences."

Deleting rendered files

When you are working on multiple projects, each with multiple sequences, render files can build up quickly.

Freeing up disk space by dumping old render files is an attractive proposition, but use caution if you are deleting render files for your current projects. Final Cut Express uses render file names that are useful to the program but unintelligible to you.

Final Cut Express will automatically delete any render file in your project that has been directly superceded by a replacement render file, but it doesn't throw out leftover render files or render files in old versions of projects. To delete render files, you'll have to sort through your project's render folder, manually weeding out obsolete files and moving them to the Trash (**Figure 18.16**).

For more information, see "Deleting Media" in Chapter 4.

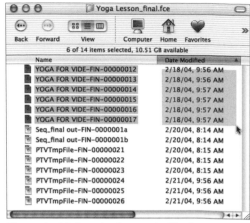

Figure 18.16 Select obsolete render files in a project's Render folder and move them to the Trash. The Date sort function in the Finder can help you find older render files.

Figure 18.17 This clip looks normal when opened from the Browser.

Figure 18.18 The same clip as it appears in the Canvas. The mismatched sequence settings override the clip settings, causing the clip to appear distorted and to play back poorly.

Rendering Strategies

To take full advantage of the media manipulation techniques that are possible with Final Cut Express, you will need to render to produce your finished results; you'll also need to render to review your sequence and evaluate any effects you've created. The rendering strategies in this section fall into three basic categories:

◆ Tips for avoiding unnecessary rendering

◆ Techniques for speeding up rendering times

◆ Schemes for preserving render files

Avoiding unnecessary rendering

Final Cut Express allows you to add source material whose frame rate and compression settings do not match your sequence settings. However, if the frame rate, frame size, or video or audio compression settings in your source media are different from the settings in your sequence, those frames need to be rendered before the sequence can be exported or printed to video.

If a particular group of source clips looks normal when you open it from the Browser window (**Figure 18.17**) but requires rendering or changes size or shape when you add it to a sequence and view it in the Canvas window (**Figure 18.18**), you probably have a settings mismatch between your source clips and your sequence settings.

Important: To avoid rendering when creating a sequence with cuts only, make sure that the sequence's editing timebase, frame size, and compression settings are the same as the frame rate, frame size, and compression settings of your source media.

continues on next page

How do you compare source clip and sequence settings? Open the clip's Item Properties window and note the clip's video rate, frame rate, frame size, and compression settings (**Figure 18.19**). Then open the Item Properties window for the sequence (**Figure 18.20**). Note the sequence's video rate (called the Vid Rate), Frame Size, and Compressor settings; these should match the clip's video rate (called the Vid Rate), Frame Size, and Compressor settings (**Figure 18.21**). For information on specifying sequence settings, see Chapter 3, "Presets and Preferences."

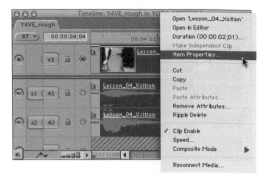

Figure 18.19 To view a clip's format settings, Control-click the clip in the Browser or the Timeline and then choose Item Properties from the shortcut menu.

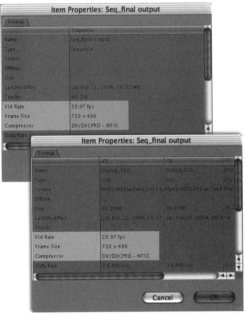

Figure 18.21 The clip's Item Properties window compared with the sequence's Item Properties window. Compare the Vid Rate, Frame Size, and Compressor settings in the two windows. Highlighted settings must match for the sequence to play in real time.

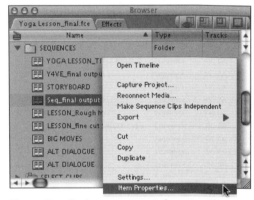

Figure 18.20 To view a sequence's format settings, Control-click the sequence in the Browser and then choose Item Properties from the shortcut menu.

Disabling rendering

There are two ways to delay rendering your sequence until you have completed your desired adjustments: you can enable the Play Base Layer Only option in the RT pop-up menu, or you can press the Caps Lock key to temporarily disable rendering.

The Play Base Layer Only option allows playback with minimal rendering. With Play Base Layer Only enabled, Final Cut Express will play the lowest opaque track in the sequence and all audio tracks rather than displaying the "Unrendered" message in areas that still require rendering. Cuts will be substituted for unrendered transitions. Motion will not be applied to clips or sequences when played back in the Viewer.

Reducing rendering time

Following are a few strategies that can help you minimize your rendering time. Using a lower-resolution draft quality saves disk space as well as time, because lower-resolution render files are smaller.

Using draft mode

Use a low-resolution render quality to perfect element positioning, motion paths, scaling, and other basic design decisions. After you are satisfied with the timing and movement of your effects sequence, start including your most calculation-intensive effects. Render short test sections first and then review them to evaluate your final image quality. If you are set up to use an external NTSC or PAL monitor, check your output on the monitor to see that your render quality is sufficient.

FCE Protocol: Nested Sequences and Rendering

When you nest, or place a sequence inside another sequence, render files for the nested sequence are saved separately, along with the nested sequence.

Nested sequences may require separate rendering in a parent sequence under the following circumstances:

◆ If a parent sequence modifies a nested sequence, the nested sequence must be re-rendered. Modifications include compositing, filters, transitions, and speed changes.

◆ If movement, such as rotation, has been applied to a sequence and then the sequence is rendered, the sequence needs to be re-rendered if it is nested inside another sequence.

◆ If a nested sequence is placed inside a parent sequence, its alpha channel type is set to Straight. If you set the alpha channel for that nested sequence to None, the clips it contains won't need to be re-rendered. Its rendered files will be retained as long as they do not need to be combined with other tracks in the sequence, but because you've turned off the alpha channel, the clip will be opaque.

RENDERING STRATEGIES

Rendering in stages

If you are building a highly complex effects sequence, you may want to render your elements in stages. For example, you might perfect just the motion paths and interactions of your composited layers and then render just that portion of your sequence in high quality by exporting and re-importing your rendered elements. The export process creates a new piece of source media, and you can continue to sculpt your sequence using the new composited clip as a fully rendered base track. Exporting to preserve a render file is described later in this chapter.

Batch rendering

Use the batch render feature to render all your projects while you're busy elsewhere.

Preserving render files

You may spend days creating a polished effects or title sequence in Final Cut Express and wait hours for your final product to render. How can you protect your time investment?

Following are a few strategies to help you hold onto your render files.

Salvaging renders with Undo

Final Cut Express allows multiple undos. If you just want to try a new idea on material you've already rendered, when you're done, you can undo (Command-Z) your experiment until you have reverted to your previously rendered file. Careful use of the Undo function can give you freedom to experiment without risking rendered sequence material.

FCE protocol dictates that when you invalidate a render file by changing a sequence, the invalid render file becomes unrecoverable either when you next save the project or when you are past the point where you can use Undo to make the render file valid again, whichever is later.

Exporting to preserve render files

Exporting creates a physical copy of your rendered file on your hard disk. Exporting is the safest way to preserve rendered material. Once you have exported render files, you can re-import and use them just as you would raw captured media. For your render file to be exported without re-rendering, the export settings must match the render file's settings.

Using nested sequences to preserve render files

You can select a group of sequence clips or a portion of a Final Cut Express sequence and, by cutting and pasting it into a separate sequence (which you then edit back into your master sequence), convert that selection into a self-contained sub-sequence. As a sub-sequence inside a parent sequence, nested sequences are treated the same as other clips in a sequence. But unlike clips, nested sequences are actually pointers, or references, to the original sequence, not copies.

A nested sequence can help preserve your render files, because even though it can be edited into another sequence in pieces just like a clip, the render files associated with the nested sequence are preserved within the nested sequence. Even if you make a change in the parent sequence that requires the nested sequence to be re-rendered, when you open the nested sequence, your original render files created within the nested sequence will still be available.

However, like everything else associated with rendering, you need to be aware of particular protocols governing the preservation of render files when a sequence is nested as a sub-sequence in another, parent sequence.

To learn how to create nested sequences, see Chapter 4, "Projects, Sequences, and Clips."

✔ Tips

■ Before rendering a sequence that you intend to nest in a parent sequence, make sure that the nested sequence has the same render settings (frame rate, frame size, and compression settings) as the parent sequence to avoid having to render the nested sequence again.

■ Final Cut Express cannot reliably track down all nested sub-sequence material that requires rendering when you perform a Render All process. If you have built multiple levels of nested, unrendered sub-sequences into your project, this tip's for you: Try rendering at least one element in each nested sequence to help FCE track down the nested rendering required. Double-check your rendered sequences before you invite your client in for a screening.

RENDERING STRATEGIES

CREATING FINAL OUTPUT

19

You've come this far. Now it's time to send your masterpiece out into the world.

Final Cut Express has a variety of output options. How do you choose the right one? The best output format for your Final Cut Express project depends on where you plan to take it next.

◆ Will you distribute your program as a DVD?

◆ Do you need a broadcast-quality master?

◆ Are you going to distribute it on VHS tape?

◆ Are you preparing a webcast?

◆ How about "all of the above"?

This chapter walks you through FCE's output options and helps you decide which one will deliver what you need.

In the first part of this chapter, you'll learn about two methods for outputting your project to tape: recording Timeline playback and printing to video.

The second part of the chapter is devoted to file export options. You can export just the editing and clip information from a sequence as a formatted text file. You can also use the file export options to convert your FCE sequence or clip to another digital format for use in computer-based media.

One of the beautiful things about digital video is the wide variety of output options available to you—right on your desktop.

Using Tape Output Modes

Final Cut Express is designed to support external video monitoring at any time using your camcorder or deck, so you can always record FCE's output. You don't need to process your FCE material unless you are exporting your sequence in a computer-compatible format.

Final Cut Express offers two tape output modes:

◆ **Recording Timeline Playback:** One of the easiest ways to record Final Cut Express's output to video tape is simply to start recording on your video deck or camcorder; then play your sequence in the Timeline. For more information, see "Recording Timeline Playback" later in this chapter.

◆ **Print to Video:** Use Print to Video to output a Final Cut Express sequence or clip to video tape. The Print to Video function lets you configure pre- and post-program elements such as color bars and a 1-kHz tone, leader, slate, and countdown. Print to Video's Loop feature allows you to print your sequence multiple times automatically.

You don't need device control to use Print to Video. Use Print to Video if you want to make a video tape copy of your FCE sequence that includes customized pre-program elements, or if you want to loop your sequence.

Figure 19.1 Set your camcorder or deck to VTR (or VCR) mode.

Setting up for recording to tape

Before you record FCE's output on video tape, make sure that your recording device is connected and receiving video and audio output from FCE, and that the sequence or clip you're outputting is set up correctly.

Use this setup checklist for both tape output modes:

◆ Make sure your camcorder or deck is set to VTR (or VCR) mode (**Figure 19.1**). Final Cut Express can't record to devices set to Camera mode.

◆ Make sure your video camcorder or deck is receiving output from Final Cut Express. Check the external video settings for your current Easy Setup. Your external video settings should send FCE's video signal to the external video device you want to record to (**Figure 19.2**). Enable the video output feed to your camcorder or deck by choosing View > Video Out > Apple FireWire.

continues on next page

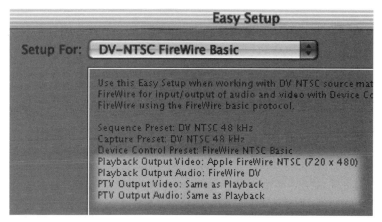

Figure 19.2 The last four settings in the Easy Setup window (highlighted here) indicate the video and audio output settings for this Easy Setup. The two PTV settings indicate video and audio output routing during a Print to Video operation. The settings shown here route video and audio output to your FireWire cable for playback and for PTV.

USING TAPE OUTPUT MODES

◆ Check the render quality settings for your sequence on the Render Control tab of the Sequence Settings window.

Both of FCE's tape output modes print the sections of your selected sequence or clip that don't require rendering at High playback quality, regardless of the video quality you selected for real-time playback (**Figure 19.3**), but you do have a choice of image quality settings for the rendered material in your sequence. The render quality settings on the Render Control tab of the Sequence Settings window (**Figure 19.4**) are the settings that will be used for rendering prior to your output operation. For more information, see "Controlling playback and rendering quality" in Chapter 18.

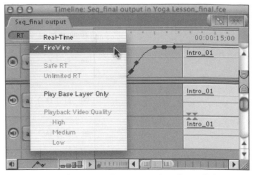

Figure 19.3 When FireWire output is selected, both RT and Video Playback quality options are dimmed. By default, FCE's FireWire output mode plays back non-rendered sections of your selected sequence or clip at High playback quality, overriding the image quality you selected for real-time playback in the Playback Video Quality section of the Timeline's RT pop-up menu.

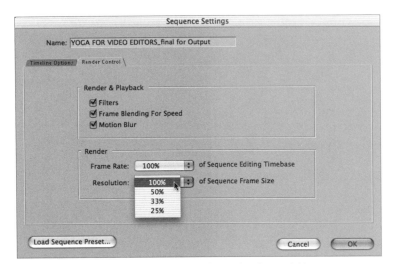

Figure 19.4 Specify image quality settings for rendered material in your sequence on the Render Control tab of the Sequence Settings window.

Figure 19.5 Set In and Out points to specify the portion you want to record.

◆ If you want to print only a selected portion of a sequence or clip, open the clip or sequence and then set In and Out points to specify the portion you want to record (**Figure 19.5**).

◆ You should enable the Report Dropped Frames During Playback preference on the General tab of the User Preferences window. Feedback on dropped frames is especially critical during final output.

If you enable dropped-frames reporting and find you're dropping frames in your external output during playback, you might try this first: Disable the Mirror on Desktop option on the A/V Devices tab of the Audio/Video Settings window. You'll immediately free up some performance power for the Print to Video functions.

See "Optimizing Performance" in Chapter 2 and "Is Your System Capture-Ready?" in Chapter 5 for more tips on eliminating dropped frames by improving FCE's performance.

◆ Test your setup by recording a section of your show to tape. Play back the test recording and scrutinize the results in your external monitoring setup. Do the rendered sections of the program match quality with the rest of the footage? Are your titles crisp? Are your video levels within the recommended brightness range for your output format, or has your video image developed hot spots? Is the audio playback level healthy but not overmodulated? Are both stereo tracks balanced properly and panned correctly? A little extra care and patience now, when you're producing your final product, will protect all the care and patience you've lavished on your project so far.

Recording Timeline Playback

If you are receiving Final Cut Express's output in your video camcorder or deck, you don't need to use Print to Video to record your FCE sequence to tape. Print to Video provides mastering options (color bars, slate, and so on). Otherwise, recording Timeline playback directly provides exactly the same output quality, and you may find it more convenient.

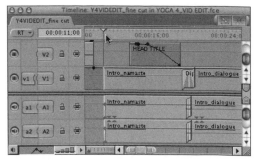

Figure 19.6 Cue your sequence in the Timeline. You don't need to set In and Out points unless you want to record less than the entire sequence.

To record Timeline playback onto tape:

1. Cue your video tape to the point where you want to start recording.

2. Cue your sequence in the Timeline (**Figure 19.6**).

3. Render any unrendered sections of your sequence. Unrendered material appears as blue, unrendered graphics when you record Timeline playback to tape.

4. Start recording on your video deck.

5. Choose Mark > Play and then select a play option from the submenu (**Figure 19.7**).

   Final Cut Express plays the contents of the Timeline as you specified and then holds on the final Timeline frame marked for playback. A freeze-frame is recorded on your tape until you stop recording.

6. Stop recording on your deck when Timeline playback is done.

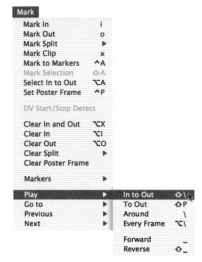

Figure 19.7 Choose Mark > Play and then select a play option from the submenu. In to Out plays only the portion of your sequence between the In and Out points.

Touching Up Your Timeline Playback

Recording your Timeline playback can be a real timesaver, but because you are making a live recording of Final Cut Express's output, you need to do a few things differently to get smooth-looking results. Here are a few pointers:

◆ You don't have to use Print to Video just because you want to add pre-program elements to your tape output. Black leader, color bars, and audio reference tone are available in the Viewer's Generator pop-up menu. You can edit your pre-program elements into the Timeline. For more information, read the introductory material in Chapter 17, "Titles and Generators."

◆ When you record Timeline playback, your camcorder or deck records whatever is sent to Final Cut Express's external video output from the instant you press your deck's Record/Play button. If the Viewer or the Canvas is active, you'll record whatever is currently displayed until you start playback of your Final Cut Express sequence. Even if you have positioned the Timeline playhead at the start of your sequence, you'll record a freeze-frame of the first frame of the sequence until you start Timeline playback. Make sure your external video output is displaying black by inserting a frame of black before the first frame in your sequence. Now the freeze-frame will appear as a solid black leader at the start of your recording.

◆ Place another frame of black at the end of your sequence, so when FCE reaches the end of the Timeline and freezes the final frame, that frame is black as well.

◆ Wait a few seconds after you start recording before you start the Timeline playback. You'll give your video tape time to get up to speed, and your picture will be rock solid from the first frame of your sequence.

Printing to Video

The Print to Video command is the correct choice when you want to make a video tape copy of a Final Cut Express sequence or clip that includes pre-program elements, such as color bars, slate, and countdown. Print to Video is also your best choice if you want to loop playback and print multiple passes of your sequence on the same tape. If you have a controllable camcorder or deck, you can set up your Device Control preset so that

FCE controls your deck during a Print to Video operation, but you don't need a deck that supports device control to use Print to Video. For information on hardware setup, see Chapter 2, "Installing and Setting Up."

If you don't need customized pre-program elements at the beginning of your dub, playing your sequence in the Timeline and recording the output directly may give you satisfactory results and save you some time as well. See "Recording Timeline Playback" earlier in this chapter.

Print to Video: Rendering Tips

◆ The quality of the render settings you specify on the Render Control tab of the Sequence Settings window before you use Print to Video is reflected in the quality and size of the playback window you see on your computer screen and on your video tape copy. In other words, what you see is what you get.

◆ If you have multiple layers of sub-sequences in your sequence (sub-sequences within sub-sequences inside the master sequence), it's a good idea to render material in the nested items at the lowest root, or sub-sequence, level first—at least for the first render. Subsequent adjustments and re-renders can be processed at the parent level, and Final Cut Express will more reliably find all the nested sub-sequence material that requires re-rendering.

◆ The pre-program elements discussed in the section "Print to Video settings checklist" must be rendered before you can print to video.

◆ If you use the same pre-program sequence frequently, you may want to use the Print to Video function to assemble your color bars, leader, slate, and countdown in advance. After your pre-program sequence has been rendered, print it to video and then capture it as a clip. You can drop your prepared pre-program clip into sequences before you print, speeding up the final output process.

Print to Video settings checklist

The Print to Video dialog box (**Figure 19.8**) displays a list of formatting options. Select the elements you want to include in your video tape copy. You can specify durations for all options.

◆ **Leader:** Select the pre-program elements you want to include in your video tape copy. Your pre-program sequence will be assembled in the same order that the elements are listed in the dialog box, which is why there are two separate Black options. Check the elements you want to include and then specify a duration (in whole seconds) for each option in the field next to the option. These elements must be rendered before printing to video can begin.

◆ **Color Bars:** Check this box to include color bars and a 1-kHz tone, preset to –12 dB, before the beginning of the sequence or clip.

◆ **Tone Level:** If necessary, adjust this slider to change the level of the preset –12-dB, 1-kHz audio reference tone. Note that this slider does not adjust the output level of your audio track, just the level of the reference tone.

◆ **Black:** Check this box to add black frames between the color bars and the slate.

◆ **Slate:** Check this box to include the slate information specified in the Slate Source pop-up menu in the adjoining field.

◆ **Slate Source pop-up menu:** Select a source for the information that appears on your slate. You can specify the sequence or clip name, a file on disk, or multiple lines of custom text.

◆ **Black:** Check this box to include black frames between a slate and a countdown (or before the beginning of the sequence or clip, if you aren't adding a slate and a countdown).

continues on next page

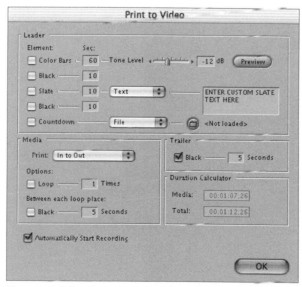

Figure 19.8 Select the pre-program elements you want to include in your video tape copy from the Print to Video dialog box.

◆ **Countdown:** Check this box to add a 10-second countdown before the sequence or clip (**Figure 19.9**). Choose FCE's built-in 10-second SMPTE standard countdown or use the corresponding pop-up menu and Browse button to specify your own custom countdown file.

◆ **Media:** Specify the material you want to include in the program section of your tape copy. You can print an entire sequence or clip or only a marked portion. You can also loop the sequence or clip selection and insert black at the end of each loop.

    ◆ **Print pop-up menu:** Choose Entire Media if you want to print the entire sequence or clip. Choose In to Out if you want to print a portion of the selected item. Specify the portion to be printed by setting In and Out points in the sequence or clip.

    ◆ **Loop:** Check this box to print your selection multiple times.

    ◆ **Times:** Specify the number of repetitions for Loop.

    ◆ **Black:** Check this box to insert black frames between repetitions for the duration specified in the Black field.

◆ **Trailer:** Check the Black box to add a black trailer at the end of the printed sequence or clip; then specify the duration in the Seconds field. If you are looping the sequence or clip, the trailer appears after the last repetition.

◆ **Duration Calculator:** These fields display the total duration of all the media you selected to print, as you have specified it.

◆ **Automatically Start Recording:** Check this box to enable FCE to automatically place your deck or camcorder into Record mode during a Print to Video operation. If you leave the box unchecked, you'll be prompted to put your deck into Record mode manually.

✔ Tip

■ Be sure your tape is long enough to record the entire program running time as calculated by the Duration Calculator. Most tape stock has a little extra capacity over the program length printed on the packaging, but it's a good idea to respect the official program-length capacity.

Figure 19.9 Final Cut Express's default countdown screen.

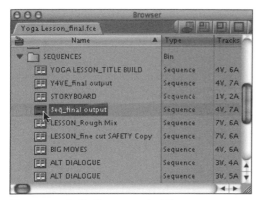

Figure 19.10 In the Browser, select the sequence you want to print to video.

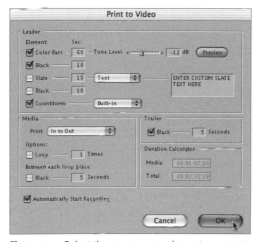

Figure 19.11 Select the pre-program elements you want to include in your video tape copy and then click OK.

Figure 19.12 If render quality settings on this sequence's Render Control tab specify less than full quality, FCE will display this warning dialog box. Click OK to proceed or cancel the operation and adjust your render quality settings.

To print a sequence or clip to video without device control:

1. Read and follow the setup process described in "Setting up for recording to tape" earlier in this chapter.

2. In the Browser, select the sequence or clip you want to print (**Figure 19.10**). Open the sequence and make the Timeline active.

3. Choose File > Print to Video.
   The Print to Video dialog box will appear.

4. Select the program elements you want to include in your program. Refer to the "Print to Video settings checklist" earlier in this chapter for explanations of your options. If you need to change any of the settings, do so now.

5. Click OK (**Figure 19.11**).
   If the sequence you select needs to be rendered before it can be printed, FCE automatically renders any unrendered sequence material, plus any additional program elements you've specified. When the rendering is complete, FCE displays a dialog box telling you to go ahead and start recording on your video deck. If render quality settings on this sequence's Render Control tab specify less than full quality, FCE will display this helpful advisory dialog box (**Figure 19.12**). Click OK to proceed with the Print to Video operation.

continues on next page

PRINTING TO VIDEO

6. Start recording on your video deck or camcorder, and when the device is up to speed, click OK to start playback of your Final Cut Express sequence.

7. When your program material has finished printing, stop recording on your deck or camcorder. Final Cut Express doesn't provide any end-of-process beep (the large black box disappears from the screen, and the interface returns), so check in at the scheduled end-of-program if you plan on recording unattended.

8. Play back your recorded sequence and check the quality.

✔ Tips

■ If you don't specify a post-program black trailer, Final Cut Express will hold on the last frame of your sequence, creating a freeze-frame that will be recorded onto your tape until you stop recording.

■ Once the Print to Video process is complete, you'll have access to the render files created for Print to Video in your regular Timeline version of the sequence.

■ HDV users take note: Because FCE uses AIC, an intermediate codec, to handle HDV footage inside the application, all HDV projects must be rendered before they can be output back to tape in HDV format. Apple recommends that you take extra care to avoid any possible interruption in this rendering process. HDV users should read Apple's Knowledge Base Article 300775, Final Cut Express HD: Tips for HDV Print to Video. This Kbase article provides a checklist of activities that could possibly interrupt your HDV Print to Video operation, and suggests ways to avoid trouble.

Output Options for HDV

If you're one of the first human beings in history to complete an HDV project, congratulations and welcome to the cutting edge—that chilly breeze blowing through your HDV-format project right now is a lack of true HD distribution options. HD-DVD and Blu-Ray—the two competing DVD formats that can handle HD video—aren't due to be released until later in 2005. What are your options right now?

FCE HD offers a wide variety of output options. These two are the best available options for HDV:

◆ You can use FCE's Print to Video function to record your HDV material back out to your HDV camcorder. FCE HD will automatically re-encode your AIC-format media files back to HDV format before recording the material back to video tape.

◆ You can export your HDV format material for use in iDVD. The export operation is the same for HDV and DV format material; both are converted to MPEG-2 for use in iDVD.

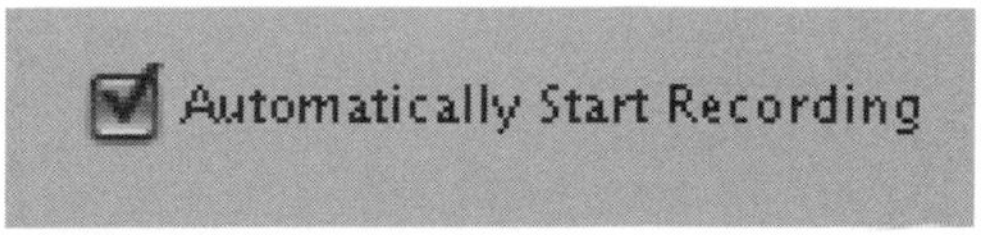

✅ Automatically Start Recording

Figure 19.13 In the Print to Video dialog box, check Automatically Start Recording to enable FCE's device control over your camcorder or deck.

To print a sequence or clip to video with device control:

1. Load the tape to which you want to record into your deck or camcorder and cue the tape to the point where you want recording to start. If you are starting your recording at the beginning of a tape, be sure to record a few seconds of black at the very head of the tape.

2. Follow steps 1 through 4 in the preceding section, "To print a sequence or clip to video without device control." When the Print to Video dialog box appears, be sure to select Automatically Start Recording to enable FCE's device control over your camcorder or deck (**Figure 19.13**); then click OK.

   If your selected settings will output video or audio at less than full quality, FCE will display an advisory dialog box. Click OK to proceed with the Print to Video operation.

   When the sequence rendering is complete, Final Cut Express will automatically place your video deck in Record mode and then start playback. When the recording is complete, FCE will stop recording on your deck, the large black box will disappear from the screen, and the interface will return.

PRINTING TO VIDEO

523

Exporting Sequences and Clips

If you want to convert a Final Cut Express sequence to another digital format for use in computer-based media, exporting is the right choice. You can also export sound files, snippets of clips, or single-frame images. Final Cut Express offers a variety of export formats.

When you export, Final Cut Express uses QuickTime's compression codec and file format conversion features to generate a media file on your hard drive in the format you choose.

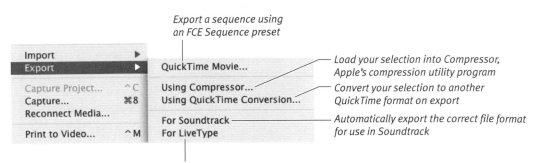

Export a sequence using an FCE Sequence preset

Load your selection into Compressor, Apple's compression utility program

Convert your selection to another QuickTime format on export

Automatically export the correct file format for use in Soundtrack

Export the correct file format for use in LiveType

Figure 19.14 When you choose File > Export, you'll see FCE's palette of media export options. LiveType and Soundtrack export options will appear only if FCE detects those applications on your computer.

Figure 19.15 Use Export > QuickTime Movie to export your sequence as a single movie using one of your Sequence presets or to export a reference movie for use with iDVD, DVD Studio Pro, or a third-party compression program.

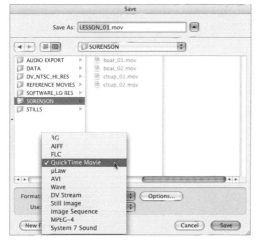

Figure 19.16 One of your QuickTime Conversion export format options, the QuickTime Movie format, is a good choice for producing highly compressed QuickTime movies for multimedia or the Web.

Here's how FCE's export options are organized:

When you choose File > Export, you'll see two QuickTime media export options: QuickTime Movie and Using QuickTime Conversion. (**Figure 19.14**).

◆ The Export > QuickTime Movie command streamlines your export configuration chores by offering very limited settings options (**Figure 19.15**). Use Export > QuickTime Movie to export your sequence as a single movie using the same format settings as your sequence or to export a reference movie for use in another compression program, such as Apple's Compressor.

QuickTime Movie is also the correct export choice if your export destination is iDVD or DVD Studio Pro.

◆ The Export > Using QuickTime Conversion command gives you access to the full range of QuickTime-supported file formats. Export > Using QuickTime Conversion is your starting point when you want to export anything from still images to compressed audio files.

One of the QuickTime format options, QuickTime Movie format (**Figure 19.16**), is a good choice for producing highly compressed QuickTime movies or media files in full-resolution, uncompressed formats. QuickTime Movie format also offers video filters that you can apply as you export a sequence.

continues on next page

EXPORTING SEQUENCES AND CLIPS

◆ These export options' settings are preset to offer streamlined export paths to Apple's family of special-purpose applications. These export options appear in the Export menu only if FCE detects the application on your computer:

- ◆ Export > Using Compressor opens your selected clip or sequence in Compressor as a reference movie.

- ◆ Export > For Soundtrack generates a file optimized for use in Soundtrack by automatically including any scoring markers you've set in your sequence.

✔ Tips

■ When you export a clip or sequence, Final Cut Express includes only the material between the In and Out points. You can set In and Out points to select a portion of your clip or sequence, but be sure to clear In and Out points before you export if you want to export the entire clip.

■ Chapter 37 of Apple's *Final Cut Express Help* PDF devotes 26 pages to the export of various QuickTime file formats—recommended reading for FCE users faced with an export format decision.

■ The two tables that follow provide a sketch of the codecs and file formats you are most likely to use with Final Cut Express and the way they're most commonly used. Note that these tables do not contain a complete list of QuickTime formats and codecs, and the summary of uses and characteristics is not comprehensive. **Table 19.1** lists the codecs most commonly used with Final Cut Express. **Table 19.2** lists the most commonly used file formats. A complete list is available at the QuickTime web site, at www.apple.com/quicktime/products/qt/specifications.html.

What's a Reference Movie?

The Export > QuickTime Movie feature offers the option of exporting your FCE clip or sequence as a reference movie. A reference movie is a bit of QuickTime media-handling wizardry. A small file that contains no media (except for a render file of your mixed sequence audio, plus video render files for parts of your exported sequence that haven't been rendered yet), a reference movie simply points to the original media files used in the exported sequence. Apple's Compressor program, which is bundled with Final Cut Pro and DVD Studio Pro, or third-party media compression programs, such as Cleaner, can use the reference movie pointer information from that small file to process the compressed version of your sequence using the larger original media files. iDVD or DVD Studio Pro can also use FCE reference movies to create a DVD disk image of your sequence.

Reference movies work with any QuickTime-compatible compression application that's installed on the same computer as your Final Cut Express system. The compression program must have access to the original QuickTime source media files for your reference movie to work.

You won't see a "Make Reference Movie" option in the Save dialog box for the Export QuickTime Movie function. The only way to export your Final Cut Express clip or sequence as a reference movie is to leave Make Movie Self-Contained unchecked. Pretty esoteric, huh?

Table 19.1

Some Useful QuickTime Codecs

FILE FORMAT	TYPE	USED FOR	ALPHA CHANNEL?
Sorenson	A/V	CD-ROM	No
Cinepak	A/V	Older CD ROM	No
QuickTime Fast Start	A/V	Web movies	No
QuickTime Streaming	A/V	Web movies	No
Animation	V	High-res digital export	Yes
M-JPEG A/M-JPEG B	V	Compressed files for editing	No
MPEG-4	A/V	Web streaming	No
DV-NTSC/DV-PAL	A/V	Importing DV into FCE	No
MPEG-2	V	DVD video	No

Table 19.2

Some Useful QuickTime File Formats

FILE FORMAT	TYPE	USED FOR	ALPHA CHANNEL?	COMPRESSION?
QuickTime Movie	A/V/Graphic/+	Cross-platform multimedia	Yes	Available
DV stream	A/V	iMovie DV media files	No	Yes
JPEG	Graphic	Graphics, video still frames	No	Available
Photoshop	Graphic	Multilayered graphics	Yes	No
PICT	Graphic	Mac format	Yes	Available
PNG	Graphic	Graphics	Yes	No
TIFF	Graphic	Graphics	Yes	Available
AIFF	A	Common audio format	N/A	Available
WAVE	A	Windows audio format	N/A	No

EXPORTING SEQUENCES AND CLIPS

Codec vs. File Format

A codec is an algorithm, or mathematical formula, for compressing and decompressing digital media. The word *codec* is techie shorthand for COmpression/DECompression. Whenever you see compression options in the QuickTime interface, you're looking at a list of codecs.

A file format is one standardized way of organizing data so it can be recognized and used by an application or operating system. You could use the same compression codec in a variety of file formats, and vice versa. QuickTime Movie is an example of a file format that supports many, many codecs.

Exporting a QuickTime movie

The Export > QuickTime Movie command is the right choice when you want to export a sequence using the same sequence settings you used in the project.

The Save dialog box for the Export QuickTime Movie function opens with your current Sequence preset already loaded. Specify whether to include audio or video, or both; then specify your marker export preference, and you're done.

QuickTime Movie is the only export format that offers the option of exporting your sequence as a QuickTime reference movie.

Because the QuickTime Movie format supports the export of both chapter markers and reference movies, it's the right export choice when you want to use iDVD or DVD Studio Pro to create a DVD of your FCE project.

To export a clip or sequence as a QuickTime movie:

1. *Do one of the following:*
   - Select a clip or sequence in the Browser.
   - In the Timeline, open the sequence you want to export.

2. Set In and Out points in your clip or sequence to mark the section you want to include in the exported file. If you want to export the entire item, clear any In and Out points from the item before export (**Figure 19.17**).

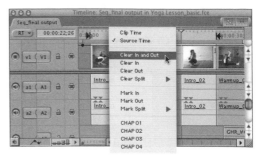

Figure 19.17 If you want to include the entire length of your sequence, be sure to clear any In and Out points before you export.

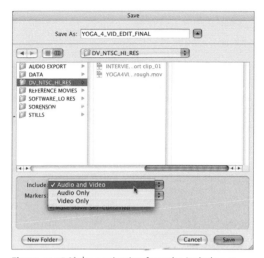

Figure 19.18 Make a selection from the Include pop-up menu. You can export audio plus video, or audio or video only.

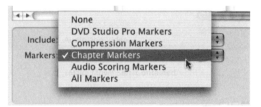

Figure 19.19 Choose Chapter Markers from the Markers pop-up menu to export chapter markers for use in iDVD 3 or DVD SP.

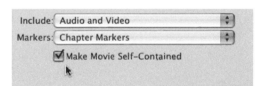

Figure 19.20 Check the Make Movie Self-Contained box to create a stand-alone movie.

3. Choose File > Export > QuickTime Movie. The Save dialog box appears. This is your opportunity to review and confirm the export format settings.

4. From the Include pop-up menu, choose Audio and Video, Audio Only, or Video Only (**Figure 19.18**).

5. If you want to export markers along with your file, select the type of markers you want to export from the Markers pop-up menu (**Figure 19.19**).

6. *Do one of the following:*

   ◆ Select Make Movie Self-Contained to export a QuickTime movie that duplicates all audio, video, and render files in one self-contained media file (**Figure 19.20**).

   ◆ Leave Make Movie Self-Contained unchecked to export a reference movie—a small movie file that contains only pointers to the original audio, video, and render files.

7. Type a name for your file in the Save As field and select a destination folder; then click Save.

✔ Tip

■ If your clip or sequence doesn't have an audio track, select Video Only from the Include pop-up menu. Even empty audio tracks will increase the file size of your exported clip.

EXPORTING SEQUENCES AND CLIPS

529

To export a Final Cut Express movie for use in iDVD or DVD Studio Pro:

1. Follow steps 1 through 4 in the previous task, "To export a clip or sequence as a QuickTime movie."

2. If you want to export chapter markers along with your file, choose Chapter Markers from the Markers pop-up menu.

3. *Do one of the following:*
   - ◆ Select Make Movie Self-Contained to make a stand-alone file that can be used with iDVD or DVD SP on this or another computer.
   - ◆ Leave Make Movie Self-Contained unchecked to export a reference movie—a small movie file that contains only pointers to the original audio, video, and render files—which can be used only with a copy of iDVD or DVD SP that is located on the same computer as your Final Cut Express project (**Figure 19.21**).

4. In the Save dialog box, type a name for your file in the Save As field and select a destination folder; then click Save.

   The exported movie contains any sequence markers you have designated as chapter markers (**Figure 19.22**).

Figure 19.21 Uncheck the Make Movie Self-Contained box to create a compact reference movie you can use in another processing program like iDVD 3 or DVD SP.

Figure 19.22 Open your exported reference movie in QuickTime Player, and you'll see a pop-up menu containing your exported chapter markers.

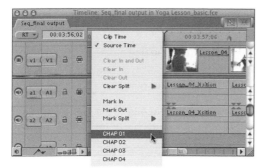

Figure 19.23 Control-click the Timeline ruler to review a list of the sequence markers in the current sequence.

✔ Tips

- If you're exporting a sequence for use in iDVD or DVD SP, remember that only sequence markers (and not clip markers) may be successfully exported as chapter markers. To learn how to set sequence markers, see "Using Markers in the Timeline and the Canvas" in Chapter 10.

- Name and number your chapter markers as you add them so you can easily spot any errors.

- Here's a quick way to review your chapter markers before you export: Control-click the Timeline ruler to see a pop-up menu of sequence markers in the current sequence (**Figure 19.23**).

EXPORTING SEQUENCES AND CLIPS

FCE Protocol: DVD Chapter Markers

It's very simple to export a QuickTime Movie with chapter markers that you can import into iDVD or DVD Studio Pro, but you should be aware of a few rules governing the number and placement of chapter markers:

♦ Final Cut Express chapter markers must be sequence markers, not clip markers.

♦ You can set a maximum of 99 chapter markers per video stream in a DVD SP project; iDVD allows no more than 36 chapter markers per project.

♦ Chapter markers must be set more than one second apart, and more than one second from the start or the end of a sequence.

Exporting Other QuickTime Formats

The Export > Using QuickTime Conversion option gives you access to the full range of QuickTime-supported file formats. Use this option to convert your FCE media to any of the following:

◆ Compressed QuickTime movies (use the QuickTime Movie format)

◆ Uncompressed, full-resolution file formats that include an alpha channel

◆ Still images in a variety of graphics file formats

◆ Audio tracks in a variety of compressed and uncompressed formats

To export a clip or sequence in another QuickTime format:

1. *Do one of the following:*

   ◆ Select a clip or sequence in the Browser (**Figure 19.24**).

   ◆ In the Timeline, open the sequence you want to export.

2. Set In and Out points in your clip or sequence to mark the section you want to include in the exported file. If you want to export the entire item, clear any In and Out points from the item before export.

3. Choose File > Export > Using QuickTime Conversion (**Figure 19.25**).

   The Save dialog box opens.

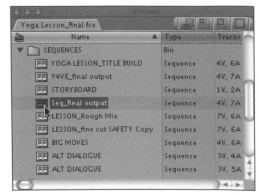

Figure 19.24 Select the sequence in the Browser.

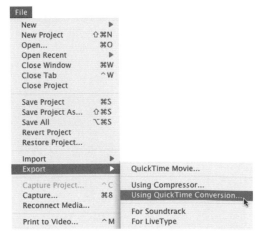

Figure 19.25 Choose File > Export > Using QuickTime Conversion. Choosing QuickTime gives you access to the full range of QuickTime's output formats.

EXPORTING OTHER QUICKTIME FORMATS

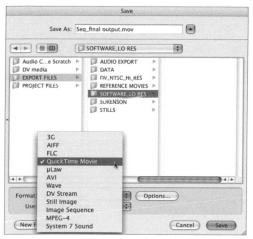

Figure 19.26 Choose an export file format from the Format pop-up menu.

4. In the Save dialog box, choose an export file format from the Format pop-up menu (**Figure 19.26**); then *do one of the following:*

- ◆ Choose one of the Export Settings presets from the Use pop-up menu (**Figure 19.27**).

- ◆ Click the Options button to access the full QuickTime settings for the format you have selected. In the settings dialog box (or boxes) that follow, confirm or modify the export format settings and then click OK. Export options will vary according to the format you have selected (**Figure 19.28**).

continues on next page

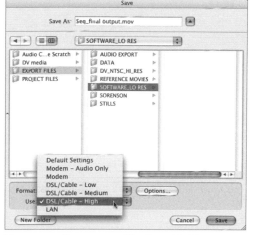

Figure 19.27 Choose one of the Export Settings presets from the Use pop-up menu. These are the export presets available for the QuickTime Movie export format.

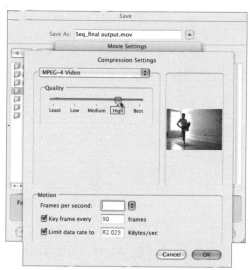

Figure 19.28 In the settings dialog boxes, confirm or modify the export format settings and click OK. Export options will vary according to the format you've selected. These are the settings dialog boxes for the MPEG 4 Video codec.

EXPORTING OTHER QUICKTIME FORMATS

5. In the Save dialog box, name your file in the Save As field (**Figure 19.29**) and then select a destination folder.

6. Click Save.

✔ Tip

■ The QuickTime Movie format gives you the option of applying QuickTime's suite of video filters, and you can choose from a range of effects and image control filters (check out the Film Noise filter!). Select the filters as you configure your export options, and they will be processed as part of the export operation. You can access the filters by clicking the Filter button in the Movie Settings window (**Figure 19.30**).

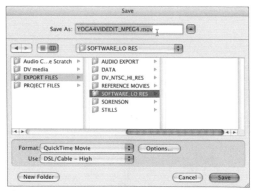

Figure 19.29 Type a name for your file in the Save dialog box's Save As field.

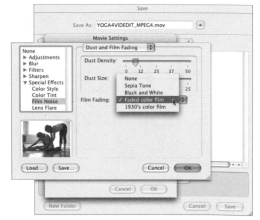

Figure 19.30 Click the Filter button in the Movie Settings window to access a palette of QuickTime filters you can apply as part of your export operation. QuickTime filters are available only in the QuickTime Movie format.

FCE Alert: Web Video Uses the Whole Video Frame

If you are converting your FCE sequence to a compressed format for Web or CD-ROM distribution, be aware that your exported file will show the entire video frame when viewed on a computer screen.

External video monitors typically don't display the edges of the video frame; that's why you're advised to keep your titles inside the title-safe area. If you have unwanted elements, such as microphones, hovering about the edges of your video frame, you may never have seen them if you've been monitoring your framing only on an external video monitor.

So check your whole video frame by viewing it on your computer monitor. If you do find that your frame has unsightly edges, you can always crop your frame before you export.

Figure 19.31 Position the Canvas or the Viewer playhead on the frame you want to export as a still frame.

To export a still image from a Canvas or a Viewer frame:

1. In the Canvas or the Viewer, position the playhead on the frame you want to export (**Figure 19.31**).

2. Choose File > Export > Using QuickTime Conversion.

3. In the Save dialog box, choose Still Image from the Format pop-up menu (**Figure 19.32**); then *do one of the following:*

   ◆ Choose one of the Still Image presets from the Use pop-up menu.

   ◆ Click the Options button to access a complete list of QuickTime still image formats and their settings. In the Export Image Sequence Settings dialog box, select an export format from the pop-up menu at the top of the dialog box (**Figure 19.33**) and then click OK.

4. In the Save dialog box, type a name for your still frame in the Save As field and select a destination folder.

continues on next page

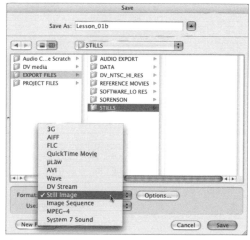

Figure 19.32 Select Still Image from the Format pop-up menu.

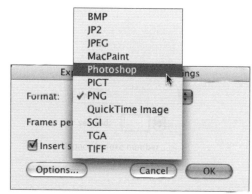

Figure 19.33 Selecting Photoshop as the export format from the pop-up menu in the Export Image Sequence Settings dialog box.

5. Click Save (**Figure 19.34**).

Final Cut Express automatically adds the correct image file extension to the name you typed.

✔ Tips

■ If you want to export multiple still frames in a batch process rather than exporting them directly (as outlined in this task), you'll first need to use the Modify > Make Freeze Frame command to create FCE still clips. When you're done selecting your freeze-frames, you can use the batch-export feature to convert them all to graphics files in one operation.

■ When you export a still frame, ignore the frames-per-second settings—they don't apply to still-frame export.

To export an image sequence:

1. *Do one of the following:*

◆ Select a clip or sequence in the Browser.

◆ In the Timeline, open the sequence you want to export.

2. Set In and Out points in your clip or sequence to mark the section you want to export as a numbered image sequence (**Figure 19.35**). If you want to export the entire item, clear any In and Out points from the item before export.

3. Choose File > Export > Using QuickTime Conversion.

Figure 19.34 In the Save dialog box, type a name for your still frame in the Save As field; then select a destination folder and click Save.

Figure 19.35 Set In and Out points in your clip or sequence to mark the section you want to include in the exported image sequence file.

EXPORTING OTHER QUICKTIME FORMATS

Figure 19.36 Select Image Sequence from the Format pop-up menu.

Figure 19.37 Select an export format from the pop-up menu at the top of the dialog box and select a frame rate for your image sequence; then click OK.

4. In the Save dialog box, choose Image Sequence from the Format pop-up menu (**Figure 19.36**); then *do one of the following:*

◆ Choose one of the Image Sequence presets from the Use pop-up menu.

◆ Click the Options button to access a complete list of QuickTime still image formats and their settings. In the Export Image Sequence Settings dialog box, select an export format from the Format pop-up menu and select a frame rate for your image sequence (**Figure 19.37**); then click OK.

5. In the Save dialog box, type a name for your still frame in the Save As field and then select a destination folder.

6. Click Save.

Your image sequence is saved as a series of still graphics in the file format you selected.

Exporting Audio Files

If you need more control over your audio
tracks than you can get inside FCE, or if
you just got off the phone with the BBC and
you have a sudden need for an audio-only
excerpt from your movie, read on. This section describes three options for exporting
audio from your Final Cut Express project.

◆ If you'd like to export just the audio from
your sequence and you need access to
export formats other than AIFF, you
can use the Export > Using QuickTime
Conversion command to convert and
export your audio in a single operation.

If you plan to finish your audio in a dedicated
audio editing workstation, you have a couple
of options:

◆ Export your edited sequence audio tracks
as individual AIFF files, and you can export
up to eight channels simultaneously, by
mapping audio tracks to specific channels.
Because each AIFF file exports as a single,
continuous piece, you'll retain volume, pan,
and filters settings, but lose edit points.

◆ Export the audio tracks from an FCE
sequence in Open Media Framework
(OMF) format, and you can transport
your edited audio to any OMF-compatible
digital audio workstation.

FCE Protocol: Exporting Audio Tracks for Finishing

If you need more control over your audio
tracks than you can get inside FCE, you
can export your edited sequence audio
tracks out of Final Cut Express as individual AIFF files and then continue your
audio finishing in a dedicated, digital
audio editing program such as Pro Tools.
FCE's audio export capability features are
limited; there's a two-channel limit for
each export operation, and the exported
audio files are continuous—you lose your
edit points. Yuck.

If you have access to a Final Cut Pro workstation, you can open your project created
in FCE and export your audio tracks in
the Open Media Framework (OMF) file
exchange format. The exported OMF file
contains the audio files, plus the audio edit
information from your project file. That
means you can export audio tracks with
the original track separations, edit points,
cross-fades, and video sync intact and then
import them into an OMF-compatible,
digital audio workstation, the kind used at
most professional, audio post-production
facilities. For more information, see "To
export audio only from a clip or sequence."

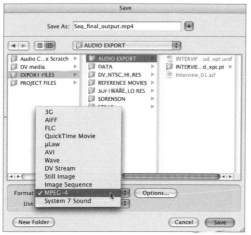

Figure 19.38 Choose File > Export > Using QuickTime Conversion and then select an audio format from the Format pop-up menu. AIFF, μLaw, and Wave are all audio formats.

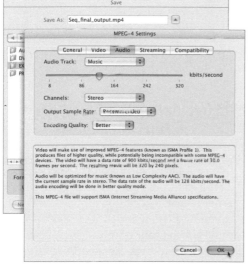

Figure 19.39 Select data-rate and compression settings from the Sound Settings dialog box and then click OK.

To export audio only from a clip or sequence:

1. Select a clip or sequence in the Browser, or open the sequence in the Timeline.

2. Set In and Out points in your clip or sequence to mark the section you want to export as an audio file.

3. Choose File > Export > Using QuickTime Conversion.

4. In the Save dialog box, choose an audio export file format from the Format pop-up menu (**Figure 19.38**); then *do one of the following:*

   ◆ Choose one of the audio export presets from the Use pop-up menu.

   ◆ Click the Options button to access the full QuickTime settings for the format you have selected. In the Sound Settings dialog box, select sample-rate (**Figure 19.39**) and compression settings; then click OK.

5. In the Save dialog box, type a name for your audio file in the Save As field, select a destination folder, and then click Save.

continues on next page

EXPORTING AUDIO FILES

✔ Tips

■ You can use the export method just described to convert the 44.1-kHz sample rate of a CD audio track. In the Sound Settings dialog box (see step 4 in the preceding procedure), choose 48 (or 32) kHz—the sample rate that matches your sequence audio's rate. Once you complete the export/sample-rate conversion, import the exported copy back into your project.

■ Final Cut Express allows you to mix audio tracks with different sample rates in the same sequence. The program can convert the sample rate of nonconforming audio on the fly as you play back a sequence. Real-time sample-rate conversion does take processor power, however and can occasionally produce nasty audible artifacts, so for best results, convert the sample rates of all your audio tracks to match the sequence settings.

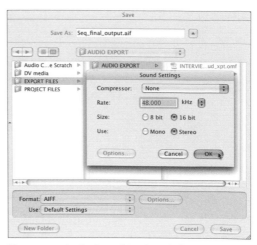

Figure 19.40 In the Sound Settings dialog box, select sample-rate and compression settings; then click OK.

To export audio in AIFF format:

1. Select a clip or sequence in the Browser, or open the sequence in the Timeline.

2. Set In and Out points in your clip or sequence to mark the section you want to export as an audio file.

3. Choose File > Export > Using QuickTime Conversion.

4. Choose AIFF from the Format pop-up menu; then click the Options button to access the full QuickTime settings for the AIFF format. In the Sound Settings dialog box, select sample-rate (**Figure 19.40**) and compression settings; then click OK.

5. Type a name for your audio file in the Save As field; then select a destination folder and click Save.

Manipulating LiveType Projects in Final Cut Express

You can import a LiveType project directly into your FCE Timeline and manipulate it just as you would a clip. There's no need to export a rendered version of your LiveType element as you refine the placement and timing of your titles, but you'll still need to open your LiveType element in LiveType if you want to adjust title elements. You can save back and forth between FCE and LiveType as many times as you need. If you aren't manipulating your sequence video as an object within LiveType, then it's best to place it as a background object so that it won't be rendered into the final title sequence.

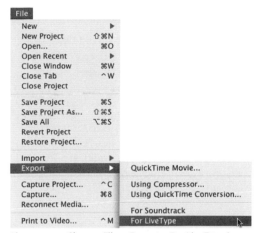

Figure 19.41 Choose File > Export > For LiveType to export a movie to use in LiveType.

Figure 19.42 To import your FCE movie as a protected layer in a Livetype project, launch Livetype, and then choose File > Place as Background Movie. You can select your FCE file from Livetype's Open dialog box.

Exporting for LiveType and Soundtrack

LiveType and Soundtrack both accept exported FCE reference movies in a variety of formats and resolutions. These application-specific Export menu commands are an amenity, but you don't actually need to use them to export a movie you can use to position and time your titles, or your music score.

To export a file for use in LiveType:

1. In the Browser, select the sequence that you want to export to LiveType, and then choose File > Export > For LiveType (**Figure 19.41**).

2. Name your exported file, and be sure to include markers if you are using them within your sequence.

   If you already have a LiveType clip in your FCE sequence when you choose File > Export > For LiveType, FCE will ask you if you want to include that LiveType clip in your exported file.

3. In the Finder, launch LiveType and create a new project.

   Do one of the following:

   ◆ Choose File > Place and select your exported FCE sequence movie file. Your file will be placed into a new, modifiable layer in LiveType.

   ◆ Choose File > Place Background Movie and select your exported FCE movie. Your file will be placed into a protected layer in LiveType (**Figure 19.42**).

✔ Tip

■ LiveType will accept exported FCE reference movies.

To export a file for use in Soundtrack:

1. In the Browser, select the sequence that you want to export to Soundtrack.

2. Choose File > Export > For Soundtrack.

3. Name your project, and be sure to include Audio Scoring Markers if you are using them within your sequence.

4. From the Finder, launch Soundtrack and create a new project.

5. Use Soundtrack's Media Manager to select the saved FCE file and drag it into the Video tab (**Figure 19.43**). (Using "Open" does not work.)

✔ Tips

■ When exporting your mixed track from Soundtrack, be sure to check "Mute audio track from video" when saving, or else you will mixdown your video's audio tracks into your new soundtrack.

■ Get the full details on FCE/Soundtrack interaction protocols in Chapter 8 of Apple's Soundtrack manual, *Working with Video in Soundtrack*.

Figure 19.43 Use Soundtrack's Media Manager pane to navigate to your exported FCE file's location on disk, and then drag it from the Media Manager pane into Soundtrack's Video tab.

EXPORTING FOR LIVETYPE AND SOUNDTRACK

ONLINE RESOURCES

Apple Computer Links

www.apple.com/finalcutexpress/

Apple's Official Final Cut Express home page is the place to go for program updates; the latest FCE news; updates on Final Cut Express and QuickTime; and the list of Apple-approved video hardware and software. Check in at the FCE home page on a regular basis.

www.apple.com/finalcutexpress/resources.html

The **Final Cut Express Resources directory page** contains a variety of resource links that Final Cut Express users will also find helpful: links to discussion groups, a complete list of Final Cut Pro user groups, general DV reference resources, and developers of software and plugins you can use in conjunction with Final Cut Pro.

www.apple.com/finalcutexpress/qualification.html

The **Final Cut Express Qualified Devices PDF** contains a complete list of DV decks and camcorders qualified to work with FCE, and the correct device control setting to use with each and every one.

www.apple.com/quicktime/

Apple's QuickTime home page.

www.apple.com/firewire/

Apple's FireWire home page.

www.info.apple.com/usen/finalcutexpress/

Apple's Final Cut Express Support site has a lot to offer; visit its home page to get an overview of the offerings. Apple changes the names and URLs of its data sites regularly. Try the URLs listed here and on the following pages.

http://kbase.info.apple.com

Apple's Knowledge Base (formerly known as the Tech Info Library, or TIL) is Apple's library of product information, technical specifications, and troubleshooting information. Search the Knowledge Base with the keywords *Final Cut* for a complete list of Apple technical documents relating to FCE (and FCP).

To access a specific Knowledge Base article:

◆ This book makes occasional mention of specific Knowledge Base reference articles. You can go directly to a specific article by using the following URL, where *XXXXX* is the document number: www.info.apple.com/kbnum/n*XXXXX*.

✔ Tip

■ Check the Knowledge Base regularly. Apple posts updates on "known issues" (a.k.a. bugs) affecting Final Cut Express in the Kbase—and nowhere else.

Online Users Forums

discussions.info.apple.com/WebX/finalcutexpress

This is **Apple's Final Cut Express Discussion**, Apple's official online support forum. For the time being, this is the most active discussion forum exclusively devoted to FCE. If you think a Final Cut Pro user might be able to assist you, try the 2-pop forums as well.

www.2-pop.com/

When Final Cut Pro was released in April 1999, the **2-pop.com site** quickly became the central exchange forum for Final Cut Pro users wanting to share information. The 2-pop site is primarily a Final Cut Pro hang-out, but its popularity makes it a good place to go for answers, FCP news and gossip, new ideas, and product critiques. A gold mine.

The action at 2-pop centers in the discussion forums. Click the Forums link on 2-pop's front page to navigate to a complete listing of 2-pop's discussion forums. Be sure to take advantage of the Search feature located at the top of most discussion boards; you'll find a wealth of detailed information by searching the archives of the 2-pop message boards.

www.creativecow.net/index.php?forumid=8

Hey! More online forums, more users, more answers for you! The **Creative Cow Final Cut Pro forum** is populated by a merry band of the usual suspects.

Reference

www.dv.com/

DV Magazine would be my first stop if I were looking for product reviews, industry analysis, and long-view technical evaluations of the current state of the digital video world.

www.adobe.com/

In addition to product-specific information on Photoshop and After Effects, **Adobe's web site** is a great source of general information on digital imaging.

www.techweb.com/encyclopedia/

Simple to use, the **TechEncyclopedia** offers more than 20,000 definitions of computer terms and concepts.

Mavens

If you are seeking alternatives to marketing department hype, these sites offer a bracing dose of opinionated candor and experienced insight, along with valuable reference material and more great links.

www.adamwilt.com/DV.html

Adam Wilt's Amazing DV FAQ. I'm an Adam Wilt fan. See for yourself.

www.kenstone.net/

Ken Stone has been quietly building an impressive online library of illustrated Final Cut Pro tutorials, reviews, and articles by Ken and other FCP scholars. Well worth the visit for FCE users.

www.digitalzoo.com.au/lunchtime/

Simon Kirby's **Lunchtime Cinema** is a chatty, pleasantly opinionated, well-organized site that's devoted to collecting helpful FCP and FCE resources.

www.joesfilters.com/

Joe's Filters is a great resource for anyone interested in using filters and transitions in Final Cut Express. Joe offers demo versions of his custom filters, and the illustrated documentation that accompanies each filter description offers a great way to learn more about using filters to create digital effects.

www.dvcentral.org/

Get subscription information at **DV & FireWire Central** for the excellent DV_L mailing list.

www.nonlinear4.com/

Michael Rubin (and co-editor Ron Diamond) are the keepers of **nonlinear4.com**, a great reference and resource site for all things digital and video. You should also visit this site to purchase *Nonlinear4* (the fourth edition of Michael Rubin's really good "field guide to digital video and film editing").

FCP User Groups

At this time, there are no Final Cut Express–only user groups out there, so you'll have to crowd in with the FCP folk.

www.apple.com/software/pro/resources/usergroups.html

Apple's Resources page contains links to all members of the **Final Cut Pro User Group Network** (20 groups and counting). Check here to see if there's a user group near you.

www.2-pop.com

2-pop's User Groups Announcements forum is a good place to check for user group action in your town. If you don't see any posts from your area, this is a good place to try to round up your neighborhood Final Cut users and start a user group of your own.

www.lafcpug.org

The **Los Angeles Final Cut Pro User Group** is a triumph of ad-hocracy (and a tribute to the energy of its prime mover, Michael Horton). Founded in June 2000, LAFCPUG now has over 1500 members on its mailing list and holds well-attended monthly meetings. The LAFCPUG web site is updated regularly and is worth a visit for the archive of fine how-to articles contributed by community-minded FCP mavens.

www.sfcutters.org

The **San Francisco Final Cut Pro User Group** web site: These guys started the first FCP user group and gleefully nagged Southern California FCP users until they started the LAFCPUG. The rest is history.

ONLINE RESOURCES

KEYBOARD SHORTCUTS

General controls

FUNCTION	KEY COMMAND	FUNCTION	KEY COMMAND
Open file	`Cmd` O	Save all	`Cmd` `Option` S
Open selected item	`Return`	Undo	`Cmd` Z
Open Item in separate window	`Shift` `Return`	Redo	`Shift` `Cmd` Z
Open Item in Editor	`Option` `Return`	Audio scrub on or off	`Shift` S
Close window	`Cmd` W	Snapping on or off	N
Quit	`Cmd` Q	Toggle Loop Playback	`Ctrl` L
Save	`Cmd` S	Close Tab	`Ctrl` W
		Open text generator	`Ctrl` X

Opening application windows

FUNCTION	KEY COMMAND
Viewer	[Cmd] 1
Canvas	[Cmd] 2
Timeline	[Cmd] 3
Browser	[Cmd] 4
Audio Meters	[Option] 4
Effects	[Cmd] 5
Trim Edit	[Cmd] 7
Log and Capture	[Cmd] 8
Item Properties	[Cmd] 9
Sequence Settings	[Cmd] 0 (zero)
User Preferences	[Option] Q

Selecting, cutting, copying, and pasting

FUNCTION	KEY COMMAND
Copy	[Cmd] C
Cut	[Cmd] X
Duplicate	[Option] D
Select In to Out	[Option] A
Paste	[Cmd] V
Paste attributes	[Option] V
Paste Insert	[Shift] V
Select all	[Cmd] A
Deselect all	[Shift] [Cmd] A

Navigation

FUNCTION	KEY COMMAND
Forward one frame	[→]
Back one frame	[←]
Forward one second	[Shift] [→]
Back one second	[Shift] [←]
Match frame in Master clip	F
Match frame in Source file	[Cmd] [Option] F
Next edit	[Shift] E or ' or [Ctrl] 8
Previous edit	[Option] E or ; or [Ctrl] 7
To next edit or In/Out	[↓]
To previous edit or In/Out	[↑]
Go to In point	[Shift] I
Go to Out point	[Shift] O

FUNCTION	KEY COMMAND
Next gap	[Shift] G
Previous gap	[Option] G
To beginning of media	[Home]
To end of media	[End] or [Shift] [Home]
To next marker	[Shift] [↓] or [Shift] M
To previous marker	[Shift] [↑] or [Option] M
Shuttle backward fast	J (tap repeatedly to increase speed)
Shuttle backward slow	J + K
Pause	K
Shuttle forward fast	L (tap repeatedly to increase speed)
Shuttle forward slow	L + K

Finding items

FUNCTION	KEY COMMAND
Find	Cmd F
Find Next (in Find results)	Cmd G or F3
Find previous (in Find results)	Shift F3

Scrolling

FUNCTION	KEY COMMAND
Horizontal scroll left	Shift Page Up
Horizontal scroll right	Shift Page Down
Vertical scroll up	Page Up
Vertical scroll down	Page Down

Screen layout and display

FUNCTION	KEY COMMAND
Custom Layout 1	Shift U
Custom Layout 2	Option U
Standard layout	Ctrl U

Projects and sequences

FUNCTION	KEY COMMAND
New project	Shift Cmd N
New sequence	Cmd N
New Sequence with Presets prompt	Cmd Option N
Import file	Cmd I

Browser

FUNCTION	KEY COMMAND
New folder	Cmd B
Open folder (List view)	→
Close folder (List view)	←
Toggle Browser View	Shift H

Timeline

FUNCTION	KEY COMMAND	FUNCTION	KEY COMMAND
Create or break link	Cmd L	Lock audio track + track no.	F5 + track no.
Create or break stereo pair	Option L	Lock all audio tracks	Shift F5
Toggle track sizes	Shift T	Toggle Audio Waveforms	Cmd Option W
Clip overlays on or off	Option W		
Delete and leave gap	Delete	Linked Selection on or off	Shift L
Ripple Delete (no gap)	Shift Delete		
Ripple Cut to Keyboard	Shift X	Modify Duration	Ctrl D
Fit sequence in window	Shift Z	Zoom Timeline In	Option + (plus sign) or Option =
Lock video track + track no.	F4 + track no.	Zoom Timeline Out	Option – (minus sign)
Lock all video tracks	Shift F4		

Logging and Capturing

FUNCTION	KEY COMMAND
Capture Project	Ctrl C
Capture Now	Shift C

Playing video

FUNCTION	KEY COMMAND
Play	L or Spacebar
Pause/Stop	K or Spacebar
Play around current	\ (backslash)
Play every frame	Option P or Option \ (backslash)
Play here to Out	Shift P
Play in reverse	Shift Spacebar or J
Play In to Out	Shift \ (backslash)

In and Out points

FUNCTION	KEY COMMAND
Set In point	I or / (slash) on keypad
Set Out point	O or * (asterisk) on keypad
Clear In	Option I
Clear Out	Option O
Clear In and Out	Option X
Make selection an In or Out	Shift A
Mark clip	X
Mark to Markers	Ctrl A
Go to In point	Shift I
Go to Out point	Shift O
Set video In only	Ctrl I
Set video Out only	Ctrl O
Set audio In only	Cmd Option I
Set audio Out only	Cmd Option O

Markers

FUNCTION	KEY COMMAND
Add marker	M or ` (accent grave)
Add and name marker	M + M
Delete marker	Cmd ` (accent grave)
Extend marker	Option ` (accent grave)
Reposition marker	Shift ` (accent grave)

FUNCTION	KEY COMMAND
Next marker	Shift M or Shift ↓
Previous marker	Option M or Shift ↑
Clear All Markers	Ctrl ` (accent grave)
Mark to Markers	Ctrl A

Tool selection

FUNCTION	KEY COMMAND	FUNCTION	KEY COMMAND
Tool Selection	A	Tool Slide	S + S
Tool Edit Select	G	Tool Razor Blade	B
Tool Group Select	G+G	Tool Razor Blade All	B + B
Tool Range Select	G+G+G	Tool Hand	H
Tool Track Forward Select	T	Tool Zoom In	Z
Tool Track Backward Select	T+T	Tool Zoom Out	Z + Z
Tool Track Select	T+T+T	Tool Crop	C
Tool All Tracks Forward Select	T+T+T+T	Tool Distort	D or C + C
Tool All Tracks Backward Select	T+T+T+T+T	Tool Pen	P
Tool Roll Edit	R	Tool Pen Delete	P + P
Tool Ripple Edit	R + R	Tool Pen Smooth	P + P + P
Tool Slip	S		

Editing

FUNCTION	KEY COMMAND	FUNCTION	KEY COMMAND
Select Closest Edit	V	Split edit	[Option] Click In or Out point
Add Edit	[Ctrl] V	Set target video + track no.	[F6] + track no.
Toggle Ripple/Roll Tool Type	U or [Shift] R	Set target video to None	[Shift] [F6]
Add Default Video Transition	[Cmd] T	Set target Audio 1 + track no.	[F7] + track no.
Add Default Audio Transition	[Cmd] [Option] T	Set target Audio 1 to None	[Shift] [F7]
Extend edit	E	Set target Audio 2 + track no.	[F8] + track no.
Insert edit*	[F9]	Set target Audio 2 to None	[Shift] [F8]
Insert with transition*	[Shift] [F9]	Trim backward one frame	[(left bracket) or , (comma)
Overwrite*	[F10]	Trim backward x frames	[Shift] [(left bracket) or [Shift] , (comma)
Overwrite with transition	[Shift] [F10]		
Replace*	[F11]	Trim forward one frame	] (rt. bracket) or . (period)
Fit to fill	[Shift] [F11]		
Superimpose	[F12]	Trim forward x frames	[Shift]] (rt. bracket) or [Shift] . (period)
Make subclip	[Cmd] U		
Slip edit	[Shift] Click In or Out point		

These FCE commands are overridden by Mac OS Exposé shortcuts

KEYBOARD SHORTCUTS

Output	
FUNCTION	KEY COMMAND
Show Current Frame on External Video	Shift F12
Toggle External Video	Cmd F12

Compositing and special effects

FUNCTION	KEY COMMAND	FUNCTION	KEY COMMAND
Nest Items	Option C	Nudge position down	Option ↓
Add Motion Keyframe	Ctrl K	Nudge position left	Option ←
Add Audio Keyframe	Cmd Option K	Nudge position right	Option →
Next Keyframe	Shift K	Nudge position up	Option ↑
Previous Keyframe	Option K	Sub pixel down	Cmd ↓
Make still frame	Shift N	Sub pixel left	Cmd ←
Render selection	Cmd R	Sub pixel right	Cmd →
Render sequence	Option R	Sub pixel up	Cmd ↑
Disable Rendering	Caps Lock	Zoom in	Cmd = (equal sign)
Speed	Cmd J	Zoom out	Cmd – (minus sign)
Toggle Image/Wireframe view	W		
Toggle RGB/RGB+A/Alpha	Shift W	Add Motion Keyframe	Ctrl K
Fit in window	Shift Z	Mixdown Audio	Cmd Option R

Quick Navigation Keys and Modifiers

This group of keyboard shortcuts for marking and navigation are arranged in what is known as a "Set-Clear-Go" scheme.

◆ The simple key command sets the edit, marker, or point.

◆ (Shift) plus the key command advances to the next edit, marker, or point.

◆ (Option) plus the key command advances to the previous edit, marker, or point.

KEY	NO MODIFIER	(Shift) + KEY	(Option) + KEY
I	Set In	Go to In	Clear In
O	Set Out	Go to Out	Clear Out
M	Set Marker	Next Marker	Previous Marker
E	Extend Edit	Next Edit	Previous Edit
G		Next Gap	Previous Gap
K		Next Keyframe	Previous Keyframe
(Ctrl) K	Add Motion Keyframe		

INDEX

INDEX

INDEX

Ready to Learn More?

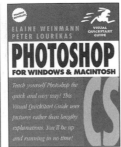

If you enjoyed this project and are ready to learn more, pick up a *Visual QuickStart Guide*, the best-selling, most affordable, most trusted, quick-reference series for computing.

With more than 5.5 million copies in print, *Visual QuickStart Guides* are the industry's best-selling series of affordable, quick-reference guides. This series from Peachpit Press includes more than 200 titles covering the leading applications for digital photography and illustration, digital video and sound editing, Web design and development, business productivity, graphic design, operating systems, and more. Best of all, these books respect your time and intelligence. With tons of well-chosen illustrations and practical, labor-saving tips, they'll have you up to speed on new software fast.

> " When you need to quickly learn to use a new application or new version of an application, you can't do better than the *Visual QuickStart Guides* from Peachpit Press."
>
> Jay Nelson
> *Design Tools Monthly*

www.peachpit.com